A SIMPLIFIED
HARMONY
— OF THE —
GOSPELS

D0839742

A SIMPLIFIED
HARMONY
— OF THE —
GOSPELS

GEORGE W. KNIGHT

HOLMAN
BIBLE PUBLISHERS

NASHVILLE, TENNESSEE

Library of Congress Cataloging-in-Publication Data

Bible. N.T. Gospels. English. Holman Christian Standard Bible. 2001
   A simplified harmony of the Gospels / George Knight.
      p. cm.
   Includes indexes.
   ISBN 0-8054-9423-5 (alk. paper)
      1. Bible. N.T. Gospels—Harmonies, English. I. Knight, George W. (George
         Wendell), 1940–   II. Title.

BS2560 .K65 2001
266'.1–dc21

2001024289

11 12 13 14 15   20 19 18 17 16

CONTENTS

EXPANDED OUTLINE: A SIMPLIFIED HARMONY   vii

ACKNOWLEDGMENTS   xix

HOW TO USE THIS BOOK   xxi

ABOUT THE HOLMAN CHRISTIAN STANDARD BIBLE   xxv

INTRODUCTION   1

I. INTRODUCTION TO THE GOOD NEWS   5

II. THE BIRTH AND CHILDHOOD OF JESUS   17

III. PREPARATION FOR THE BEGINNING OF JESUS' MINISTRY   27

IV. THE MINISTRY OF JESUS IN GALILEE   47

V. THE FINAL YEAR: JESUS' MINISTRY IN JUDEA AND PEREA   103

VI. JESUS' FINAL DAYS IN JERUSALEM   183

VII. TRIAL AND CRUCIFIXION   223

VIII. RESURRECTION, POST-RESURRECTION
APPEARANCES, AND ASCENSION   243

A SYSTEMATIC READING PLAN   257

SCRIPTURE INDICES   259
Matthew Scripture Index   259
Mark Scripture Index   260
Luke Scripture Index   260
John Scripture Index   262

SUBJECT INDEX   263
Miracles of Jesus   266
Major Parables of Jesus   267

EXPANDED OUTLINE: *A Simplified Harmony*

	Matthew	Mark	Luke	John
		⌞ SYNOPTIC ⌟		

I. INTRODUCTION TO THE GOOD NEWS

	Matthew	Mark	Luke	John
1. Luke's Preface and Dedication			1:1–4	
2. John's Introduction				1:1–18
3. Announcement of the Birth of John the Baptizer			1:5–25	
4. Announcement of the Birth of Jesus			1:26–38	
5. Mary Visits Elizabeth			1:39–56	
6. Birth of John the Baptizer			1:57–66	
7. Zachariah's Song at John's Birth			1:67–80	
8. Jesus' Genealogy as Traced through Joseph	1:1–17			
9. Jesus' Genealogy as Traced through Mary			3:23–38	
10. Joseph's Reassuring Dream	1:18–25			

II. THE BIRTH AND CHILDHOOD OF JESUS

	Matthew	Mark	Luke	John
11. Jesus Born in Bethlehem			2:1–7	
12. Good News to the Shepherds			2:8–20	
13. The Circumcision and Naming of Jesus	1:25		2:21	
14. Jesus' Presentation as an Infant in the Temple			2:22–38	
15. The Wise Men Visit Jesus	2:1–12			
16. Jesus and His Family Flee to Egypt	2:13–15			
17. Slaughter of Innocent Children by Herod	2:16–18			
18. Jesus and His Family Return to Nazareth	2:19–23		2:39–40	
19. The Boy Jesus among the Teachers in Jerusalem			2:41–52	

	Matthew	Mark	Luke	John
III. PREPARATION FOR THE BEGINNING OF JESUS' MINISTRY				
20. John the Baptizer Preaches and Baptizes	3:1–12	1:1–8	3:1–18	
21. Jesus Baptized by John	3:13–17	1:9–11	3:21–23	
22. Jesus Tempted by Satan	4:1–11	1:12–13	4:1–13	
23. John Identifies Jesus as the Messiah				1:19–34
24. Jesus Calls His First Disciples				1:35–51
25. Jesus' First Miracle: Water into Wine				2:1–11
26. Jesus Visits the City of Capernaum in Galilee				2:12
27. Jesus' First Cleansing of the Temple				2:13–25
28. Jesus Explains the New Birth to Nicodemus				3:1–21
29. Jesus and His Disciples in Judea				3:22–24
30. John the Baptizer Points People to Jesus				3:25–36
31. John Imprisoned by Herod	14:1–5	6:17–20	3:19–20	
*32. Jesus Goes through Samaria on His Way to Galilee	4:12	1:14	4:14–15	4:1–4
33. Jesus Talks with the Woman at the Well in Samaria				4:5–44
IV. THE MINISTRY OF JESUS IN GALILEE				
34. Jesus Begins Preaching in Galilee	4:17	1:14–15		4:45
35. Jesus Heals the Son of a Royal Official				4:46–54
36. Jesus' Identification with the Suffering Servant			4:16–21	
37. Rejected at Nazareth, Jesus Moves to Capernaum	4:13–16		4:22–31	
38. Calling of Peter and Andrew, James and John	4:18–22	1:16–20	5:1–11	
39. Healing of a Demon-Possessed Man		1:21–26	4:31–35	
40. Amazement at Jesus' Authority		1:22,27–28	4:32,36–37	

	Matthew	Mark	Luke	John
41. Healing of Peter's Mother-in-Law	8:14–15	1:29–31	4:38–39	
42. Healing of Many People in Capernaum	8:16–17	1:32–34	4:40–41	
43. A Healing and Preaching Tour throughout Galilee	4:23–25	1:35–39	4:42–44	
44. A Leper Healed	8:1–4	1:40–45	5:12–16	
45. Healing of a Paralyzed Man	9:1–8	2:1–12	5:17–26	
46. Jesus Calls Matthew	9:9–13	2:13–17	5:27–32	
47. Observations on Fasting	9:14–17	2:18–22	5:33–39	
48. Jesus Heals a Lame Man on the Sabbath				5:1–15
49. Jesus Defends His Sabbath Healing				5:16–47
50. Criticism for Picking Grain on the Sabbath	12:1–8	2:23–28	6:1–5	
51. Jesus Heals a Man's Paralyzed Hand on the Sabbath	12:9–14	3:1–6	6:6–11	
52. Many People Healed at Lake Galilee	12:15–21	3:7–12		
53. Jesus Selects His Twelve Disciples	10:2–4	3:13–19	6:12–16	
54. The Sermon on the Mount	5:1–7:29		6:17–49	
55. Jesus Heals a Centurion's Slave	8:5–13		7:1–10	
56. Jesus Raises a Widow's Son			7:11–17	
57. A Question from John the Baptizer	11:1–19		7:18–35	
58. Galilean Cities Condemned because of Their Unbelief	11:20–24			
59. An Invitation to the Weary	11:25–30			
60. Jesus Anointed by a Sinful Woman			7:36–50	
61. Another Tour of Galilee			8:1–3	
62. The Healing of a Blind Man	12:22–24			
63. Jesus Answers the Blasphemous Charge of the Pharisees	12:25–37	3:20–30		
64. Condemnation of the Sign Seekers	12:38–45			
65. The Mother and Brothers of Jesus	12:46–50	3:31–35	8:19–21	
66. The Parable of the Sower	13:1–9	4:1–9	8:4–8	

	Matthew	Mark	Luke	John
67 Why Jesus Spoke in Parables	13:10–17	4:11–12	8:10	
68 The Parable of the Sower Explained	13:18–23	4:10,13–20	8:9–15	
69. The Lamp on a Lampstand		4:21–25	8:16–18	
70. The Seed of God's Kingdom		4:26–29		
71. The Parable of the Wheat and the Weeds	13:24–30			
72. The Parable of the Mustard Seed and the Parable of the Yeast	13:31–35	4:30–34	13:18–21	
73. The Parable of the Wheat and the Weeds Explained	13:36–43			
74. The Parable of the Hidden Treasure	13:44			
75. The Parable of the Priceless Pearl	13:45–46			
76. The Parable of the Net	13:47–51			
77. The Parable of the Landowner	13:52			
78 Jesus Stills the Storm	8:18,23–27	4:35–41	8:22–25	
79 Jesus Heals a Wild Man among the Tombs	8:28–34	5:1–20	8:26–39	
80 The Healing of Jairus's Daughter and a Woman with a Hemorrhage	9:18–26	5:21–43	8:40–56	
81. Two Blind Men and a Demon-Possessed Man Healed	9:27–38			
82. Jesus Visits Nazareth and Is Rejected Again	13:53–58	6:1–6		
83 Jesus Sends His Disciples out to Preach and Heal	10:1,5–42	6:7–13	9:1–6	
84. The Death of John the Baptizer	14:6–12	6:17–29		
85. Herod Wonders about Jesus		6:14–16	9:7–9	

V. THE FINAL YEAR: JESUS' MINISTRY IN JUDEA AND PEREA

	Matthew	Mark	Luke	John
86. Feeding of the Five Thousand	14:13–21	6:30–44	9:10–17	6:1–15
87. Jesus Walks on the Water	14:22–36	6:45–56		6:16–21
88. Jesus' Message on the Bread of Life				6:22–71

	Matthew	Mark	Luke	John
89. Pharisees Criticize Jesus because of Unwashed Hands	15:1–20	7:1–23		
90. Jesus Heals the Daughter of a Canaanite Woman	15:21–28	7:24–30		
91. Jesus Heals a Deaf Man		7:31–37		
92. Feeding of the Four Thousand	15:29–38	8:1–10		
93. Pharisees and Sadducees Ask for a Sign	15:39–16:4	8:11–12		
94. Jesus Warns about the Influence of Pharisees and Sadducees	16:5–12	8:13–21		
95. Jesus Heals a Blind Man at Bethsaida		8:22–26		
96. Peter's Great Confession about Jesus	16:13–20	8:27–30	9:18–20	
97. Jesus Predicts His Death and Resurrection	16:21–28	8:31–9:1	9:21–27	
98. Jesus Is Transformed before His Disciples	17:1–8	9:2–8	9:28–36	
99. Jesus Discusses John the Baptizer and Elijah	17:9–13	9:9–13		
100. Jesus Casts a Stubborn Demon out of a Boy	17:14–21	9:14–29	9:37–42	
101. Jesus Again Predicts His Death and Resurrection	17:22–23	9:30–32	9:43–45	
102. Jesus Produces a Coin to Pay the Temple Tax	17:24–27			
103. Jesus Teaches about Service	18:1–11	9:33–50	9:46–50	
104. Jesus Teaches about Reclamation and Forgiveness	18:15–22			
105. Jesus Refuses to Destroy a Samaritan Village			9:51–56	
106. The Parable of the Unforgiving Slave	18:23–35			
107. Jesus Challenges His Followers to Full Commitment	8:19–22		9:57–62	

	Matthew	Mark	Luke	John
108. Jesus Hesitates about Going to Jerusalem				7:1–9
109. Jesus' Discussion at the Festival of Tabernacles				7:10–52
110. Jesus Forgives a Woman Accused of Adultery				7:53–8:11
111. Jesus Claims to Be the Light of the World				8:12–59
112. Jesus Heals a Man Blind from Birth				9:1–41
113. Jesus Claims to Be the Good Shepherd				10:1–21
114. Jesus Sends Seventy Followers on a Preaching Mission			10:1–24	
115. The Parable of the Good Samaritan			10:25–37	
116. Jesus Visits Mary and Martha in Bethany			10:38–42	
117. Jesus Teaches the Disciples How to Pray	6:9–13		11:1–13	
118. Jesus Accused of Healing through Beelzebul			11:14–28	
119. The Sign of Jonah			11:29–36	
120. Jesus Criticized by a Pharisee and an Expert in the Law			11:37–54	
121. Jesus Warns about the Deception of the Pharisees			12:1–12	
122. The Parable of the Rich Fool			12:13–21	
123. The Wildflowers and the Ravens			12:22–34	
124. Jesus Discusses His Second Coming			12:35–48	
125. Jesus Predicts His Death by Crucifixion			12:49–59	
126. The Parable of the Barren Fig Tree			13:1–9	
127. Jesus Heals a Woman with a Crooked Back			13:10–17	
128. Jesus Claims to Be One with God				10:22–42
129. The Narrow Way of Salvation			13:22–30	

	Matthew	Mark	Luke	John
130. Jesus Is Warned about Herod			13:31–33	
131. Jesus Expresses His Sorrow over Jerusalem	23:37–39		13:34–35	
132. Jesus Heals a Man Whose Body Was Swollen with Fluid			14:1–6	
133. Jesus Teaches about Humility			14:7–14	
134. The Parable of the Large Banquet			14:15–24	
135. The Cost of Following Jesus			14:25–35	
136. The Parable of the Lost Sheep	18:12–14		15:1–7	
137. The Parable of the Lost Coin			15:8–10	
138. The Parable of the Lost Son			15:11–32	
139. The Parable of the Dishonest Manager			16:1–18	
140. The Parable of the Rich Man and Lazarus			16:19–31	
141. Jesus Teaches about Faith and Service			17:1–10	
142. Jesus Raises Lazarus from the Dead				11:1–44
143. The Sanhedrin's Plot against Jesus				11:45–54
144. Jesus Heals Ten Lepers on His Way to Jerusalem			17:11–19	
145. Jesus Teaches about the Advent of the Kingdom			17:20–37	
146. Parables on Prayer: The Persistent Widow and the Proud Pharisee			18:1–14	
147. Jesus Discusses Divorce and Remarriage	19:1–12	10:1–12		
148. Jesus Welcomes Little Children	19:13–15	10:13–16	18:15–17	
149. Jesus and the Rich Young Ruler	19:16–30	10:17–31	18:18–30	
150. The Parable of the Vineyard Workers	20:1–16			
151. Jesus Again Discusses His Death and Resurrection	20:17–19	10:32–34	18:31–34	

	Matthew	Mark	Luke	John
152. James and John Ask for Prominent Places in Jesus' Kingdom	20:20–28	10:35–45		
153. Jesus Heals Blind Bartimaeus	20:29–34	10:46–52	18:35–43	
154. Jesus Talks with Zacchaeus			19:1–10	
155. The Parable of the Minas			19:11–27	

VI. JESUS' FINAL DAYS IN JERUSALEM

	Matthew	Mark	Luke	John
156. The Sanhedrin Plots against Jesus and Lazarus				11:55– 12:1,9–11
157. Jesus' Triumphal Entry into Jerusalem	21:1–11	11:1–11	19:28–44	12:12–19
158. Jesus Curses a Fig Tree and Cleanses the Temple	21:12–19	11:12–19	19:45–48	
159. Greeks Ask to See Jesus				12:20–50
160. The Message of the Withered Fig Tree	21:19–22	11:20–26		
161. The Sanhedrin Questions Jesus' Authority	21:23–27	11:27–33	20:1–8	
162. The Parable of the Two Vineyard Workers	21:28–32			
163. The Parable of the Vineyard Owner	21:33–46	12:1–12	20:9–19	
164. The Parable of the Wedding Banquet	22:1–14			
165. Jesus Questioned about Paying Taxes to Caesar	22:15–22	12:13–17	20:20–26	
166. The Sadducees Question Jesus about the Resurrection	22:23–33	12:18–27	20:27–40	
167. Jesus Discusses the Greatest Commandment	22:34–40	12:28–34		
168. Jesus Discusses the Deity of the Davidic Messiah	22:41–46	12:35–37	20:41–44	
169. Jesus Condemns the Scribes and Pharisees	23:1–36	12:38–40	20:45–47	
170. A Sacrificial Offering by a Poor Widow		12:41–44	21:1–4	

	Matthew	Mark	Luke	John
171. Jesus' Great Prophetic Discourse	24:1–51	13:1–37	21:5–38	
172. The Parable of the Ten Virgins	25:1–13			
173. The Parable of the Talents	25:14–30			
174. The Sheep and the Goats	25:31–46			
175. The Sanhedrin Continues Its Plot against Jesus	26:1–5	14:1–2	22:1–2	
176. Mary of Bethany Anoints Jesus	26:6–13	14:3–9		12:2–8
177. Judas Plans to Betray Jesus	26:14–16	14:10–11	22:3–6	
178. Preparations Made for the Memorial Supper	26:17–19	14:12–16	22:7–13	
179. Jesus Washes the Disciples' Feet				13:1–20
✳180. Jesus Identifies Judas as the Betrayer	26:20–25	14:17–21	22:21–23	13:21–30
✳181. Jesus Predicts That His Disciples Will Deny Him	26:31–35	14:27–31	22:31–38	13:31–38
182. Jesus Teaches about True Greatness			22:24–30	
183. Jesus Institutes the Memorial Supper	26:26–30	14:22–26	22:14–20	
184. Jesus' Farewell to His Disciples				14:1–16:33
185. Jesus' Intercessory Prayer for His Disciples				17:1–26
186. Jesus' Agony in the Garden of Gethsemane	26:36–46	14:26, 32–42	22:39–46	

VII. TRIAL AND CRUCIFIXION

	Matthew	Mark	Luke	John
✳187. Jesus Betrayed and Arrested	26:47–56	14:43–52	22:47–53	18:1–12
188. Hearing before Annas				18:12–14, 19–23
✳189. Jesus Appears before Caiaphas	26:57–68	14:53–65	22:54, 63–65	18:24
✳190. Peter Denies Jesus	26:58, 69–75	14:54, 66–72	22:54–62	18:15–18, 25–27
191. Jesus Condemned by the Sanhedrin	27:1–2	15:1	22:66–23:1	

	Matthew	Mark	Luke	John
192. Judas Iscariot Commits Suicide	27:3–10			
*193. Jesus' First Hearing before Pilate	27:2,11–14	15:1–5	23:2–5	18:28–38
194. Pilate Sends Jesus to Herod Antipas			23:6–10	
195. Herod Sends Jesus Back to Pilate			23:11–12	
*196. Jesus Condemned to Die	27:15–26	15:6–15	23:13–25	18:39–19:16
197. Jesus Mocked by the Soldiers	27:27–31	15:16–20		
198. Simon Carries the Cross to the Crucifixion Site	27:32	15:21	23:26–31	
*199. Jesus Is Crucified	27:33–37	15:22–26	23:32–34	19:17–24
*200. Jesus' Mother and Other Women at the Cross	27:55–56	15:40–41	23:49	19:25–27
201. Jesus Mocked by the Crowd	27:39–43	15:29–32	23:35–38	
202. Two Criminals Are Crucified with Jesus	27:38,44	15:27–28	23:39–43	
*203. Supernatural Events Surrounding Jesus' Death	27:45–54	15:33–39	23:44–48	19:28–30
204. Soldiers Pierce the Side of Jesus				19:31–37
*205. Jesus Buried in Joseph's Tomb	27:57–60	15:42–46	23:50–54	19:38–42
206. Women Mourn at the Guarded Tomb	27:61–66	15:47	23:55–56	

VIII. RESURRECTION, POST-RESURRECTION APPEARANCES, AND ASCENSION

	Matthew	Mark	Luke	John
207. Jesus Is Resurrected	28:2–4			
208. Women Visit the Tomb to Anoint Jesus' Body	28:1	16:1–4	24:1–2	
*209. Women Discover the Empty Tomb	28:5–8	16:5–8	24:3–8	20:1–2
210. Peter and John Hurry to the Tomb			24:9–12	20:3–10
211. Jesus Appears to Mary Magdalene		16:9–11		20:11–18
212. Jesus Sends the Women to Tell the Disciples	28:8–10			
213. Soldiers Bribed by the Sanhedrin	28:11–15			

	Matthew	Mark	Luke	John
214. Jesus Appears to Two Followers at Emmaus			24:13–32	
215. Simon Peter Sees Jesus			24:33–35	
216. Jesus Appears to His Disciples, but Thomas Is Absent			24:36–43	20:19–25
217. Jesus Appears to Thomas and the Other Disciples				20:26–29
218. A Miraculous Catch of Fish at Lake Galilee				21:1–14
219. Jesus Reinstates Peter				21:15–19
220. Jesus and Peter Discuss the Future of the Apostle John				21:20–24
221. Jesus Commissions His Disciples to Continue His Work	28:16–20	16:15–18		
222. Jesus Ascends to His Father			24:44–53	
223. John's Statement of Purpose and Conclusion for His Gospel				20:30–31; 21:25

ACKNOWLEDGMENTS

This book is the fulfillment of a dream I have had for many years. Most dreams are more than solo performances, and I have certainly found this true in the pursuit of this project. My thanks to the following people for their contribution.

Steve Bond, editor at Broadman & Holman Publishers, Nashville, Tennessee, encouraged me in this project when I first mentioned it to him more than three years ago. He sold his coworkers on the idea and provided helpful suggestions along the way. Thanks, Steve, for your enthusiasm and support.

Several other people at Broadman & Holman also deserve a special word of thanks. Editor Lawrence Kimbrough kept me on track, helping me polish and refine my approach. David Shepherd, editorial director, also gave me valuable formatting and marketing input. Editor John Landers made a major contribution by reviewing the manuscript and comparing it carefully with other Gospel harmonies, especially *A Harmony of the Gospels* by A. T. Robertson. My thanks to him for his valuable insights and helpful suggestions. Lloyd Mullens and Kim Overcash also helped out by directing me to resource materials and keeping me informed about issues regarding the Holman Christian Standard Bible.

I'm also grateful to Broadman & Holman for giving me permission to adapt material from *Broadman Comments* for use in this book. Many of the notes on the Gospels are drawn from the past ten years or so of this popular annual Bible lesson commentary. This material was written originally by Bob Dean and the late Donald Ackland, former colleagues of mine at LifeWay Christian Resources, Nashville. My thanks to these two fine Bible students for their insights into the life and ministry of Jesus as portrayed by the Gospel writers.

A special thanks to my wife Dorothy, who served as word processor, research associate, and general helper on this project. Her computer skills made the impossible doable. And her positive attitude and encouragement kept me focused on the goal. I'm fortunate to have her on my writing and editorial team.

Finally, I'm indebted to a class of senior adult men at Haywood Hills Baptist Church, Nashville, Tennessee, for keeping me excited about studying the Word of God—especially the life of Jesus. Their eager questions and comments have been a constant source of inspiration and motivation to me as their teacher. I have tried to keep everyday Bible students like them in mind as I have worked on this book. I send it forth with the prayer that it may bring people to a greater knowledge and understanding of Him of whom it was said:

"Who can this be? He commands even the winds and the waves, and they obey Him!" (Luke 8:25).

"Who is this man who even forgives sins?" (Luke 7:49).

George W. Knight
Nashville, Tennessee

The writer of the Book of Ecclesiastes declared, "There is no end to the making of many books" (Eccl. 12:12). If this Old Testament writer had been living in the centuries after the New Testament, he might have said the same thing about Gospel harmonies. Many harmonies of the life of Jesus from the four Gospels have been published over the years, so why do we need another?

This book reflects my conviction that there is a need for a *simplified* harmony directed to a *popular* audience—laypeople, ministers, Bible teachers, and other nonspecialist Bible students. Most harmonies are designed for scholars and other specialists who know the original Greek language. There is certainly a place for these books. But in my own Bible-teaching ministry, I have often wished for a harmony that was simple, straightforward, and easy to use. I have designed the *Simplified Harmony of the Gospels* to meet this need.

This book also goes a step beyond most harmonies by including explanatory notes on the Gospel narratives. The purpose of these comments is to help the reader understand and apply the life and teachings of Jesus. Space limitations have kept these notes brief, but they still provide helpful information for general Bible students who do not have access to longer commentaries on the Gospels.

The text of the Gospels that appears in the *Simplified Harmony* is from the Holman Christian Standard Bible (HCSB). This new and fresh rendering of God's Word is as close as it can be to a literal translation of the actual words of the Greek text. But it is also easy to read and understand at the same time. A translation of this type is especially appropriate for a harmonistic study of the life and ministry of Jesus. See the accompanying introductory comments, "About the Holman Christian Standard Bible," for a discussion of more distinctives of this new translation.

In the text of the *Simplified Harmony,* the life and ministry of Jesus is divided into 223 individual segments. These segments are numbered and arranged chronologically for easy comparison and comprehension. These numbers also help the reader find a specific Gospel segment quickly, since the expanded outline of the *Harmony* at the front of the book is keyed to this numbering system.

A quick glance at the expanded outline (see p. vii) reveals a major benefit of studying the life of Jesus in harmonistic fashion. For example, consider segment 11, "Jesus Born in Bethlehem" (Luke 2:1–7). Only Luke gives any details about the actual birth of Jesus. But Matthew records the visit of the Magi to Jesus when He was about two years old (see segment 15, "The Wise Men Visit Jesus," Matt. 2:1–12). This event is unique to Matthew's Gospel. And so it goes throughout the life of Jesus: each of the Gospels includes events not reported by any other Gospel writer. Neither Matthew, Mark, Luke, nor John alone gives the total story of Jesus' life and ministry. We get a better picture of who He was and what

He did when we organize the information from all four Gospels in chronological order and study His life and ministry in harmonistic fashion.

Most people who have studied the life of Jesus also realize there is duplication and overlap among the Gospels. They often report the same event from His life and teachings. But these individual accounts sometimes emphasize a different part of the story or give different details. For example, look at segment 79, "Jesus Heals a Wild Man among the Tombs" (p. 91)—an event reported by Matthew, Mark, and Luke. These accounts differ slightly from one another. Notice that different details from each of these Gospels have been woven into one single, unified account of this event. The different Gospel passages are identified with superscripts in the text (for example, $^{Mk\ 5:1-5}$Then they came to the other side of the sea).

Note in this example that words in italics within brackets show alternative readings from the various Gospels. For example, [$^{Mt\ 8:28b}$ *two demon-possessed men*] means that Matthew reports two men came out of the tombs to meet Jesus, while Mark and Luke mention only one man.

Major differences like this among parallel Gospel accounts are generally pointed out in the accompanying notes as well as highlighted in the Gospel text. All this information should enable Bible students to do careful comparative analysis and detailed study of the life and ministry of Jesus as presented by the individual Gospel writers.

The *Simplified Harmony of the Gospels* can also be used as a guide for reading through the harmonized life of Jesus. Just follow the suggestions at the back of the book (see "A Systematic Reading Plan," p. 257).

At the back of this book you will find four indices—Matthew, Mark, Luke, and John—to help you locate parallel Gospel passages quickly and easily. For example, let's assume you are preparing a Bible study on Luke's account of the feeding of the five thousand (Luke 9:10–17). You would like to know if the other Gospels report this event and what they say about it.

Turn to the "Luke Scripture Index" (see p. 260). Luke 9:10–17 sends you to page 103 in the *Simplified Harmony,* where you find segment 86, "Feeding of the Five Thousand." You note that all four Gospels report this event. You can read each Gospel writer's account in its entirety from your own Bible, study the merged account in the Holman Christian Standard Bible translation in the *Harmony,* or study the notes on this event in the *Harmony* for insights to use in your Bible class.

Finally, you will find a subject index to the *Harmony* at the back of the book (p. 263). This index is helpful in locating any person, place, or event covered in the Gospel accounts of the life of Jesus. For example, let's assume you would like to find the account of Jesus' discussion with Nicodemus about the new birth. You look under *Nicodemus* in the subject index. This directs you to segment 28, "Jesus Explains the New Birth to Nicodemus."

The *Simplified Harmony of the Gospels* is a vast treasury of information for leisurely Bible reading, serious study, and lesson preparation. It should keep you excited for many years about studying the life of Jesus—an inexhaustible subject that is always fresh and new.

Bible study is the road God's people take to hear and obey our Creator and Savior. The Holman Christian Standard Bible™ offers believers in the third millennium an up-to-date translation designed specifically for the needs of students of Scripture. It seeks to provide a translation as close to the words of the Hebrew and Greek texts as possible while still maintaining the literary quality and ease of reading that invite and enable people to read, study, and obey God's Word. To reach God's people effectively, a translation must provide a reverent, exalted text that is also within reach of its readers.

Translating the Bible into English offers a double challenge. First, each language has its own vocabulary, grammar, and syntax that cannot be rendered exactly into another language. Second, contemporary culture so honors relativism and individual freedom that it distrusts claims to absolute authority.

Precision with Clarity

The first challenge means that English translators must avoid creating a special form of the language that does not communicate well to modern readers. For example, John 1:6 in Greek reads, "was a man having been sent from God, name to him John." The English translator must provide a word order and syntax that follow the dynamics of the English language and that are familiar to English readers. In this instance, the Holman Christian Standard Bible reads, "There was a man named John who was sent from God." This accurately represents the Greek text but also presents it in a form that readers should find inviting and natural.

On the other hand, the Holman Christian Standard Bible is not based on a theory of translation that considers completely dispensable the form of the original language. Rules governing word order are very different in Hebrew, Greek, and English. But English shares with Hebrew and Greek certain grammatical forms such as nouns, verbs, prepositional phrases, independent and dependent clauses, and so forth. In most cases these forms perform similar functions in English as they do in Hebrew or Greek.

Therefore, since grammatical form is one way that language communicates, we have retained the grammatical form of the original whenever it can be rendered into English with sufficient accuracy and clarity. Nevertheless, this is not a strict word-for-word translation, since it is often impossible to render one and only one English word for every Hebrew or Greek word. Language differences often require several English words to render one Hebrew or Greek word, and sometimes a Hebrew or Greek phrase may be more accurately and clearly translated by one word in English.

Communicating with Authority

The second challenge, that of contemporary culture, means translators must hold firm to traditional beliefs about the authority of Scripture and avoid modern temptations to rewrite the Bible to say what modern readers want to hear. Translators must remember that the divine Author of the Bible inspired His Word for people today and for all time just as much as for the original audience. The Holman Christian Standard Bible stands on the authority of God and has attempted to provide an accurate and readable translation of the ancient texts.

The mission of the Holman Christian Standard Bible is to produce as precise a translation of the Hebrew, Aramaic, and Greek Scriptures as possible with the use of newly-published lexicons, grammars, and computer programs. The goal of this kind of translation is to encourage in-depth Bible study, but this translation also seeks to be highly readable (for public and private use) and also useful for personal memorization.

Jesus and the Four Gospels

Since the four Gospels were not written as formal biographies, they don't tell us everything we would like to know about Jesus. The purpose of the Gospel writers was to show how God revealed Himself uniquely in the life and ministry of His Son. Precise details about His life were not so important to them as the realization by their readers that Jesus was one in whom they could place their faith and trust. They wrote to call people to commitment to Him as Lord and Savior (see John 20:31).

Because of this faith orientation of the Gospels, reproducing a precise chronology of Jesus' days on earth from the information they contain is difficult. But a general outline of His life and ministry emerges from the four Gospels.

Summary of Jesus' Life

1. Jesus was born in 6/5 B.C. in Bethlehem of Judea, the southernmost province of Palestine. He and His family eventually settled in the northernmost province of Galilee in the village of Nazareth—hometown of His earthly parents Mary and Joseph. In Nazareth Jesus grew to manhood with His brothers and sisters—all born to Mary and Joseph by natural means after His own miraculous conception and birth.

2. When He was "about thirty years old" (Luke 3:23), Jesus announced the beginning of His public ministry by identifying with the message of repentance being preached by John the Baptizer in Judea. He also submitted to baptism at the hands of John, whom He recognized as His forerunner. The Baptizer, a relative of Jesus, was about six months older than Jesus. Their ministries must have overlapped by about six to twelve months. But John's work came to an end when he was arrested by Herod Antipas, Roman governor of Judea. Jesus redirected His ministry away from Herod's territory by moving north into the province of Galilee.

3. Rejected by the people of His hometown, Nazareth, Jesus moved to Capernaum near Lake Galilee. This city served as the headquarters for His great Galilean ministry, which lasted about eighteen months. During these months, He selected His twelve disciples and began to train them for the mission they would assume after His death, resurrection, and ascension. Galilee was the setting for His Sermon on the Mount, other major teachings, and many of His parables and healing miracles.

4. When Jesus learned that John the Baptizer had been executed by Herod Antipas, He began to withdraw from Galilee as the focus of His ministry. His

popularity with the Galileans was declining because they realized He was not going to be a political or military Messiah. The Jewish religious leaders grew more and more hostile toward Him because He ignored their cherished traditions and claimed to be the Son of God. He stepped up His training of the disciples as He sensed the time of His death was drawing near. During the final year of Jesus' earthly life, He concentrated His ministry in Judea, Jerusalem, and a region known as Perea. Situated east of the Jordan River, Perea was populated mostly by Gentiles.

5. Jesus' earthly ministry came to an end during the Jewish Passover celebration in Jerusalem, probably in A.D. 30. The Jewish ruling council, the Sanhedrin, determined that He must die because of His blasphemous claim to be the Son of God. They convinced Pontius Pilate, the Roman governor of Judea, that He was a dangerous revolutionary who challenged the authority of Rome.

6. Executed by crucifixion and placed in a borrowed tomb, Jesus was gloriously resurrected, as He had predicted. Before His ascension to the Father, He spent forty days with His followers, proving that He was alive and strengthening them for their mission of proclaiming His gospel to all the world.

The Witness of the Gospels

For at least twenty to twenty-five years after Jesus' ascension, stories of His life and ministry must have circulated mainly in oral form. People who had known Jesus in the flesh—particularly the apostles of Jesus—told others what they remembered from their firsthand observance of His teachings and miracles. But as these eyewitnesses grew older and began to pass from the scene, they realized the need to put these accounts in writing so they could be passed down to future generations.

Mark's Gospel was probably the first to appear, written about A.D. 62. This was followed within a few years by Luke and Matthew. These three Gospels circulated for twenty to twenty-five years before the fourth and final Gospel appeared. The Gospel of John, according to most New Testament scholars, was written about A.D. 85–90.

Matthew, Mark, and Luke are known as the Synoptic Gospels because they take basically the same approach to reporting on the life and ministry of Jesus. The word *synoptic* comes from a Greek word *synopsis,* meaning "a seeing together." They report many of the same events from Jesus' life, using similar wording, content, and chronological arrangement.

For example, look at the expanded outline of the *Harmony* at the front of the book. Notice segments 20, 21, and 22 are parallel passages from each of these three Gospels. They report on these events almost as if they were written by the same writer, including some of the same details. Look under the Matthew, Mark, and Luke columns throughout the expanded outline and you will notice a consistent pattern of "seeing together" by these three Gospels.

Since Mark was probably the first Gospel written, many scholars believe Luke and Matthew followed Mark's lead. They probably used some of Mark's material, supplementing it with accounts contributed by other eyewitnesses. As the shortest Gospel, Mark contains only a few verses that have no parallel in Matthew or Luke. On the other hand, Matthew and Luke contain a great deal of material that appears in no other Gospel. Again, check this principle by looking at the Matthew and Luke columns in the expanded outline of the *Harmony* at the front of the book.

Matthew, Mark, and Luke may have been well known to the author of John by the time he wrote his Gospel. Perhaps this is why he took a different approach to the life and ministry of Jesus. He was not satisfied just to report what Jesus said and did. He went beyond the obvious to tell us the theological meaning of His sayings and miracles.

For example, not a single parable of Jesus appears in the Gospel of John. Only a few of Jesus' short sayings so typical in Matthew, Mark, and Luke appear in his Gospel. Instead, John chooses to expand upon an incident and give its deeper meaning. Two good examples of this technique are Jesus' discussion with Nicodemus (John 3:1–21) and Jesus' healing of the man blind from birth (John 9:1–41).

John's Gospel also supplements the Synoptic Gospels by giving us a more accurate picture of the length and chronology of Jesus' public ministry. Matthew, Mark, and Luke report that Jesus taught and healed in the province of Galilee, but they mention only one journey of Jesus to Jerusalem to celebrate the Jewish Passover. One might conclude from reading only the Synoptic Gospels that Jesus' ministry lasted less than one year.

But the Gospel of John tells us that Jesus made at least three trips to the Holy City to observe the Passover (John 2:13, 23; 6:4; 12:1). He also cites longer periods of ministry in the southern province of Judea. John's chronology is probably a better portrait of the length and scope of Jesus' ministry.

We are fortunate that we have four separate accounts of the life of Jesus. Even the Synoptics, though similar, give us three distinctive views of Him. This enriches our understanding of who Jesus was and what He did. The four Gospels were written to different audiences and for different purposes. The following unique portraits of Jesus emerge from Matthew, Mark, Luke, and John, respectively.

Matthew, written primarily to Jews, portrays Jesus as the Messiah—the fulfillment of Old Testament prophecy. As the first book of the New Testament, Matthew serves as a natural bridge between God's old covenant with the Jewish nation and His new covenant with all Christian believers.

Mark describes Jesus as a man of decisive action who identifies with humanity through the human side of His nature as the God-man. Mark directed his Gospel to a non-Jewish audience, particularly people of Roman background.

Luke, a Gentile physician, wanted other Gentiles to realize through his Gospel that Jesus is the universal Savior who feels compassion particularly for the poor and outcast.

John describes Jesus as the eternal Word who participated with God in the creation of the universe. Jesus' miracles are "signs" that identify Him as the divine Son of God. John wrote his Gospel for the widest possible readership, using both Jewish and Greek ideas. In John, Jesus speaks not to any specific nation or ethnic group but to all people everywhere.

Look for these and other portraits of Jesus as you study this *Harmony* of Jesus' life and ministry. Better still, expect to be surprised by some new discovery about Him that will enrich your life. Jesus is still surprising people and changing lives, just as He did almost two thousand years ago. As Mark reported of the crowds who observed Jesus: "They were extremely astonished and said, 'He has done everything well! He even makes deaf people hear, and people unable to speak, talk!'" (Mark 7:37).

I. INTRODUCTION TO THE GOOD NEWS

All the Gospels except Mark contain information of an introductory nature that sets the stage for the birth of Jesus. Luke contains the most information of this type. His Gospel tells us about the events surrounding the birth of John the Baptizer; the announcement to Mary of the forthcoming birth of Jesus; Mary's visit to her relative Elizabeth, the mother of John the Baptizer; and the genealogy of Jesus as traced through Mary.

Matthew enumerates the family line of Jesus as traced through Joseph and tells us about Joseph's reassuring dream regarding Mary's pregnancy. The Gospel of John contributes its famous prologue that describes Jesus as the true Light and the Word made flesh.

1. LUKE'S PREFACE AND DEDICATION

Luke 1:1–4

¹Since many have undertaken to compile a narrative about the events that have been fulfilled among us, ²just as the **original eyewitnesses** and servants of the word handed them down to us, ³it also seemed good to me, having carefully investigated everything from the very first, to write to you in orderly sequence, **most honorable Theophilus**, ⁴so that you may know the certainty of the things about which you have been instructed.

2. JOHN'S INTRODUCTION

John 1:1–18

¹**In the beginning was the Word**, and the Word was with God, and the **Word was God**. ²He was with God in the beginning. ³**All things were created**

---

1. LUKE'S PREFACE AND DEDICATION

original eyewitnesses: In writing his Gospel, Luke depended on people who had been with Jesus during His earthly ministry. A Gentile physician (Col. 4:14), Luke became a close companion of the apostle Paul and author of the Book of Acts who recorded Paul's missionary journeys. He had many opportunities to meet people who knew Jesus personally. Luke investigated their accounts of Jesus' life and ministry "carefully" and "from the very first" before writing his Gospel.

most honorable Theophilus: The purpose of Luke's Gospel was to show people of Greek and Roman background that Jesus was the humble servant of God. Thus, Luke dedicated his Gospel (and the Book of Acts) to this unknown Gentile of high official rank. Theophilus may have been the chief magistrate of some city in Greece or Asia Minor.

2. JOHN'S INTRODUCTION

In the beginning was the Word: These words call to mind Genesis 1:1, but they go beyond creation into eternity itself to affirm the preexistence of Jesus Christ as the eternal Word.

Word was God: With these words John affirmed the full deity of Jesus Christ. This claim was John's answer to a growing heresy of his times, Gnosticism, which minimized the importance of Jesus by making Him just one of many spiritual entities linking heaven with earth.

All things were created through Him: The eternal Word participated in the creation of all things. God the Father is

through Him, and apart from Him not one thing was created that has been created. [4]In Him was life, and that **life** was the **light** of men. [5]That light shines in the darkness, yet the darkness did not overcome it.

The Incarnation of Jesus

The introduction to the Gospel of John contains one of the strongest affirmations of the doctrine of the incarnation in the entire New Testament. The word incarnation means "embodied in flesh." John declares that Jesus—the divine Son of God—took on a human body as a necessary step for carrying out God's plan of redemption in the world. Jesus is the God-man—fully human and fully divine—who can be experienced and understood by us as human beings.

[6]There was a **man named John** who was sent from God. [7]He came as a witness to testify about the light, so that all might believe through him. [8]**He was not the light**, but he came to testify about the light. [9]The **true light**, who gives light to everyone, was coming into the world. [10]He was in the world, and the world was created through Him, yet the **world did not know Him**. [11]He came to His own, and His own people did not receive Him. [12]But to all who did receive Him, He gave them the right to be children of God, to those who believe in His name, [13]who were born, not of blood, or of the will of the flesh, or of the will of man, but of God.

[14]The **Word became flesh** and took up residence among us. We observed His glory, the glory as the only Son from the Father, **full of grace and truth**.

---

the source of divine creation, but He created all things through the Word.

life . . . light: In His creative capacity, the Word bestowed life, and in His redemptive work He offered eternal life. By becoming "alive" in the form of a human being, Jesus brought the light of God's revelation into the world.

man named John: John the Baptizer broke a four-hundred-year silence when he appeared in the wilderness of Judea in the role of the ancient prophets. Notice the contrast between the words used to describe the Word and John. John "came," but the eternal Word "was." John was "a man," but the Word was "with God." John was "sent from God," but the Word "was God."

He was not the light: John had an important, God-given mission—to bear witness to Jesus in such a way that people would believe in Him. However, the Baptizer must not be confused with the One to whom he bore witness.

true light: As the eternal Light, Jesus would make the truth of God available to every person. He is the only source of this true knowledge.

world did not know Him: The irony is that Jesus came to the world He had created, but the world rejected Him. Especially tragic was the rejection of the Word by the very people who had been prepared to receive Him. He was born a Jew, but many of His countrymen rejected Him. But not everyone rejected Him. John and all the earliest believers were Jews. Later they were joined by a host of Gentile believers.

Word became flesh: This phrase describes the reality, glory, and purpose of the incarnation of the Son of God. The word *flesh* shows the full humanity of the eternal Word. The phrase "the glory as the only Son from the Father" shows His full deity. The Gnostics claimed that the Son of God only appeared to become human; John insisted that He became fully human.

full of grace and truth: Jesus was the vehicle of divine grace expressed in His deeds of mercy and sacrificial love. He was also the vehicle of divine truth as He taught His listeners about God and themselves, about God in His holiness and justice, and about themselves in their sinful condition and need for salvation.

[15](John testified concerning Him and exclaimed, "This was the One of whom I said, 'The One coming after me has surpassed me, because He existed before me.'") [16]For we have all received grace after grace from His fullness. [17]For the **law was given through Moses**; grace and truth came through Jesus Christ.

[18]No one has ever seen God. The only Son—the One who is at the Father's side—**He has revealed Him**.

3. ANNOUNCEMENT OF THE BIRTH OF JOHN THE BAPTIZER

Luke 1:5–25

[5]In the days of **King Herod** of Judea, there was a **priest of Abijah's division** named Zachariah. His wife was from the **daughters of Aaron**, and her name was Elizabeth. [6]**Both were righteous** in God's sight, living without blame according to all the commandments and requirements of the Lord. [7]But they had no children because Elizabeth could not conceive, and both of them were well along in years.

[8]When his division was on duty, and he was serving as priest before God, [9]it happened that he was chosen by lot, according to the custom of the priesthood, to enter the sanctuary of the Lord and burn incense. [10]At the **hour of incense** the whole assembly of the people was praying outside. [11]**An angel of the Lord** appeared to him, standing to the right of the altar of incense. [12]When Zachariah saw him, he was startled and overcome with fear.

---

law was given through Moses: God made Himself known in an intimate way through Moses. But not even Moses saw God in the full sense in which He later revealed Himself in His Son Jesus. Jesus declared, "Believe in me and you shall have life eternal." This is the message of divine grace. It offers blessing not as a reward for good works but as a free gift.

He has revealed Him: Jesus came into the world to be the revealer of the Father. This was the reason for the incarnation—that God might be made known in all His love, compassion, justice, and redemptive purpose.

3. ANNOUNCEMENT OF THE BIRTH OF JOHN THE BAPTIZER

King Herod: Herod the Great reigned under Roman authority from 40 to 4 B.C. He was responsible for rebuilding the temple in Jerusalem. He was also a ruthless tyrant, polluting the land with pagan institutions and imposing death on any who resisted him. Luke introduced his Gospel against this somber background.

priest of Abijah's division . . . daughters of Aaron: Priests who served in the temple were divided into twenty-four groups, or orders. There were thousands of these priests, serving a week at a time as the turn for their order came around. Zachariah was a priest, and his wife Elizabeth was a priest's daughter. They were childless.

Both were righteous: Zachariah and Elizabeth were godly people who kept the Ten Commandments and observed the requirements of their religion.

hour of incense: Priests were chosen by lot to officiate at certain rituals. Because there were so many priests, no one offered incense more than once during his life. So this was Zachariah's big day—when he served at the altar of incense. The incense symbolized the prayers of the priest and people going up to God. While Zachariah was inside the temple offering the incense, the people were praying outside the area in which the priests served.

An angel of the Lord: While engaged in this task, Zachariah was confronted by the angel Gabriel. He was troubled and terrified by this heavenly messenger. The angel reassured Zachariah by quieting his fears.

The Angel Gabriel

Gabriel was an archangel, a heavenly being higher in rank than an angel. As a special messenger from God, he appeared to Daniel in the Old Testament (Dan. 8:16). Gabriel's appearance to Zachariah and to the virgin Mary (Luke 1:26–38) was a dramatic statement from God that the Messiah would soon appear. Some interpreters believe Gabriel is the archangel whose voice will be heard when Christ appears in the clouds (1 Thess. 4:16).

[13]But the angel said to him: "Do not be afraid, Zachariah, because your prayer has been heard. Your wife Elizabeth will **bear you a son**, and you will name him John. [14]There will be joy and delight for you, and many will rejoice at his birth. [15]For he will be great in the sight of the Lord, and will never drink wine or beer. And he will be filled with the Holy Spirit while still in his mother's womb. [16]He will turn many of the sons of Israel to the Lord their God. [17]And he will go before Him in the spirit and power of Elijah, to turn the hearts of fathers to their children, and the disobedient to the understanding of the righteous, to make ready for the Lord a prepared people."

[18]"How can I know this?" Zachariah asked the angel. "For **I am an old man**, and my wife is well along in years."

[19]The angel answered him, "I am Gabriel, who stands in the presence of God, and I was sent to speak to you and tell you this good news. [20]Now listen! You will become **silent and unable to speak** until the day these things take place, because you did not believe my words, which will be fulfilled in their proper time."

[21]Meanwhile, the people were waiting for Zachariah, amazed that he stayed so long in the sanctuary. [22]When he did come out, he could not speak to them. Then they realized that he had seen a vision in the sanctuary. He kept making signs to them and remained speechless. [23]And when the days of his ministry were completed, he went back home.

[24]After these days his wife **Elizabeth** conceived, and **kept herself in seclusion** for five months. She said, [25]"The Lord has done this for me. He has looked with favor in these days to take away my disgrace among the people."

---

bear you a son: Zachariah and his wife had been praying for a son; it was every Jewish woman's hope that she might be the mother of the Messiah. The child of Gabriel's promise would not fulfill this hope, but he would be the forerunner of the long-expected deliverer.

I am an old man: As a priest, Zachariah must have been familiar with the story of Abraham and Sarah, to whom God gave a son in their old age (Gen. 21:1–7). But he could not believe that he and his wife would produce a child in their advanced years.

silent and unable to speak: Zachariah wanted some evidence of the angel's authority and of the truth of his message. The sign he received was that he would be unable to speak until the day that the promise of a child was fulfilled. This sign was also a penalty for his unbelief. Zachariah would have nine months of enforced silence to reflect on his lack of spiritual perception and the wonder of God's providence and power.

Elizabeth . . . kept herself in seclusion: Why did Elizabeth hide for five months? During her barren years, perhaps she had seen looks of scorn and heard words of reproach about her childlessness. She did not want to endure any more of these when she was pregnant. Thus, she avoided people until she was a mother or at least until her pregnancy was apparent.

4. Announcement of the Birth of Jesus

Luke 1:26–38

[26]In the **sixth month**, the angel Gabriel was sent by God to **a town in Galilee called Nazareth**, [27]to a virgin **engaged** to a man named Joseph, of the house of David. The virgin's name was Mary. [28]And he came to her and said, "Rejoice, **favored woman**! The Lord is with you."

[29]But she was **deeply troubled** by this statement and was wondering what kind of greeting this could be.

[30]Then the angel told her: "Do not be afraid, Mary, for you have found favor with God. [31]Now listen: You will conceive and give birth to a son, and you will **call His name JESUS**. [32]He will be great and will be called the Son of the Most High, and the Lord God will give Him the **throne of His father David**. [33]He will reign over the house of Jacob forever, and His kingdom will have no end."

[34]Mary asked the angel, "**How can this be**, since I have not been intimate with a man?"

[35]The angel replied to her: "The Holy Spirit will come upon you, and the power of the Most

The Virgin Birth of Jesus

The miraculous conception of Jesus and His birth to a virgin mother was just as puzzling for Mary as it is for most of us today (see Luke 1:34). But God did not give Mary— or us—a medical explanation. In some strange and mysterious way, God would "overshadow" Mary by His Spirit to bring about a miraculous conception. Once formed in Mary's womb, Jesus was born through the normal process that brings children into the world.

Thus, from the beginning Jesus had two natures. His divine nature as God's Son was joined with a human nature, in Mary's womb, by a direct act of the Author of all creation. God is not limited in His work by our human understanding.

---

4. Announcement of the Birth of Jesus

sixth month . . . engaged: In the "sixth month" of Elizabeth's pregnancy, the angel Gabriel appeared to Mary. She was engaged to Joseph. This involved a contract between the two as solemn as marriage itself.

a town in Galilee called Nazareth: Nazareth may have been small, but it was not isolated, since it was near important trade routes.

favored woman: These words indicate a person of unusual character and spirituality. God chose a human mother for His Son with careful attention to her qualifications. Mary was an exemplary woman who cooperated with God's plan of redemption. Mary is to be esteemed among Christians for being the chosen of God for this glorious purpose.

deeply troubled: Mary's encounter with Gabriel, together with the words with which he greeted her, caused confusion in Mary's mind. She was a girl of humble circumstances, and her home was an obscure Palestinian village. She felt unworthy to be called "favored woman."

call His name JESUS: Mary, though not married, would bear a son whose name would be Jesus. This name, identical with the Old Testament name *Joshua,* meant "the Lord is salvation." This was a popular name among Jewish people and was probably borne by other boys in Nazareth. But the child of promise would be unique in His relationship to both God and Israel. He would be called "the Son of the Most High" and would fulfill the hopes of His people for a successor to David who would be the Messiah-King.

throne of His father David: To David had been given the promise of an unnamed descendant who would "establish the throne of his kingdom permanently" (2 Sam. 7:13) as the promised Messiah. According to Gabriel, this person was Mary's child, who would establish an everlasting kingdom among all people.

How can this be: Mary wondered how she, an unmarried girl who had not experienced sexual relations, could become a mother.

High will overshadow you. Therefore the holy child to be born will be called the Son of God. ³⁶And **consider Elizabeth your relative**—even she has conceived a son in her old age, and this is the sixth month for her who was called barren. ³⁷For nothing will be impossible with God."

³⁸"**Consider me the Lord's slave**," said Mary. "May it be done to me according to your word." Then the angel left her.

5. MARY VISITS ELIZABETH

Luke 1:39–56

³⁹In those days **Mary** set out and hurried to a town in the hill country of Judah, ⁴⁰where she entered Zachariah's house and **greeted Elizabeth**. ⁴¹When Elizabeth heard Mary's greeting, the baby leaped inside her, and Elizabeth was filled with the Holy Spirit. ⁴²Then she exclaimed with a loud cry: "Blessed are you among women, and **blessed is your offspring**! ⁴³How could this happen to me, that the mother of my Lord should come to me? ⁴⁴For you see, when the sound of your greeting reached my ears, the baby leaped for joy inside me! ⁴⁵Blessed is she who has believed that what was spoken to her by the Lord will be fulfilled!"

⁴⁶And Mary said: "**My soul proclaims the greatness of the Lord**, ⁴⁷and my spirit has rejoiced in God my Savior, ⁴⁸because He has looked with favor on the humble condition of His slave. Surely, from now on all generations will call me blessed, ⁴⁹because the Mighty One has done great things for me, and holy is His

---

consider Elizabeth your relative: Mary apparently was not aware of the pregnancy of Elizabeth. The two lived at a distance, Mary in Galilee and Elizabeth in Judea. So the angel's news was both a surprise and a stimulant to Mary's faith. Knowing Elizabeth's advanced age, Mary would readily agree that "nothing will be impossible with God," even motherhood for Elizabeth. The precise relationship between Elizabeth and Mary is not disclosed by the word translated as "relative," but it does indicate a blood relationship. Thus, in the broadest sense, Jesus and John the Baptizer were "cousins."

Consider me the Lord's slave: Overwhelmed by what she heard, Mary submitted to God's will. She probably had many questions about how the miracle would happen, how Joseph would respond, and how she could raise Jesus as the Son of God. But she trusted God to accomplish His word and placed herself in His hands to work out His will.

5. MARY VISITS ELIZABETH

Mary . . . greeted Elizabeth: With whom could Mary share her secret? With none more suitably than Elizabeth, whom she hurried to visit. Since Mary lived in Nazareth in Galilee, this trip involved a journey of many miles to the hill country of Judea. During the five months in which Elizabeth "kept herself in seclusion" (Luke 1:24), perhaps she was prepared for Mary's coming. There seemed to be no need for explanations when Mary showed up at Elizabeth's house. Even the unborn child within her womb responded to the sound of Mary's voice.

blessed is your offspring: Zachariah had probably told Elizabeth what Gabriel had revealed about John and also about Jesus (Luke 1:13–17). Thus, Elizabeth's words to Mary reflected the theme of the superiority of Mary's son to her own.

My soul proclaims the greatness of the Lord: Mary gave expression to her deep feelings in a beautiful song known as the *Magnificat*. She gave thanks to God for the honor He had conferred on her. She saw in her experience a reversal of the accepted order. Through the action of God, the humble and hungry—not the rich and mighty—would be blessed. She looked back to the promise given to Abraham (Gen. 12:3) that was now coming to fulfillment in the anticipated birth of Jesus.

name. ⁵⁰His mercy is from generation to generation on those who fear Him. ⁵¹He has done a mighty deed with His arm; He has scattered the proud because of the thoughts of their hearts; ⁵²He has toppled the mighty from their thrones and exalted the lowly. ⁵³He has satisfied the hungry with good things and sent the rich away empty. ⁵⁴He has helped His servant Israel, mindful of His mercy, ⁵⁵just as He spoke to our forefathers, to Abraham and his descendants forever."

⁵⁶And Mary stayed with her about three months; then she returned to her home.

6. Birth of John the Baptizer

Luke 1:57–66

⁵⁷Now the time for Elizabeth to give birth was completed, and she bore a son. ⁵⁸Then her **neighbors and relatives** heard that the Lord had shown her His great mercy, and they **rejoiced** with her.

⁵⁹When they came to circumcise the child on the eighth day, they were going to name him Zachariah, after his father. ⁶⁰But his mother responded, "No! He will be called John."

⁶¹Then they said to her, "None of your relatives has that name." ⁶²So they motioned to his father to find out what he wanted him to be called. ⁶³ᵃHe asked for a writing tablet, and wrote: **"His name is John."**

⁶³ᵇAnd they were all amazed. ⁶⁴Immediately his mouth was opened and his tongue freed, and he began to speak, praising God. ⁶⁵Fear came upon all those who lived around them, and all these things were being talked about throughout the hill country of Judea. ⁶⁶All who heard took them to heart, saying, "What then will this child become?" For, indeed, the Lord's hand was with him.

7. Zachariah's Song at John's Birth

Luke 1:67–80

⁶⁷Then his father Zachariah was filled with the Holy Spirit and prophesied: ⁶⁸**"Blessed is the Lord**, the God of Israel, because He has visited and provided

---

6. Birth of John the Baptizer

neighbors and relatives . . . rejoiced: Elizabeth's joy was fulfilled when she gave birth to a son. Her neighbors and relatives came to rejoice with her because of God's mercy.

His name is John: In his message to Zachariah, the angel Gabriel had said that the promised child was to bear the name John, meaning "the Lord is merciful" or "gift of God's grace." When the time came for naming the baby, family and friends expected that he would bear his father's name. But Zachariah called for a writing tablet on which he wrote, "His name is John." By this act of obedience Zachariah affirmed his faith in the God who had wrought wonders. Once again he was able to speak.

7. Zachariah's Song at John's Birth

Blessed is the Lord: In beautiful words known as the *Benedictus*, Zachariah expressed his gratitude to God for the com-

redemption for His people, [69]and has raised up a horn of salvation for us in the house of His servant David, [70]just as He spoke by the mouth of His holy prophets of old: [71]salvation from our enemies and from the clutches of those who hate us. [72]He has dealt mercifully with our fathers and remembered His holy covenant—[73]the oath that He swore to our father Abraham. He has granted us that, [74]having been rescued from our enemies' clutches, we might serve Him without fear [75]in holiness and righteousness in His presence all our days. [76]And you, child, will be called a **prophet of the Most High**, for you will go before the Lord to prepare His ways, [77]to give His people knowledge of salvation through the forgiveness of their sins, [78]because of our God's merciful compassion by which the Dawn from on high will visit us, [79]to shine on those who live in darkness and the shadow of death, to guide our feet into the way of peace."

[80]The child grew up and became strong in spirit, and he was in the wilderness until the day of His public appearance to Israel.

8. Jesus' Genealogy as Traced through Joseph

Matthew 1:1–17

[1]The historical record of **Jesus Christ**, the Son of David, the **Son of Abraham**: [2]**Abraham fathered** Isaac, Isaac fathered Jacob, Jacob fathered Judah and his brothers, [3]Judah fathered Perez and Zerah by **Tamar**, Perez fathered Hezron, Hezron fathered Aram, [4]Aram fathered Amminadab, Amminadab fathered Nahshon, Nahshon fathered Salmon, [5]Salmon fathered Boaz by **Rahab**, Boaz fathered Obed by **Ruth**, Obed fathered Jesse, [6a]and Jesse fathered King David.

---

ing deliverer and revealed his understanding of the future mission of his son. He portrayed the Messiah in terms of a national champion who would bring deliverance "from our enemies' clutches." But at the same time, He would cause people to "serve . . . in holiness and righteousness."

prophet of the Most High: This spiritual mission of the Messiah is more explicitly recognized in the second part of the song in which John's role is described. He would prepare the way for the Lord and would "give His people knowledge of salvation through the forgiveness of their sins."

8. Jesus' Genealogy as Traced through Joseph

Jesus Christ: The name or title "Christ" means "Anointed One." It refers to the Messiah-King for whom the Jews looked, based on God's covenant with David (2 Sam. 7:11–16). Thus, Jesus Christ as the son of David was the fulfillment of Old Testament prophecy.

Son of Abraham: Jesus also was the son of Abraham. He fulfilled God's promises to Abraham (Gen. 12:1–3), which were renewed with the other patriarchs Isaac and Jacob.

Abraham fathered: This listing of Jesus' ancestors reveals much about who Jesus is and what He came to do. The names emphasize Jesus as the son of David. Verses 2–6a go from Abraham to David; verses 6b–11 go from David to the exile, which seemed the end of David's line of kings; verses 12–16 go from the exile and show that Jesus was the true King.

Tamar . . . Rahab . . . Ruth . . . Uriah's wife . . . Mary: This genealogy is unusual in that it mentions five women. The first four were probably added to remind readers of the inclusiveness of Jesus' mission. He came for women as well as men. He came for Gentiles as well as Jews (Rahab and Ruth were foreigners). He came to save sinners (Tamar, Rahab, and Bathsheba [Uriah's wife] were involved in sexual sins). Mary is included because she was the mother of Jesus.

Matthew: A Gospel for Jews

Matthew wrote his Gospel for his own Jewish countrymen to show that Jesus was the Messiah who had been foretold in the Old Testament. This genealogy of Jesus at the very beginning of Matthew has a thoroughly Jewish orientation. Matthew traced Jesus' family line all the way back to Abraham, the father of the Jewish nation.

Matthew also contains more quotations from the Old Testament than any of the other Gospels. After reporting on an event in the life of Jesus, Matthew often cites an Old Testament passage with this introductory phrase, "So that what was spoken through the prophet . . . might be fulfilled" (Matt. 8:17). He used this technique to show that Jesus was the Promised One whom the Jewish people had been expecting for several centuries.

---

⁶ᵇThen David fathered Solomon by **Uriah's wife**, ⁷Solomon fathered Rehoboam, Rehoboam fathered Abijah, Abijah fathered Asa, ⁸Asa fathered Jehoshaphat, Jehoshaphat fathered Joram, Joram fathered Uzziah, ⁹Uzziah fathered Jotham, Jotham fathered Ahaz, Ahaz fathered Hezekiah, ¹⁰Hezekiah fathered Manasseh, Manasseh fathered Amon, Amon fathered Josiah, ¹¹and Josiah fathered Jechoniah and his brothers at the time of the exile to Babylon.

¹²Then after the exile to Babylon Jechoniah fathered Shealtiel, Shealtiel fathered Zerubbabel, ¹³Zerubbabel fathered Abiud, Abiud fathered Eliakim, Eliakim fathered Azor, ¹⁴Azor fathered Zadok, Zadok fathered Achim, Achim fathered Eliud, ¹⁵Eliud fathered Eleazar, Eleazar fathered Matthan, Matthan fathered Jacob, ¹⁶and Jacob fathered Joseph the husband of **Mary**, who gave birth to Jesus who is called Messiah.

¹⁷So all the generations from Abraham to David were 14 generations; and from David until the exile to Babylon, 14 generations; and from the exile to Babylon until the Messiah, 14 generations.

9. JESUS' GENEALOGY AS TRACED THROUGH MARY

Luke 3:23–38

²³As He began His ministry, Jesus was about **30 years old** and was thought to be the son of Joseph, son of Heli,

²⁴son of Matthat, son of Levi, son of Melchi, son of Jannai, son of Joseph,

²⁵son of Mattathias, son of Amos, son of Nahum, son of Esli, son of Naggai,

---

9. JESUS' GENEALOGY AS TRACED THROUGH MARY

30 years old: Jesus was thirty years old when He began His public ministry. This was the age at which the Levitical priests began their service (Num. 4:47).

²⁶son of Maath, son of Mattathias, son of Semein, son of Josech, son of Joda,
²⁷son of Joanan, son of Rhesa, son of Zerubbabel, son of Shealtiel, son of Neri,
²⁸son of Melchi, son of Addi, son of Cosam, son of Elmadam, son of Er,
²⁹son of Joshua, son of Eliezer, son of Jorim, son of Matthat, son of Levi,
³⁰son of Simeon, son of Judah, son of Joseph, son of Jonan, son of Eliakim,
³¹son of Melea, son of Menna, son of Mattatha, son of Nathan, son of David,
³²son of Jesse, son of Obed, son of Boaz, son of Salmon, son of Nahshon,
³³son of Amminadab, son of Ram, son of Hezron, son of Perez, son of Judah,
³⁴son of Jacob, son of Isaac, son of Abraham, son of Terah, son of Nahor,
³⁵son of Serug, son of Reu, son of Peleg, son of Eber, son of Shelah,
³⁶son of Cainan, son of Arphaxad, son of Shem, son of Noah, son of Lamech,
³⁷son of Methuselah, son of Enoch, son of Jared, son of Mahalaleel, son of Cainan,
³⁸son of Enos, son of Seth, **son of Adam, son of God**.

10. JOSEPH'S REASSURING DREAM

Matthew 1:18–25

¹⁸The birth of Jesus Christ came about this way: After His mother **Mary had been engaged to Joseph**, before they came together, she was **found to be with child** by the Holy Spirit. ¹⁹So Joseph, her husband, being a righteous man, and not wanting to disgrace her publicly, decided to **divorce her secretly**.

²⁰But after he had considered these things, an angel of the Lord suddenly appeared to him in a dream, saying, "Joseph, son of David, don't be afraid to take Mary as your wife, because what has been conceived in her is **by the Holy**

---

son of Adam, son of God: Matthew and Luke give different genealogies for Jesus (see segment 8, "Jesus' Genealogy as Traced through Joseph," p. 12). Matthew, writing for Jews, wanted to show that Jesus' line of descent was through Abraham and David. Thus, Jesus fulfilled the Jewish prophecy that the Messiah would claim the throne of David. Luke's genealogy traces Jesus' lineage all the way back to Adam. This line of descent emphasized that Christ as man is related through Adam to the whole human race. As the Second Adam, born of a woman but conceived of the Holy Spirit, His life and ministry have universal meaning. He came not only for Israel, but for the whole world.

10. JOSEPH'S REASSURING DREAM

Mary had been engaged to Joseph: Mary and Joseph were engaged, but not yet married. First-century Jewish engagements were more binding than modern engagements. A formal agreement or contract bound them to become married. This relationship could be broken only by a divorce.

found to be with child: Although Joseph is called Mary's "husband," the word *engaged* and the phrase "before they came together" emphasized that they were not living together as husband and wife. During this period, Joseph became aware that Mary was expecting a child.

divorce her secretly: The custom of the day was for the man to subject his unfaithful fiancée to divorce and public humiliation. Joseph chose not to do this. He is described as "a righteous man." He did not want a wife who was guilty of adultery, but he was not a vindictive man. Mercy tempered his sense of doing what was right. So he made plans to divorce Mary but to do so as quietly as possible.

by the Holy Spirit: God sent an angel to speak to Joseph in a dream and to tell him what an angel had revealed to Mary months before. She was not guilty of adultery; the child was miraculously conceived by the Holy Spirit.

Spirit. ²¹She will give birth to a son, and you are to name Him Jesus, because He will save His people from their sins."

²²Now all this took place to fulfill what was spoken by the Lord through the prophet: ²³"See, the virgin will be with child and give birth to a son, and they will name Him Immanuel," which is translated "God is with us."

²⁴When **Joseph** woke up from his sleep, he **did as the Lord's angel had commanded** him. He took his wife home, ²⁵but he did not know her intimately until she gave birth to a son. And he named Him Jesus.

Joseph . . . did as the Lord's angel had commanded: We honor Mary for her trust and obedience. Joseph showed the same kind of trust and obedience. He did not question the angel's unusual explanation for Mary's pregnancy, nor did he delay in obeying what the Lord told him to do. Instead of divorcing Mary, he married her. He refrained from sexual relations with her until after she had borne her firstborn son. When the child was born, Joseph named Him Jesus—as the angel had told him to do.

II. The Birth and Childhood of Jesus

The Gospels of Mark and John contain no information about the birth and childhood of Jesus. If not for Matthew and Luke, we would know nothing about Him until He launched His public ministry at about 30 years of age. But thanks to these two Gospel writers, we know several important things about Jesus' early life.

Matthew and Luke tell us that Jesus was born in Bethlehem of Judea in fulfillment of Old Testament prophecy; that He was circumcised and presented as an infant in the temple in Jerusalem in accordance with Jewish law; that wise men from the east visited Him in Bethlehem when He was about two years old; that Jesus and His family fled to Egypt to escape the wrath of Herod the Great; that He and His family eventually settled in Nazareth of Galilee; and that Jesus was discovered in the temple in Jerusalem when He was 12 years old, discussing the Jewish law with the learned religious teachers.

11. Jesus Born in Bethlehem

Luke 2:1–7

¹In those days a decree went out from **Caesar Augustus** that the whole empire should be registered. ²This first registration took place while Quirinius was governing Syria. ³So everyone went to be registered, each to his own town.

⁴And Joseph also went up from the town of **Nazareth** in Galilee, to Judea, to the city of David, which is called **Bethlehem**, because he was of the house and family line of David, ⁵to be registered **along with Mary**, who was engaged to him and was pregnant. ⁶While they

When Was Jesus Born?

Most scholars believe Jesus was born around 6 to 4 B.C. How can this be, since our calendar supposedly reckons time beginning at A.D. 1 as the year of His birth? (A.D. is the abbreviation for the Latin phrase anno Domini, meaning "in the year of our Lord.")

The simple answer is that the calendar we use today (the Gregorian calendar) was systemized and recalculated in the 1500s by Pope Gregory. This refiguring pushed some early years of the A.D. period back into the B.C. period.

How can we be certain that Jesus was born in the 6 to 4 B.C. period? It had to be no later than 4 B.C. because Jesus was born "in the days of King Herod" (Matt. 2:1). We know from secular history that Herod the Great died in 4 B.C.

---

11. Jesus Born in Bethlehem

Caesar Augustus: God used an emperor's decree to bring fulfillment to Israel's long-cherished hope for a Messiah. The emperor of the Roman Empire, Caesar Augustus, ordered a census, probably for the purpose of future taxation of all subjects in the lands that Rome controlled.

Nazareth . . . Bethlehem: Jewish custom required that census enrollment take place in the ancestral cities of all citizens. This is why Joseph traveled from Nazareth to his ancestral city of Bethlehem, about ninety miles away.

along with Mary: Why did Joseph take Mary on this trip? Perhaps he did not want to leave her alone to face criticism

were there, it happened that the days were completed for her to give birth. [7]Then she gave birth to her firstborn Son, and she **wrapped Him snugly** in cloth and laid Him in a manger—because there was **no room** for them **at the inn**.

12. GOOD NEWS TO THE SHEPHERDS

Bethlehem: The City of David

Bethlehem was known as "the city of David" (Luke 2:11) because King David had grown up in this village about one thousand years before Jesus was born. The prophet Micah predicted that the Messiah would be born in Bethlehem (Mic. 5:2). The Jewish people believed the Messiah would be a descendant of David, the most popular king in their history.

According to early Christian tradition, Jesus was born in a cave that served as a stable for the inn at Bethlehem. This site is marked today by the Church of the Nativity, a place visited every year by thousands of Holy Land tourists.

Luke 2:8–20

[8]In the same region, **shepherds** were living **out in the fields** and keeping watch at night over their flock. [9]Then an angel of the Lord stood before them, and the glory of the Lord shone around them, and they were terrified. [10]But the angel said to them, "Do not be afraid, for you see, I announce to you good news of great joy, which will be **for all the people**: [11]because today in the city of David was born for you a **Savior**, who is **Christ the Lord**. [12]This will be the sign for you: you will find a baby wrapped snugly in cloth and lying in a manger."

[13]Suddenly there was a multitude of the heavenly host with the angel, praising God and saying: [14]"Glory to God in the highest heaven, and **peace on earth** to people He favors!"

[15]When the angels had left them and returned to heaven, the shepherds said to one another, "**Let's go** straight to Bethlehem **and see** this thing that has taken place, which the Lord has made known to us."

[16]And they hurried off and found both Mary and Joseph, and **the baby** who was **lying in the manger**. [17]After seeing them, they reported the message they were told about this

---

and accusation in Nazareth after the birth of her child. He may have recalled the prophecy that the Messiah was to be born in Bethlehem. He could have seen the census as an outworking of divine purpose by which Mary's child would be born in the place of prophecy.

wrapped Him snugly: According to the practice of the Jews, Mary probably wrapped the baby Jesus in swathing bands after she had washed Him and rubbed salt into His body as an antiseptic (see Ezek. 16:4).

no room . . . at the inn: Bethlehem would have been crowded with people who were responding to the Roman call for registration. This explains why there was no room in the inn. An inn of New Testament times was a primitive structure with a central courtyard for animals, surrounded by cubicles to accommodate travelers. Such inns had a bad reputation, and they were clearly unsuitable for the birthing of a child. The innkeeper at Bethlehem may have been a kindly person who went out of his way to provide privacy for Mary and Joseph.

12. GOOD NEWS TO THE SHEPHERDS

shepherds . . . out in the fields: A group of shepherds was watching their sheep when the good news of Jesus' birth came to them. Shepherds were outside the circle of religious respectability because their occupation kept them from

child, [18]and all who heard it were amazed at what the shepherds said to them. [19]But Mary was **treasuring** up all these things in her heart **and meditating** on them. [20]The shepherds returned, glorifying and praising God for all they had seen and heard, just as they had been told.

13. The Circumcision and Naming of Jesus

Matthew 1:25; Luke 2:21

Lk 2:21When the eight days were completed for His circumcision, He was **named JESUS**—the name given by the angel before He was conceived.

14. Jesus' Presentation as an Infant in the Temple

Luke 2:22–38

[22]And when the **days of their purification** according to the law of Moses were completed, they brought Him **up to Jerusalem** to present Him to the Lord [23](just as it is written in the law of the Lord: "Every firstborn male will be called

---

observing the requirements and rituals of the Jewish faith. The coming of this revelation to them magnifies the grace of God and anticipates the ministry of Jesus "to preach good news to the poor" (Luke 4:18).

for all the people: Some religious people in the first century tried to exclude certain people from the circle of God's love. The good news of God in Christ is that no one is excluded. By sending the message of Jesus' birth first to shepherds, God declared that the good news is for everyone.

Savior . . . Christ the Lord: The angels' announcement to the shepherds was associated with the name of David, whose home had been in Bethlehem. It told of the coming of One for whom a threefold claim was made: He was a Savior, the Messiah (Christ), and the Lord, thus establishing a relationship to sinners, to the Jewish people, and to God Himself. Yet He would not be found in a palace or temple, but in a cattle shed.

peace on earth: The world under Caesar Augustus enjoyed a remarkable period of peace, the *Pax Romana* as it was called. But the world needed a peace more enduring than any emperor could give—God's peace. The coming of Jesus was a declaration of the Father's desire for peace between Himself and sinful humanity. He came on a mission of redemption and reconciliation.

Let's go . . . and see: What the shepherds had seen was hard to believe. This encounter with heavenly beings was staggering enough, but the message they delivered was even more astounding. This announcement of the birth of "Christ the Lord"—could it mean that the long-expected Messiah had arrived? The shepherds decided to go and see for themselves.

the baby . . . lying in the manger: The shepherds found a crude shelter, a makeshift cradle, a young mother from Galilee, a carpenter by her side, and a little child in the manger. Yet they believed that this infant was all that the angel had said, and they left the scene to tell others the good news.

treasuring . . . and meditating: Mary locked all these things away in her memory, and she gave considerable thought to all she had experienced. A similar insight is mentioned after Jesus' trip to the temple at age 12 (Luke 2:51).

13. The Circumcision and Naming of Jesus

named JESUS: Circumcision was the badge of membership in the covenant community of Israel. The rite was performed eight days after Jesus' birth, probably in Bethlehem. At the time of circumcision, the name *Jesus* was bestowed on Mary's child.

14. Jesus' Presentation as an Infant in the Temple

days of their purification: Leviticus 12 describes how a woman was to be ritually purified after childbirth. The purification was to take place 33 days after the child's circumcision on the eighth day.

up to Jerusalem: A visit to the Jerusalem temple was necessary for the baby Jesus' circumcision and presentation. The

holy to the Lord") ²⁴and to offer a sacrifice (according to what is stated in the law of the Lord: "a pair of turtledoves or two young pigeons").

²⁵There was a man in Jerusalem whose name was **Simeon**. This man was **righteous and devout**, looking forward to Israel's consolation, and the Holy Spirit was upon him. ²⁶It had been revealed to him by the Holy Spirit that he would not see death before he saw the Lord's Messiah. ²⁷Guided by the Spirit, he entered the temple complex. When the parents brought in the child Jesus to perform for Him what was customary under the law, ²⁸Simeon took Him up in his arms, praised God, and said: ²⁹"Now, Master, You can **dismiss Your slave in peace**, according to Your word. ³⁰For my eyes have seen Your salvation, ³¹which You have prepared in the presence of all peoples; ³²a light for revelation to the Gentiles and glory to Your people Israel."

³³His **father and mother were amazed** at what was being said about Him. ³⁴Then Simeon blessed them and told His mother Mary: "Indeed, this child is destined to cause the fall and rise of many in Israel, and to be a sign that will be opposed—³⁵and a **sword will pierce your own soul**—that the thoughts of many hearts may be revealed."

³⁶There was also **a prophetess, Anna**, a daughter of Phanuel, of the tribe of Asher. She was well along in years, having lived with a husband seven years after her marriage, ³⁷and was a widow for 84 years. She did not leave the temple complex, serving God night and day with fastings and prayers. ³⁸At that very moment, she came up and began to thank God and to speak about Him to all who were looking forward to the redemption of Jerusalem.

---

offering made by Joseph and Mary showed their poverty. Under the law, a lamb was to be offered as a cleansing sacrifice. If a woman could not afford a lamb, the offering was to be two doves or young pigeons. Luke 2:24 implies that Mary offered two birds rather than a lamb.

Simeon . . . righteous and devout: Simeon was a righteous man with a deep devotion to God. His consuming goal in life was to see the Messiah. Simeon also lived under the direction of the Spirit of God, who had promised him that he would see the Messiah before he died.

dismiss Your slave in peace: Simeon took the infant Jesus in his arms. He was ready to die, now that he had seen the Promised One. He hailed Jesus as God's instrument of blessing for Jews and Gentiles alike. Quoting one of Isaiah's prophecies about the Messiah (Isa. 49:6), Simeon echoed the promises of God through Isaiah that the Servant-Messiah would be a light to all people.

father and mother were amazed: Although Joseph and Mary knew things about Jesus that others did not know, they were still amazed at what Simeon said. Perhaps it was the universal scope of the mission of Jesus that surprised them. They may also have been surprised that this old man recognized immediately who Jesus was.

sword will pierce your own soul: Simeon foretold the sharp division that the child in his arms would create, the hostility that He would arouse, the sorrow that would befall His mother, and the exposure of people's thoughts and attitudes that would result from His ministry. Perhaps Simeon was still thinking of the Servant foretold by Isaiah and remembering that Isaiah predicted that He would be a Suffering Servant (see Isa. 53).

a prophetess, Anna: An elderly prophetess named Anna apparently overheard Simeon's ecstatic speech. Her concept of the "redemption of Jerusalem" went beyond political freedom to embrace spiritual deliverance. Agreeing with Simeon's pronouncements, she gave thanks to God and began to share this good news about Jesus with others.

15. THE WISE MEN VISIT JESUS

Matthew 2:1–12

¹After Jesus was born in Bethlehem of Judea in the **days of King Herod**, **wise men from the east** arrived unexpectedly in **Jerusalem**, ²saying, "Where is He who has been born King of the Jews? For we saw **His star in the eas**t and have come to worship Him."

³When King **Herod** heard this, he **was deeply disturbed**, and **all Jerusalem with him**. ⁴So he **assembled all the chief priests** and scribes of the people and asked them where the Messiah would be born.

⁵"In Bethlehem of Judea," they told him, "because this is what was written through the prophet: ⁶'And you, Bethlehem, in the land of Judah, are by no means least among the leaders of Judah: because out of you will come a Leader who will shepherd My people Israel.'"

⁷Then Herod **secretly summoned the wise men** and learned from them the time when the star appeared. ⁸He sent them to Bethlehem and said, "Go and search carefully for the child. When you find Him, report back to me so that I too can go and worship Him."

⁹After hearing the king, they went on their way. And there it was—the star they had seen in the east! It led them until it came and stopped above the place where the child was. ¹⁰When they saw the star, they were overjoyed beyond measure. ¹¹Entering **the house**, they saw the child with Mary His mother, and falling to their knees, they worshiped Him. Then they opened their treasures and presented Him with gifts:

The Star of Bethlehem

Some facts about the star that led the wise men to Bethlehem are clear, but much remains a mystery. We do know that the wise men saw the star while they were in the east, and they concluded that it proclaimed the birth of the King of the Jews (Matt. 2:2). Matthew 2:9–10 reveals these additional facts: The star led them as they left Jerusalem, it stopped over where Jesus was in Bethlehem, and they felt great joy as a result.

What is not clear is where the star was when the wise men traveled from their home to Jerusalem. Either the star had not been visible since they first saw it, or it had been stationary over Judea. The Creator of the universe put this star in the sky as His messenger to people outside the borders of Israel to guide them to the young King, Mary's firstborn son. The star's reappearance and course in the sky brought them to Bethlehem, not more than five miles south of Jerusalem.

---

15. THE WISE MEN VISIT JESUS

days of King Herod: The Herods were a line of princes who ruled Palestine for about 150 years. They were Idumeans (Edomites) who gained favor with Rome so that one of their number, Herod the Great, was appointed king in 40 B.C. It was during his reign that Jesus was born in Bethlehem.

wise men from the east: These wise men, or *Magi* (meaning "diviner"), could have come from Persia (modern Iran) or from some place farther east. Legend has played a large part in our modern concept of these men, expressed in a carol that begins, "We three kings of Orient are." The Bible does not say how many wise men there were, and it does not

gold, frankincense, and myrrh. [12]And being **warned in a dream** not to go back to Herod, they returned to their own country by another route.

16. JESUS AND HIS FAMILY FLEE TO EGYPT

Matthew 2:13–15

[13]After they [the wise men] were gone, an angel of **the Lord** suddenly **appeared to Joseph** in a dream, saying, "Get up! Take the child and His mother, flee to Egypt, and stay there until I tell you. For Herod is about to search for the child to destroy Him." [14]So he got up, took the child and His mother during the night, and **escaped to Egypt**. [15]He stayed there until Herod's death, so that what

---

describe them as kings. They were more likely a type of priest. They studied the heavens for light on coming events, much as astrologers do today.

Jerusalem: It was natural that the wise men should seek direction in Jerusalem. Herod's palace was there, and he had gained fame for his reconstruction of the Jewish temple.

His star in the east: A new star in the sky was understood by these men to signal the birth of a king. Throughout the world at that time was expectation of a great deliverer. It was the motion of the star that brought them to Jerusalem. They must have been aware of the Jewish hope of a Messiah, and they associated the star with that hope.

Herod . . . was deeply disturbed: The aging Herod lived with the suspicion that others were conspiring to steal his throne. The wise men asked about someone "born King of the Jews." Herod had not been born king. Rather, he had obtained this rank through political intrigue. He thought he might be facing a serious competitor in this new-born king.

all Jerusalem with him: The words of the wise men shocked the city of Jerusalem. These foreigners from the east did not know that Herod had spent much of his reign killing people whom he suspected of aspiring to be king of the Jews. But the people of Jerusalem knew what Herod was like. They were troubled because the coming of the wise men might set off a new blood bath.

assembled all the chief priests: Herod knew enough about Jewish religion to recognize "King of the Jews" as the title of the long-awaited Messiah of the Jews. He called in the biblical scholars to tell him where the Messiah or Christ was to be born. They quoted to Herod the well-known prophecy of Micah 5:2, which named Bethlehem as the place of His birth.

secretly summoned the wise men: Herod was a schemer who knew how to use deceit to get what he wanted. Now that he knew where the Messiah was to be born, he pumped the wise men for information about when they first saw the star. If he could learn this, he would know the age of the child and whom to target in his murderous scheme.

the house: The wise men moved on to Bethlehem, where they found Jesus and His earthly mother Mary in "the house." They had moved from the temporary shelter of the stable into a home of some kind. Jesus must have been about two years old at the time of this visit, since Herod later ordered the execution of all children in the region who were two years old and under.

gold, frankincense, and myrrh: The gifts presented by the wise men were normal for these times, especially for royal recipients. The gold was appropriate for royalty. The frankincense suggested worship accorded to divinity. The myrrh, used in embalming, was a provision against death. Each gift had its own special significance in the life and ministry of Jesus.

warned in a dream: The wise men were about to send word to Herod about this new king, as he had requested. But God warned them in a dream about the scheming king. God told them not to let Herod know they had found Jesus. Leaving Bethlehem, they returned to their country by another route. Their act of faith and courage was the first part of God's plan to thwart Herod's murderous intentions.

16. JESUS AND HIS FAMILY FLEE TO EGYPT

the Lord . . . appeared to Joseph: Joseph was a key human figure in God's deliverance of His Son. Joseph immediately obeyed the divine warning to flee Bethlehem by taking Jesus and Mary out of the region to safety.

escaped to Egypt: A strong Jewish colony had existed in Egypt since before the prophet Jeremiah's time (see Jer. 44:1). Though under Roman rule, that country was outside Herod's jurisdiction.

was spoken by the Lord through the prophet might be fulfilled: "**Out of Egypt** I called My Son."

17. Slaughter of Innocent Children by Herod

Matthew 2:16–18

16Then Herod, when he saw that he had been outwitted by the wise men, flew into a rage. He gave orders to **massacre all the male children** in and around Bethlehem who were two years old and under, in keeping with the time he had learned from the wise men. 17Then what was spoken through Jeremiah the prophet was fulfilled: 18"A voice was heard in Ramah, weeping, and great mourning, **Rachel weeping** for her children; and she refused to be consoled, because they were no more."

18. Jesus and His Family Return to Nazareth

Matthew 2:19–23; Luke 2:39–40

Mt 2:19–21**After Herod died**, an angel of the Lord suddenly appeared in a dream to Joseph in Egypt, 20saying, "Get up! Take the child and His mother and go to the land of Israel, because those who sought the child's life are dead." 21So he got up, took the child and His mother, and entered the land of Israel.

22But when he heard that Archelaus was ruling over Judea in place of his father Herod, he was afraid to go there. And being warned in a dream, he withdrew to the region of Galilee Lk 2:39ato **their own town of Nazareth**, Mt 2:23b to fulfill what was spoken through the prophets, that He will be called a Nazarene.

Out of Egypt: This quotation is from Hosea 11:1. Matthew compared Jesus with the nation of Israel. Both went to Egypt in their infancy, and both were called out by the Lord as a part of His purpose of world redemption.

17. Slaughter of Innocent Children by Herod

massacre all the male children: Herod estimated that Jesus had been born about two years before. Thus, he ordered the slaughter of all children in and around Bethlehem who were two years old and under. This cruel and jealous king thought nothing of murdering innocent children to destroy a single victim.

Rachel weeping: Matthew quoted an Old Testament passage from Jeremiah. This prophet portrayed Rachel, the mother of Joseph and Benjamin, as weeping for the nation of Israel when the people were carried away as captives into Babylonia (Jer. 31:15). Her lament for her countrymen was particularly appropriate for the innocent children of Bethlehem.

18. Jesus and His Family Return to Nazareth

After Herod died: The death of Herod the Great allowed Joseph, Mary, and Jesus to return from Egypt. Archelaus, the son of Herod, was ruling over southern Palestine. Thus, Joseph settled his family north of Judea in the province of Galilee in case this Herod might carry on the evil traditions of his father.

their own town of Nazareth: A small town in lower Galilee about halfway between the Mediterranean Sea and Lake Galilee, Nazareth was the former home of Mary and Joseph, according to Luke 1:26–27; 2:39. It was natural for them to settle here when warned away from Judea.

Lk 2:40The boy **grew up and became strong**, filled with wisdom, and God's grace was on Him.

The Herods of the New Testament

The Herods were a dynasty of Roman rulers in Palestine during New Testament times. Four different Herods are mentioned in the Gospels:
- *Herod the Great (ruled 37 to 4 B.C.), who tried to murder the baby Jesus;*
- *Herod Archelaus (ruled 4 B.C. to A.D. 6), son and successor of Herod the Great as ruler over Judea;*
- *Herod Antipas (ruled 4 B.C. to A.D. 39), who executed John the Baptizer (Mark 6:17–29) and who returned Jesus for sentencing by Pilate (Luke 23:6–12); and*
- *Herod Philip (ruled 4 B.C. to A.D. 33), ruler in extreme northern Galilee when Jesus began His public ministry (Luke 3:1, 19–20).*

Two additional Herods mentioned in the New Testament are Herod Agrippa I (ruled A.D. 37–44), who executed James, the leader of the Jerusalem church (Acts 12:1–19); and Herod Agrippa II (ruled A.D. 50–100), before whom the apostle Paul made his defense at Caesarea (Acts 25:13–26:32).

---

19. THE BOY JESUS AMONG THE TEACHERS IN JERUSALEM

Luke 2:41–52

41Every year His parents traveled **to Jerusalem for the Passover** Festival. 42**When He was twelve years old**, they went up according to the custom of the festival. 43After those days were over, as they were returning, the boy **Jesus stayed behind** in Jerusalem, but His parents did not know it. 44Assuming He was in the traveling party, they went a day's journey. Then **they began looking** for Him among their relatives and friends. 45When they did not find Him, they returned to Jerusalem to search for Him.

---

grew up and became strong: These words describe a growing child, normal in every respect except for His relationship to God. He developed mentally, physically, and spiritually, with expanding awareness of His mission and His divine sonship.

19. THE BOY JESUS AMONG THE TEACHERS IN JERUSALEM

to Jerusalem for the Passover: All adult males were required to attend this annual festival in Jerusalem. It commemorated the mercy of God in causing the angel of death to "pass over" the houses of the Israelites on the night when all the firstborn of Egypt were killed (Exod. 12).

When He was twelve years old: This visit of Jesus to Jerusalem is the only event reported during the period between His return from Egypt and His thirtieth year.

Jesus stayed behind . . . they began looking: Mary and Joseph didn't know Jesus was missing until they had traveled a day's journey back toward Nazareth. Jews going to and from their festivals traveled in caravans. In the daytime the children mingled with one another among all the travelers. But in the evening when they made camp, the members of each family came together. This must have been when Joseph and Mary discovered that Jesus was not with the caravan.

⁴⁶After three days, they **found Him** in the temple complex sitting **among the teachers**, listening to them and asking them questions. ⁴⁷And all those who heard Him were astounded at His understanding and His answers. ⁴⁸When His **parents** saw Him, they **were astonished**, and His mother said to Him, "Son, **why have You treated us like this?** Here Your father and I have been anxiously searching for You."

⁴⁹"**Why were you searching for Me?**" He asked them. "Didn't you know that I must be involved in My Father's interests?" ⁵⁰But **they did not understand** what He said to them.

⁵¹Then He went down with them and came to Nazareth, and was **obedient to them**. His mother kept all these things in her heart. ⁵²And Jesus increased in wisdom and stature and in favor with God and with people.

Nazareth: Jesus' Hometown

Nazareth, in lower Galilee, was an isolated village surrounded by high hills and located just south of the Lebanon mountain range. Here in this insignificant place Jesus grew to manhood, probably working as a carpenter with Joseph and His four brothers.

Lack of respect for this out-of-the-way crossroads must have been widespread. When Philip told Nathanael about Jesus and indicated where He was from, Nathanael asked with obvious sarcasm, "Can anything good come out of Nazareth?" (John 1:46). After Jesus began His public ministry, He visited Nazareth twice but was not well received by the townspeople (Mark 6:1–6; Luke 4:28–30). Like Nathanael, they also seemed to believe that nothing good could come from their village.

Modern Nazareth draws many tourists to the Latin Church of the Annunciation, so named because the announcement of Jesus' birth was made to the virgin Mary at Nazareth (Luke 1:26).

---

found Him . . . among the teachers: When they didn't find Jesus among the travelers, Jesus' parents returned to Jerusalem to search for Him. The boy Jesus was sitting among the teachers as an eager student. The rabbinical method of instruction was to state cases or problems that called for interpretation or application of the law by the students.

parents . . . were astonished: Mary and Joseph stood in awe of these respected teachers. They were astonished that their young son was sitting among them, asking and answering questions.

why have You treated us like this? Mary's language implies that Jesus had been instructed about the time when His parents and the caravan would depart for home. They were upset that He had not followed orders.

Why were you searching for Me? These are the first recorded words of Jesus. He made it clear that Mary, knowing all that had been revealed to her about Jesus, should have expected to find Him in the temple, "involved in My Father's interests" (Luke 2:49).

they did not understand: It may seem strange that Mary—the one to whom the angel had revealed the scope of Jesus' ministry (Luke 1:26–38)—did not grasp the meaning of His words. But He would face this problem of slow understanding of His mission by others during His entire ministry. Christ spoke plainly, but human ears were slow to understand.

obedient to them: Jesus returned to Nazareth with His parents, and He lived in obedience to them during His growing-up years. He probably learned the trade of Joseph (Mark 6:3). Joseph is not mentioned after this passage, and the probability is that he died while Jesus was a boy.

III. PREPARATION FOR THE BEGINNING OF JESUS' MINISTRY

When Jesus was about 30 years old, He began to make preparations for the launching of His public ministry. This time of preparation lasted about six months. He identified publicly with John the Baptizer, His forerunner, and John's message of repentance by coming to John to be baptized. Jesus' close connection with John's ministry is emphasized especially by the Gospel of John, which reports that Jesus' first disciples were followers of John the Baptizer.

After His baptism by John, Jesus faced temptation by Satan, who challenged Him to take the easy way out by becoming a "bread Messiah" whom people would eagerly follow and by impressing the crowds as a miracle worker.

During this period of preparation, Jesus circulated mostly in the province of Judea in southern Palestine, the area where John the Baptizer was calling people to repentance. But He did make at least one trip to the northerly province of Galilee, where He turned water into wine at Cana of Galilee.

After John the Baptizer was imprisoned by Herod Antipas, Roman governor of Judea, Jesus apparently decided to move to Galilee and make this area the main focus of His ministry. On His way from Judea to Galilee, He stopped over in Samaria, where He talked with the Samaritan woman at Jacob's well.

20. JOHN THE BAPTIZER PREACHES AND BAPTIZES

Matthew 3:1–12; Mark 1:1–8; Luke 3:1–18

Lk 3:1–2In the fifteenth year of the reign of Tiberius Caesar, while Pontius Pilate was governor of Judea, Herod was tetrarch of Galilee, his brother Philip tetrarch of the region of Iturea and Trachonitis, and Lysanias tetrarch of Abilene, ²during the high priesthood of Annas and Caiaphas, God's word came to John the son of Zachariah **in the wilderness**.

Mt 3:1aJohn the Baptist came, Mk 1:4b**preaching a baptism of repentance** for the forgiveness of sins, Mt 3:2–3aand saying, "Repent, because the kingdom of heaven has come near!" ³aFor he is the one spoken of through the prophet Isaiah, Mk 1:2b–3"Look, I am sending My messenger ahead of You, who will prepare Your way. ³A voice of one crying out in the wilderness: 'Prepare the way for the

---

20. JOHN THE BAPTIZER PREACHES AND BAPTIZES

in the wilderness: John was ministering in the barren area east of the Dead Sea. Luke 1:80 tells us that John had lived in the wilderness from an early age. His food was what he could forage in that bleak region. His clothing and appearance reminded people of Elijah the prophet (2 Kgs. 1:8). Malachi 4:5–6 had predicted that God would send Elijah the prophet before the day of the Lord. John was the fulfillment of that promise.

preaching a baptism of repentance: When a Gentile became a Jew, he went through a kind of baptism. But this had nothing to do with repentance, and it was self-administered. John's baptism differed in three ways: (1) it required repentance; (2) it was for Jews as well as Gentiles; and (3) it was administered by John. His preaching was basically a call to repent. Repentance involves sincere confession of one's sins. God forgave sins as people confessed and forsook their sins.

Lord; **make His paths straight!** ^Lk 3:5–6^Every valley will be filled, and every mountain and hill will be made low; the crooked will become straight, the rough ways smooth, ⁶and everyone will see the salvation of God.'"

^Mt 3:4–6^John himself had a camel hair garment with a leather belt around his waist, and his food was locusts and wild honey. ⁵Then Jerusalem, all Judea, and all the vicinity of the Jordan were flocking to him, ⁶and they were baptized by him in the Jordan River as they confessed their sins.

⁷When he saw many of the Pharisees and Sadducees coming to the place of his baptism, he said to them, "**Brood of vipers!** Who warned you to flee from the coming wrath? ⁸Produce fruit consistent with repentance. ⁹And don't presume to say to yourselves, 'We have Abraham as our father.' For I tell you that God is able to raise up children for Abraham from these stones! ¹⁰Even now the ax is ready to strike the root of the trees! Therefore, every tree that doesn't produce good fruit will be cut down and thrown into the fire."

^Lk 3:10^"What then should we do?" the crowds were asking him.

¹¹He replied to them, "The one who has two shirts must **share with someone** who has none, and the one who has food must do the same."

¹²Tax collectors also came to be baptized, and they asked him, "Teacher, what should we do?"

¹³He told them, "**Don't collect any more** than what you have been authorized."

¹⁴ᵃSome soldiers also questioned him: "What should we do?"

¹⁴ᵇHe said to them, "Don't take money from anyone by force or false accusation; **be satisfied with your wages.**"

---

make His paths straight! When important persons traveled in Old Testament times, roads had to be made, or improved, to ease their journey. John saw himself as a voice calling for such a work of preparation not for a king or a general but for a Savior.

Brood of vipers! John condemned the Pharisees and Sadducees because he knew they had not come to confess their sins. If they had come to repent, the fruits of their sincere repentance would have been evident in deeds of true righteousness. John knew these leaders were trusting in their ancestry as descendants of Abraham, not in the transforming power of God.

share with someone: John echoed the preaching of the early prophets. He did not tell his listeners to attend temple services, to keep the annual feasts, or to perform the rituals of the law. He charged them to engage in right relationships toward others. Love for God must be demonstrated in loving acts toward others, particularly the poor.

Don't collect any more: Tax collectors under the Roman system paid for the privilege of collecting taxes. Anything over what they paid was theirs to keep. This led to widespread dishonesty and extortion, in which the common people were the victims. Repentance on the part of these tax collectors meant behaving with honesty.

be satisfied with your wages: The soldiers who came to John were possibly Jews, in which case they were not part of the Roman army but perhaps temple guards. They may have worked with the tax collectors and therefore shared their guilt in extorting money. John told them to quit using violence and making false accusations. They should be content with what they were paid and not seek to boost their income by fraudulent practices.

more powerful than I: John had baptized with water, but the Messiah for whom he prepared the way would baptize people with the Holy Spirit. This promise was fulfilled at Pentecost (Acts 2:1–13).

strap of His sandals: Sandals were tied on the feet with a thong. Slaves performed this menial task for important people. John declared that he was unworthy of being Jesus' slave.

¹⁵Now the people were waiting expectantly, and all of them were debating in their minds whether John might be the Messiah. ¹⁶John answered them all, "I baptize you with water. But One is coming who is **more powerful than I**. I am not worthy to untie the **strap of His sandals**. He will baptize you **with the Holy Spirit and fire**. ¹⁷His winnowing shovel is in His hand to clear His threshing floor and gather the wheat into His barn, but the chaff He will burn up with a fire that never goes out." ¹⁸Then, along with many other exhortations, he announced good news to the people.

21. JESUS BAPTIZED BY JOHN

Matthew 3:13–17; Mark 1:9–11; Luke 3:21–23

Mk 1:9aIn those days, Lk 3:21awhen all the people were baptized, Mk 1:9b**Jesus** came from Nazareth in Galilee and was baptized in the Jordan by **John**. Mt 3:14But **John tried to stop Him**, saying, "I need to be baptized by You, and yet You come to me?"

¹⁵**Jesus answered him**, "Allow it for now, because this is the way for us to fulfill all righteousness." Then he allowed Him to be baptized.

¹⁶After Jesus was baptized, He went up immediately from the water. The heavens suddenly opened for Him, and He saw the **Spirit of God descending like a**

The Jordan River

By Western standards, the Jordan is not much of a river—only about one hundred feet wide and three to ten feet deep in most places. But it has been memoralized for all time as the stream in which Jesus was baptized by John the Baptizer. The Jordan cuts a circuitous path through the entire length of modern Israel, falling more than sixteen hundred feet along its seventy miles before emptying into the Dead Sea. This drastic fall is reflected in its name, which means "the descender."

---

with the Holy Spirit and fire: John emphasized that his baptism in water foreshadowed a baptism of the Spirit. The One to whom he pointed would perform this Spirit baptism. When God sent His Spirit at Pentecost, He inaugurated an age when the risen Lord continued His work in His people through His Spirit (Acts 2:1–13).

21. JESUS BAPTIZED BY JOHN

Jesus . . . John: This was Jesus' first public appearance in preparation for launching His ministry. The news of John's activities, preaching and baptizing, must have been the signal to Him that His public ministry was due to begin. Jesus stepped out of 30 years of obscurity and silence and made His way to the place where John was baptizing. He asked to be baptized by John.

John tried to stop Him: John recognized Jesus as the sinless One for whose coming he had been preparing the people. He objected to baptizing Jesus. Instead, Jesus the sinless One should be baptizing John the unworthy servant.

Jesus answered him: Jesus' answer to John, together with God's words from heaven, are our best clues to why Jesus wanted to be baptized. Jesus set an example for all who would later follow Him in the obedience of baptism. This event also pointed ahead to how Jesus would fulfill divine righteousness through His death and resurrection. He was not one of the sinners who confessed their sins as John baptized them, but Jesus publicly identified Himself with these sinners, whom He had come to save.

Spirit of God descending like a dove: The vision of the dove was the Father's assurance that the full power of His Spirit rested on Jesus.

dove and coming down on Him. [17]And there came a **voice from heaven**: "This is My beloved Son. I take delight in Him!"

Lk 3:23aAs He began His ministry, Jesus was about 30 years old.

22. JESUS TEMPTED BY SATAN

Matthew 4:1–11; Mark 1:12–13; Luke 4:1–13

Lk 4:1aThen Jesus returned from the Jordan, full of the Holy Spirit. Mk 1:12–13Immediately the **Spirit drove Him into the wilderness**. [13]He was in the wilderness 40 days, **being tempted by Satan**. He was **with the wild animals**, and the angels began to serve Him. Lk 4:2b**He ate nothing during those days**, and when they were over, He was hungry.

Mt 4:3Then the tempter approached Him and said, "**If You are the Son of God**, tell these stones to become bread."

[4]But He answered, "It is written: '**Man must not live on bread alone**, but on every word that comes from the mouth of God.'"

[5]Then the Devil took Him to the holy city, had Him stand on the **pinnacle of the temple**, [6]and said to Him, "If You are the Son of God, throw Yourself down. For it is written: 'He will give His angels orders concerning you,' and, 'In their hands they will lift you up, so you will not strike your foot against a stone.'"

---

voice from heaven: The heavenly voice quoted parts of two important strands of Old Testament prophecy about the mission of the Messiah. The first part was from Psalm 2:7, which pictured the anointed One who would fulfill the royal role of son of David and Son of God. The latter part was from Isaiah 42:1, one of the prophet's famous Servant passages. Jesus could become King only by way of the cross. He was committing Himself to this kind of mission. And God placed His stamp of approval on this commitment.

22. JESUS TEMPTED BY SATAN

Spirit drove Him into the wilderness: The Spirit with which Jesus had just been anointed immediately led Jesus into the wilderness. The word *led* emphasizes that this was God's will and direction for Him at that time.

being tempted by Satan: James 1:13–15 denies that God is tempted by evil or that God ever tempts anyone to do evil. The same Greek word can mean either "test" or "tempt." God leads us into situations in which our faith is tested, but His purpose is that our faith be strengthened.

with the wild animals: Only the Gospel of Mark mentions this detail, apparently to emphasize the intensity of Satan's attacks. But there was divine aid available and freely given as angels came to help Jesus.

He ate nothing during those days: As Jesus prepared to launch His public ministry, He went without food. Because Jesus had not eaten for so long, He was hungry. The Devil attacked at the point of Jesus' physical needs.

If You are the Son of God: The tempter was not casting doubt on who Jesus was; he was challenging the Son of God to use His divine power to turn stones into bread. Jesus was tempted to use His power to perform a miracle to satisfy His own hunger.

Man must not live on bread alone: Jesus quoted Deuteronomy 8:3, which summarizes what God tried to teach the Israelites during their forty years in the wilderness (Deut. 8:2). Bread meets the needs of our bodies for physical life, but the Word of God is essential for the kind of deeper life that comes through faith in God.

pinnacle of the temple: In the second temptation, Satan took Jesus to the highest point of the Jewish temple in Jerusalem. Then he quoted Psalm 91:11–12, implying that Jesus should jump off to prove that God would protect Him. In this spectacular act, Jesus would impress the people and gain an immediate following.

⁷Jesus told him, "It is also written: '**You must not tempt the Lord** your God.'"

⁸Again, the Devil took Him to a very high mountain and showed Him **all the kingdoms of the world** and their splendor. ⁹And he said to Him, "I will give You all these things if You will fall down and worship me."

¹⁰Then Jesus told him, "Go away, Satan! For it is written: 'You must **worship the Lord** your God, and you must **serve Him only**.'"

Lk 4:13After the Devil had finished every temptation, he departed from Him for a time. Mt 4:11bAnd immediately angels came and began to serve Him.

23. JOHN IDENTIFIES JESUS AS THE MESSIAH

John 1:19–34

¹⁹This is John's testimony when the **Jews** from Jerusalem **sent priests and Levites** to ask him, "**Who are you?**"

²⁰He confessed and did not deny, declaring, "I am not the Messiah."

²¹a"What then?" they asked him. "**Are you Elijah?**"

²¹b"I am not," he said.

²¹c"**Are you the Prophet?**"

²¹d"No," he answered.

You must not tempt the Lord: Jesus rejected the Devil's interpretation of Psalm 91:11–12. He saw that doing what Satan suggested would not be placing trust in God but putting God to the test. Thus, Jesus quoted Deuteronomy 6:16. Jesus often used signs and wonders, but He never did this to impress people and to gain an easy following from the fickle crowds.

all the kingdoms of the world: In the third temptation, Satan offered Jesus a shortcut to achieving His mission. Satan suggested that Jesus could accomplish His goals without suffering and without dying for sin. Throughout His ministry Jesus reminded His disciples that His way involves humble, self-giving service. People worship Satan when they adopt his methods of achieving their goals. People give in to the tempter's suggestion that the good end justifies whatever is necessary to achieve it. Those who look for the quick, easy way to achieve goals often are bowing before the Devil, whose first commandment is, "The end justifies the means."

worship the Lord . . . serve Him only: At this reply from Jesus, the Devil left Him, but passages like Matthew 16:23; 26:36–46 show that Satan continued to tempt Jesus. Then the angels came and ministered to Jesus. As in the case of Elijah, their ministry probably included feeding Jesus (1 Kgs. 19:5–8).

23. JOHN IDENTIFIES JESUS AS THE MESSIAH

Jews . . . sent priests and Levites: A delegation was sent from Jerusalem to investigate John the Baptizer. These Jewish leaders included priests and Levites, whose work related to temple worship. John himself was from a priestly family (Luke 1:5–25). They were concerned because the crowds were anxious to hear John (Mark 1:5).

Who are you? John quickly denied that he was the Christ. *Messiah* is the Hebrew word for "anointed one," or king. "Christ" is the Greek translation. The Jewish people were looking for the king of David's line whom the Lord promised to David (2 Sam. 7:12–16). Messianic expectations were running high, and some people were wondering if John was the Messiah (Luke 3:15).

Are you Elijah? Some Jews thought that the prophet Elijah, who had been taken directly to heaven (2 Kgs. 2:9–14), would reappear before the coming of the Messiah (Mal. 4:5). But John denied that he was Elijah.

Are you the Prophet? The Jewish leaders had in mind the prophet like Moses, predicted in Deuteronomy 18:15–18. Some of the Jewish people thought of this prophet as the Messiah (John 6:1–15); others saw this prophet as a forerunner of the Messiah (John 7:40–41).

²²"Who are you, then?" they asked. "We need to give an answer to those who sent us. **What can you tell us about yourself?**"

²³He said, "I am 'A voice of one crying out in the wilderness: Make straight the way of the Lord'—just as Isaiah the prophet said."

²⁴Now they had been sent from the Pharisees. ²⁵So they asked him, "**Why then do you baptize** if you aren't the Messiah, or Elijah, or the Prophet?"

²⁶"I baptize with water," John answered them. "But among you stands Someone you don't know. ²⁷He is the One coming after me, whose sandal strap **I'm not worthy** to untie."

²⁸All this happened in Bethany across the Jordan, where John was baptizing.

²⁹The next day John saw Jesus coming toward him and said, "**Here is the Lamb of God**, who takes away the sin of the world! ³⁰This is the One I told you about: 'After me comes a man who has surpassed me, because He existed before me.' ³¹I didn't know Him, but I came baptizing with water so He might be revealed to Israel."

³²And John testified, "I watched the Spirit descending from heaven like a dove, and He rested upon Him. ³³I didn't know Him, but He who sent me to baptize with water told me, 'The One on whom you see the Spirit descending and resting—He is the One baptizing in the Holy Spirit.' ³⁴I have seen and testified that He is the Son of God!"

24. JESUS CALLS HIS FIRST DISCIPLES

John 1:35–51

³⁵Again the next day, **John** was standing **with two of his disciples**. ³⁶When he saw Jesus passing by, he said, "Look! The Lamb of God!"

What can you tell us about yourself? John answered this question by quoting Isaiah 40:3. He was a herald who went before a king to announce his approach and to prepare the way for him. "Make straight the way of the Lord" pictured the herald as a road builder who made a straight, level road for the king.

Why then do you baptize: The Pharisees were the largest and most influential religious party in the land. They regarded themselves as protectors of the law and the traditions of the Jewish religion. They were concerned about John's message and baptism. John defended his baptizing by telling the Pharisees that the Messiah was already in their midst but that they had not recognized Him.

I'm not worthy: John declared that he was only a lowly servant of the Messiah. The Messiah came after him in historical sequence, but the Messiah was before him in eternity and superior to him in every way. Tying or untying a leather strap that held a person's sandals was a job for the lowest slave. John said he was unworthy to do even this for the One who was coming.

Here is the Lamb of God: In Israel's sacrificial system, the lamb played a prominent role, particularly in the observance of Passover. Isaiah spoke prophetically of One who would be "led like a lamb to the slaughter" (Isa. 53:7 NIV). These and other Old Testament Scriptures would have been in John's mind as he described Jesus as "the Lamb of God."

24. JESUS CALLS HIS FIRST DISCIPLES

John . . . with two of his disciples: This passage about two of John's disciples shows clearly that some who followed John became followers of the Messiah through John's ministry as the forerunner.

³⁷The two disciples heard him say this and followed Jesus. ³⁸ᵃWhen Jesus turned and noticed them following Him, He asked them, "**What are you looking for?**"

³⁸ᵇThey said to Him, "Rabbi" (which means "Teacher"), "**where are You staying?**"

³⁹"Come and you'll see," He replied. So they went and saw where He was staying, and they stayed with Him that day. It was about ten in the morning.

⁴⁰**Andrew**, Simon Peter's brother, **was one of the two** who heard John and followed Him. ⁴¹**He** first **found his own brother Simon** and told him, "We have found the Messiah!" (which means "Anointed One") ⁴²ᵃand brought him to Jesus.

⁴²ᵇWhen Jesus saw him, He said, "You are Simon, son of John. You will be called Cephas" (which means "Rock").

⁴³The next day He decided to leave for Galilee. **Jesus found Philip** and told him, "Follow Me!"

⁴⁴Now Philip was from Bethsaida, the hometown of Andrew and Peter. ⁴⁵**Philip found Nathanael** and told him, "We have found the One of whom Moses wrote in the law (and so did the prophets): Jesus the son of Joseph, from Nazareth!"

Titles of Jesus

Notice the many different titles for Jesus that appear in John 1:35–51:

- *Lamb of God (v. 36)*
- *Rabbi (vv. 38, 49)*
- *Messiah (v. 41)*
- *Anointed One (v. 41)*
- *Son of God (v. 49)*
- *King of Israel (v. 49)*
- *Son of Man (v. 51)*

All these titles for Jesus reflect the rich diversity of His divine nature and personhood. But the one title that He consistently used for Himself throughout His ministry was "Son of Man."

In some Jewish writings, the "Son of Man" was a figure of power and glory associated with the end times. But Jesus interpreted this title in light of the Suffering Servant of Isaiah. Jesus was emphasizing that the Son of Man must suffer and be rejected before He would be exalted to a position of power and glory.

What are you looking for? . . . where are You staying? These two disciples of John wanted to sit down with Jesus and hear His response to the witness of John the Baptizer. So Jesus invited them to the place where He was staying. They spent the rest of the day in fellowship and conversation with Him.

Andrew . . . was one of the two: Andrew, Simon Peter's brother, was one of the two who went to Jesus. The other disciple remains anonymous. However, since the writer of the Gospel of John obscured his identity by such phrases as "one of His disciples, whom Jesus loved" (John 13:23), this disciple was probably John, the son of Zebedee (see also Matt. 4:21).

He [Andrew] . . . found his own brother Simon: Andrew and Peter, sons of a man named John, were engaged in commercial fishing on Lake Galilee (Matt. 4:18). Andrew made the startling announcement to his brother that he had found the Messiah, the long-promised deliverer of His people.

Jesus found Philip: Jesus took the initiative in recruiting His next disciple, Philip. On His way from the site where John was baptizing, east of the Jordan River, to the predominantly Gentile area of Galilee, He met this man whose home was near that of Andrew and Peter. Perhaps these two men had suggested Philip as a suitable member for their newly formed fellowship. Philip responded immediately to Christ's words, "Follow me." This suggests that he had some previous contact with Jesus. Like Andrew, John, and Peter, he had probably been a disciple of John the Baptizer, from whom he had learned about Jesus.

Philip found Nathanael . . . Come and see: The next recruit was different than those already called. Nathanael had

^{46a}"Can anything good come out of Nazareth?" Nathanael asked him.

^{46b}"**Come and see**," Philip answered.

⁴⁷Then Jesus saw Nathanael coming toward Him and said about him, "Here is a true Israelite in whom is no deceit."

^{48a}"**How do you know me?**" Nathanael asked.

^{48b}"Before Philip called you, when you were **under the fig tree**, I saw you," Jesus answered.

⁴⁹"Rabbi," Nathanael replied, "You are the Son of God! You are **the King of Israel!**"

⁵⁰Jesus responded to him, "Do you believe only because I told you I saw you under the fig tree? You will see greater things than this." ⁵¹Then He said, "I assure you: You will see heaven opened and the angels of God ascending and descending upon the Son of Man."

25. JESUS' FIRST MIRACLE: WATER INTO WINE

John 2:1–11

¹On the third day **a wedding** took place in Cana of Galilee. **Jesus' mother** was there, and ²Jesus and His disciples were invited to the wedding as well. ³**When the wine ran out, Jesus' mother told Him**, "They don't have any wine."

⁴"What has this concern of yours to do with Me, woman?" Jesus asked. "**My hour has not yet come**."

⁵"Do whatever He tells you," His mother told the servants.

---

not been prepared for the encounter with Jesus. When Philip told him that he and others had met a person who fulfilled Old Testament prophecies, Nathanael raised an objection: "Can anything good come out of Nazareth?" He was probably puzzled because there was no reference to Nazareth in messianic Scriptures. Philip urged Nathanael to come and meet Jesus.

How do you know me? Jesus already knew enough about Nathanael to greet him as "a true Israelite in whom is no deceit." Nathanael was surprised about Jesus' assessment of him as a no-nonsense, open-minded, sincere person.

under the fig tree: According to the Jews, the shadow of a fig tree was the ideal place for studying and meditating on the Hebrew Scriptures. Jesus paid tribute to Nathanael as a devout Jew who paid high regard to the written Word.

the King of Israel: Nathanael acknowledged Jesus as "Son of God" and "King of Israel"—the complete fulfillment of the prophetic Scriptures. Such faith would be rewarded.

25. JESUS' FIRST MIRACLE: WATER INTO WINE

a wedding: Marriage ceremonies among the Jews usually began at twilight. The feast after the marriage was held at the home of the bridegroom. Sometimes this event would last for several days (Gen. 29:27). But the financial status of this family must have limited the wedding feast to one day.

Jesus' mother: The apostle John in his Gospel never called Jesus' mother by name. He assumed she was known to his readers.

When the wine ran out: The arrival of Jesus and His disciples may have hastened the depletion of the supply of wine. This must have been a humiliating and embarrassing situation for the host family.

Jesus' mother told Him: The interest that Mary took in the wedding feast suggests that she was a friend of the bridegroom's family. Her statement, "They don't have any wine," was a strong suggestion that Jesus should remedy the situation.

My hour has not yet come: This response by Jesus indicated that Mary wanted Him to show Himself as the Messiah.

⁶Now **six stone water jars** had been set there **for Jewish purification**. Each contained twenty or thirty gallons.

⁷"Fill the jars with water," Jesus told them. So they filled them to the brim. ⁸Then He said to them, "Now draw some out and take it to the chief servant." And they did.

⁹When the chief servant tasted the water (after it had become wine), he did not know where it came from—though the servants who had drawn the water knew. He called the groom ¹⁰and told him, "Everybody sets out the fine wine first, then, after people have drunk freely, the inferior. But you have kept the fine wine until now."

¹¹Jesus performed **this first sign** in Cana of Galilee. He **displayed His glory**, and His disciples believed in Him.

The Seven Signs of John's Gospel

According to the Gospel of John, this miracle of the turning of water into wine was the first of seven signs that signified Jesus was the divine Son of God. This sign showed that Jesus was the source of life. The other six signs and their meaning are:

- *healing of a nobleman's son, emphasizing Jesus as master over distance (4:46–54);*
- *healing of a paralyzed man in Jerusalem, showing Jesus as master over time (5:1–9);*
- *feeding of the five thousand, demonstrating that Jesus is the bread or sustenance of life (6:5–14);*
- *walking on the water, showing Jesus' mastery of nature (6:15–21);*
- *healing of a man born blind, emphasizing Jesus as the light of the world (9:1–7); and*
- *the raising of Lazarus, indicating that Jesus has power over death (11:38–44).*

His miracles were secondary manifestations of His messiahship, but His suffering and death were the supreme manifestations (John 8:28; Matt. 12:38–40). Jesus called this supreme sign His "hour." His mother wanted a supreme sign, but only a secondary sign could be given at this point in His ministry.

six stone water jars . . . for Jewish purification: These details suggest that John was an eyewitness of this event. The Jews regarded themselves as ceremonially unclean if they did not wash their hands before eating (Matt. 15:2).

this first sign . . . displayed His glory: The value of this miracle was that it showed the glory of God. Jesus dramatized the inadequacy of the waterpots, long associated with the Old Testament ritual of cleansing, to meet the needs of people. In these same waterpots, Jesus turned the water into wine.

26. Jesus Visits the City of Capernaum in Galilee

John 2:12

¹²After this He went **down to Capernaum**, together with His mother, **His brothers**, and His disciples, and they **stayed there only a few days**.

27. Jesus' First Cleansing of the Temple

John 2:13–25

¹³The Jewish Passover was near, so Jesus went up to Jerusalem. ¹⁴**In the temple complex** He found **people selling oxen, sheep, and doves**, and He also found the money changers sitting there. ¹⁵After making a whip out of cords, He drove everyone out of the temple complex with their sheep and oxen. He also **poured out the money changers' coins** and overturned the tables. ¹⁶He told those who were selling doves, "**Get these things out of here!** Stop turning **My Father's house into a marketplace!**"

¹⁷And His disciples remembered that it is written: "Zeal for Your house will consume Me."

¹⁸So the Jews replied to Him, "**What sign of authority** will You show us for doing these things?"

¹⁹Jesus answered, "**Destroy this sanctuary**, and I will **raise it up in three days**."

²⁰Therefore the Jews said, "This sanctuary took forty-six years to build, and will You raise it up in three days?"

---

26. Jesus Visits the City of Capernaum in Galilee

down to Capernaum: After leaving Cana in the hills, Jesus went "down" to Capernaum, a city by Lake Galilee, about six hundred feet below sea level.

His brothers: Six passages in the Gospels speak of Jesus' brothers in connection with His mother (Matt. 12:46; 13:55; Mark 3:32; 6:3; Luke 8:19–20; John 2:12). Jesus was the firstborn son of Mary, and she had at least four other sons.

stayed there only a few days: This record of a brief visit to Capernaum shows that the natural ties of kinship with His earthly family were not immediately broken by Jesus. Until He went to Jerusalem for the first Passover, He apparently lived with His mother and His brothers in Nazareth.

27. Jesus' First Cleansing of the Temple

In the temple complex: The Jewish temple in Jerusalem had four sections, ranging from the most sacred inner section, where only priests were allowed, to the outer court, where Gentiles were allowed. The buying and selling were going on in this outer or Gentiles' court.

people selling oxen, sheep, and doves: This market was for the convenience of worshipers in Jerusalem to celebrate the Passover Festival. Oxen and doves were needed for sacrificial purposes. The members of each family who ate the Passover meal required a lamb.

poured out the money changers' coins: Each adult Jewish male was required to pay one half-shekel annually for the support of the temple (Exod. 30:13; Matt. 17:24). These money changers provided a service to worshipers from outside Palestine by changing their foreign money into the required Jewish half-shekel coins.

Get these things out of here! Although Jesus cleansed the temple of this merchandise, He did not destroy any property. The sheep and oxen were safe outside the temple, the scattered money could be picked up from the stone pavement, and the doves were not set free from their cages.

²¹But He was speaking about the sanctuary of His body. ²²So when He was raised from the dead, His disciples remembered that He had said this. And they believed the Scripture and the statement Jesus had made.

²³While He was in Jerusalem at the Passover Festival, many trusted in His name when they saw the signs He was doing. ²⁴Jesus, however, would not entrust Himself to them, since He knew them all ²⁵and because He did not need anyone to testify about man; for He Himself knew what was in man.

Two Cleansings of the Temple?

John places Jesus' cleansing of the temple at the beginning of His public ministry. But the other Gospel writers report that He cleansed the temple as His ministry drew to a close about three and one-half years later (see segment 158, "Jesus Curses a Fig Tree and Cleanses the Temple," p. 185).

Were there two separate cleansings of the temple or only one? Scholars disagree on this issue. Some believe that Jesus cleansed the temple only one time. They theorize that John placed this event early in Jesus' ministry to show that He clashed with the Jewish religious leaders from the very beginning, while the writers of Matthew, Mark, and Luke wanted to show that this event sealed Jesus' doom.

Other scholars point out that two separate cleansings of the temple are a distinct possibility. For example, A. T. Robertson in his A Harmony of the Gospels *declares: "There is no inherent difficulty in the repetition of such an act when one reflects on the national indignation of Jesus at the desecration of the temple on his visits during his ministry and considers that Jesus may have wished to make one last protest at the close of his ministry. Certainty, of course, is not possible in such an argument one way or the other" (p. 25).*

My Father's house into a marketplace! Jesus based His authority over the temple on His relationship to Him for whom the temple was built. As a Son, He purged the temple that belonged to His Father. He challenged the right of the Jewish religious leaders to appropriate His Father's house to their secular uses. The rebuke of Jesus was addressed to the priests, since the market belonged to them and the money changers were their agents.

What sign of authority: The religious leaders felt that only a divinely commissioned person could interfere with the ordering of the temple. They called on Jesus to give them a sign as evidence that He had such a commission.

Destroy this sanctuary . . . raise it up in three days: Jesus replied by using the Greek word *naos,* or sanctuary—the structure which was the seat of God's presence. The sanctuary was a symbol of the body of Christ. His words were a prediction that just as the religious leaders were desecrating the physical temple, so they would destroy His body, which the temple symbolized.

28. JESUS EXPLAINS THE NEW BIRTH TO NICODEMUS

John 3:1–21

¹There was a man from the Pharisees named Nicodemus, a ruler of the Jews. ²This man came to Him **at night** and said, "Rabbi, we know that You have come **from God as a teacher**, for no one could perform these signs You do unless God were with him."

³Jesus replied, "I assure you: Unless someone is **born again**, he cannot see the kingdom of God."

⁴"But how can anyone be **born when he is old**?" Nicodemus asked Him. "Can he enter his mother's womb a second time and be born?"

⁵Jesus answered: "I assure you: Unless someone is born of water and the Spirit, he cannot enter the kingdom of God. ⁶Whatever is born of the flesh is flesh, and whatever is born of the Spirit is spirit. ⁷Do not be amazed that I told you that you must be born again. ⁸**The wind blows** where it pleases, and you hear its sound, but you don't know where it comes from or where it is going. So it is with everyone born of the Spirit."

⁹"**How can these things be?**" asked Nicodemus.

¹⁰"Are you a teacher of Israel and don't know these things?" Jesus replied. ¹¹"I assure you: We speak what We know and We testify to what We have seen, but you do not accept Our testimony. ¹²If I have told you about things that happen on earth and you don't believe, how will you believe if I tell you about **things of heaven**? ¹³No one has ascended into heaven except the One who descended from

---

28. JESUS EXPLAINS THE NEW BIRTH TO NICODEMUS

at night: Why did Nicodemus come to Jesus "at night"? The plural pronoun "we" suggests that he came in behalf of himself and others among the religious leadership of the people. In this circumstance, a night visit could have been a course of discretion.

from God as a teacher: Nicodemus was a sincere seeker of truth, not someone who was trying to trap Jesus. Nicodemus was aware of the miraculous signs Jesus had performed (John 2:23), but he had not yet arrived at true faith for himself personally.

born again: Jesus' response to what Nicodemus intended as a polite compliment must have startled the Pharisee. The word translated "again" can also mean "anew" or "from above." People must be born again, but it must be a new kind of birth, not a second physical birth. And this new birth is possible only if it is a birth from above (from God).

born when he is old: Nicodemus probably understood that Jesus was using symbolic language to say that adults can make a new beginning in life comparable to being born again. His problem was that he could not believe this was possible.

The wind blows: Jesus pointed out to Nicodemus that we don't know where the wind comes from or where it is going, but we know the wind is blowing because we feel it and see its effects. The new birth by the Spirit is not something that human beings can achieve for themselves; neither can we fully understand it. Yet those who experience it see and feel its reality.

How can these things be? Divine truth was eluding Nicodemus because he was seeking an intellectual answer. Truth would come to him not by reasoning but by revelation.

things of heaven: Jesus' words are reliable because He alone has come from heaven with God's truth for humanity. Nicodemus may not have been able to understand such things as the mysterious workings of God's Spirit, but he could trust the word of the Son of Man that God's Spirit is able to do it.

heaven—the Son of Man. ¹⁴Just as **Moses lifted up the serpent** in the wilderness, so the **Son of Man must be lifted up**, ¹⁵so that everyone who believes in Him will have eternal life.

¹⁶"For God loved the world in this way: He gave His only Son, so that everyone who believes in Him will **not perish but have eternal life**. ¹⁷For God did not send His Son into the world that He might judge the world, but that the world might be saved through Him. ¹⁸Anyone who **believes in Him** is not judged, but anyone who does not believe is already judged, because he has not believed in the name of the only Son of God.

¹⁹"This, then, is the **judgment**: the light has come into the world, and people loved **darkness** rather than the light, because their deeds were evil. ²⁰For everyone who practices wicked things hates the light and avoids it, so that his deeds may not be exposed. ²¹But anyone who lives by the truth comes to the light, so that his works may be shown to be accomplished by God."

Nicodemus: An Open-Minded Pharisee

Throughout His ministry Jesus clashed with the Pharisees because of their legalism, hypocrisy, and inflexible approach to religion. But Nicodemus was different. Although he was a Pharisee (John 3:1), probably a member of the Sanhedrin ("a ruler of the Jews," John 3:1), and most certainly a respected Jewish teacher (John 3:10), he was interested in what Jesus had to say. He was open to Jesus' teachings about the new birth and life in the Spirit.

Nicodemus never made an open declaration of faith in Jesus, as far as we know. But he did come to Jesus' defense on one occasion (John 7:50). Along with Joseph of Arimathea, he claimed Jesus' body after His crucifixion and helped prepare it for burial (John 19:39; see segment 205, "Jesus Buried in Joseph's Tomb," p. 240). He may have been an undeclared or "secret" follower of Jesus.

Moses lifted up the serpent: The phrase "eternal life" appears for the first time in verse 15. Jesus compared His death on the cross to Moses' lifting up the replica of a serpent in the wilderness (Num. 21:4–9). The people of Israel were dying because of their sins. But when they looked in faith upon the serpent that Moses lifted up on a pole at God's command, the people lived.

Son of Man must be lifted up: Not only did the Son of Man descend from heaven to reveal God, but He also came so perishing sinners might have eternal life. "Lifted up" referred to Jesus' being lifted up on the cross. These words also implied His being lifted up from the grave and later being lifted up to heaven. Jesus' point was that His own death and resurrection are the means by which God would make the new birth possible for sinners.

not perish but have eternal life: The verse magnifies the love of God that stands behind the new birth and all that God does for us. The scope of His love is the entire world.

believes in Him: Believing in Jesus is more than accepting the facts of the Good News. Believing involves personal trust in and commitment to Jesus Christ as Lord and Savior.

judgment . . . darkness: Those who believe have been saved already, but those who have not believed stand under the condemnation of their sins (John 3:18). People's responses to Jesus reveal whether they love light or darkness. Those who love light come to the light, but those who love darkness retreat further into the darkness of sin (John 3:19–21).

29. JESUS AND HIS DISCIPLES IN JUDEA

John 3:22–24

[22]After this **Jesus** and His disciples went **to the Judean countryside**, where He spent time with them and **baptized**. [23]John also was baptizing in Aenon near Salim, because there was plenty of water there. And people were coming and being baptized, [24]since **John had not yet been thrown into prison**.

30. JOHN THE BAPTIZER POINTS PEOPLE TO JESUS

John 3:25–36

[25]Then a dispute arose between John's disciples and a Jew about purification. [26]So they came to John and told him, "Rabbi, **the One you testified about**, and who was with you across the Jordan, is baptizing—and everyone is flocking to Him."

[27]John responded, "No one can receive a single thing **unless it's given to him from heaven**. [28]You yourselves can testify that I said, 'I am not the Messiah, but I've been sent ahead of Him.' [29]He who has the bride is the **groom**. But the **groom's friend**, who stands by and listens for him, rejoices greatly at the groom's voice. So this joy of mine is complete. [30]He must **increase**, but I must **decrease**."

---

29. JESUS AND HIS DISCIPLES IN JUDEA

to the Judean countryside: Jesus left Jerusalem, the capital of Judea, and went into the surrounding rural districts. Followers whom He enlisted in these areas included Mary, Martha, and Lazarus.

Jesus . . . baptized: The baptism conducted by Jesus was a continuation of the baptism performed by John the Baptizer. The fact that John was also baptizing is a further indication that the baptism administered by Jesus was done in preparation for the founding of the church.

John had not yet been thrown into prison: The ministry of Jesus was well under way before John the Baptizer was arrested by Herod. Their ministries probably overlapped by several months.

30. JOHN THE BAPTIZER POINTS PEOPLE TO JESUS

the One you testified about: John's disciples argued with a Jewish leader about the purifying effects of John's baptism. This caused them to notice that Jesus was baptizing more disciples than John. They believed Jesus owed His popularity to John's testimony, so they were surprised to find that Jesus was surpassing John. They thought this showed ingratitude on the part of Jesus.

unless it's given to him from heaven: John compared himself as a mere man to Jesus as the Son of God. A person can take only what is given him; but the Son of God takes what He chooses. A friend receives only what hospitality extends to him, but the heir takes what he desires since he is the owner of the house.

groom . . . groom's friend: John compared his relationship to Jesus with that of the groom's friend to the groom in a wedding. The groom's friend was responsible for demanding the hand of the bride and preparing everything for the reception of the bride and groom. Thus, John was more than a passive observer of the coming of the Messiah. He was a vital part of God's plan for getting everything ready for the coming of God's Son into the world.

increase . . . decrease: John was the last of the Jewish prophets. As the power of the new order under Christ began to grow in popularity, the old order was growing obsolete and would soon vanish.

³¹The One who comes from above is above all. The one who is from the earth is earthly and speaks in earthly terms. **The One who comes from heaven** is above all. ³²He testifies to what He has seen and heard, yet no one accepts His testimony. ³³The one who has accepted His testimony has affirmed that God is true. ³⁴For He whom God sent speaks God's words, since He **gives the Spirit without measure**. ³⁵The Father loves the Son and has given all things into His hands. ³⁶The one who believes in the Son has eternal life, but the one who refuses to believe in the Son will not see life; instead, the **wrath of God remains on him**.

31. JOHN IMPRISONED BY HEROD

Matthew 14:1–5; Mark 6:17–20; Luke 3:19–20

Lk 3:19–20But **Herod** the tetrarch, being rebuked by him [John the Baptizer] about Herodias, his brother's wife, and about all the evil things Herod had done, ²⁰added this to everything else—he **locked John up in prison**. Mt 14:3–4For Herod had arrested John, chained him, and put him in prison on account of Herodias, his brother Philip's wife, ⁴because John had been telling him, "It's not lawful for you to have her!"

Mk 6:19So Herodias held a grudge against him and wanted to kill him. But she could not. Mt 14:5Though he wanted to kill him, he feared the crowd, since they regarded him as a prophet. Mk 6:20a**Herod was in awe of John** and was protecting him, knowing he was a righteous and holy man.

The One who comes from heaven: To John, Jesus was so far above all earthly prophets that no person could reveal Him. Jesus Himself would have to reveal His character through His words and deeds.

gives the Spirit without measure: To give anything by measure indicates a paltry amount (Ezek. 4:16). The Spirit of God, even through inspired prophets, was only a partial revelation of God's grace (Heb. 1:1). But in Jesus, the Son of God, the Spirit of God is revealed fully and completely (Col. 1:19).

wrath of God remains on him: Those who have not confessed Jesus as Savior and Lord and repented of their sins reside under the wrath of God. John the Baptizer had already warned the Jewish people of the wrath to come if they rejected the Messiah. In his last recorded words, he repeated this warning.

31. JOHN IMPRISONED BY HEROD

Herod . . . locked John up in prison: Herod Antipas was the Roman procurator or governor of Galilee and Perea. He had John the Baptizer arrested and imprisoned because John had condemned Herod's marriage to Herodias, the former wife of Herod's brother.

Herod was in awe of John: Although Herod's wife wanted John executed, Herod refused to do so. He knew that John was a righteous man, and he seemed to respect his boldness and opposition to wrongdoing.

32. JESUS GOES THROUGH SAMARIA
ON HIS WAY TO GALILEE

Matthew 4:12; Mark 1:14; Luke 4:14–15; John 4:1–4

^Jn 4:1–2^Jesus knew that the Pharisees heard He was making and baptizing more disciples than John ²(though Jesus Himself was not baptizing, but His disciples were). ^Mt 4:12a^But after He heard that John had been arrested, He ^Lk 4:14a^returned to Galilee **in the power of the Spirit,** ^Mk 1:14b^preaching the good news of God, ^Lk 4:14b^and news about Him spread throughout the entire vicinity. ^Jn 4:4^He had to travel through Samaria.

33. JESUS TALKS WITH THE WOMAN
AT THE WELL IN SAMARIA

John 4:5–44

⁵So He came to **a town of Samaria called Sychar** near the property that Jacob had given his son Joseph. ⁶Jacob's well was there, and Jesus, worn out from His journey, sat down at the well. It was about six in the evening.

⁷ᵃA woman of Samaria came to draw water.

⁷ᵇ**"Give Me a drink,"** Jesus said to her, ⁸for His disciples had gone into town to buy food.

⁹"How is it that **You, a Jew,** ask for a drink from me, a Samaritan woman?" she asked. For **Jews do not associate with Samaritans.**

---

32. JESUS GOES THROUGH SAMARIA ON HIS WAY TO GALILEE

in the power of the Spirit: Jesus launched His ministry after John the Baptizer was arrested. Jesus would also be arrested and killed, but His death would atone for the sins of the world. Luke's parallel account of this event tells us that Jesus "returned to Galilee in the power of the Spirit" (Luke 4:14a). Throughout his Gospel, Luke emphasizes the work of the Holy Spirit in the life and ministry of Jesus. The power of God was present in Jesus through the Spirit.

33. JESUS TALKS WITH THE WOMAN AT THE WELL IN SAMARIA

a town of Samaria called Sychar: Many Jews would go around Samaria rather than pass through it. Jesus, however, felt compelled to go through this region as He headed north from Judea (John 4:1–4). When He and the disciples reached Sychar, Jesus rested beside a well known as Jacob's Well while they went to buy food. A woman approached as Jesus rested there.

Give Me a drink: Jesus was thirsty and tired, so He asked the woman for a drink of water. He had nothing with which to draw the water (4:11).

You, a Jew: When He asked the woman for a drink, Jesus crossed three social barriers: (1) He was a Jew, and she was a Samaritan. (2) He was a man, and she was a woman. (3) He was a Jewish religious teacher, and she was a woman with a bad reputation.

Jews do not associate with Samaritans: The two groups did not relate to each other socially. A Jew and a Samaritan certainly would not drink from the same cup of water.

¹⁰Jesus answered, "If you knew the gift of God, and who is saying to you, 'Give Me a drink,' you would ask Him, and He would give you **living water**."

¹¹"Sir," said the woman, "You don't even have a bucket, and the well is deep. So where do you get this 'living water'? ¹²You aren't **greater than our father Jacob**, are you? He gave us the well and drank from it himself, as did his sons and livestock."

¹³Jesus said, "Everyone who drinks from this water will get thirsty again. ¹⁴But whoever drinks from the water that I will give him will **never get thirsty again**—ever! In fact, the water I will give him will become a well of water springing up within him for eternal life."

¹⁵"Sir," the woman said to Him, "**give me this water** so I won't get thirsty and come here to draw water."

¹⁶"Go call your husband," He told her, "and come back here."

¹⁷ᵃ"I don't have a husband," she answered.

¹⁷ᵇ"**You have correctly said**, 'I don't have a husband,'" Jesus said. ¹⁸"For you've had five husbands, and the man you now have is not your husband. What you have said is true."

Jews and Samaritans

The feud between Jews and Samaritans extended over many centuries. According to 2 Kings 17:24, after the Assyrian conquest of 722 B.C., the cities of the Northern Kingdom (Israel) were repopulated by foreigners from Babylonia, Syria, and several other pagan nations. The Jews in this region intermarried with these foreigners. This produced a mixed race of "half-breed" Jews who grew to the point where they knew nothing of the religion of Israel. They rejected the temple in Jerusalem and substituted their own shrine at Mount Gerizim.

Judah, the Southern Kingdom, also fell to a foreign power. Its leading citizens were deported to Babylonia, but they returned seventy years later with their Jewish bloodline intact. These full-bloodied Jews of Judah looked down on the Samaritans because of their mixed marriages and pagan worship. The hostility between these two groups was so severe that this Samaritan woman was amazed that Jesus would talk to her.

---

living water: Jesus told the woman that if she knew who He was, she could have asked and received from Him living water. He had water to give that would quench a person's thirst forever.

greater than our father Jacob: The woman's question was phrased as if she assumed a "no" answer. She obviously did not think that this Jewish stranger was greater than Jacob, who was revered as a patriarch by the Samaritans as well as the Jews.

never get thirsty again: Pointing to the well, Jesus said that whoever drank physical water would always need more water. But He was speaking of a different kind of water—the kind that satisfies the spirit forever because it springs up inside to everlasting life. This was the life-giving presence of the Spirit within a person's heart.

give me this water: Was this woman being serious, sarcastic, or flippant in her request? If her tone was flippant, she was not only denying faith in what Jesus said; she was also taunting Him for such a ridiculous claim.

You have correctly said: Jesus knew this woman's past was marred by moral failures. He also knew she was tired of her life and yearned to be something she thought she could never be. Jesus was offering her a new start and new life from

[19]"Sir," the woman replied, "I see that **You are a prophet**. [20]**Our fathers worshiped** on this mountain, yet you Jews say that the place to worship is in Jerusalem."

[21]Jesus told her, "Believe Me, woman, an hour is coming when you will worship the Father neither on this mountain nor in Jerusalem. [22]You Samaritans worship what you do not know. We worship what we do know, because salvation is from the Jews. [23]But an hour is coming, and is now here, when the true worshipers will worship the Father **in spirit and truth**. Yes, the Father wants such people to worship Him. [24]God is Spirit, and those who worship Him must worship in spirit and truth."

[25]The woman said to Him, "I know that **Messiah is coming**" (who is called Christ). "When He comes, He will explain everything to us."

[26]"**I am He**," Jesus told her, "the One speaking to you."

The Ripened Harvest

[27]Just then **His disciples arrived**, and they were amazed that He was talking with a woman. Yet no one said, "What do You want?" or "Why are You talking with her?"

[28]Then the woman left her water jar, went into town, and **told the men**, [29]"Come, see a man who told me everything I ever did! Could this be the Messiah?" [30]They left the town and made their way to Him.

[31]In the meantime the disciples kept urging Him, "Rabbi, eat something."

---

where she was. He was not trying to embarrass her. He was trying to force her to take seriously the offer of living water.

You are a prophet: The woman tried to move the conversation away from her and her need. Her recognition of Jesus as a prophet was probably sincere. How else could this stranger know all her secrets?

Our fathers worshiped: The woman spoke in the past tense when she said, "Our fathers worshiped on this mountain," perhaps pointing at nearby Mount Gerizim with its empty summit. The Samaritan temple on this mountain had been destroyed more than one hundred years before.

in spirit and truth: Jesus declared that worship in special places and buildings was about to give place to worship without such limitations—"neither on this mountain nor in Jerusalem" (John 4:21b). True worshipers would have no need to seek out historic shrines in order to communicate with God, but they would worship "in spirit and truth." God Himself is Spirit, not a physical being confined to one place. He is everywhere present and accessible to everyone.

Messiah is coming: The woman replied that she would wait for the Messiah, who would tell them all things. Both Jews and Samaritans were looking for such a deliverer as God's answer to human problems.

I am He: Jesus cut through this excuse by declaring that He was the Messiah. He did not make this claim when dealing with Jews. Their distorted concept of messiahship, based on a narrow nationalism, compelled His silence; but to this half-Jew, a foreigner, He freely admitted that He was their long-promised deliverer and Savior. He was this not only for Jews but also for Samaritans.

His disciples arrived: About that time, the disciples returned and found Jesus talking to this woman. This must have shocked them, since Jewish males did not talk with women in public, not even their own wives. Yet Jesus was conversing with a Samaritan woman. The woman hurried away from the well so abruptly that she left her water jar.

told the men: This woman was a social outcast, yet she told the men of Sychar about Jesus. She framed her testimony in the form of a question instead of a statement. Her question in Greek can be translated, "Surely this man can't be the Messiah, can He?" Perhaps she wanted to stir their curiosity without causing them to reject what was said by a woman

[32]But He said, "I have food to eat that you don't know about."

[33]The disciples said to one another, "Could someone have brought Him something to eat?"

[34]"**My food** is to do the will of Him who sent Me and to finish His work," Jesus told them. [35]"Don't you say, 'There are still four more months, then comes the harvest'? Listen to what I'm telling you: Open your eyes and look at the fields, for they are ready for harvest. [36]The reaper is already receiving pay and gathering fruit for eternal life, so the sower and reaper can rejoice together. [37]For in this case the saying is true: 'One sows and another reaps.' [38]I sent you to reap what you didn't labor for; others have labored, and you have benefited from their labor."

The Savior of the World

[39]Now **many** Samaritans from that town **believed in Him** because of what the woman said when she testified, "He told me everything I ever did." [40]Therefore, when the Samaritans came to Him, they asked Him to stay with them, and He stayed there two days. [41]Many more believed because of what He said. [42]And they told the woman, "We no longer believe because of what you said, for we have heard for ourselves and know that this really is the Savior of the world."

[43]After **two days** He left there for Galilee. [44]Jesus Himself testified that a prophet has no honor in his own country.

---

of her reputation. She invited the men of the village to come and see for themselves by meeting Jesus. They could make up their own minds.

My food: Meanwhile, the disciples were surprised when Jesus turned down their request that He eat. He explained that He was nourished by His preoccupation with the needs of the Samaritans. To Jesus, the Samaritans were like a ripe harvest field that someone else had sown; now He and the disciples could reap the harvest.

many . . . believed in Him: When the men of the village came out to see Jesus for themselves, they also believed in Him. Each became a believer on his own.

two days: Anyone else might have regarded this event as an interruption, but Jesus saw it as a rich opportunity. He accepted the Samaritans' invitation to stay, remaining two days. During that time, many others came to Jesus and believed.

IV. The Ministry of Jesus in Galilee

The period of Jesus' life known as the great Galilean ministry must have lasted for at least eighteen months. It was the most prolific segment of His entire ministry of about three and one-half years. During these months, He selected and trained His twelve disciples; delivered most of His major teachings, including the Sermon on the Mount; and performed most of His miracles. This period was also marked by increasing hostility and resentment toward Jesus by the Jewish religious leaders.

34. Jesus Begins Preaching in Galilee

Matthew 4:17; Mark 1:14–15; John 4:45

Jn 4:45When they entered Galilee, the Galileans welcomed Him because they had seen everything He did in Jerusalem during the festival. For they also had gone to the festival. Mt 4:17aFrom then on Jesus began to preach Mk 1:14b–15**the good news of God**: 15**"The time is fulfilled**, and the kingdom of God has come near. **Repent and believe** in the good news!"

35. Jesus Heals the Son of a Royal Official

John 4:46–54

46Then He went again to Cana of Galilee, where He had turned the water into wine. There was **a certain royal official** whose son was ill at Capernaum. 47When this man heard

Cana of Galilee

The village of Cana was only about six miles northeast of Nazareth, Jesus' hometown. But this royal official who came to Jesus at Cana was from Capernaum near Lake Galilee, about twenty miles away. He probably walked the distance to ask Jesus to heal his son. Although Cana was an insignificant village, it was a place where Jesus worked two miracles (see John 4:47). One of Jesus' twelve disciples, Nathanael, was from Cana (John 21:2).

---

34. Jesus Begins Preaching in Galilee

the good news of God: The ministry of John the Baptizer had been the beginning of the good news of Jesus Christ (Mark 1:1). Now in Galilee Jesus began His public ministry by proclaiming the good news.

The time is fulfilled: For centuries, God's prophets had been promising that God would visit and redeem His people. Jesus announced that the decisive time in God's redemptive plan had arrived.

Repent and believe: John the Baptizer had called people to repent in preparation for the Coming One. Jesus called people to repent and believe because He was that One. Repenting is turning from sin; believing is turning to God.

35. Jesus Heals the Son of a Royal Official

a certain royal official: This man was probably an officer of Herod Antipas, the Roman ruler over the province of Galilee.

that Jesus had come from Judea into Galilee, he went to Him and pleaded with Him to come down and heal his son, for he was about to die.

⁴⁸Jesus told him, "**Unless you people see signs and wonders**, you will not believe."

⁴⁹"Sir," the official said to Him, "**come down before my boy dies!**"

⁵⁰"**Go**," Jesus told him, "**your son will live**." The man believed what Jesus said to him and departed.

⁵¹While he was still going down, his slaves met him saying that his boy was alive. ⁵²He asked them at what time he got better. "Yesterday at seven in the morning **the fever left him**," they answered. ⁵³The father realized this was the very hour at which Jesus had told him, "Your son will live." Then **he** himself **believed, along with his** whole **household**.

⁵⁴This therefore was the second sign Jesus performed after He came from Judea to Galilee.

36. JESUS' IDENTIFICATION WITH THE SUFFERING SERVANT

Luke 4:16–21

¹⁶He came to Nazareth, where He had been brought up. As usual, He **entered the synagogue** on the Sabbath day and stood up to read. ¹⁷The scroll of the prophet Isaiah was given to Him, and unrolling the scroll, He found the place where it was written: ¹⁸"The Spirit of the Lord is upon Me, because He has anointed Me to preach good news to the poor. He has sent Me to proclaim freedom to the **captives** and recovery of sight to the **blind**, to set free the **oppressed**, ¹⁹to proclaim the **year of the Lord's favor**."

Unless you people see signs and wonders: Jesus wanted people to believe in Him because of His character and His words (John 15:22–24). But many people insisted on having their faith undergirded by miracles. *Signs* and *wonders* indicate two different responses to miracles. To those who were inclined toward faith, Jesus' miracles were *signs* that He acted under the authority of God. To those who were skeptical and unconvinced, they were mere *wonders*. The people were startled by their strangeness but not moved to faith in the miracle worker.

come down before my boy dies: The father knew he was in a race with death. He also thought that Jesus had to be physically present to heal his son.

Go . . . your son will live: Jesus enlarged the royal official's conception of His divine power by showing that His words would bring healing across time and space.

the fever left him: The father expected that the fever in his son would go down slowly. But the reply of the servants to his question shows that it had gone away instantly the day before at the very moment when Jesus had declared his son healed.

he . . . believed, along with his . . . household: This royal official believed first in the power of Jesus' *presence*, then in the power of Jesus' *word*, and finally in Jesus Himself. His faith was infectious because his household shared his belief.

36. JESUS' IDENTIFICATION WITH THE SUFFERING SERVANT

entered the synagogue: Synagogues were local places of prayer, worship, and instruction. Their services allowed for a measure of freedom. After a selected reading from the Hebrew Scriptures by a synagogue official, a respected visitor might be called on to read from the Scriptures and add his comments. Jesus took advantage of this opportunity for communicating His message.

captives . . . blind . . . oppressed: Jesus read passages from Isaiah 61:1–2 and 58:6. These words focused on people in

[superscript]20[/superscript]He then rolled up the scroll, gave it back to the attendant, and sat down. And the eyes of everyone in the synagogue were fixed on Him. [superscript]21[/superscript]He began by saying to them, "Today this Scripture has been fulfilled in your hearing."

37. Rejected at Nazareth, Jesus Moves to Capernaum

Matthew 4:13–16; Luke 4:22–31

Lk 4:22They were all speaking well of Him and were amazed by the gracious words that came from His mouth, yet they said, "**Isn't this Joseph's son?**"

[superscript]23[/superscript]Then He said to them, "No doubt you will quote this proverb to Me: 'Doctor, heal Yourself.' 'All we've heard that took place in Capernaum, do here in Your hometown also.'"

[superscript]24[/superscript]He also said, "I assure you: No prophet is accepted in his hometown. [superscript]25[/superscript]But I say to you, there were certainly many widows in Israel in Elijah's days, when the sky was shut up for three years and six months while a great famine came over all the land. [superscript]26[/superscript]Yet **Elijah** was not sent to any of them, except to a widow at Zarephath in Sidon. [superscript]27[/superscript]And there were many lepers in Israel in the prophet **Elisha's** time, yet not one of them was cleansed except Naaman the Syrian."

[superscript]28[/superscript]When they heard this, all who were in the synagogue were enraged. [superscript]29[/superscript]They got up, drove Him out of town, and brought Him to the edge of the hill on which their town was built, **intending to hurl Him over the cliff.** [superscript]30[/superscript]But He passed right through the crowd and went on His way.

Mt 4:13–16He left Nazareth behind and went to live in Capernaum by the sea, in the region of Zebulun and Naphtali. [superscript]14[/superscript]This was to fulfill what was spoken through the prophet Isaiah: [superscript]15[/superscript]"O land of Zebulun and land of Naphtali, along the sea road, beyond the Jordan, Galilee of the Gentiles! [superscript]16[/superscript]The people who live

---

great economic and physical need—the poor, the captives, the blind. While Jesus came primarily to proclaim the "gospel," or good news, of salvation from sin, He also expressed great compassion for the underprivileged, especially through His healing ministry.

year of the Lord's favor: These words referred to the coming of the messianic age. Jesus declared that this new age had arrived in Him. God was establishing a new relationship with people through the incarnation of His Son.

37. Rejected at Nazareth, Jesus Moves to Capernaum

Isn't this Joseph's son? Joseph had been the village carpenter. The way the question was asked meant, "Who does this Jesus think He is?"

Elijah . . . Elisha: This critical attitude reminded Jesus of treatment received by men of God in the past—Elijah and Elisha. It was true for them, as it was now for Him, that "no prophet is accepted in his hometown" (Luke 4:24). When Old Testament prophets met with indifference or hostility among their own people, they sought a hearing among Gentiles. For example, Elijah was instructed to go to Phoenicia, the home territory of the evil queen Jezebel (see 1 Kgs. 17:2–6). There a Gentile widow gave him food and drink.

intending to hurl Him over the cliff: Jesus' Jewish listeners were proud of their unique relationship with God. So great was their anger about His suggestion that foreigners might be blessed by God that they rushed Jesus out of the synagogue to throw Him down to His death. But He slipped away from them and made His way to Capernaum, where He resumed His work.

in darkness have seen a great light, and for those living in the shadowland of death, light has dawned."

38. CALLING OF PETER AND ANDREW, JAMES AND JOHN

Matthew 4:18–22; Mark 1:16–20; Luke 5:1–11

Lk 5:1 As the crowd was pressing in on Jesus to hear God's word, He was standing by Lake Gennesaret. ²He saw two boats at the edge of the lake; the fishermen had left them and were washing their nets. ³He **got into one of the boats**, which belonged to Simon, and asked him to put out a little from the land. Then He sat down and was teaching the crowds from the boat.

Fishing on Lake Galilee

Lake Galilee in northern Palestine was the center of the commercial fishing business for the Jewish nation during New Testament times. Fresh fish were sold in the local markets. Fish were also preserved by salting, then shipped to Jerusalem in the south and even exported to major markets such as Rome.

Casting nets from small boats and pulling in the catch was hard, messy work. And there was always something for fishermen to do even when on shore—patching and washing their nets, taking care of their boats, buying supplies, and preserving the fish for shipment.

This passage from Luke shows clearly that at least four of Jesus' twelve disciples were commercial fishermen—the brothers Peter and Andrew and the brothers James and John. Other disciples may also have been involved in the fishing business.

---

38. CALLING OF PETER AND ANDREW, JAMES AND JOHN

got into one of the boats: Crowds thronged Jesus to benefit from His healing powers and to listen to His message. On the shore of Lake Galilee (Gennesaret), this became a problem. For Jesus to see the people as He spoke, and for them to see Him, He used Peter's small fishing boat as a pulpit.

let down your nets: After teaching the people, Jesus told Peter to push away from shore and let down his fishing nets. Peter and his companions had been out all night fishing, with no success. There was even less likelihood of finding fish in the daylight hours. But Peter did as Jesus directed.

the other boat: This second boat belonged to James and John and their father Zebedee. Their obedience of Jesus' command resulted in such a large catch that Peter and his crew were unable to handle it. They called for help from their partners. Both boats were so loaded that "they began to sink."

Depart from me: Peter thought he knew all there was to know about fishing. But when Jesus filled Peter's nets with fish, Peter realized he was in the presence of God. (For another instance of a miraculous catch of fish, see segment 218, "A Miraculous Catch of Fish at Lake Galilee," p. 251.) He pleaded with Jesus to leave him because he was "a sinful man." But Jesus stayed in the boat to enlist Peter for greater service.

catching people: Peter, Andrew, James, and John were offered the opportunity to exchange fishing for a more significant task; they would "catch people." This invitation was appropriate for persons in the fishing business. Jesus calls people to devote their interests and skills to His service.

they . . . left everything: They went with Jesus, leaving their vocation as commercial fishermen. They did not immediately become all they needed to be, but they launched out as followers and learners.

⁴When He had finished speaking, He said to Simon, "Put out into deep water and **let down your nets** for a catch."

⁵"Master," Simon replied, "we've worked hard all night long and caught nothing! But at Your word, I'll let down the nets." ⁶When they did this, they caught a great number of fish, and their nets began to tear. ⁷So they signaled to their partners in **the other boat** to come and help them; they came and filled both boats so full that they began to sink.

⁸When Simon Peter saw this, he fell at Jesus' knees and said, "**Depart from me**, because I'm a sinful man, Lord!" ⁹For he and all those with him were amazed at the catch of fish they took, ¹⁰ᵃand so were James and John, Zebedee's sons, who were Simon's partners.

¹⁰ᵇ"Don't be afraid," Jesus told Simon. "From now on you will be **catching people!**" ¹¹Then **they** brought the boats to land, **left everything**, and followed Him.

39. HEALING OF A DEMON-POSSESSED MAN

Mark 1:21–26; Luke 4:31–35

ᴹᵏ ¹:²¹Then they went into **Capernaum**, and right away He entered **the synagogue** on the Sabbath and began to teach. . . . ²³Just then a man with **an unclean spirit** [ᴸᵏ ⁴:³³*unclean demonic spirit*] was in their synagogue. He cried out, ²⁴"What do You have to do with us, **Jesus—Nazarene**? Have You come to destroy us? I know who You are—the Holy One of God!"

Jesus in Galilee

From His headquarters city, Capernaum on Lake Galilee, Jesus traveled throughout the surrounding province of Galilee—preaching, teaching, and healing. Galilee was the most northerly of the three provinces of Palestine—Galilee, Samaria, and Judea.

In this region of the country, known as "Galilee of the Gentiles" (Isa. 9:1; Matt. 4:15), Jesus spent the first two years of His ministry. The Galileans, influenced by both Jewish and Gentile customs, were probably more open to Jesus' message than the citizens of the southern part of the country, where the Pharisees and scribes were strong and influential.

Jesus Himself was a native of Galilee, and all His disciples except Judas were from this province. He was known as Judas Iscariot, indicating he was from the town of Kerioth in southern Judah (Luke 6:16; Josh. 15:25).

---

39. HEALING OF A DEMON-POSSESSED MAN

Capernaum: This town on the northwest coast of Lake Galilee was the home of Simon and Andrew (Mark 1:29). It became the home base for Jesus' ministry in Galilee (Mark 2:1; Matt. 9:1).

the synagogue: When Jesus entered the synagogue at Capernaum, He had already established a reputation as a teacher, so He was invited to speak during the service.

an unclean spirit: Jesus was interrupted by the cries of a man who was possessed by demons. This encounter was the first of many confrontations of Jesus with demon-possessed people.

Jesus—Nazarene: The demons recognized Jesus and used His name, apparently in an attempt to influence Him to leave them alone.

[25]But Jesus rebuked him and said, "**Be quiet**, and come out of him!" [26]And the unclean spirit convulsed him, shouted with a loud voice, and **came out of him**.

40. Amazement at Jesus' Authority

Mark 1:22, 27–28; Luke 4:32, 36–37

[Mk 1:22]They were astonished at His teaching because, unlike the scribes, He was **teaching them as one having authority**. [Lk 4:36]They were all struck with amazement and kept saying to one another, "What is this message? For with authority and power He commands the unclean spirits, [Mk 1:27b–28]and they obey Him." [28]His **fame then spread** throughout the entire vicinity of Galilee.

41. Healing of Peter's Mother-in-Law

Matthew 8:14–15; Mark 1:29–31; Luke 4:38–39

[Mk 1:29–31]As soon as they left the synagogue, they went into Simon and Andrew's house with James and John. [30]**Simon's mother-in-law** was lying in bed with a fever, and they told Him about her at once. [31]So He went to her, took her by the hand, and raised her up. The fever left her, and she began to serve them.

42. Healing of Many People in Capernaum

Matthew 8:16–17; Mark 1:32–34; Luke 4:40–41

[Lk 4:40a]When the **sun was setting**, all those who had anyone sick with various diseases brought them to Him. [Mk 1:33]The whole town was assembled at the door.

Be quiet: Why did Jesus tell the demons to be silent? Perhaps He felt the testimony of demons would do more to discredit Him than to help Him. Another possibility may be the same reason why Jesus later told the cleansed leper not to say what had happened (Mark 1:44) and Peter not to tell anyone that Jesus was the Messiah (Mark 8:30). Jesus feared that many people would see Him only as a miracle-working Christ who had come to be an earthly king.

came out of him: A number of people in Jesus' day claimed to have the ability to cast out demons. They used elaborate rituals and formulas, but Jesus simply ordered the demons to leave the man. With terrible convulsions and loud cries, they came out of the man.

40. Amazement at Jesus' Authority

teaching them as one having authority: The scribes and Pharisees taught the people by quoting other authorities and experts. The people were amazed that Jesus taught on His own authority—without quoting someone else. His authority came directly from God.

fame then spread: Probably the man whom Jesus healed was well known in the synagogue. The people were amazed, and they began to ask questions about someone with such authority that even the demons obeyed Him. News of this miracle spread quickly.

41. Healing of Peter's Mother-in-Law

Simon's mother-in-law: Jesus healed Peter's mother-in-law by taking her by the hand and lifting her up from the bed. She showed her gratitude by waiting on the guests in the house.

Lk 4:40b As He **laid His hands on each one** of them, He would heal them. Mt 8:17 So that what was spoken through the prophet Isaiah might be fulfilled: "He Himself took our weaknesses and carried our diseases." Lk 4:41 Also, demons were coming out of many, shouting and saying, "You are the Son of God!" But **He rebuked them** and would not allow them to speak, because they knew He was the Messiah.

43. A Healing and Preaching Tour throughout Galilee

Matthew 4:23–25; Mark 1:35–39; Luke 4:42–44

Mk 1:35–37 Very early in the morning, while it was still dark, He got up, went out, and made His way to a deserted place. And **He was praying there**. ³⁶Simon and his companions went searching for Him. ³⁷They found Him and said, "Everyone's looking for You!"

³⁸And He said to them, "**Let's go on to the neighboring villages**, so that I may preach there too. [Lk 4:43 *I must proclaim the good news about the kingdom of God to the other towns also*]. This is why I have come." ³⁹So He went into all of Galilee, preaching in their synagogues and driving out demons.

Mt 4:24–25 Then the news about Him spread throughout Syria. So they brought to Him all those who were afflicted, those suffering from various diseases and intense pains, the demon-possessed, the epileptics, and the paralytics. And He healed them. ²⁵Large crowds followed Him from Galilee, Decapolis, Jerusalem, Judea, and beyond the Jordan.

---

42. Healing of Many People in Capernaum

sun was setting: The Jews began their days at sunset. This sunset meant the Sabbath day was ending. The traditions of the elders forbade traveling or carrying a sick person on the Sabbath. Thus, the people waited until the Sabbath was over before bringing their sick and afflicted to Jesus at Peter's house for healing.

laid His hands on each one: News of the exorcism in the synagogue and the healing of Peter's mother-in-law had spread quickly. People brought those who were sick and those possessed with demons to Jesus for healing.

He rebuked them: Jesus also cast out many demons, ordering them not to speak. He repudiated such witness from demonic sources. Perhaps He also wanted to suppress references to Himself as the Messiah. The Messiah, so people thought, would liberate them from their enemies and restore Israel's prestige and power. But Jesus had come as a spiritual deliverer.

43. A Healing and Preaching Tour throughout Galilee

He was praying there: The greater the demands made on Jesus, the more He felt the need for quiet communion with God. He also saw the dangers in His growing popularity. Large crowds draw attention. This would be especially true in Galilee, an area notorious for its insurrections and rebellion against Rome. He was also sensitive to the danger of being regarded as a public benefactor whom the people would like to turn into a political leader.

Let's go on to the neighboring villages: Jesus refused to restrict His ministry to the city of Capernaum. He went to the people in the surrounding villages and towns to proclaim the kingdom of God and to heal their sicknesses.

44. A Leper Healed

Matthew 8:1–4; Mark 1:40–45; Luke 5:12–16

Mk 1:40Then **a leper** [Lk 5:12*a man covered with leprosy*] came to Him, and begged on his knees [Lk 5:12*fell on his face*] before Him, saying, "If You are willing, You can make me clean."

41**Moved with compassion**, Jesus reached out His hand and **touched him**. "I am willing," He told him. "Be made clean." 42Immediately the leprosy left him, and he was made clean. 43Then He sternly warned him and sent him away at once, 44telling him, "See that you **say nothing to anyone**; but go and show yourself to the priest, and offer what Moses prescribed for your cleansing, as a testimony to them."

45Yet he went out and began to proclaim it widely and to spread the news, with the result that Jesus could no longer enter a town openly. But He was out in deserted places, and **they** [Lk 5:15*large crowds*] **would come to Him from every-where** Lk 5:15b–16to hear Him and to be healed of their sicknesses. 16Yet He often withdrew to deserted places and prayed.

45. Healing of a Paralyzed Man

Matthew 9:1–8; Mark 2:1–12; Luke 5:17–26

Mt 9:1So He got into a boat, crossed over, and came to His own town Mk 2:1b–2aCapernaum again. After some days, it was reported that He was at home. 2aSo many people gathered together that there was no more room, even near the door.

Lk 5:17On one of those days **while He was teaching**, Pharisees and teachers of the law were sitting there who had come from every village of Galilee and Judea,

---

44. A Leper Healed

a leper: Under Jewish law a person with leprosy also became an unclean outcast (Lev. 13). This leper broke the law by coming to Jesus. He had confidence that Jesus could make him well.

Moved with compassion . . . touched him: Jesus showed His compassion by touching the unclean outcast. Touching is mentioned often in connection with His miracles (Mark 3:10; 6:56; 7:33; 8:22–23). Jesus also spoke powerful words of healing. His miracles were signs of the divine authority of the Son of God (Matt. 12:28).

say nothing to anyone: Jesus told the man to go to the priest and offer the proper sacrifices. This was necessary for him to be officially declared no longer an unclean outcast. Why did Jesus want to keep His miracles and His identity a secret? He knew that many people were expecting a Messiah who would be an earthly king. He did not want stories of His miracles to strengthen this false idea.

they would come to Him from everywhere: When the man disobeyed and spread the news of his healing, large crowds sought Jesus as a healer. So many people came that Jesus could no longer minister in a town. He sought privacy in the open country.

45. Healing of a Paralyzed Man

while He was teaching: Jesus returned to Capernaum and "was at home" (Mark 2:1b). This was probably the home of Simon and Andrew. While Jesus was teaching, people crowded about the door.

and also from Jerusalem. And the Lord's power to heal was in Him. ^{Mk 2:2b}And He was speaking the message to them.

^{Lk 5:18–19}Just then some men came, carrying on a stretcher **a man who was paralyzed**. They tried to bring him in and set him down before Him. ^{19a}Since they could not find a way to bring him in because of the crowd, they went up on the roof ^{Mk 2:4b}[and] removed the roof above where He was. And when they had broken through, they ^{Lk 5:19b}**lowered him** on the stretcher **through the roof tiles** into the middle of the crowd before Jesus.

^{20a}**Seeing their faith** He said, ^{Mt 9:2b}"Have courage, son, **your sins are forgiven**."

^{Lk 5:21}Then the scribes and the Pharisees **began to reason**: "Who is this man who speaks blasphemies? Who can forgive sins but God alone?"

²²But perceiving their thoughts, Jesus replied to them, "Why are you reasoning this in your hearts? ²³Which is easier: to say, 'Your sins are forgiven you,' or to say, 'Get up and walk'? ²⁴But so you may know that the Son of Man has **authority** on earth **to forgive sins**"—He told the paralyzed man, "I tell you: get up, pick up your stretcher, and go home."

²⁵Immediately he got up before them, picked up what he had been lying on, and went home glorifying God. ²⁶Then everyone was astounded, and they were giving glory to God. And they were filled with awe and said, "We have seen incredible things today!"

---

a man who was paralyzed: This man may have been a paraplegic, dependent on others for mobility. His bed would have resembled a stretcher that took four men to carry. Unable to break through the crowd around Jesus, the men who carried the paralyzed man took extreme measures.

lowered him . . . through the roof tiles: The houses of that day had flat roofs that were accessible by outside stairs. The roof over where Jesus stood was not solid enough to keep these determined men from breaking through. Their access to Jesus through the roof was probably done with Peter's permission.

Seeing their faith: The faith that Jesus noticed must have included the faith of the four friends as well as the faith of the sick man.

your sins are forgiven: Jesus perceived that the man's condition was the result of a sinful lifestyle. Perhaps his manner of life was so well known in Capernaum that Jesus used him to warn of the consequences of sinfulness. Before he could recover, he needed to know that his spiritual problem as well as his physical disability had been remedied.

began to reason: The scribes and Pharisees heard what Jesus said to the sick man. They thought this was blasphemy because He claimed to do something that only God could do. But no blasphemy was involved since Jesus had divine power to forgive sins.

authority . . . to forgive sins: Jesus told the scribes and Pharisees that He would show them He had the power and authority to forgive sins. He told the man to get up, pick up his stretcher, and go to his house. Immediately, the man obeyed. The people were amazed at this miracle of forgiveness and healing.

Matthew the Tax Collector

Tax collectors such as Matthew were Jews who gathered taxes from their fellow Jews for the Roman government as independent contractors. The Romans placed taxes on land, goods produced and sold in Palestine, and products that passed through the region. These tax agents were allowed to keep any money they raised above the amount levied by the Romans—a practice that led to extortion and corruption. They were hated by other Jews—particularly the Pharisees—because they sold themselves into the employ of the Roman Empire. But Jesus associated with these despised tax collectors, showing that God's grace extends to all people.

46. JESUS CALLS MATTHEW

Matthew 9:9–13; Mark 2:13–17; Luke 5:27–32

Lk 5:27–28 After this, Jesus went out [Mk 2:13a *went out again beside the sea*] and saw **a tax collector named Levi** [Mt 9:9 *Matthew*] [Mk 2:14a *Levi the son of Alphaeus*] sitting at the tax office, and He said to him, "Follow Me!" 28So, leaving everything behind, he got up and began to follow Him.

29Then Levi hosted **a grand banquet** for Him at his house. Now there was a large crowd of tax collectors and others who were guests with them. 30But the Pharisees and their scribes were complaining to His disciples, "**Why do you eat** and drink **with tax collectors and sinners?**"

31Jesus replied to them, "**The healthy** don't need a doctor, but **the sick** do. Mt 9:13 Go and learn what this means: 'I desire mercy and not sacrifice.' For I didn't come to call the righteous, but sinners."

---

46. JESUS CALLS MATTHEW

a tax collector named Levi: Like Simon Peter, Matthew (Levi) had two names. He collected customs fees, probably on goods passing along one of the roads near Capernaum.

a grand banquet: After accepting Jesus' call, Matthew hosted a sumptuous meal for Jesus and His disciples, inviting some of his fellow tax collectors and other guests.

Why do you eat . . . with tax collectors and sinners? The Pharisees were offended that Jesus would associate with such people. The Pharisees considered just about everyone except themselves as "sinners." Having table fellowship with unclean people was a flagrant abuse of their rules. To the Pharisees, one of Jesus' "sins" was being a friend of sinners (Luke 15:1–2).

The healthy . . . the sick: Jesus and the Pharisees had different strategies of evangelism. Because the Pharisees feared contamination, they avoided any contact with sinners. They would accept repentant sinners if they came to the Pharisees, confessed their sins, and began to live by their standards of righteousness. But Jesus sought out sinners, befriended them, and showed them God's love in order to lead them to repent (Luke 15:3–32; 19:10). Since He had come to heal those who were diseased by sin, He needed to spend time with those who were sick.

47. OBSERVATIONS ON FASTING

Matthew 9:14–17; Mark 2:18–22; Luke 5:33–39

Mk 2:18Now John's disciples and the Pharisees were fasting. People came and asked Him, "Why do John's disciples and the Pharisees' disciples fast [Lk 5:33a*fast often and say prayers*], **but Your disciples do not fast?**"

Mt 9:15Jesus said to them, "Can the **wedding guests** be sad while the **groom** is with them? The days will come when the groom is taken away from them, and then they will fast."

Lk 5:36aHe also told them a parable: Mk 2:21–22a"No one sews a patch of **unshrunk cloth on an old garment**. Otherwise, the new patch pulls away from the old cloth, and a worse tear is made. 22aAnd no one puts new wine into old wineskins. Otherwise, the wine will burst the skins, and the wine is lost as well as the skins. Lk 5:38–39But new wine should be put into fresh wineskins. 39And no one, after drinking old wine, wants new, because he says, 'The old is better.'"

48. JESUS HEALS A LAME MAN ON THE SABBATH

John 5:1–15

1After this a Jewish festival took place, and Jesus went up to Jerusalem. 2By **the Sheep Gate** in Jerusalem there is **a pool**, called Bethesda in Hebrew, which has five colonnades. 3Within these lay **a multitude of the sick**—blind, lame, and paralyzed—**waiting for the moving of the water**, 4because an angel would go down into the pool from time to time and stir up the water. Then the first one who got in after the water was stirred up recovered from whatever ailment he had.*

The words "waiting for the moving of the water" in verse 3 and all of verse 4 do not appear in some New Testament manuscripts.

---

47. OBSERVATIONS ON FASTING

but Your disciples do not fast: The disciples of John the Baptizer had great respect for fasting, and they noticed that Jesus and His disciples did not observe this ritual. As honest inquirers, they wondered why.

wedding guests . . . groom: Jesus answered by comparing Himself to the groom at a wedding. As long as the groom was with his friends, He pointed out, these friends should be happy; there was no need to fast. The groom's friends were called "sons of the bride chamber." They went with the groom to the bride's house and escorted her to her new home. After they arrived, a great feast began. Mourning and fasting would be out of place on such an occasion.

unshrunk cloth on an old garment: The disciples of John the Baptizer thought of Jesus as a reformer of Judaism, but He corrected this false assumption with an illustration. New cloth could not be used as a patch on old clothes. In the same way, the kingdom of God that had arrived in Jesus could not conform to the rites of the Pharisees. The Old Testament law was inadequate. He was attempting to move the law to a higher level, represented by God's love and grace.

48. JESUS HEALS A LAME MAN ON THE SABBATH

the Sheep Gate . . . a pool: Jesus went to a pool called Bethesda near a gate in the city wall of Jerusalem. The word *Bethesda* means "house of mercy." It was probably a double pool surrounded by porches.

a multitude of the sick . . . waiting for the moving of the water: Many sick and disabled people had been drawn to this pool by the legend that the bubbling spring waters had magical healing properties. They believed that the first person to enter the pool after an angel stirred the waters would be healed.

⁵**One man** was there who had been **sick for 38 years**. ⁶When Jesus saw him lying there and knew he had already been there a long time, He said to him, "Do you want to get well?"

⁷"Sir," the sick man answered, "I don't have a man to put me into the pool when the water is stirred up, but while I'm coming, someone goes down ahead of me."

⁸"Get up," Jesus told him, "pick up your bedroll and walk!" ⁹ᵃInstantly the man got well, picked up his bedroll, and started to walk.

⁹ᵇNow that day was the Sabbath, ¹⁰so the Jews said to the man who had been healed, "**This is the Sabbath**! It's illegal for you to pick up your bedroll."

¹¹He replied, "**The man who made me well told me**, 'Pick up your bedroll and walk.'"

¹²"Who is this man who told you, 'Pick up your bedroll and walk'?" they asked.

¹³But the man who was cured did not know who it was, because Jesus had slipped away into the crowd that was there.

¹⁴After this Jesus found him in the temple complex and said to him, "See, you are well. Do not sin any more, so that something worse doesn't happen to you." ¹⁵The **man** went and **reported to the Jews** that it was Jesus who had made him well.

49. JESUS DEFENDS HIS SABBATH HEALING

John 5:16–47

¹⁶Therefore, the Jews began persecuting Jesus because He was doing these things on the Sabbath. ¹⁷But Jesus responded to them, "My Father is still working, and **I also am working**." ¹⁸This is why the Jews began trying all the more to

---

One man . . . sick for 38 years: Jesus noticed a man lying there in hopes of being healed. He asked him if he wanted to be healed. The man complained that other sick people always got into the pool ahead of him. In an act of compassion, Jesus healed the helpless man.

This is the Sabbath: The Pharisees grumbled that Jesus and this man had broken the Sabbath law—Jesus by healing him, and the man by carrying his bed.

The man who made me well told me: The man put the blame for his Sabbath transgression on Jesus, the person who had told him to walk. His words indicate that he did not know who Jesus was.

man . . . reported to the Jews: The healed man probably had no malicious intent in reporting back to Jesus' critics about his healing. He probably thought of these religious leaders as persons of integrity. But they began to make a case against Jesus for healing on the Sabbath.

49. JESUS DEFENDS HIS SABBATH HEALING
I also am working: Jesus referred to the original Sabbath commandment that prohibited work because the Lord rested on the seventh day (Exod. 20:11). He clearly did not interpret this to mean that God stopped all activity, but that He

kill Him: not only was He breaking the Sabbath, but He was even **calling God His own Father**, making Himself equal with God.

[19]Then Jesus replied, "I assure you: The Son is not able to do anything on His own, but only what He sees the Father doing. For whatever the Father does, these things the Son also does in the same way. [20]For the Father loves the Son and shows Him everything He is doing, and He will show Him greater works than these so that you will be amazed. [21]And just as the Father raises the dead and gives them life, so also the Son gives life to whomever He wishes. [22]The Father, in fact, judges no one but has given all judgment to the Son, [23]so that all people will honor the Son just as they honor the Father. Anyone who does not honor the Son does not honor the Father who sent Him.

Life and Judgment

[24]"I assure you: Anyone who hears My word and believes Him who sent Me has eternal life and will not come under judgment, but has passed from death to life.

[25]"I assure you: An hour is coming, and is now here, when the dead will hear the voice of the Son of God, and those who hear will live. [26]For just as the Father has life in Himself, so also He has granted to the Son to have life in Himself. [27]And He has granted Him the right to pass judgment, because He is the Son of Man. [28]Do not be amazed at this, because a time is coming when all who are in the graves will hear His voice [29]and come out—those who have done good things, to the resurrection of life, but those who have done wicked things, to the resurrection of judgment.

[30]"I can do nothing on My own. Only as I hear do I judge, and My judgment is righteous, because I do not seek My own will, but the will of Him who sent Me.

[31]"If I testify about Myself, My testimony is not valid. [32]There is Another who testifies about Me, and I know that the testimony He gives about Me is valid. [33]You people have sent messengers to John, and he has testified to the truth. [34]I don't receive man's testimony, but I say these things so that you may be saved. [35]John was a burning and shining lamp, and for an hour you were willing to enjoy his light.

---

rested from the work of creation. Jesus claimed that the Father had continued His activity. As God's Son, He was engaged in similar deeds of compassion on the Sabbath.

calling God His own Father: The anger of the religious leaders grew even hotter. Now Jesus was claiming God as His Father and making Himself equal with God. Jesus went on to claim that the Father honored the Son by empowering Him to raise the dead. They must accept Him and His message and gain everlasting life, or face future condemnation.

Testimony of Jesus' Acts

³⁶"But I have a greater testimony than John's because of the works that the Father has given Me to accomplish. These very works I am doing testify about Me that **the Father has sent Me**. ³⁷The Father who sent Me has Himself testified about Me. You have not heard His voice at any time, and you haven't seen His form. ³⁸You don't have His word living in you, because you don't believe the One He sent. ³⁹You pore over the Scriptures because you think you have eternal life in them, yet they testify about Me. ⁴⁰And you are not willing to come to Me that you may have life.

⁴¹"I do not accept glory from men, ⁴²but I know you—that you have no love for God within you. ⁴³I have come in My Father's name, yet you don't accept Me. If someone else comes in his own name, you will accept him. ⁴⁴How can you believe? While accepting glory from one another, you don't seek the glory that comes from the only God. ⁴⁵Do not think that I will accuse you to the Father. Your accuser is Moses, on whom you have set your hope. ⁴⁶For if you believed Moses, you would believe Me, because he wrote about Me. ⁴⁷But if you don't believe his writings, how will you believe My words?"

50. CRITICISM FOR PICKING GRAIN ON THE SABBATH

Matthew 12:1–8; Mark 2:23–28; Luke 6:1–5

^{Lk 6:1}On a Sabbath, He **passed through the grainfields**. His disciples were picking heads of grain, rubbing them in their hands, and eating them. ^{Mt 12:2}But when the Pharisees saw it, they said to Him, "Look, Your disciples are doing what is **not lawful to do on the Sabbath!**"

³He said to them, "Haven't you read **what David did when he was hungry**, and those who were with him—^{4a}how he entered the house of God ^{Mk 2:26a}in the time of Abiathar the high priest, ^{Mt 12:4b–7}and they ate the sacred bread, which is

---

the Father has sent Me: The religious leaders had already charged Jesus with blasphemy. He seemed to be providing more and more reasons for this charge. As though anticipating their reaction, He mentioned four witnesses to the truth of His claims: John the Baptizer, His miracles, His Father, and the Scriptures (John 5:31–47).

50. CRITICISM FOR PICKING GRAIN ON THE SABBATH
passed through the grainfields: The Mosaic Law allowed people using footpaths through cropland to help themselves to whatever was growing—but not to gather more than enough to satisfy their hunger (Deut. 23:24–25). The disciples picked grain from the stalks of wheat and rubbed it between their hands to remove the husks.
not lawful to do on the Sabbath: The Pharisees condemned this act because they considered it Sabbath labor, a breach of the law. They had listed a number of trifling activities that were prohibited on the Sabbath, including tying or untying a knot and writing two letters of the alphabet. In their eyes, the disciples' action was the same as reaping and winnowing grain.
what David did when he was hungry: Jesus argued that ritual laws must give place to human need. In an emergency, David and his men had eaten showbread, which was reserved for the use of priests alone (see 1 Sam. 21:1–6). Jesus claimed that He was "greater than the temple," and that He was "Lord of the Sabbath." These claims were sufficient, in the opinion of the Pharisees, to condemn Him for blasphemy.

not lawful for him or for those with him to eat, but only for the priests? ⁵Or haven't you read in the law that on Sabbath days the priests in the temple violate the Sabbath and are guiltless? ⁶But I tell you that something greater than the temple is here! ⁷If you had known what this means: 'I desire mercy and not sacrifice,' you would not have condemned the guiltless."

Mk 2:27–28Then He told them, "The Sabbath was made for man, and not man for the Sabbath. ²⁸Therefore the Son of Man is Lord even of the Sabbath."

51. JESUS HEALS A MAN'S PARALYZED HAND ON THE SABBATH

Matthew 12:9–14; Mark 3:1–6; Luke 6:6–11

Lk 6:6–8On another Sabbath He entered the synagogue and was teaching. A man was there whose right hand was paralyzed. ⁷The **scribes and Pharisees were watching Him** closely, to see if He would heal on the Sabbath, so that they might find a charge against Him. ⁸But He knew their thoughts and told the man with the paralyzed hand, "Get up and stand here." So he got up and stood there.

Mt 12:11–12aBut He said to them, "What man among you, **if he had a sheep** that fell into a pit on the Sabbath, wouldn't take hold of it and lift it out? ¹²ᵃA man is worth far more than a sheep."

Lk 6:9Then Jesus said to them, "I ask you: is it lawful on the Sabbath to do good or to do evil, to save life or to destroy it?" Mk 3:4b–5But they

Pharisees and Herodians

Mark's account of this event reports that "the Pharisees went out and started plotting with the Herodians" how they might kill Jesus (see Mark 3:6).

This was a strange alliance, since the Pharisees and the Herodians were natural enemies. The Herodians, a political party, were favorable toward Greek customs and Roman law. But the Pharisees, a religious group, hated everything about foreign culture and wanted to reestablish a purely Jewish way of life.

The Pharisees and the Herodians also joined forces in an attempt to trap Jesus on the issue of paying taxes to the Roman government (see segment 165, "Jesus Questioned about Paying Taxes to Caesar," p. 192). Although these two groups had no love for each other, they were willing to work together to get rid of Jesus, whom they considered a dangerous enemy.

---

51. JESUS HEALS A MAN'S PARALYZED HAND ON THE SABBATH

scribes and Pharisees were watching Him: The local synagogue furnished another setting for the Pharisees to expose Jesus' attitude toward the Sabbath. They were in the synagogue not to worship but to trap Jesus. A man with a paralyzed hand was present, and they were watching to see if Jesus would heal him.

if he had a sheep: Jesus surprised His critics with a statement that exposed their inconsistency. Many of them kept sheep. If one of these fell into a pit on the Sabbath, they would get it out immediately. Then He declared, "A man is worth far more than a sheep" (Matt. 12:12a). Jesus laid down the principle that "it is lawful to do good on the Sabbath," that a good deed is appropriate any day of the week. In a situation where the observance of the Sabbath interfered with the performance of deeds of mercy and kindness, the observance must yield to human need.

were silent. [5]After looking around at them **with anger and sorrow** at the hardness of their hearts, He told the man, "Stretch out your hand." So he stretched it out, and his hand was restored.

[Mk 3:6a]Immediately the Pharisees went out, [Lk 6:11a]**filled with rage**, [Mk 3:6b] and started plotting with the Herodians against Him, how they might destroy Him.

52. MANY PEOPLE HEALED AT LAKE GALILEE

Matthew 12:15–21; Mark 3:7–12

[Mk 3:7–11]**Jesus departed** with His disciples **to the sea**, and a great multitude followed from Galilee, Judea, [8]Jerusalem, Idumea, beyond the Jordan, and around Tyre and Sidon. The great multitude came to Him because they heard everything He was doing. [9]Then He told His disciples to have a small boat ready for Him, so the crowd would not crush Him. [10]Since He had healed many, all who had diseases were pressing toward Him to touch Him. [11]Whenever the unclean spirits saw Him, they would fall down before Him and cry out, "You are the Son of God!"

[12]And He would strongly warn them not to make Him known, [Mt 12:17–21]so that **what was spoken through the prophet Isaiah** might be fulfilled: [18]"Here is My Servant whom I have chosen, My beloved in whom My soul delights; I will put My Spirit on Him, and He will proclaim justice to the nations. [19]**He will not argue or shout**, and no one will hear His voice in the streets. [20]He will not break a **bruised reed**, and He will not put out a **smoldering wick**, until He has led justice to victory. [21]The nations will hope in His name."

---

with anger and sorrow: The actions of the Pharisees stirred two emotions in Jesus. He was angry at their indifference to the man's needs and He was sad because their actions showed how hard and stubborn their hearts were becoming. Although He knew they would try to use it against Him, Jesus healed the man.

filled with rage: The reaction of the Pharisees was quick and extreme. Jesus had embarrassed them publicly, and they began to look for a way to get rid of Him.

52. MANY PEOPLE HEALED AT LAKE GALILEE

Jesus departed . . . to the sea: Jesus withdrew with His disciples to Lake Galilee to get away from the scribes and Pharisees. People came to Him from many different places—from Galilee in the north to Judea in the south and even from the Phoenician cities of Tyre and Sidon. His reputation as a teacher and healer was spreading over a broad geographic area.

what was spoken through the prophet Isaiah: Matthew 12:15–21 is a quotation from one of the Servant Songs of the prophet Isaiah (Isa. 42:1–4). Jesus was the humble servant of God who brought salvation to the world through His redemptive suffering. He was a servant in form (Phil. 2:7) and in obedience (Heb. 10:9).

He will not argue or shout: Jesus had already fulfilled this prophecy in His confrontation with the Pharisees. He did not argue or quarrel with them. Rather, He silenced them with His humble response, then withdrew quietly from their presence.

bruised reed . . . smoldering wick: These two images represent the sick, lame, and blind—sinners, according to the Pharisees—who came to Jesus to be healed. He would not break their battered spirits or extinguish their weak, flickering flame. Rather, He would heal their bruises and fan their dying energies and resolutions into a roaring blaze.

53. Jesus Selects His Twelve Disciples

Matthew 10:2–4; Mark 3:13–19; Luke 6:12–16

^{Lk 6:12–13}During those days He went out to the mountain to pray and spent all night in prayer to God. ¹³When daylight came, **He summoned His disciples**,

---

The Twelve and the Three

A comparison of the lists of Jesus' twelve disciples in Matthew, Mark, and Luke yields some interesting results. Another list also appears in Acts 1:13. All the names in these three lists are not the same. The differences are explained by the fact that some of the disciples were known by more than one name.

Here's a complete list of the Twelve, with the variant names noted and a brief description of each:

Disciple/Apostle	Description
1. Simon (Peter)	A fisherman from Galilee; Andrew's brother
2. Andrew	A fisherman from Galilee; Peter's brother
3. James	A fisherman from Galilee: son of Zebedee; John's brother
4. John	A fisherman from Galilee: son of Zebedee; James's brother
5. Philip	From Bethsaida
6. Bartholomew (Nathanael)	From Cana in Galilee
7. Thomas (Didymas)	Perhaps a fisherman
8. Matthew (Levi)	A tax collector from Capernaum
9. James (not the same as James, son of Zebedee)	Son of Alphaeus
10. Lebbaeus Thaddaeus (Judas)	Called Judas son of James to distinguish him from Judas Iscariot
11. Simon (the Zealot)	From Cana; associated with the Zealots, revolutionaries opposed to Rome
12. Judas Iscariot	From Kerioth in southern Judah; probably the only disciple from outside Galilee

Among these twelve men, Peter, James, and John were considered the "inner circle" disciples. They accompanied Jesus on some of the most important events in His ministry, including the transformation/transfiguration (Matt. 17:1–8) and His agonizing prayer in the Garden of Gethsemane (Mark 14:32–33).

---

53. Jesus Selects His Twelve Disciples

He summoned His disciples: *Disciples* were pupils who attached themselves to a special teacher, often as live-in students. The Twelve were not the only followers of Jesus called disciples. He had many other such followers during His

and from them He chose 12, whom **He also named apostles**: Mk 3:14b–15that they might be with Him and that He might send them out to preach 15and to have authority to drive out demons: Lk 6:14Simon, whom He also named Peter, and Andrew his brother; James and John [Mk 3:17b *He gave the name "Boanerges," (that is, "Sons of Thunder")*]; Philip and Bartholomew; Mt 10:3bMatthew the tax collector Lk 6:15–16and Thomas; James the son of Alphaeus, and Simon called the Zealot [Mk 3:18b *Simon the Zealot*]; 16Judas the son of James, and Judas Iscariot, who became a traitor.

54. THE SERMON ON THE MOUNT

Matthew 5:1–7:29; Luke 6:17–49

Mt 5:1–2When He saw the crowds, He went up on the mountain [Lk 6:17a *After coming down with them, He stood on a level place*], and after He sat down, His disciples came to Him. 2Then He began to teach them, saying:

3"**Blessed** are the **poor in spirit** [Lk 6:20b *Blessed are you who are poor*], because the kingdom of heaven is theirs [Lk 6:20c *because the kingdom of God is yours*].

4"Blessed are **those who mourn**, because they will be comforted.

5"Blessed are **the gentle**, because they will inherit the earth.

6"Blessed are **those who hunger and thirst for righteousness**, because they will be filled.

---

public ministry (Matt. 8:21). A person usually became a disciple by seeking out a teacher and joining his school. But Jesus took the initiative in seeking and calling His disciples.

He also named apostles: From among all His followers, Jesus selected 12 as His apostles. An apostle was a witness of the risen Lord who was commissioned by Him as a bearer of His message to all the world. Jesus trained these special disciples to continue His ministry after He was gone. The New Testament is the inspired record of the unique testimony and teachings of these apostles. They have no successors; the Spirit of the risen Lord speaks to us through their writings in the New Testament. Another list of these apostles is also found in Acts 1:13.

54. THE SERMON ON THE MOUNT

Blessed: The word *blessed* means "happy" or "fortunate." True blessedness is a deep sense of peace and joy in the knowledge that we are doing God's will. The kind of blessedness Jesus described is not primarily something we feel, but something we are. Any joy that comes as a result of God's blessedness is a fruit of what He is doing in and through us.

poor in spirit: Jesus declared that the kingdom of heaven is made up of the poor in spirit—those who are spiritually destitute and who desperately need the grace of God. This is the first quality a person must have to enter the kingdom of God.

those who mourn: True followers of Christ mourn over their sins and the plight of others. Jesus knew nothing of sorrow over His own sins because He had no sins. But He wept over the moral and spiritual plight of others (Luke 19:41).

the gentle: Gentleness is the opposite of those who lay claim to everything for themselves. The gentle are those who claim nothing for themselves. They will inherit the earth because God rewards gentleness and unselfishness. The paradox was stated by Jesus: "Whoever wants to save his life will lose it, but whoever loses his life because of Me will find it" (Matt. 16:25).

those who hunger and thirst for righteousness: Jesus was referring to spiritual hunger rather than physical hunger. Hunger and thirst are the strongest possible words to describe a deep yearning and searching for something. We find true fulfillment by seeking God and His kingdom.

[7]"Blessed are **the merciful**, because they will be shown mercy.

[8]"Blessed are **the pure in heart**, because they will see God.

[9]"Blessed are **the peacemakers**, because they will be called sons of God.

[10]"Blessed are **those** who are **persecuted for righteousness**, because the kingdom of heaven is theirs.

[11]"Blessed are you when they insult you and persecute you, and say every kind of evil against you falsely because of Me. [12]**Be glad and rejoice** [Lk 6:23b *leap for joy*], because your reward is great in heaven. For that is how they persecuted the prophets who were before you.

Lk 6:24–26"But woe to you who are rich, because you have received your comfort. [25]Woe to you who are full now, because you will be hungry. Woe to you who are laughing now, because you will mourn and weep. [26]Woe to you when all people speak well of you, because this is the way their forefathers used to treat the false prophets.

Salt and Light

Matt 5:13"You are the **salt of the earth**. But if the salt should lose its taste, how can it be made salty? It's no longer good for anything but to be thrown out and trampled on by men.

[14]"You are the **light of the world**. A city situated on a hill cannot be hidden. [15]No one lights a lamp and puts it under a basket, but rather on a lampstand, and it gives light for all who are in the house. [16]In the same way, let your light shine before men, so that they may see your good works and give glory to your Father in heaven.

---

the merciful: God is loving and merciful in His dealings with people. He expects His followers to treat other people the same way.

the pure in heart: The pure in heart are people with a single-minded devotion to God that is reflected in a life of moral purity. Many people have no desire to see God because they will experience Him only as judge. But the pure in heart who walk with God in this life are anxious to see Him face to face (1 Cor. 13:12).

the peacemakers: God Himself is the great peacemaker. Through Jesus Christ, He calls sinners to find peace with God (Rom. 5:1). Christ also reconciles people to one another, thus making peace (Eph. 2:14). Those who know the Lord have a ministry of reconciliation as peacemakers in His name.

those . . . persecuted for righteousness: Jesus knew that His mission would end in rejection and crucifixion. He also knew that His followers would be subjected to ridicule and misunderstanding. He pronounced the blessing of God on those who were persecuted for their righteous behavior. Those who are persecuted can rejoice and be glad. In times of trouble, followers of Christ can dare to rejoice.

Be glad and rejoice: This final beatitude shows the striking contrast between the joy that comes from Christ and the kind of happiness sought by people who don't know Christ. Worldly people assume that happiness depends on outward circumstances. Christ said that joy depends only on being in the center of God's will.

salt of the earth: Salt is used to season food. It can be irritating to a wound, or it can create thirst in a person. It is also used as a preservative. Christian believers are called to be all of these things. Jesus spoke of the tragedy of salt losing its distinctive character. Such salt is worthless. Believers should never lose their saltiness as witnesses in the world.

light of the world: Light is meant to illuminate; it is not meant to be hidden. It should be placed on display in full view of others. We are to shine for God so He will be glorified.

[17]"Don't assume that I came to destroy the Law or the Prophets. I did not come to destroy but to fulfill. [18]For I assure you: Until heaven and earth pass away, not the smallest letter or one stroke of a letter will ever pass from the law until all things are accomplished. [19]Therefore, whoever breaks one of the least of these commandments and teaches people to do so will be called least in the kingdom of heaven. But whoever practices and teaches these commandments will be called great in the kingdom of heaven. [20]For I tell you, unless your righteousness surpasses that of the scribes and Pharisees, you will never enter the kingdom of heaven.

[21]"You have heard that it was said to our ancestors, '**You shall not murder,**' and whoever murders will be subject to judgment. [22]But I tell you, everyone who is angry with his brother will be subject to judgment. And whoever says to his brother, 'Fool!' will be subject to the council. But whoever says, 'You moron!' will be subject to hellfire. [23]So if you are offering your gift on the altar, and there you remember that your brother has something against you, [24]leave your gift there in front of the altar. First go and be reconciled with your brother, and then come and offer your gift. [25]Reach a settlement quickly with your adversary, while you're on the way with him, or your adversary will hand you over to the judge, the judge to the officer, and you will be thrown into prison. [26]I assure you: You will never get out of there until you have paid the last penny!

[27]"You have heard that it was said, '**You shall not commit adultery.**' [28]But I tell you, everyone who looks at a woman to lust for her has already committed adultery with her in his heart. [29]If your right eye causes you to sin, gouge it out and throw it away. For it is better that you lose one of your members than for your whole body to be thrown into hell. [30]And if your right hand causes you to sin, cut it off and throw it away. For it is better that you lose one of your members than for your whole body to go into hell!

[31]"It was also said, 'Whoever divorces his wife must give her a written notice of divorce.' [32]But I tell you, everyone who divorces his wife, except in a case of sexual immorality, causes her to commit adultery. And whoever marries a divorced woman commits adultery.

[33]"Again, you have heard that it was said to our ancestors, 'You must not break your oath, but you must keep your oaths to the Lord.' [34]But I tell you, don't take an oath at all: either by heaven, because it is God's throne; [35]or by the earth, because it is His footstool; or by Jerusalem, because it is the city of the great King. [36]Neither should you swear by your head, because you cannot make a sin-

---

You shall not murder: Obeying the commandment against murder (Exod. 20:13) involves more than refraining from the act of killing people. It also includes guarding the heart against uncontrolled anger, which is the root of murder. Jesus condemned the act as well as the inner attitudes that lead a person to commit murder.

You shall not commit adultery: Jesus condemned the lust in the heart that leads to adultery. We must not treat others as objects of sexual lust and gratification.

gle hair white or black. ³⁷But let your word 'yes,' be 'yes,' and your 'no,' be 'no.' Anything more than this is from the evil one.

³⁸"You have heard that it was said, 'An eye for an eye' and 'a tooth for a tooth.' ³⁹But I tell you, **don't resist an evildoer**. On the contrary, if anyone **slaps you on your right cheek**, turn the other to him also. ⁴⁰As for the one who wants to sue you and take away your **shirt**, let him have your **coat** as well. ⁴¹And if anyone forces you to go one mile, **go with him two**. ⁴²Give to the one who asks you, and don't turn away from the one who wants to borrow from you.

Love Your Enemies

⁴³"You have heard that it was said, 'You shall love your neighbor and hate your enemy.' ⁴⁴But I tell you, **love your enemies**, and pray for those who persecute you, ⁴⁵so that you may be sons of your Father in heaven. For He causes His sun to rise on the evil and the good, and sends rain on the righteous and the unrighteous.

^{Lk 6:30}"Give to everyone who asks from you, and from one who takes away your things, don't ask for them back. ^{Mt 5:46–47}For if you love those who love you, what reward will you have? **Don't** even the **tax collectors do the same?** ⁴⁷And if you greet only your brothers, what are you doing out of the ordinary? Don't even the Gentiles do the same? ^{Lk 6:32–34}If you love those who love you, what credit is that to you? Even sinners love those who love them. ³³If you do good to those who do good to you, what credit is that to you? Even sinners do that. ³⁴And if you lend to those from whom you expect to receive, what credit is that to you? Even sinners lend to sinners to be repaid in full. ^{Mt 5:48}**Be perfect**, therefore, as your heavenly Father is perfect [^{Lk 6:36}*Be merciful, just as your Father also is merciful*].

---

don't resist an evildoer: Jesus was speaking about not trying to get even with people who hurt us. Our natural tendency is to try to hurt them as they have hurt us. Jesus expects His followers to show love, not to seek revenge.

slaps you on your right cheek: Striking a person on the right cheek suggests a backhanded slap by a right-handed person. This was a form of insult in Jesus' day. "Turning the other cheek" means to accept personal insults without striking back at the person who has insulted us.

shirt . . . coat: Jesus spoke of a situation in which one of His followers was being sued for damages. The person was being asked to give up his shirt. Jesus said that His follower should voluntarily give up his coat as well.

go with him two: Roman soldiers in Jesus' time were allowed to compel a Jew to carry their personal belongings for one mile—but no farther. Jesus declared that His followers should voluntarily carry the load a second mile. They should be willing to go beyond the law in showing consideration for others.

love your enemies: Some people in Jesus' day limited their neighborliness to people of their own kind. Jesus broadened the concept of "neighbor" to include all people. He intended for His followers to love their enemies. We show ourselves to be children of God when we do good for our enemies.

Don't . . . tax collectors do the same? The Jews hated tax collectors, considering them no better than pagans. Jesus taught that loving our own kind of people is no different from the love of an unbelieving world. All people naturally love those who love them. But Jesus expected more of His followers. We must also seek to do good for those who hate us.

Be perfect: None of us is perfect; but perfection remains our goal. The heavenly Father calls each of us to the highest and best. When we fail, He forgives and encourages us.

Mt 6:1"Be careful not to practice your righteousness in front of people, to be seen by them. Otherwise, you will have no reward from your Father in heaven. ²So whenever you give to the poor, don't sound a trumpet before you as the hypocrites do in the synagogues and in the streets, to be applauded by people. I assure you: They've got their reward! ³But when you give to the poor, don't let your left hand know what your right hand is doing, ⁴so that your giving may be in secret. And your Father who sees in secret will reward you.

How to Pray

⁵"Whenever you pray, you must not be like the hypocrites, because they love to pray standing in the synagogues and on the street corners to be seen by people. I assure you: They've got their reward! ⁶But when you pray, **go into your private room**, shut your door, and pray to your Father who is in secret. And your Father who sees in secret will reward you. ⁷When you pray, **don't babble like the idolaters**, since they imagine they'll be heard for their many words. ⁸Don't be like them, because **your Father knows** the things you need **before you ask** Him.

⁹"Therefore, you should pray like this: '**Our Father in heaven**, Your name be honored as holy. ¹⁰Your kingdom come. **Your will be done** on earth as it is in heaven. ¹¹**Give us today our daily bread**. ¹²And **forgive us our debts**, as we also have forgiven our debtors. ¹³And **do not bring us into temptation**, but deliver

---

go into your private room: Jesus was not forbidding praying in public. He was warning against praying in order to be seen and praised by others. The foundation of a believer's prayer life must be private prayer. This enables us to shut out distractions and to be aware of God's presence.

don't babble like the idolaters: The pagan religions of Jesus' day believed that prayer consisted of repeating certain words and phrases. They thought such fervent praying would move their gods to do their bidding. But Jesus warned against using such empty words in prayer. He came to reveal a different God from the false gods of the pagans. We do not win His favor by repeating formulas but by placing our lives in His will.

your Father knows . . . before you ask: God is aware of our needs and eager to care for us. His gifts depend on our awareness of need and our openness to receive His gifts.

Our Father in heaven: We generally call Matthew 6:9–13 the Lord's Prayer or the Model Prayer. Jesus gave it as a model because it contains all the elements of prayer. It begins with praise. The striking difference between Christian prayer and pagan prayer is the God to whom we pray. Jesus taught us to pray to the eternal God who created heaven and earth, who is also our loving heavenly Father. The "name" of God stands for who and what He is. Believers pray that God will be hallowed or honored.

Your will be done: A worldly person seeks his own selfish interests. A believer in God longs for the kingdom of God and His righteousness. We should pray that God's will will be done in our lives.

Give us today our daily bread: Rather than being anxious about material needs, believers ask God for daily bread and thank Him for this provision. Arrogant unbelievers think they provide their own food through their work. Believers know that life itself is a gift and so is every good thing in life.

forgive us our debts: This is one part of the Model Prayer that Jesus never prayed. Since He had no sin, He did not pray for forgiveness. But the rest of us are sinners who need forgiveness. Confession of sins is part of all genuine prayer.

do not bring us into temptation: God allows us to pass through experiences that test our faith, but He uses these tests

us from the evil one. For Yours is the kingdom and the power and the glory forever, Amen.'*

[14]"For if you forgive people their wrongdoing, your heavenly Father will forgive you as well. [15]**But if you don't forgive people**, your Father will not forgive your wrongdoing.

[16]"Whenever you fast, don't be sad-faced like the hypocrites. For they make their faces unattractive so they may show their fasting to people. I assure you: They've got their reward! [17]But when you fast, brush your hair and wash your face, [18]so that you don't show your fasting to people, but to your Father who is in secret. And your Father who sees in secret will reward you.

[19]"Don't collect for yourselves **treasures on earth**, where moth and rust destroy and where thieves break in and steal. [20]But collect for yourselves **treasures in heaven**, where neither moth nor rust destroys, and where thieves don't break in and steal. [21]For where your treasure is, there your heart will be also.

[22]"The eye is the lamp of the body. If your eye is generous, your whole body will be full of light. [23]But if your eye is stingy, your whole body will be full of darkness. So if the light within you is darkness—how deep is that darkness!

[24]"No one can be a **slave of two masters**, since either he will hate one and love the other, or be devoted to one and despise the other. You cannot be slaves of God and of money.

The Cure for Anxiety

[25]"This is why I tell you: **Don't worry about your life**, what you will eat or what you will drink; or about your body, what you will wear. Isn't life more than

---

The words "For Yours is the kingdom and the power and the glory forever, Amen" do not appear in some New Testament manuscripts.

---

to mature our faith. But Satan turns these tests into temptations to do evil. Jesus taught His followers to be aware of their own weaknesses and of the strength of the evil one. We should ask God to deliver us from the power of evil when we are tempted.

But if you don't forgive people: Forgiveness is not a one-way street in which the only direction for forgiveness is from God into our hearts and lives. Forgiveness is like a two-way street in which traffic flows in both directions: from God to us and from us to others. The person who closes his heart in either direction closes it in the other. The person whose heart is open to receive God's forgiveness is also a person who offers forgiveness to others. A heart that is closed to forgiveness flowing out is closed to forgiveness flowing in.

treasures on earth . . . treasures in heaven: Jesus encouraged us to lay up treasures in heaven because these are the only secure riches. Our earthly lives and possessions are temporary, but we can invest time, money, and other resources in God's eternal kingdom. If our treasures are in heaven, we live for God and serve others.

slave of two masters: A slave belonged to only one master. Jesus applied this to people's relationship to God. Mammon was a money-god worshiped by many ancient people. Jesus taught that we cannot serve the true God and the money-god at the same time.

Don't worry about your life: Jesus warned about anxiety over food and clothing. Most people of Jesus' time struggled to put bread on the table, clothes on their backs, and a roof over their heads. While the poor were preoccupied with

food and the body more than clothing? [26]Look at the **birds of the sky**: they don't sow, or reap, or gather into barns, yet your heavenly Father feeds them. Aren't you worth more than they?

[27]"Can any of you add **a single cubit to his height** by worrying? [28]And why do you worry about clothes? Learn how **the wildflowers of the field** grow: they don't labor or spin thread. [29]Yet I tell you that not even Solomon in all his splendor was adorned like one of these! [30]If that's how God clothes the grass of the field, which is here today and thrown into the furnace tomorrow, won't He do much more for you—you of little faith? [31]So don't worry, saying, 'What will we eat?' or 'What will we drink?' or 'What will we wear?' [32]For the **Gentiles** eagerly **seek all these things**, and your heavenly Father knows that you need them. [33]But seek first the kingdom of God and His righteousness, and **all these things will be provided** for you. [34]Therefore don't worry about tomorrow, because **tomorrow will worry about itself**. Each day has enough trouble of its own.

Do Not Judge

Mt 7:1"**Do not judge**, so that you won't be judged. [2]For with the judgment you use, you will be judged, and with the measure you use, it will be measured to you. Lk 6:37b–38Forgive, and you will be forgiven. [38]Give, and it will be given to you; a good measure, pressed down, shaken together, and running over will be poured into your lap. For with the measure that you use, it will be measured back to you."

---

food and clothing; the rich were caught up in their quest for wealth. Jesus warned both the rich and the poor that life consists of more than material possessions.

birds of the sky: Birds neither sow nor reap, but God takes care of them. Since humans are created in God's image, how much more will God care for us? This is not an argument for idleness, because even the birds forage for food. Their food is a gift from God. So is ours. We may feel that we have earned our own bread, but God is the giver of every good and perfect gift (James 1:17). We should give thanks to God for our daily bread (Matt. 6:11).

a single cubit to his height: Worry does not increase either our height or our life span. In fact, anxiety contributes to emotional and physical ailments. Obsessive worrying can actually shorten life.

the wildflowers of the field: Humans are created in the image of God, and they are capable of knowing God. If God clothes the flowers in the meadows, how much more will He supply our daily necessities?

Gentiles . . . seek all these things: Anxiety about material things is typical of unbelievers. Jesus pointed out that His followers were acting like pagans when they became anxious and preoccupied with material things. He assured them that their heavenly Father knows what they need. He encouraged them to replace anxiety with trust in the heavenly Father.

all these things will be provided: Jesus called His followers to seek first the kingdom of God. Such people honor God, live by His righteous standards, and advance His cause. This priority shapes all their attitudes and actions. If they seek God first, then food, clothing, and other necessities will be provided.

tomorrow will worry about itself: People who worry about the future are less prepared to handle what comes up each day. Many of our worst fears never happen.

Do not judge: Jesus warned against harsh, condemning criticism of other people. He pointed out that God will judge us by the same severe standard we use to judge others. He used the comical picture of a person with a log in his eye trying to remove a spot from the eye of another person. It is hypocritical for a person with a big fault to criticize someone else for a minor problem.

Lk 6:39He also told them a parable: "Can the blind guide the blind? Won't they both fall into a pit? 40A disciple is not above his teacher, but everyone who is fully trained will be like his teacher. 41Why do you look at the speck in your brother's eye, but don't notice the log in your own eye? 42Or how can you say to your brother, 'Brother, let me take out the speck that is in your eye,' when you yourself don't see the log in your eye? Hypocrite! First take the log out of your eye, and then you will see clearly to take out the speck in your brother's eye.

Mt 7:6"**Don't give what is holy to dogs** or toss your pearls before pigs, or they will trample them with their feet, turn, and tear you to pieces.

7"**Keep asking**, and it will be given to you. Keep **searching**, and you will find. Keep **knocking**, and the door will be opened to you. 8For everyone who asks receives, and the one who searches finds, and to the one who knocks, the door will be opened. 9What man among you, if his son asks him for bread, will give him a stone? 10Or if he asks for a fish, will give him a snake? 11If you, then, who are evil know how to give good gifts to your children, how much more will your Father in heaven give good things to those who ask Him! 12Therefore, whatever you want others to do for you, do also the same for them—this is the Law and the Prophets.

Sermon on the Mount or Sermon on the Plain?

The Sermon on the Mount is so named because Jesus taught His disciples from a mountainside, according to Matthew's account (Matt. 5:1). But Luke's Gospel, in the parallel narrative, states that He "stood on a level place" as He taught (Luke 6:17). Was the setting for this sermon a mountain or a plain?

Actually, it was probably both. Jesus must have delivered His Sermon on the Mount on a plateau on a mountain. His healing had attracted widespread attention, and many people gathered to hear His teaching. A large level place would have been needed to accommodate the crowds (see Luke 6:17–19).

The traditional site of the Sermon on the Mount is marked today by a beautiful little church called the Chapel on the Mount of Beatitudes. This is one of the major stopping points for tourists visiting the Holy Land.

Don't give what is holy to dogs: Some people, represented by the "dogs" in His warning, do not know the difference between what is holy and what is unholy. A follower of Jesus must use discernment to decide how and with whom to share the truths of God.

Keep asking . . . searching . . . knocking: Jesus emphasized the need for us to persist in our prayers. Our persistence shows that we are serious about the things we pray for and that we have faith in the Father to whom we pray. We can be assured that He will give us what we need when we come to Him in earnest prayer.

Entering the Kingdom

¹³"**Enter through the narrow gate**; because the gate is wide and the road is broad that leads to destruction, and there are many who go through it. ¹⁴How narrow is the gate and difficult the road that leads to life; and few find it.

¹⁵"**Beware of false prophets** who come to you in sheep's clothing, but inwardly are ravaging wolves. ¹⁶You'll recognize them by their fruit. Are grapes gathered from thornbushes or figs from thistles? ¹⁷In the same way, every good tree produces good fruit, but a bad tree produces bad fruit. ¹⁸A good tree can't produce bad fruit; neither can a bad tree produce good fruit. ¹⁹Every tree that doesn't produce good fruit is cut down and thrown into the fire. Lk 6:45A good man produces good out of the good storeroom of his heart, and an evil man pro-

Ten Principles for Kingdom Citizens

The purpose of Jesus' Sermon on the Mount was to teach His followers how to live as citizens of the kingdom of God. Here's a thumbnail summary of the ten major sections of the sermon that support this central theme:

1. *The Beatitudes (Matt. 5:3–12). The rewards for those who live as citizens of God's kingdom.*
2. *Salt and light (Matt. 5:13–16). How Christian living by kingdom citizens affects the world.*
3. *Genuine righteousness (Matt. 5:17–48). Living by the deeper meaning of God's law.*
4. *Avoiding hypocrisy (Matt. 6:1–18). Giving, praying, and fasting from the right motives.*
5. *Setting priorities (Matt. 6:19–34). Putting God's kingdom first frees us from anxiety over lesser matters.*
6. *Don't judge (Matt. 7:1–6). The dangers of judging people in a harsh and careless manner.*
7. *Lessons in prayer (Matt. 7:7–12). How to claim the privilege and blessings of prayer.*
8. *Choosing between the two ways (Matt. 7:13–14). The narrow way leads to life; the broad way to destruction.*
9. *Fruit-bearing (Matt. 7:15–20). By our fruits or deeds we will be known and judged.*
10. *Deeds, not talk (Matt. 7:21–29). It's better to obey God than to talk about our commitment to Him.*

duces evil out of the evil storeroom. For his mouth speaks from the overflow of the heart. ^{Mt 7:20} So you'll recognize them by their fruit.

^{Mt 7:21}"**Not everyone** who says to Me, 'Lord, Lord!' **will enter the kingdom** of heaven, but the one who does the will of My Father in heaven. ²²On that day many will say to Me, 'Lord, Lord, didn't we prophesy in Your name, drive out demons in Your name, and do many miracles in Your name?' ²³Then I will announce to them, 'I never knew you! Depart from Me, you lawbreakers!'

²⁴"Therefore, everyone who hears these words of Mine and acts on them will be like a sensible man who built his **house on the rock**. ²⁵The rain fell, the rivers rose, and the winds blew and pounded that house. Yet it didn't collapse, because its foundation was on the rock. ²⁶But everyone who hears these words of Mine and doesn't act on them will be like a foolish man who built his **house on the sand**. ²⁷The rain fell, the rivers rose, the winds blew and pounded that house, and it collapsed. And its collapse was great!"

²⁸When Jesus had finished this sermon, the crowds were astonished at His teaching. ²⁹For He was teaching them like one who had authority, and not like their scribes.

55. Jesus Heals a Centurion's Slave

Matthew 8:5–13; Luke 7:1–10

^{Lk 7:1–5}When He had concluded all His sayings in the hearing of the people, He entered Capernaum. ²**A centurion's slave**, who was highly valued by him, was sick and about to die. ³Having heard about Jesus, he sent some Jewish elders to Him [^{Mt 8:5b}*a centurion came to Him*], requesting Him to come and save his slave's life. ⁴When they reached Jesus, they pleaded with Him earnestly, saying,

---

Enter through the narrow gate: The way to God is not the broad and easy way that most people follow. To find God and His kingdom, we must enter through the narrow gate—the self-disciplined way that demands submission to God and service to others.

Beware of false prophets: Jesus warned His followers about false teachers who would lead the flock astray. His followers could tell the difference between a true prophet and a false prophet by examining their "fruit" (v. 16). Evil and sinful actions and deeds would mark these deceitful people.

Not everyone . . . will enter the kingdom: Jesus made it clear that some people who think they are citizens of His kingdom do not really belong to Him. This includes some who have even performed miracles in His name. The acid test of discipleship is obedience to God and His will. In the day of judgment, God will declare that He never knew those who refused to obey Him.

house on the rock . . . house on the sand: Jesus concluded His Sermon on the Mount with the parable of the two builders. One man took the easy way out and built his house on unstable soil. But the other built more deliberately and carefully on a solid rock foundation. This house withstood the storms, while the sand-based building collapsed. The person who builds on Jesus and His teachings will be able to weather all the storms of life.

55. Jesus Heals a Centurion's Slave

A centurion's slave: A centurion was the commander of one hundred foot soldiers in a Roman legion. This centurion may have been assigned to the army of Herod Antipas, the Roman governor of Galilee and Perea. This centurion had heard of Jesus' healing miracles. He sent several Jewish officials to ask Jesus to heal his servant, who was gravely ill.

"He is worthy for You to grant this, ⁵because **he** loves our nation, and **has built us a synagogue**."

⁶Jesus went with them, and when He was not far from the house, the centurion sent friends to tell Him, "Lord, don't trouble Yourself, since I am not worthy to have You come under my roof. ⁷That is why I didn't even consider myself worthy to come to You. **But say the word**, and my servant will be cured. ⁸For I too am a man placed under authority, having soldiers under my command. I say to this one, 'Go!' and he goes; and to another, 'Come!' and he comes; and to my slave, 'Do this!' and he does it."

⁹Hearing this, **Jesus was amazed** at him, and turning to the crowd following Him, said, "I tell you, I have not found so great a faith even in Israel! ᴹᵗ ⁸:¹¹⁻¹³I tell you that many will come from east and west, and recline at the table with Abraham, Isaac, and Jacob in the kingdom of heaven. ¹²But the sons of the kingdom will be thrown into the outer darkness. In that place there will be weeping and gnashing of teeth." ¹³Then Jesus told the centurion, "Go. As you have believed, let it be done for you." And his servant was cured that very moment.

56. Jesus Raises a Widow's Son

Luke 7:11–17

¹¹Soon afterward He was on His way to **a town called Nain**. His disciples and a large crowd were traveling with Him. ¹²Just as He neared the gate of the town, a dead man was being carried out. He was **his mother's only son**, and **she was a widow**. A large crowd from the city was also with her. ¹³When the Lord saw her, **He had compassion on her** and said, "Don't cry." ¹⁴Then He came up and

---

he . . . has built us a synagogue: The Jewish officials recommended that Jesus heal the servant, since the centurion had helped them build a local synagogue for Jewish worship. The centurion probably believed in God and worshiped with them at the synagogue, although he was a Gentile.

But say the word: As Jesus approached the centurion's house, the Roman official sent word that he was not worthy to have Jesus enter his house. He must have known that most Jews refused to enter Gentile houses because they considered them unclean. He was probably trying to save Jesus any embarrassment. But he had such a strong faith that he was certain Jesus could heal his servant from a distance.

Jesus was amazed: Such faith expressed by a Gentile astounded Jesus, perhaps because He had seen such lack of faith among His own Jewish countrymen. He honored the centurion's faith by restoring his servant to health.

56. Jesus Raises a Widow's Son

a town called Nain: This village, situated in a mountainous region, was about 25 miles south of Capernaum.

his mother's only son . . . she was a widow: The death of an only child is one of the most devastating losses imaginable. But this mother's sorrow was deepened by the fact that she was a widow. She was probably dependent upon her son for support. He had comforted her when her husband died. Now that her son was dead, who would console her?

He had compassion on her: As the funeral procession came out of the gate of the city, they met Jesus with His disciples coming in. Jesus must have sensed the situation immediately, and His heart went out to this distraught widow.

touched the open coffin, and the pallbearers stopped. And He said, "**Young man**, I tell you, **get up!**"

[15]The dead man sat up and began to speak, and Jesus gave him to his mother. [16]Then fear came over everyone, and they glorified God, saying, "**A great prophet** has risen among us," and "God has visited His people." [17]This **report about Him went throughout Judea** and all the vicinity.

57. A QUESTION FROM JOHN THE BAPTIZER

Matthew 11:1–19; Luke 7:18–35

Mt 11:1–3When Jesus had finished giving orders to His twelve disciples, He moved on from there to teach and preach in their towns. [2]When John heard in prison what the Messiah was doing, he sent a message by his disciples [3]and asked Him, "**Are You the Coming One**, or should we expect someone else?"

[4]Jesus replied to them, "Go and report to John what you hear and see: [5]the blind see, the lame walk, lepers are cleansed, the deaf hear, the dead are raised, and the poor are told the good news. [6]And if anyone is not offended because of Me, he is blessed."

[7]As these men went away, Jesus began to speak to the crowds about John: "**What did you go out** into the wilderness **to see?** A reed swaying in the wind? [8]What then did you go out to see? A man dressed in soft clothes? Look, those who wear soft clothes are in kings' palaces. [9]But what did you go out to see? A prophet? Yes, I tell you, and **far more than a prophet**. [10]This is the one of whom it is written: 'Look, I am sending My messenger ahead of You; he will prepare Your way before You.' [11]I assure you: Among those born of women no

---

Young man . . . get up! Jesus spoke directly to the young man in the coffin. He issued this command with confidence and authority—an authority that came from His heavenly Father. The young man's life was restored, and he and his mother were reunited.

A great prophet: For years the Jewish people had expected the return of one of the prophets. The people of Nain connected Jesus with this popular expectation.

report about Him went throughout Judea: This great miracle caused the fame of Jesus to spread throughout the province of Judea to the south as well as the northern province of Galilee, where Jesus was teaching and healing.

57. A QUESTION FROM JOHN THE BAPTIZER

Are You the Coming One: In answering this question from John the Baptizer, Jesus called attention to His actions of compassion and grace that were foreshadowed in such passages as Isaiah 35:5–6; 42:6–7; and 61:1–3. He told the disciples of John to tell the Baptizer what they had seen Jesus doing. This should put John's doubts to rest.

What did you go out . . . to see? As these followers of John went away, Jesus' concern for John's reputation led Him to ask a number of questions. At the height of his popularity, the Baptizer drew crowds from all over Palestine. What did these people go to see? A weakling? The obvious answer was no. John's experience with doubt must not change opinions about him. Jesus said that people went to the wrong place, the wilderness, if they wanted to see a man elegantly dressed. John's physical appearance witnessed to his moral and spiritual strength. John stood in the tradition of the ancient prophets.

far more than a prophet: But John the Baptizer was more than a prophet. He bridged the gap between God's spokesmen of old and the future messengers of the gospel. John prepared the way for Christ and His gospel.

one greater than John the Baptist has appeared, but the least in the kingdom of heaven is **greater than he**.

[12]"From the days of John the Baptist until now, the kingdom of heaven has been suffering violence, and the violent have been seizing it by force. [Lk 7:29–30](And when all the people, including the tax collectors, heard this, they acknowledged God's way of righteousness, because they had been baptized with John's baptism. [30]But since the Pharisees and experts in the law had not been baptized by him, they rejected the plan of God for themselves.)

[Mt 11:13–15]"For all the prophets and the law prophesied until John; [14]if you're willing to accept it, he is **the Elijah who is to come**. [15]Anyone who has ears should listen!

[16]"To what should I compare this generation? It's like children sitting in the marketplaces who call out to each other: [17]'We played the flute for you, but you didn't dance; we sang a lament, but you didn't mourn!' [18]For John did not come eating or drinking [[Lk 7:33a]*For John the Baptist did not come eating bread or drinking wine*], and they say, 'He has a demon!' [19]The Son of Man came eating and drink-

---

Why Did John the Baptizer Doubt?

During his imprisonment, John the Baptizer heard about the ministry of Jesus. In his isolation and loneliness, he was eager for news. But when word about Jesus reached him, it was not what he expected.

When we look at terms used by John in proclaiming Christ, we can understand his perplexity. He had seen himself as the herald of a coming conqueror (Matt. 3:3), and had spoken of Him wielding an ax (Matt. 3:10) and separating wheat from chaff (Matt. 3:12). But the ministry of Jesus did not conform to this expectation. To compound John's perplexity, Jesus had done nothing to free John from imprisonment by Herod.

It is hard to accept God's way of doing things when His way does not line up with what we expected. Matthew does not tell us how John reacted to the message that Jesus sent back by John's followers. Perhaps Matthew wanted to leave us with the same question that John faced: You see the deeds and hear the words of Jesus. Do you believe that He is the Messiah?

---

greater than he: According to Jesus, there was no prophet greater than John. He compared John to Elijah, considered the greatest of the prophets. But John's message preceded the preaching of the gospel based on Christ's ministry, death, and resurrection—events that were still in the future. Those who responded to that gospel would belong to a higher level of ministry even than John.

the Elijah who is to come: The equating of John with Elijah is based on Malachi 4:5—a prophetic statement that the prophet Elijah would reappear in a role preparatory to the coming of God's kingdom. Jesus was saying that John the Baptizer fulfilled the role associated with Elijah.

The City of Capernaum

Jesus lived in Capernaum during His Galilean ministry. But this major city was subject to the same unbelief that characterized the other towns of this region. Jesus condemned Capernaum because of its lack of faith (Matt. 11:23–24).

The citizens of Capernaum witnessed several miracles performed by Jesus, including the healing of Peter's mother-in-law (Mark 1:29–31), the healing of a centurion's servant (Matt. 8:5–13), and the healing of a lame man let down through the roof of a house by his friends (Mark 2:1–12).

Capernaum was known for its commercial fishing industry during New Testament times. Four of Jesus' "fishermen disciples"—Peter, Andrew, James, and John—were apparently from Capernaum. Jesus also called Matthew the tax collector away from his toll booth in or near Capernaum to become His disciple (Mark 2:1, 13–14).

ing, and they say, 'Look, a glutton and a drunkard, a friend of tax collectors and sinners!' Yet wisdom is vindicated by her deeds."

58. Galilean Cities Condemned because of Their Unbelief

Matthew 11:20–24

²⁰Then **He proceeded to denounce the towns** where most of His miracles were done, because they did not repent: ²¹"Woe to you, **Chorazin**! Woe to you, **Bethsaida**! For if the miracles that were done in you had been done in Tyre and Sidon, they would have repented in sackcloth and ashes long ago! ²²But I tell you, it will be more tolerable for Tyre and Sidon on the day of judgment than for you.

²³"And you, **Capernaum**, will you be exalted to heaven? You will go down to Hades. For if the miracles that were done in you had been done in Sodom, it would have remained until today. ²⁴But I tell you, it will be more tolerable for the land of Sodom on the day of judgment than for you."

---

58. Galilean Cities Condemned because of Their Unbelief

He proceeded to denounce the towns: Jesus condemned the people in the area around Lake Galilee where He conducted most of His ministry. They refused to recognize the presence of the kingdom in Him and His mighty acts.

Chorazin . . . Bethsaida: These were two cities in the province of Galilee in which Jesus had performed many miracles. The people of these cities would suffer harsh condemnation because they did not recognize the wisdom of God.

Capernaum: Proud Capernaum, the city that served as Jesus' headquarters during His Galilean ministry, would suffer destruction just as Sodom had in Old Testament times. In the day of judgment, the citizens of Capernaum would be punished for their unbelief.

59. AN INVITATION TO THE WEARY

Matthew 11:25–30

²⁵At that time Jesus said, "I praise You, Father, Lord of heaven and earth, because You have hidden these things from **the wise and learned** and **revealed them to infants**. ²⁶Yes, Father, because this was Your good pleasure. ²⁷**All things have been entrusted to Me** by My Father. No one **knows the Son** except the Father, and no one **knows the Father** except the Son and anyone to whom the Son desires to reveal Him.

²⁸"Come to Me, all you who are weary and burdened, and I will give you rest. ²⁹**Take My yoke** upon you and **learn from Me**, because I am gentle and humble in heart, and you will find rest for your souls. ³⁰For My yoke is easy and My burden is light."

60. JESUS ANOINTED BY A SINFUL WOMAN

Luke 7:36–50

³⁶Then one of the Pharisees invited Him to eat with him. **He entered the Pharisee's house** and reclined at the table. ³⁷And **a woman** in the town **who was a sinner** found out that Jesus was reclining at the table in the Pharisee's house. She brought an alabaster flask of fragrant oil ³⁸and stood behind Him at His feet, weeping, and began to wash His feet with her tears. She wiped His feet with the hair of her head, kissing them and anointing them with the fragrant oil.

³⁹When the Pharisee who had invited Him saw this, he said to himself, "This man, if He were a prophet, would know who and what kind of woman this is who is touching Him—that **she's a sinner!**"

⁴⁰ᵃJesus replied to him, "Simon, I have something to say to you."

⁴⁰ᵇ"Teacher," he said, "say it."

---

59. AN INVITATION TO THE WEARY

the wise and learned: Jesus was referring to the selfish and shrewd, the scribes and Pharisees, who were wise in their own conceit and foolishness.

revealed them to infants: These were pure and childlike people like His disciples who were free from prejudice, pride, and bigotry. The proud despised Jesus, but the common people received Him gladly.

All things have been entrusted to Me: All things needed for the full execution of His office as Lord of the kingdom had been granted to Jesus by His heavenly Father. This authority became clear to His disciples after His resurrection when He gave them the Great Commission to carry on His work (Matt. 28:18).

knows the Son . . . knows the Father: Correct knowledge of God comes only through revelation. Jesus began the revelation of the Father in this world, and He will complete it in the world to come.

Take My yoke . . . learn from Me: All who labor and are burdened down are invited to come to Jesus. Here they will find rest by taking His yoke upon them in exchange for the legalistic teachings of the scribes and Pharisees.

⁴¹"A creditor had **two debtors**. One owed five hundred denarii, and the other fifty. ⁴²Since they could not pay it back, he graciously forgave them both. So, which of them will love him more?"

⁴³ᵃSimon answered, "I suppose the one he forgave more."

⁴³ᵇ"You have judged correctly," He told him. ⁴⁴Turning to the woman, He said to Simon, "Do you see this woman? I entered your house; **you gave Me no water** for My feet, **but she**, with her tears, **has washed My feet** and wiped them with her hair. ⁴⁵You gave Me no kiss, but she hasn't stopped kissing My feet since I came in. ⁴⁶You didn't anoint My head with oil, but she has anointed My feet with fragrant oil. ⁴⁷Therefore I tell you, her many sins have been forgiven; that's why she loved much. But the one who is forgiven little, loves little." ⁴⁸Then He said to her, **"Your sins are forgiven."**

⁴⁹Those who were at the table with Him began to say among themselves, "Who is this man who even forgives sins?"

⁵⁰And He said to the woman, "Your faith has saved you. Go in peace."

Two Anointings of Jesus

This anointing of Jesus during His Galilean ministry is similar to another that occurred as His earthly ministry was drawing to a close (see segment 176, "Mary of Bethany Anoints Jesus," p. 206). But the details of each anointing are different, and they are considered two separate and distinct events.

The woman who anointed Jesus here is described as a "sinner," while the woman in the second anointing is identified by the Gospel of John as Mary of Bethany (John 12:3). Jesus was a close friend of Mary and her sister Martha and brother Lazarus (see John 11:1–44).

---

60. Jesus Anointed by a Sinful Woman

He entered the Pharisee's house: Jesus accepted this invitation from a Pharisee because of His mission to all people. He was willing to take risks, whether by eating a meal with social outcasts or a critical Pharisee, if He could touch hearts and change lives.

a woman . . . who was a sinner: This woman knew that Jesus was a guest in Simon's home. Perhaps she had been looking for an opportunity to honor Him. She was a great sinner, probably a prostitute well known in the community. She began to anoint Jesus' feet with an expensive perfume, and she let her hair down to dry His feet.

she's a sinner: Simon the Pharisee obviously knew this woman. He turned against his guest with a double criticism: The woman was a sinner, and Jesus was certainly not a religious man because He let her touch Him.

two debtors: Jesus used a short parable about two debtors to make a point with Simon. One debtor owed five hundred denarii (well over a year's pay for a working person) and the other fifty. The generous creditor forgave them both. Which one of them would have the most gratitude? Simon did not hesitate to reply that the greater the debt forgiven, the greater the gratitude one should have.

you gave Me no water . . . but she . . . has washed My feet: Jesus contrasted the thoughtless attitude of the Pharisee with the thoughtful actions of this woman. Jesus was a guest in Simon's house, but he did not extend to Him any of the common courtesies usually expressed by a host. But this woman made up for Simon's lack of hospitality with her acts of extravagant love and affection.

Your sins are forgiven: Jesus declared the woman forgiven because of this demonstration of her love and faith.

61. Another Tour of Galilee

Luke 8:1–3

[1]Soon afterward He was traveling from one town and village to another, preaching and telling the good news of the kingdom of God. **The Twelve were with Him**, [2]and also some women who had been healed of evil spirits and sicknesses: **Mary, called Magdalene**, from whom seven demons had come out; [3]Joanna the wife of Chuza, Herod's steward; Susanna; and **many others who were supporting them** from their possessions.

62. The Healing of a Blind Man

Matthew 12:22–24

[22]Then a demon-possessed man who was blind and unable to speak was brought to Him. He healed him, so that the man both spoke and saw. [23]And all the crowds were astounded and said, "Perhaps this is **the Son of David!**"

[24]When the Pharisees heard this, they said, "The man **drives out demons** only **by Beelzebul**, the ruler of the demons."

63. Jesus Answers the Blasphemous Charge of the Pharisees

Matthew 12:25–37; Mark 3:20–30

Mk 3:20–22[20]Then He went into a house, and the crowd gathered again so that they were not even able to eat. [21]When His family heard this, they set out to restrain Him, because they said, "He's out of His mind." [22]And the scribes who had come down from Jerusalem said, "He has Beelzebul in Him!" and, "He drives out demons by the ruler of the demons!"

---

61. Another Tour of Galilee

The Twelve were with Him: Journeying from place to place throughout Galilee, Jesus was constantly preaching the gospel to the people and instructing His disciples. The Twelve were serving an apprenticeship in the work He would soon leave in their hands.

Mary, called Magdalene: Mary's name indicates she was a native of Magdala. She was one of a group of women who had been healed of various diseases, apparently by Jesus.

many others who were supporting them: The financial support of these women shows the poverty of Jesus and His disciples. It also explains how they were able to devote themselves to a teaching and healing ministry among the people. Many followers may have contributed to their ministry.

62. The Healing of a Blind Man

the Son of David! A line of prophecy that stirred Jewish hopes of national restoration concerned promises made to David that "your throne will be established permanently" (2 Sam. 7:16). The Messiah was expected to be a descendant of that famous king. Notice the crowd's reaction to this miracle: "Perhaps this is the Son of David!"

drives out demons . . . by Beelzebul: This popular acclaim provoked Jesus' enemies to deeper hostility. They accused Him of performing miracles with Satan's help.

The Unforgivable Sin

Considerable discussion swirls around what Jesus meant by the sin that "will not be forgiven." Whatever it was, it was committed by people opposed to Jesus, not His followers. It also had to do with rejecting God's revelation in Christ as signified by the power of God's Spirit.

The most narrow interpretation limits the unpardonable sin to attributing the work of the Holy Spirit to Satan. This was how the sin was expressed in this specific situation. But many people see this as only one expression of a broader sin—persistently rejecting God's revelation of Himself in Christ as the Spirit convicts people of sin and seeks to point them to Jesus.

Persistently refusing to believe in Christ in the full light of God's revelation is to choose darkness rather than light (John 3:17–21; 9:37–41). The Pharisees knew that Jesus was God's Son, but they rejected Him in the full light of that knowledge. Thus, the unpardonable sin is refusing God's offer of pardon.

Mt 12:25–28 Knowing their thoughts, He told them: "Every **kingdom divided against itself** is headed for destruction, and no city or house divided against itself will stand. ²⁶If Satan drives out Satan, he is divided against himself. How then will his kingdom stand? ²⁷And if I drive out demons by Beelzebul, **by whom do your sons drive them out?** For this reason they will be your judges. ²⁸If I drive out demons by the Spirit of God, then **the kingdom of God has come** to you.

²⁹"How can someone enter a strong man's house and steal his possessions unless he first ties up the strong man? Then he can rob his house. ³⁰Anyone who is not with Me is against Me, and anyone who does not gather with Me scatters. ³¹Because of this, I tell you, people will be forgiven every sin and blasphemy, but the blasphemy against the Spirit will not be forgiven. ³²Whoever speaks a word against the Son of Man, it will be forgiven him. But whoever speaks against the Holy Spirit, it will not be forgiven him, either in this age or in the one to come.

---

63. JESUS ANSWERS THE BLASPHEMOUS CHARGE OF THE PHARISEES

kingdom divided against itself: Jesus began His response to the charge of the Pharisees with a statement of the obvious. A city divided into warring factions cannot survive. By the same token, Satan is doomed if he wages war against himself by casting out some of his own evil forces. Thus, the charge that Satan would help Jesus cast out demons was nonsense.

by whom do your sons drive them out? Some of the Pharisees were exorcists who claimed they had power to cast out evil spirits. Jesus asked if they also were using Satan's power to perform exorcisms. If Jesus was casting out demons by Satan's power, then all exorcists must rely on the Devil's power. The Pharisees certainly were not willing to make such a charge against their own.

the kingdom of God has come: If Jesus did not rely on Satan for His power, He depended on the power of the Holy Spirit—the true enemy of Satan. If He was casting out demons by the Spirit's power, then this was one of many signs that the kingdom of God had come.

33"Either make the tree good and its fruit good, or make the tree bad and its fruit bad; for a tree is known by its fruit. 34Brood of vipers! How can you speak good things when you are evil? For the mouth speaks from the overflow of the heart. 35A good man produces good things from his storeroom of good, and an evil man produces evil things from his storeroom of evil. 36I tell you that on the day of judgment people will have to account for every careless word they speak. 37For by your words you will be acquitted, and by your words you will be condemned."

64. Condemnation of the Sign Seekers

Matthew 12:38–45

38Then some of the scribes and Pharisees said to Him, "Teacher, **we want to see a sign from You**."

39But He answered them, "**An evil and adulterous generation** demands a sign, but no sign will be given to it except **the sign of the prophet Jonah**. 40For as Jonah was in the belly of the great fish three days and three nights, so the Son of Man will be in the heart of the earth three days and three nights. 41The men of Nineveh will stand up at the judgment with this generation and condemn it, because they repented at Jonah's proclamation; and look—something greater than Jonah is here! 42The queen of the south will rise up at the judgment with this generation and condemn it, because she came from the ends of the earth to hear the wisdom of Solomon; and look—something greater than Solomon is here!

43"When an unclean spirit comes out of a man, it roams through waterless places looking for rest, but doesn't find any. 44Then it says, 'I'll go back to my house that I came from.' And when it arrives, it finds the house vacant, swept, and put in order. 45Then off it goes and brings with it seven other spirits more evil than itself, and they enter and settle down there. As a result that man's last condition is worse than the first. That's how it will also be with this evil generation."

65. The Mother and Brothers of Jesus

Matthew 12:46–50; Mark 3:31–35; Luke 8:19–21

Mt 12:46He was still speaking to the crowds when suddenly **His mother and brothers** were standing outside **wanting to speak to Him,** Lk 8:19bbut they

---

64. Condemnation of the Sign Seekers

we want to see a sign from You: A number of miracle workers lived in Jesus' day, but the Pharisees requested a sure sign from heaven that Jesus was who He claimed to be. A sign was different from an ordinary miracle.

An evil and adulterous generation: Demanding that Jesus prove Himself by a special sign from heaven was evidence of arrogant unbelief. Jesus knew the hearts of the Pharisees were so evil that they would not accept a sign, even if He gave one.

The Brothers of Jesus

The Gospels of Matthew and Mark reveal the specific number of Jesus' brothers and tell us their names: "James, Joseph (Joses, Mark 6:3), Simon, and Judas" (Matt. 13:55). We also learn from Matthew and Mark that Jesus had sisters as well, but their names are not cited (Matt. 13:56; Mark 6:3).

Actually, "half brothers" is a better word for these relatives of Jesus, since His conception occurred through the action of the Holy Spirit (Luke 1:35). After Jesus was born to Mary, she obviously gave birth to other children through the normal reproductive process.

During Jesus' earthly ministry, His brothers took a skeptical attitude toward Him and His work as a wandering teacher and healer. John declared in his Gospel, "Not even His brothers believed in Him" (John 7:5).

But at least one of His brothers, James, changed his mind and became a believer after Jesus' death and resurrection. He became an early leader of the church in Jerusalem (Acts 15:12–19; 21:17–18). James also probably wrote the epistle in the New Testament that bears his name.

Some scholars believe that another brother of Jesus, Judas (Jude), was also active in the early church. They point to him as the probable author of the epistle of Jude in the New Testament.

---

could not meet with Him because of the crowd. [Mt 12:47] And someone told Him, "Look, Your mother and Your brothers are standing outside, wanting to speak to You."

48But He replied to the one who told Him, "Who is My mother and who are My brothers?" 49And stretching out His hand toward His disciples [[Mk 3:34a] *looking about at those who were sitting in a circle around Him*], He said, "**Here are My mother and My brothers!** 50For whoever does the will of My Father in heaven, that person is My brother and sister and mother."

---

the sign of the prophet Jonah: Jesus' reference to Jonah and the great fish foreshadowed His death, burial, and resurrection. This was the only sign the Pharisees would be given, He declared.

65. THE MOTHER AND BROTHERS OF JESUS

His mother and brothers . . . wanting to speak to Him: We learn just before this passage in Mark's Gospel that Jesus' family came to "restrain Him" because they thought He was out of His mind (Mark 3:21). Perhaps this is why they came in a group. They wanted to force Him to come back to Nazareth. They sent word to Jesus inside the house where He was speaking that they wanted to see Him outside.

Here are My mother and My brothers! Jesus' response shows that fellowship in the kingdom of God does not follow the line of family ties. The old covenant had been administered primarily in terms of the family; the new covenant would deal with individual obedience. The true family of God consists of those who do the will of God.

66. THE PARABLE OF THE SOWER

Matthew 13:1–9; Mark 4:1–9; Luke 8:4–8

^{Mt 13:1a}On that day Jesus went out of the house. ^{Mk 4:1a}Again He began to **teach by the sea**, and a very large crowd gathered around Him ^{Lk 8:4b}from every town. ^{Mk 4:1b}So He got into a boat on the sea and sat down, while the whole crowd was on the shore facing the sea. ²He taught them many things in parables, and in His teaching He said to them: ³"Listen! Consider the **sower who went out to sow.** ⁴As he sowed this occurred: Some seed **fell along the path** [^{Lk 8:5b}*it was trampled on*], and the birds came and ate it up. ⁵Other seed **fell on rocky ground** where it didn't have much soil, and it sprang up right away, since it didn't have deep soil. ⁶When the sun came up, it was scorched, and since it didn't have a root, it

---

The Parables of Jesus

The word parable *means "a casting alongside." In His teaching Jesus compared one thing with another to communicate truth. He picked up incidents from everyday life and compared them with a deeper, more abstract truth to help His audience understand spiritual realities.*

For example, in this parable of the sower Jesus described a Palestinian farmer who sowed seed in a field. The people who were listening got the picture immediately. But the various soils upon which the seed fell—representing different reactions to the gospel or the word of God—was the spiritual point of the story.

The advantage of such stories is that they arrest the listeners' attention with a vivid, memorable picture of the truth. But this does not mean that Jesus' parables were always easy to understand. Even Jesus' disciples were sometimes puzzled about the meaning of His parables, as they were about the parable of the wheat and the weeds (Matt. 13:36). Jesus patiently explained the meaning of the parable to them because they were open-minded and teachable. But His parables sometimes concealed the truth from those who were stubborn and disobedient, especially the Pharisees (Luke 8:9–10).

---

66. THE PARABLE OF THE SOWER

teach by the sea: Although Jesus sometimes taught in the synagogues and in the temple, He often taught elsewhere. In this situation, He got into a boat and taught the crowds on the shore.

sower who went out to sow: This is often called "the parable of the sower," but a more appropriate title is "the parable of the soils." The parable has only one sower and one kind of seed, but it focuses on four types of soil.

fell along the path: Public right-of-ways crossed fields in Palestine. The soil along these pathways became hardened by the passage of many feet. Seed falling on this hard surface would remain where it fell until eaten by birds.

withered. [7]Other seed **fell among thorns**, and the thorns came up and choked it, and it didn't produce a crop. [8]Still others **fell on good ground** and produced a crop that increased 30, 60, and a 100 times what was sown."

Lk 8:8b As He said this, He called out, "Anyone who has ears to hear should listen!"

67. WHY JESUS SPOKE IN PARABLES

Matthew 13:10–17; Mark 4:11–12; Luke 8:10

Mt 13:10 Then the disciples came up and asked Him, "Why do You speak to them in parables?"

[11]He answered them, "**To know the secrets** of the kingdom of heaven **has been granted to you,** but to them [Mk 4:11b *those outside*] it has not been granted. [12]For whoever has, more will be given to him, and he will have more than enough. But whoever does not have, even what he has will be taken away from him. [13]For this reason I speak to them in parables, because **looking they do not see**, and hearing they do not listen or understand.

[14]"In them the prophecy of Isaiah is fulfilled that says: 'You will listen and listen, yet never understand; and you will look and look, yet never perceive. [15]For this people's heart has grown callous; their ears are hard of hearing, and they have shut their eyes; otherwise they might see with their eyes and hear with their ears, understand with their hearts and turn back—and I would cure them.'

[16]"But your eyes are blessed because they do see, and your ears because they do hear! [17]For I assure you: Many prophets and righteous people longed to see the things you see, yet didn't see them; to hear the things you hear, yet didn't hear them."

---

fell on rocky ground: Much of the soil of Palestine was stony. Seed sown in such soil might survive long enough to send up shoots. But there was not enough soil to withstand the heat of the sun, so the plants soon withered and died.

fell among thorns: Plants may begin to grow in such conditions, but they will eventually be choked by the thorns.

fell on good ground: A farmer would not waste good seed on a field that offered no promise of harvest. Even though some of the soil is bad, he concentrates on the good ground that will reward his efforts.

67. WHY JESUS SPOKE IN PARABLES

To know the secrets . . . has been granted to you: Sometimes Jesus rebuked His disciples for being slow in their understanding. But they had at least made a commitment by responding to His call to discipleship. To them, therefore, He gave "the secrets of the kingdom of heaven," truths hidden from those who had made no commitment. These revealed "secrets" were only gradually comprehended by the disciples, but they became the foundation for the message they declared after Jesus' resurrection.

looking they do not see: These words of Jesus must be understood in light of His total ministry. He did not obscure truth but made it plain. The fault was in His listeners. They chose not to see or hear, so they failed to understand.

68. THE PARABLE OF THE SOWER EXPLAINED

Matthew 13:18–23; Mark 4:10, 13–20; Luke 8:9–15

Mk 4:10, 13a When He was in private, those who were around Him, along with the Twelve, **asked Him about the parables**. . . . 13aThen He said to them: "Do you not understand this parable?

Lk 8:11–14"This is the meaning of the parable: The seed is the word of God. 12The seeds along the path are those who have heard. Then the Devil [Mk 4:15 Satan] comes and takes away the word from their hearts, so that they may not believe and be saved. 13And the seeds on the rock [Mk 4:16 rocky ground] are those who, when they hear, welcome the word with joy. Having no root, these believe for a while and depart in a time of testing. 14As for the seed that fell among thorns, these are the ones who, when they have heard, go on their way and are choked with worries, riches, and pleasures of life, and produce no mature fruit.

Mt 13:23 "But the one sown on the good ground—this is one who hears and understands the word, who does bear fruit and produce: some a 100, some 60, some 30 times what was sown."

69. THE LAMP ON A LAMPSTAND

Mark 4:21–25; Luke 8:16–18

Mk 4:21 He also said to them, "Is a **lamp** brought in to be put **under a basket** or under a bed? Isn't it to be put on a lampstand? 22For nothing is concealed except to be revealed, and nothing hidden except to come to light. 23If anyone has ears to hear, he should listen!" 24Then He said to them, "Pay attention to what you hear. By the measure you use, it will be measured and added to you. 25For to the one who has, it will be given, and from the one who does not have, even what he has will be taken away."

---

68. THE PARABLE OF THE SOWER EXPLAINED

asked Him about the parables: After the people left, the disciples asked Jesus the meaning of the parable. He explained that the sower sowed the word of God. The soils represent four different kinds of responses to the word of God: (1) The seed on the path represents those from whose hearts Satan snatches the word. They have hard hearts that fail to receive the word. (2) Others are superficial hearers, whose initial enthusiasm gives way to indifference and rejection. (3) Others hear the word and it takes root, but it never bears fruit because worldly ambitions and anxieties choke it out. (4) But some people hear, develop roots, grow, and bear fruit. They show they have truly heard the word of God by the fruitfulness of their lives.

69. THE LAMP ON A LAMPSTAND

lamp . . . under a basket: Jesus was referring to small oil-burning lamps that were used to illiminate rooms. No homeowner would light such a lamp and put it under a basket. He would place it on a stand so it could send its light into every corner of the room. Each Christian believer is like a lamp, lighted and placed on a stand to send the light of God's love into the lives of others.

70. The Seed of God's Kingdom

Mark 4:26–29

26"The kingdom of God is like this," He said. "A man scatters seed on the ground; 27night and day he sleeps and gets up, and the seed sprouts and grows—**he doesn't know how**. 28The soil produces a crop by itself—first the blade, then the head, and then the ripe grain on the head. 29But as soon as the crop is ready, he sends for the sickle, because harvest has come."

71. The Parable of the Wheat and the Weeds

Matthew 13:24–30

24He presented another parable to them: "The kingdom of heaven may be compared to a man who sowed good seed in his field. 25But while people were sleeping, his **enemy** came, **sowed weeds among the wheat**, and left. 26When the plants sprouted and produced grain, then the weeds also appeared. 27The landowner's slaves came to him and said, 'Master, didn't you sow good seed in your field? Then where did the weeds come from?'

28a"'An enemy did this!' he told them.

28b"'So, do you want us to go and gather them up?' the slaves asked him.

29"'No,' he said. 'When you gather up the weeds, you might also uproot the wheat with them. 30Let both grow together until the harvest. At harvest time I'll tell the reapers, "Gather the weeds first and tie them in bundles to burn them, but store the wheat in my barn."'"

72. The Parable of the Mustard Seed and the Parable of the Yeast

Matthew 13:31–35; Mark 4:30–34; Luke 13:18-21

Mt 13:31a He presented another parable to them: Lk 13:18b "What is the kingdom of God like, and to what should I compare it? Mt 13:31b–32 The kingdom of heaven is **like a mustard seed** that a man took and sowed in his field

---

70. The Seed of God's Kingdom

he doesn't know how: This farmer sowed seed and went about his other activities. The seed grew to harvest in ways he did not control or understand. Jesus' point is that the kingdom of God is God's work. We are privileged to sow the seed, but God causes the seed to grow and develop until harvest time.

71. The Parable of the Wheat and the Weeds

enemy . . . sowed weeds among the wheat: The plant sowed among the wheat was probably a weed known as darnel. These plants looked just like wheat until the grain was almost mature. At harvest time the worthless weeds could be separated from the wheat. This parable teaches that the kingdom of God has come, but society is to continue in a mixed condition until the final judgment. Then the children of the kingdom and the children of the evil one will be separated.

72. The Parable of the Mustard Seed and the Parable of the Yeast

like a mustard seed: The mustard seed is proverbial for its small size; yet a huge tree grows from this tiny seed. From the

[Lk 13:19a*sowed in his garden*]. ³²It's the smallest of all the seeds, but when grown, it's taller than the vegetables and becomes a tree [Mk 4:32a*produces large branches*], so that the birds of the sky come and nest in its branches [Mk 4:32b*nest in its shade*]."

³³He told them another parable: "The kingdom of heaven is **like yeast** that a woman took and **mixed into three measures of flour** until it spread through all of it."

³⁴Jesus told the crowds all these things in parables, and He would not speak anything to them without a parable, ³⁵so that what was spoken through the prophet might be fulfilled: "I will open My mouth in parables; I will declare things kept secret from the foundation of the world."

73. THE PARABLE OF THE WHEAT AND THE WEEDS EXPLAINED

Matthew 13:36–43

³⁶Then He dismissed the crowds and went into the house. And His disciples approached Him and said, "**Explain the parable** of the weeds in the field to us."

³⁷He replied: "The One who sows the good seed is the Son of Man; ³⁸the field is the world; and the good seed—these are the sons of the kingdom. The weeds are the sons of the evil one, and ³⁹the enemy who sowed them is the Devil. The harvest is the end of the age, and the harvesters are angels. ⁴⁰Therefore just as the weeds are gathered and burned in the fire, so it will be at the end of the age. ⁴¹The Son of Man will send out His angels, and they will gather from His kingdom everything that causes sin and those guilty of lawlessness. ⁴²They will throw them into the blazing furnace where there will be weeping and gnashing of teeth. ⁴³Then the righteous will shine like the sun in their Father's kingdom. Anyone who has ears should listen!"

---

world's point of view, the coming of Jesus was an insignificant event. His life, death, and resurrection made only a tiny ripple in the waters of the first-century world. When the Christians preached Christ crucified, their message seemed weak and foolish to the world (1 Cor. 1:18–24). But Christians saw in that mustard seed the power of God that would eventually triumph.

like yeast . . . mixed into three measures of flour: The leaven is very small in relation to the three measures of flour. But it will eventually leaven the whole lump by working quietly within the dough. The kingdom of heaven may be minute and barely noticeable to the world. But it works quietly and effectively, transforming the values of the people and the society in which they live.

73. THE PARABLE OF THE WHEAT AND THE WEEDS EXPLAINED

Explain the parable: The disciples were curious about the parable of the wheat and the weeds. Jesus gave them a thorough explanation of its message. He Himself was the sower of the good seed. The field in which the seed was sowed represented the world. The enemy who sowed the weeds among the wheat was Satan. The harvest represented the final judgment. The fire symbolized hell, the final destination of unbelievers. As Lord of the harvest, Jesus directs the sowing and harvesting process. At the final judgment, He will separate believers from unbelievers and send them to the eternal destinies that they have determined for themselves.

74. The Parable of the Hidden Treasure

Matthew 13:44

⁴⁴"The kingdom of heaven is like **treasure, buried in a field**, that a man found and reburied. Then in his joy he goes and sells everything he has and buys that field."

75. The Parable of the Priceless Pearl

Matthew 13:45–46

⁴⁵"Again, the kingdom of heaven is like a merchant in search of fine pearls. ⁴⁶When he found one priceless pearl, he went and **sold everything** he had, **and bought it**."

76. The Parable of the Net

Matthew 13:47–51

⁴⁷"Again, the kingdom of heaven is like a large net thrown into the sea. It **collected every kind of fish**, ⁴⁸and when it was full, they dragged it ashore, sat down, and gathered the good fish into containers, but threw out the worthless ones. ⁴⁹So it will be at the end of the age. The angels will go out, separate the evil who are among the righteous, ⁵⁰and throw them into the blazing furnace. In that place there will be weeping and gnashing of teeth.

⁵¹ᵃ"Have you understood all these things?"

⁵¹ᵇ"Yes," they told Him.

---

74. The Parable of the Hidden Treasure

treasure, buried in a field: People of Jesus' time hid their valuables in unusual places. This man apparently found a treasure that someone had buried and forgotten. He bought the field in order to claim the treasure. The message is that the kingdom of God is of supreme value. No cost is too great for those who want to belong to this kingdom.

75. The Parable of the Priceless Pearl

sold everything . . . and bought it: This parable delivers the same message as the parable of the hidden treasure: We should be willing to pay any price in order to claim the riches of God's kingdom.

76. The Parable of the Net

collected every kind of fish: This parable is similar to the parable of the wheat and the weeds (see segment 71, "The Parable of the Wheat and the Weeds," p. 87). It teaches that the kingdom of God brings within its influence people who are both good and bad. But a final separation will occur at the day of judgment when the evil will be taken away. The truth of this parable was demonstrated in Jesus' own life and ministry. One of the Twelve, Judas, turned Him over to His enemies for 30 pieces of silver (Matt. 26:15).

77. The Parable of the Landowner

Matthew 13:52

⁵²"Therefore," He said to them, "every student of Scripture instructed in the kingdom of heaven is like a landowner who brings out of his storeroom what is **new and** what is **old.**"

78. Jesus Stills the Storm

Matthew 8:18, 23–27; Mark 4:35–41; Luke 8:22–25

Mk 4:35–38On that day, when evening had come [Mt 8:18a *When Jesus saw large crowds around Him*], He told them, "Let's **cross over to the other side** of the lake." ³⁶So they left the crowd and took Him along since He was in the boat. And there were other boats with Him. ³⁷A fierce windstorm arose, and the waves

---

Storms on Lake Galilee

The body of water where Jesus' disciples were caught in this storm was known as the Sea of Galilee. It was not really a sea but a fresh-water lake, about thirteen miles long and eight miles wide at its widest point.

At least four of Jesus' disciples—the two sets of brothers, Peter and Andrew and James and John—made their living as commercial fishermen on this lake (see segment 38, "Calling of Peter and Andrew, James and John," p. 50). They must have known everything about Lake Galilee. How could such seasoned fishermen be caught in such a sudden storm on the open water?

The unique topography of the lake provides the answer. Lake Galilee sits 690 feet below sea level in a deep depression. It is surrounded on three sides by steep cliffs and high mountains, some as high as 2,700 feet. Cool winds often rush down from these steep slopes and mix with the warmer air rising from the surface of the lake. The resulting turbulence creates violent storms that strike without warning.

---

77. The Parable of the Landowner

new and . . . old: A landowner would use both his new and old possessions to provide for the needs of his family. Jesus' disciples should combine the spiritual truths they already knew with the new insights He was teaching them in order to meet the needs of others.

78. Jesus Stills the Storm

cross over to the other side: Tired from a day of hard work, Jesus sought rest from the multitude by going with His disciples to the sparsely settled district on the east side of Lake Galilee.

in the stern, sleeping on the cushion: Jesus probably rolled up the cushion on the seat in the rear of the boat and used it for a pillow as He laid down to rest. While He was sleeping, a fierce thunderstorm struck. Notice the contrast between the behavior of Jesus and the disciples in the midst of the storm. He was fast asleep, and the frightened disciples had to wake Him up.

were breaking over the boat, so that the boat was already being swamped. [38]But He was **in the stern, sleeping on the cushion**. So they woke Him up and said to Him, "Teacher! Don't you care that we're going to die?"

[39a]He got up, **rebuked the wind** [Lk 8:24]and the raging waves, [Mk 4:39b–40]and **said to the sea**, "Silence! **Be still!**" The wind ceased, and **there was a great calm**. [40]Then He said to them, "Why are you fearful? **Do you still have no faith?**"

[41]And they were terrified and said to one another, "Who then is this? **Even the wind and the sea obey Him!**"

79. Jesus Heals a Wild Man among the Tombs

Matthew 8:28–34; Mark 5:1–20; Luke 8:26–39

[Mk 5:1–5]Then they came to the other side of the sea, to the **region of the Gerasenes**. [2]As soon as He got out of the boat, **a man** [[Mt 8:28b] *two demon-possessed men*] with an unclean spirit **came out of the tombs** and met Him. [3]He lived in the tombs; and no one was able to restrain him any more—even with chains, [4]because he often had been bound with shackles and chains, but had snapped off the chains and smashed the shackles. No one was strong enough to subdue him. [5]And always, night and day, among the tombs and in the mountains, he was crying out and cutting himself with stones.

[6]When he saw Jesus from a distance, he ran and knelt down before Him. [7]And he cried out with a loud voice, "**What do You have to do with me**, Jesus, Son of the Most High God? I beg You before God, don't torment me!" [Lk 8:29]For He had

---

rebuked the wind: Jesus did not regard the wind and waves as evil spirits, but He saw in this particular storm the actions of the Devil. In rebuking them, He condemned the ministers of Satan who were making use of the storm. The powers of evil were attempting to swamp the boat.

said to the sea . . . Be still! Jesus spoke to the winds and waves as if they were persons to emphasize His authority over the natural order.

there was a great calm: This calm showed the perfection of the miracle. The waves of a lake in such a storm would normally continue to roll long after the winds died down.

Do you still have no faith? On one hand, the disciples had little faith or they would not have been so frightened. On the other hand, they had some faith or they would not have appealed to Jesus.

Even the wind and the sea obey Him! It was beginning to dawn upon His disciples that the ordinary categories of human experience were not adequate to describe the power of Jesus.

79. Jesus Heals a Wild Man among the Tombs

region of the Gerasenes: Jesus and His disciples crossed over to the eastern side of Lake Galilee to the region known as the Decapolis—a territory inhabited mostly by Gentiles of Greek background.

a man . . . came out of the tombs: This demon-possessed man (according to Matthew, two men; Matt. 8:28b) was suicidal and self-destructive. Apparently the people of the area had tried unsuccessfully to restrain him with shackles and chains. Now he was living as an outcast in the burial caves on this rocky shore, battling with the demons that controlled his life.

What do You have to do with me: The question asked of Jesus by the afflicted man meant, "What do we have in common with You?" The demons recognized the unique personality of Jesus and addressed Him as the Son of God. The demons knew judgment awaited them, and they feared it might be imposed immediately.

commanded the unclean spirit to come out of the man. Many times it had seized him, and although he was guarded, bound by chains and shackles, he would snap the restraints and be driven by the demon into deserted places.

Mk 5:9a"**What is your name?**" He asked him.

9b"**My name is Legion**," he answered Him, "because we are many." 10And **he kept begging Him** not to send them out of the region [Lk 8:31*And they begged Him not to banish them to the abyss*].

11Now a large herd of pigs was there, feeding on the hillside. 12The demons begged Him, "Send us to the pigs, so we may enter them." 13And He gave them permission. Then the unclean spirits came out and **entered the pigs**, and the herd of **about two thousand** rushed down the steep bank into the sea and drowned there. 14The men who tended them ran off and reported it in the town and the countryside, and people went to see what had happened. 15They came to Jesus and saw the man who had been demon-possessed by the legion sitting there, dressed and in his right mind; and they were afraid. 16The eyewitnesses described to them what had happened to the demon-possessed man and told about the pigs.

Lk 8:37Then all the people of the Gerasene region **asked Him to leave** them, because they were gripped by great fear. So getting into the boat, He returned.

Lk 8:38-39The man from whom the demons had departed kept begging Him to be with Him. But He sent him away and said, 39"Go back to your home [Mk 5:19a*Go back home to your own people*], and tell [Mk 5:19*report*] all that God has done for you [Mk 5:19b*and how He has had mercy on you*]." And off he went, **proclaiming** throughout the town [Mk 5:20a*in the Decapolis*] **all that Jesus had done for him**. Mk 5:20bAnd they were all amazed.

What is your name? Jesus did not respond to this question from the demons, but He asked the man to identify himself. He recognized him as a person created in God's image, although this had been obscured by the presence of these demons.

My name is Legion: A Roman legion consisted of six thousand soldiers. The man probably did not have six thousand demons; this was his way of admitting he was controlled by a large number of evil spirits.

he kept begging Him: One demon in the man spoke for the others. He knew that Jesus had the power to cast them out. They asked not to be sent "out of the region." They considered this wild Gentile place their own country.

entered the pigs . . . about two thousand: When the demons left the man, they entered a large herd of pigs nearby. They caused the pigs to rush down the steep hillside into Lake Galilee to their death. Some people wonder about this destruction of property associated with a miracle of Jesus. There is no simple answer to this question. But note that while Jesus gave the demons permission to enter the pigs, He did not command them to cause the pigs to drown.

asked Him to leave: We are not told the reason for the action of the townspeople in asking Jesus to leave. Was it anger at the loss of the pigs? Or fear over all that had happened? Perhaps both. Whatever the reason, they dismissed Jesus and His message, more concerned over the loss of their property than the salvation of their souls.

proclaiming . . . all that Jesus had done for him: The healed man wanted to go with Jesus and His disciples. But Jesus asked him to remain in his own region as a witness to others. Imagine what an impression he must have made on those who remembered when he was known as "the wild man among the tombs."

Demons and Demon Possession

According to some interpreters, this man who lived among the tombs was suffering from nothing more than a severe form of mental illness. He was certainly wild and out of his mind, but it is clear that his condition was caused by the "unclean spirits" or demons that possessed him. Note that when the demons left the man, he returned to "his right mind" (Mark 5:15).

Demons and demon possession cannot be explained away simply as mental illness. Jesus accepted the reality of demons, and He exercised control over them during His public ministry by casting them out of several people. Demons sometimes caused physical ailments, including deafness (Mark 9:25), blindness (Matt. 12:22), and bodily deformities (Luke 13:10–17). But not all the sicknesses that Jesus healed were caused by demons. The Gospels make a distinction between normal sickness and demon possession (Matt. 4:24; Luke 6:17–18).

In Jesus' time some of the Pharisees claimed they had the power to cast evil spirits out of people (see Matt. 12:27). But they did so through elaborate rituals and magical incantations. Jesus simply ordered demons through His spoken word to come out of people. This showed clearly that Jesus was master over Satan and his evil forces.

---

80. The Healing of Jairus's Daughter and a Woman with a Hemorrhage

Matthew 9:18–26; Mark 5:21–43; Luke 8:40–56

$^{Mk\ 5:21-24}$When Jesus had crossed over again by boat to the other side, a large crowd gathered around Him [$^{Lk\ 8:40b}$ *the crowd welcomed Him, for they were all expecting Him*] while He was by the sea. ^{22}One of the synagogue leaders, named **Jairus**, came, and when he saw Jesus he fell at His feet ^{23}and kept begging Him [$^{Lk\ 8:41b}$*pleaded with Him to come to his house*], "**My little daughter** [$^{Lk\ 8:42a}$*because he had an only daughter about 12 years old*] **is at death's door**. Come and lay Your hands on her, so that she may get well and live." ^{24}So Jesus went with him [$^{Mt\ 9:19b}$*and His disciples got up and followed Him*], and **a large crowd** was following and **pressing against Him**.

---

80. The Healing of Jairus's Daughter and a Woman with a Hemorrhage

Jairus: As the leader of a synagogue, Jairus was responsible for arrangements for the worship service and for the building itself. This was a position of trust and honor. When Jairus saw Jesus, he fell down at His feet. He was a desperate man with a critical need.

My little daughter is at death's door: Jairus felt that his daughter was dead or as good as dead. He showed great faith in asking Jesus to help his loved one who was caught in the clutches of death.

a large crowd . . . pressing against Him: Jesus listened to this distressed father and went with him. But His progress was slowed by the large number of people who pressed against Him on all sides.

²⁵**A woman** suffering from bleeding for 12 years ²⁶had endured much under many doctors. She had spent everything she had [ᴸᵏ ⁸:⁴³ᵇ *had spent all she had on doctors*], and was not helped at all. On the contrary, she became worse. ²⁷Having heard about Jesus, she came behind Him in the crowd and touched His robe [ᴸᵏ ⁸:⁴⁴ᵃ *touched the tassel of His robe*]. ²⁸For she said [ᴹᵗ ⁹:²¹ᵃ *said to herself*], "**If I can just touch His robes**, I'll be made well!" ²⁹Instantly her flow of blood ceased, and she sensed in her body that she was cured of her affliction.

³⁰At once Jesus realized in Himself that **power had gone out from Him**. He turned around in the crowd and said, "Who touched My robes?"

ᴸᵏ ⁸:⁴⁵ᵇWhen they all denied it, Peter said, ᴹᵏ ⁵:³¹ᵇ"You see the crowd pressing against You, and You say, 'Who touched Me?'"

ᴸᵏ ⁸:⁴⁶"Somebody did touch Me," said Jesus. "I know that power has gone out from Me." ᴹᵏ ⁵:³²So He was looking around to see who had done this.

ᴸᵏ ⁸:⁴⁷⁻⁴⁸When the woman saw that she was discovered, she came trembling [ᴹᵏ ⁵:³³ᵃ *came with fear and trembling*] and fell down before Him. In the presence of all the people, she declared the reason she had touched Him and how she was instantly cured. ⁴⁸"Daughter," He said to her, "**your faith has made you well** [ᴹᵏ ⁵:³⁴ᵇ *be free from your affliction*]. Go in peace." ᴹᵗ ⁹:²²ᵇAnd the woman was made well from that moment.

ᴹᵏ ⁵:³⁵While He was still speaking, people came from the synagogue leader's house and said, "**Your daughter is dead**. Why bother the Teacher any more?"

³⁶But when Jesus overheard what was said, He told the synagogue leader, "Don't be afraid. **Only believe**, ᴸᵏ ⁸:⁵⁰ᵇand she will be made well." ᴹᵏ ⁵:³⁷He did not let anyone accompany Him except Peter, James, and John, James's brother.

A woman: In the crowd was a woman with a desperate need of her own. She had been losing blood for 12 years. She had been to many doctors. All her money was gone, and she was getting worse. Her condition was not only debilitating, but it also made her a social outcast. Leviticus 15:25–30 declared her condition ceremonially unclean. No pious Jew would have any contact with her.

If I can just touch His robes: This woman was reluctant to get in front of Jesus and make her request. So she touched His robe, hoping this might bring healing.

power had gone out from Him: At her touch, Jesus felt power flow from Him. This gives us insight into the cost of His ministry. He expended Himself in order to serve others.

your faith has made you well: The woman fell at Jesus' feet and confessed she had touched Him. Why didn't Jesus let her slip away unnoticed? Probably because, in view of the private nature of her condition, she would have had difficulty persuading others that she was healed. The obstacles to sharing normal religious and social activities would not have been removed. Jesus calmed her fears and assured her that her faith had healed her.

Your daughter is dead: We can only imagine how Jairus must have felt during this delay. Then messengers arrived with the shocking news: "Your loved one is dead."

Only believe: Jesus overheard what the messengers told Jairus. He instructed the synagogue leader to stop being afraid and to keep on believing. Jairus had dared to believe that Jesus had power to heal the sick, even those at the point of death. He was about to discover that Jesus also had power to call the dead back to life.

people weeping and wailing: As Jesus approached Jairus's house, He heard the familiar sounds of a first-century Jewish mourning for the dead. The bereaved family hired flute players to play sad music and mourners to wail.

the girl isn't dead, but sleeping: Jesus was not denying that the girl was really dead. He was saying that from God's

Victorious over Death

The Gospels give three examples of Jesus bringing dead people back to life: Jairus's daughter, the son of the widow of Nain (Luke 7:11–17), and Lazarus (John 11:1–44). Each of these miracles was a restoration to physical life. But they were resuscitations rather than resurrections. Each of these people would later die again.

These victories over death foreshadowed the unique resurrection of Jesus Himself. Jesus was not just restored to physical life, later to die. He conquered death once and for all. He has dominion over death and is alive forever. And because He lives, those who know Him as Lord and Savior will live also.

Mk 5:38–39a They came to the synagogue leader's house and He saw a commotion—**people weeping and wailing** loudly [Mt 9:23b *saw the flute players and a crowd lamenting loudly*]. 39a He went in and said to them, Mt 9:24 "Leave . . . because **the girl isn't dead, but sleeping.**" And they started laughing at Him [Lk 8:53 *started laughing at Him, because they knew she was dead*].

Mk 5:40b–42a But **He put them all outside.** He took the child's father, mother, and those who were with Him, and entered the place where the child was. 41 Then He took the child by the hand and said to her, *"Talitha koum!"* (which is translated, "Little girl, I say to you, get up!"). 42a Immediately the girl got up and began to walk. (She was 12 years old.)

Mk 5:42b–43 At this they were utterly astounded. 43 Then He gave them strict orders that no one should know about this, and said that she should be given something to eat. Mt 9:26 And this news spread throughout that whole area.

81. Two Blind Men and a Demon-Possessed Man Healed

Matthew 9:27–38

27 As Jesus went on from there, **two blind men** followed Him, **shouting,** "Have mercy on us, Son of David!"

28a When He entered the house, the blind men approached Him, and Jesus said to them, "**Do you believe** that I can do this?"

---

point of view, the condition of the dead is not hopeless and lifeless. He declared that He had the power to overcome death and cause the dead to live.

He put them all outside: The scornful laughter of the mourners shows they did not believe in Jesus' power over death; it also raises questions about the sincerity of their grief. His response was to force them to leave.

Talitha koum! Jesus used two Aramaic words to call the girl back from the dead. These were the words a loving parent would use when arousing a child from sleep. Jesus touched her, and she got up and began to walk. The others were astonished. Jesus ordered them not to spread the word about this miracle—another example of His desire not to become known as a wonder worker.

81. Two Blind Men and a Demon-Possessed Man Healed

two blind men . . . shouting: As these two men groped along after Jesus, they cried out loudly for Him to show mercy on them. Jesus acted as if He had not heard them.

Do you believe: Jesus' failure to respond immediately must have tested their faith. After they assured Jesus that they truly believed, Jesus touched their eyes, and they were healed. Then He healed a demon-possessed man who was unable to speak.

28b"Yes, Lord," they answered Him.

29Then He touched their eyes, saying, "Let it be done for you according to your faith!" 30And their eyes were opened. Then Jesus warned them sternly, "Be sure that no one finds out!" 31But they went out and spread the news about Him throughout that whole area.

32Just as they were going out, a demon-possessed man who was unable to speak was brought to Him. 33When the demon had been driven out, the man spoke. And the crowds were amazed, saying, "Nothing like this has ever been seen in Israel!"

34The Pharisees however, said, "He drives out demons by the ruler of the demons!"

35Then Jesus went to all the towns and villages, teaching in their synagogues, preaching the good news of the kingdom, and healing every disease and every sickness. 36When He saw the crowds, He felt compassion for them, because they were weary and worn out, like sheep without a shepherd. 37Then He said to His disciples, "The **harvest is abundant**, but the **workers are few**. 38Therefore, pray to the Lord of the harvest to send out workers into His harvest."

82. JESUS VISITS NAZARETH AND IS REJECTED AGAIN

Matthew 13:53–58; Mark 6:1–6

Mt 13:53When Jesus had finished these parables, He left there Mk 6:1b–3and came to **His hometown**, and His disciples followed Him. 2When the Sabbath came, He began to teach in **the synagogue**, and many who heard Him were astonished. "Where did this man get these things?" they said. "What is this wisdom given to Him, and these miracles performed by His hands? 3**Isn't this**

---

harvest is abundant . . . workers are few: Jesus had compassion on the crowds. He described them as a mature crop ready for the harvest. The field of harvest was too great in proportion to the number of available laborers. He prayed that God would send more workers to help gather the harvest.

82. JESUS VISITS NAZARETH AND IS REJECTED AGAIN

His hometown . . . the synagogue: An interesting congregation gathered in Nazareth's synagogue one Sabbath morning. Jesus was there with His disciples, along with His mother and her family, plus a variety of friends and neighbors. Jesus was asked to expound the reading from the Old Testament. But what He said, and the way He said it, aroused the hostility of the people.

Isn't this the carpenter: This is the only place in Scripture where Jesus is called "the carpenter." By this time Joseph was dead, and Jesus had probably followed his trade. But on the lips of His critics, the statement was derogatory: He was not an educated person but only a manual worker.

A prophet is not without honor: Jesus reacted with a proverbial saying that He elaborated to include His own relatives and His own household. Most prophets had been rejected by the people to whom they were sent, some even being put to death.

He laid His hands on a few sick people: This phrase does not suggest any loss of healing power on the part of Jesus. But the majority of the people of Nazareth placed themselves beyond the possibility of healing by their unbelief.

the carpenter, the son of Mary, and the brother of James, Joses, Judas, and Simon? And aren't His sisters here with us?

Mt 13:56b "So where does He get all these things?" Mk 6:3bSo they were offended by Him.

4Then Jesus said to them, "**A prophet is not without honor** except in his hometown, among his relatives, and in his household." 5So He was not able to do any miracles there, except that **He laid His hands on a few sick people** and healed them. 6And He was amazed at their unbelief. Now He was going around the villages in a circuit, teaching.

83. Jesus Sends His Disciples out to Preach and Heal

Matthew 10:1, 5–42; Mark 6:7–13; Luke 9:1–6

Mt 10:1aSummoning His 12 disciples, He Mk 6:7a**began to send them out in pairs.** Mt 10:1b[He] gave them authority over unclean spirits, to drive them out, and to heal every disease and every sickness Lk 9:2a[and] to proclaim the kingdom of God.

Mt 10:5–8Jesus sent out these 12 after giving them instructions: "Don't take the road leading to other nations, and don't enter any Samaritan town. 6Instead, **go to the lost sheep** of the house **of Israel**. 7As you go, announce this: 'The kingdom of heaven has come near.' 8Heal the sick, raise the dead, cleanse the lepers, drive out demons. You have received free of charge; give free of charge.

Lk 9:3"**Take nothing for the road,**" He told them, "no walking stick, no backpack, no bread, no money; and don't have an extra shirt Mt 10:10bor sandals, or a walking stick [Mk 6:8a–9 *He instructed them to take nothing for the road except a walking stick . . . 9but to wear sandals*], for the worker is worthy of his food. Lk 9:4–5**Whatever house you enter, stay there** and leave from there. 5Wherever

---

83. Jesus Sends His Disciples out to Preach and Heal

began to send them out in pairs: There was more than provision of companionship in sending the disciples out in pairs. In the Old Testament, truth was established in the mouths of two witnesses (Deut. 17:6). Since the mission of the disciples was to Jews, their message would be more impressive if it came from two people. The dual witness also made rejection all the more serious.

go to the lost sheep . . . of Israel: These words are a distinct contrast to Jesus' farewell instructions to His disciples, "Go, therefore, and make disciples of all nations" (Matt. 28:19). They indicate that the mission of the Twelve in this instance was a temporary approach. Jesus had limited time to get His message across. He focused His efforts on His fellow Jews probably because He could teach more of them during His brief ministry.

Take nothing for the road: The mission was to be brief and urgent. Time was of the essence. So the disciples were to take no excess baggage; they were to depend on the hospitality of others. For food they were to depend on those to whom they ministered. According to the Gospel of Mark, two essentials were permitted—walking stick and sandals (Mark 6:8–9). Walking sticks would serve as a walking aid, since they had to walk wherever they went. They also might be needed for protection against unfriendly animals.

Whatever house you enter, stay there: Jesus told the disciples they were to stay with the accommodations they were first offered for the duration of a visit to a community. Temptation to exchange inadequate or uncomfortable lodging

Sending Out the Twelve and the Seventy

Just as Jesus sent His 12 disciples on a preaching and healing mission here, He later sent 70 of His followers on a similar mission (see segment 114, "Jesus Sends Seventy Followers on a Preaching Mission," p. 140).

Jesus gave each group instructions on how to perform its mission. The procedures they were to follow (traveling in pairs, what to take with them, where to lodge, etc.) are similar. But each group seems to have been sent out with a distinct purpose.

The purpose of the disciples' preaching mission was to announce the nearness of the kingdom of God. They were to determine the response of the people to Jesus as Messiah. But Jesus' sending of the 70 had a broader missionary purpose. These 70 believers pointed to the time in the future when the followers of Jesus would be sent out to preach the gospel to all nations. The number 70 is significant, reflecting the 70 Gentile nations listed in Genesis 10.

---

they do not welcome you, when you leave that town, **shake off the dust** from your feet as a testimony against them." ^{Mt 10:15}I assure you: It will be more tolerable on the day of judgment for the land of Sodom and Gomorrah than for that town.

Persecutions Predicted

¹⁶"Look, I'm sending you out like **sheep among wolves**. Therefore be as shrewd as serpents and harmless as doves. ¹⁷Because people will hand you over to **sanhedrins** and flog you in their synagogues, beware of them. ¹⁸You will even be brought before **governors** and **kings** because of Me, to bear witness to them and to the nations. ¹⁹But when they hand you over, don't worry about how or what you should speak. For you will be given what to say at that hour, ²⁰because you are not speaking, but the Spirit of your Father is speaking in you.

---

for something better would be strong. But to move on would be an insult to their hosts and would violate the spirit of humility that Jesus' followers should display.

shake off the dust: A custom among the Jews was to shake dust from their feet on leaving Gentile territory—a gesture of separation from unbelievers. For the disciples to do this was a testimony against people who rejected their message—a warning of judgment to come.

sheep among wolves: Jesus warned the Twelve that they would be vulnerable and subject to persecution. Their sincerity and honesty should be tempered with good judgment and common sense as they conducted themselves "as shrewd as serpents and harmless as doves."

sanhedrins . . . governors . . . kings: Jesus warned that the disciples might face three kinds of court trials. They might be dragged before the local Jewish councils (sanhedrins), local Roman officials (governors), and high-level Roman rulers (kings). These trials would bring opportunity for them to bear witness for Christ. The disciples should not worry about what to say during these trials. God's Spirit would give them the appropriate words.

Brother will betray brother: Jesus' disciples would also face another type of persecution. Even family members would turn against them because of their commitment to Him and His teachings.

²¹"**Brother will betray brother** to death, and a father his child. Children will even rise up against their parents and have them put to death. ²²You will be hated by everybody because of My name. And the one who endures to the end will be delivered. ²³But when they persecute you in one town, move on to another. For I assure you: You will not have covered the towns of Israel before the Son of Man comes. ²⁴A disciple is not above his teacher, or a slave above his master. ²⁵It is enough for a disciple to become like his teacher and a slave like his master. If they called the head of the house 'Beelzebul,' how much more the members of his household.

Fear God

²⁶"Therefore, **don't be afraid of them**, since there is nothing covered that won't be uncovered, and nothing hidden that won't be made known. ²⁷What I tell you in the dark, speak in the light. What you hear in a whisper, proclaim on the housetops. ²⁸Don't fear those who kill the body but are not able to kill the soul; but rather, fear Him who is able to destroy both soul and body in hell. ²⁹Aren't two sparrows sold for a penny? Yet not one of them falls to the ground without your Father's consent. ³⁰But even the hairs of your head have all been counted. ³¹Don't be afraid therefore; you are worth more than many sparrows.

³²"Therefore, everyone who will acknowledge Me before men, I will also acknowledge Him before My Father in heaven. ³³But whoever denies Me before men, I will also deny him before My Father in heaven. ³⁴Don't assume that I came to bring peace on the earth. I did not come to bring peace, but a sword. ³⁵For I came to turn 'A man against his father, a daughter against her mother, a daughter-in-law against her mother-in-law; ³⁶and a man's enemies will be the members of his household.' ³⁷The person who loves father or mother more than Me is not worthy of Me; the person who loves son or daughter more than Me is not worthy of Me. ³⁸And whoever doesn't take up his cross and follow Me is not worthy of Me. ³⁹Anyone finding his life will lose it, and anyone losing his life because of Me will find it.

A Cup of Cold Water

⁴⁰"The one who welcomes you welcomes Me, and the one who welcomes Me welcomes Him who sent Me. ⁴¹Anyone who welcomes a prophet because he is a prophet will receive a prophet's reward. And anyone who welcomes a righteous person because he's righteous will receive a righteous person's reward. ⁴²And

---

don't be afraid of them: The disciples were encouraged not to be afraid of their persecutors. Whatever the charges brought against them, the truth would win out. They should not hesitate to proclaim "in the light" what Jesus had taught them in secret.

whoever gives just a cup of cold water to one of these little ones because he is a disciple—I assure you: He will never lose his reward!"

Lk 9:6aSo they went out and traveled from village to village, proclaiming the good news and Mk 6:12b–13that people should repent. 13And they were driving out many demons, anointing many sick people with oil, and healing.

84. THE DEATH OF JOHN THE BAPTIZER

Matthew 14:6–12; Mark 6:17–29

Mk 6:17–20For **Herod himself** had given orders to arrest John and to chain him in prison on account of **Herodias, his brother Philip's wife**, whom he had married. 18John had been telling Herod, "It is not lawful for you to have your brother's wife!" 19So **Herodias held a grudge** against him and wanted to kill him. But she could not, 20because **Herod was in awe of John** and was protecting him, knowing he was a righteous and holy man. When Herod heard him he would be very disturbed, yet would hear him gladly.

21Now **an opportune day came** on his birthday, when Herod gave a banquet for his nobles, military commanders, and the leading men of Galilee. 22When **Herodias's own daughter** came in and **danced**, she pleased Herod and his guests. The king said to the girl, "**Ask me** whatever you want, and **I'll give it to you**." 23So he swore oaths to her: "Whatever you ask me I will give you, up to half my kingdom."

24aThen she **went** out and said **to her mother**, "What should I ask for?"

So they went out: The mission of the Twelve was an extension of Jesus' ministry. They preached repentance, healed the sick, and cast out demons. By words and works the Twelve were heralds of God's kingdom, setting a pattern that is followed in missionary service today.

84. THE DEATH OF JOHN THE BAPTIZER
Herod himself: This was Herod Antipas, the son of Herod the Great. Herod Antipas was the Roman governor over the province of Galilee and the area known as Perea on the eastern side of the Jordan River.
Herodias, his brother Philip's wife: Herod had divorced his own wife in order to marry a woman named Herodias, the wife of his own brother Philip of Rome.
Herodias held a grudge: John the Baptizer condemned this illicit relationship between Herod and Herodias, thus incurring the hatred of Herodias. Herod had John imprisoned in Machaerus, a fortress near the Dead Sea.
Herod was in awe of John: Herod feared John and his influence among the Jewish people. His fear of the man as a prophet caused him to protect John against any attempts his angry wife might make to have him executed.
an opportune day came: This was a day suited to the purposes of Herodias. She would not rest until John was dead.
Herodias's own daughter . . . danced: This girl was Salome, the niece of Herod and the daughter of his brother Philip. She performed her voluptuous and suggestive dancing to entertain Herod and his guests.
Ask me . . . I'll give it to you: Herod was pleased with Salome's performance. In a rash spirit of generosity before his guests, he promised to give her anything she wanted as a reward.
went . . . to her mother: Salome may have been told by her mother in advance what to ask for if Herod made such an offer. Perhaps she went to Herodias to make sure John's execution was still what her mother desired.
hurried to the king: Salome probably wanted to make her mother's request known before Herod had time to put limitations on his offer.

²⁴ᵇ"John the Baptist's head!" she said.

²⁵Immediately she **hurried to the king** and said, "I want you to give me **John the Baptist's head on a platter**—right now!"

²⁶Though the king was deeply distressed, **because of his oaths and the guests** he did not want to refuse her. ²⁷The king immediately sent for an executioner and commanded him to bring John's head. So he went and beheaded him in prison, ²⁸brought his head on a platter, and gave it to the girl. Then **the girl gave it to her mother.** ²⁹When his disciples heard about it, they came and removed his corpse and placed it in a tomb.

85. HEROD WONDERS ABOUT JESUS

Mark 6:14–16; Luke 9:7–9

ᴸᵏ ⁹:⁷ᵃ**Herod the tetrarch** heard about everything that was going on ᴹᵏ ⁶:¹⁴ᵃbecause Jesus' name had become well known. ᴸᵏ ⁹:⁷ᵇHe was perplexed, because some said that **John had been raised from the dead.**

ᴹᵏ ⁶:¹⁵But others said, "He's **Elijah**." Still others said, "He's a prophet—like **one of the prophets.**"

ᴸᵏ ⁹:⁹"I beheaded John," Herod said. "But who is this I hear such things about?" And **he wanted to see Him.**

John the Baptist's head on a platter: She asked for the prophet's head so she and her mother could see with their own eyes that John was dead. They wanted indisputable proof.

because of his oaths and the guests: Herod's oath to Salome, by itself, may not have compelled him to grant her request. But his guests were a complicating factor. He had made a promise in their presence. To save face, he felt he had to keep his word. Perhaps his guests even joined with the evil women against the man of God and shamed Herod into this murderous act.

the girl gave it to her mother: John's severed head must have seemed like a great gift to Herodias, since it assured her that the voice of her most dangerous enemy was now silent. But Herod and Herodias's sense of security was short-lived. Herod was soon filled with superstitious fears that John had risen from the dead in the person of Jesus (Luke 9:7).

85. HEROD WONDERS ABOUT JESUS

Herod the tetrarch: This was Herod Antipas, Roman governor of Galilee and Perea, who had executed John the Baptizer (see segment 84, "The Death of John the Baptizer," p. 100).

John had been raised from the dead: The people of the ancient world believed departed spirits had superhuman powers. Herod may have thought the risen John had brought these powers with him from the spirit world.

Elijah . . . one of the prophets: People had several opinions about who Jesus was. Some thought Elijah might have returned or that Jesus was a prophet like the great prophets of the Old Testament.

he [Herod] wanted to see Him: Jesus kept away from Herod because He knew how dangerous and scheming the Roman governor was (Luke 13:32). Herod apparently never saw Jesus face to face until the day of Jesus' crucifixion (Luke 23:8–12; see segment 194, "Pilate Sends Jesus to Herod Antipas," p. 231).

V. The Final Year: Jesus' Ministry in Judea and Perea

This period marks a turning point in Jesus' ministry. With the execution of John the Baptizer by Herod Antipas, He must have been graphically reminded of the fate that awaited Him. His popularity in Galilee began to wane as people realized He was not a military Messiah who would deliver them from Roman domination. The Pharisees and other religious leaders grew increasingly hostile in their opposition to Him and His teachings.

All these factors led Jesus to begin a series of strategic withdrawals from Galilee. He spent more time in seclusion with His disciples, training them for the mission that He planned to leave in their hands after His departure. And He warned them of His forthcoming death to prepare them for the tough times ahead.

During this final year of His ministry, Jesus also ministered more than He had done up to this point to the people in the surrounding Gentile regions—particularly in Perea, the area east of the Jordan River. He must have sensed the increasing rejection of the Jewish nation, so He was determined to give non-Jews the opportunity to respond to His message.

Jesus also confronted the Pharisees and other religious leaders on their home turf, where they were strongest and most influential—the province of Judea and the city of Jerusalem. He even raised Lazarus from the dead at the village of Bethany, just a few miles from the Holy City. Jesus was a spiritual Messiah and not a military figure, but He was no stranger to courage and decisive action.

86. Feeding of the Five Thousand

Matthew 14:13–21; Mark 6:30–44; Luke 9:10–17; John 6:1–15

Mk 6:30The apostles gathered around Jesus and reported to Him all that they had done and taught. Lk 9:10bHe took them along and [they] withdrew privately, Jn 6:1b**crossed the Sea of Galilee** (or Tiberias) Mk 6:32–33in the boat by themselves to a remote place, 33but many saw them leaving and recognized them. Then they ran there on foot from all the towns and arrived ahead of them.

Jn 6:2And a huge crowd was following Him because they saw the signs that He was performing on the sick. Lk 9:11bHe welcomed them, spoke to them about the kingdom of God, and cured those who needed healing. Mk 6:34He . . . had

---

86. Feeding of the Five Thousand

crossed the Sea of Galilee: Jesus and His disciples probably set out from Capernaum and sailed to a sparsely populated place on the opposite shore of Lake Galilee about five miles away. They were trying to get away from the crowds for some much-needed rest. But the crowds followed Jesus and His party by running along the northern shore of the lake. They traveled faster than the boat and were waiting for Him when He arrived.

compassion on them, because they were like sheep without a shepherd. Then He began to teach them many things.

^Jn 6:4^Now **the Passover**, a Jewish festival, **was near**. ^Lk 9:12^Late in the day, the Twelve approached and said to Him, "Send the crowd away, so they can go into the surrounding villages and countryside to find food and lodging, because we are in a deserted place here."

^Mt 14:16^"They don't need to go away," Jesus told them. "You give them something to eat." ^Jn 6:5b–6^**He asked Philip**, "Where will we buy bread so these people can eat?" ^6^He asked this to test him, for He Himself knew what He was going to do.

^7^Philip answered, "Two hundred denarii worth of bread wouldn't be enough for each of them to have a little."

Five Loaves and Two Fish

^8^One of His disciples, Andrew, Simon Peter's brother, said to Him, ^9^"There's a boy here who has **five barley loaves and two fish**—but what are they for so many?"

Two Feedings of the Crowds

The feeding of the five thousand is the only miracle of Jesus that appears in all four Gospels. But He also fed another crowd of people in a similar miracle a little later in His ministry (see segment 92, "Feeding of the Four Thousand," p. 114). This has to be a separate and distinct event because it is recorded as such by Matthew (15:29–38) and Mark (8:1–9).

Some of the details in these miracles are similar. For example, Jesus multiplied a few pieces of bread and fish to feed both crowds. But there are also distinct differences in these two events. The five thousand were a Jewish crowd in Jewish territory. The four thousand were a predominantly Gentile crowd in a Gentile region.

By recording the second feeding miracle, perhaps Matthew and Mark wanted to show the progressive breaking down of the wall of prejudice through Jesus' ministry. Jesus showed no partiality toward people because of their race. What He did for Jews He also did for Gentiles. He is the universal Savior.

---

the Passover . . . was near: This statement helps to explain the gathering of so many people in this isolated region. Pilgrims on their way to the Passover Festival in Jerusalem would gladly go several miles out of their way to see the great prophet whom they had heard about perform a miracle.

He asked Philip: According to Luke's account, the disciples were the first to approach Jesus about the crowds and their plight (Luke 9:12). Perhaps they were hungry themselves. Their own discomfort made them think about the problem the people were facing. Jesus tested Philip to see how he would respond to this problem. He asked Philip where they could buy bread to feed the people, knowing He had the power to work a miracle on their behalf. But Philip wondered where they would get the money to buy bread for the crowd.

five barley loaves and two fish: Another disciple, Andrew, had inquired among the crowd to see what food was available. He found a boy with two sardine-size fish and several small barley rolls—typical fare for the poor people of that area. Andrew knew these scant provisions were inadequate. "What are they for so many?" he asked.

Mt 14:18"Bring them here to Me," He said. Jn 6:10a**"Have the people sit down** Lk 9:14b**in groups of about fifty each."**

Jn 6:10bThere was plenty of grass in that place, so the men sat down Mk 6:39bon the green grass. Lk 9:14a(For **about five thousand men** were there.)

Mk 6:41–42Then He took the five loaves and the two fish, and looking up to heaven, He blessed and broke the loaves. And He **kept giving them to His disciples to set before the people.** He also divided the two fish among them all. 42Everyone ate and was filled.

Jn 6:12–13When they were full, He told His disciples, "**Collect the leftovers** so that nothing is wasted." 13So they collected them and filled twelve baskets with the pieces from the five barley loaves that were left over by those who had eaten.

Jn 6:14When the people saw the sign He had done, they said, "This really is the Prophet who was to come into the world!"

Mk 6:45Immediately He made His disciples get into the boat and go ahead of Him to the other side, to Bethsaida, while He dismissed the crowd.

Jn 6:15aTherefore, when Jesus knew that they were about to come and **take Him by force to make Him king**, Mt 14:23bHe went up on the mountain by Himself to pray. When evening came, He was there alone.

87. Jesus Walks on the Water

Matthew 14:22–36; Mark 6:45–56; John 6:16–21

Jn 6:16–18When evening came, His disciples went down to the sea, 17got into a boat, and started across the sea to Capernaum. Darkness had already set in, but Jesus had not yet come to them. 18Then a high wind arose, and the sea began to churn.

Have the people sit down: By arranging the people in small groups, Jesus saved His apostles time and labor in distributing the food. He ensured that each person was fed and that the reality of the miracle could not be questioned. This was also a convenient way of determining how many men were fed.

about five thousand men: Because of the distance of this site from Capernaum, probably not many women and children were present. They were not included in the count because Jewish custom did not permit the women to sit with the men.

kept giving them to His disciples to set before the people: After giving thanks, Jesus began distributing the food to His disciples (Mark 6:41b). They in turn passed it on to the people. Miraculously, the meager food supply never ran out. Not only did everyone eat, but they were "filled" (Mark 6:42). This showed His sufficiency in the face of the inadequacy of all other resources.

Collect the leftovers: So thorough was this miracle that food remained after the crowd had eaten. Jesus directed His disciples to collect the leftovers so nothing would be wasted. He set a good example for His followers in His stewardship of resources.

take Him by force to make Him king: Food has a way of making people agreeable, so it is not surprising that some in the crowd decided that Jesus was "the Prophet who was to come into the world"—a reference to Deuteronomy 18:15, 18. Others ascribed to Him messianic qualities and decided He was the kind of person they would like to have as king. But this was far from Jesus' intentions, so He slipped away to a mountain retreat.

Mt 14:24But the boat was already over a mile from land [Jn 6:19a*After they had rowed about three or four miles*], battered by the waves, because **the wind was against them**. Mk 6:48aHe [Jesus] saw them being battered as they rowed. . . . Around three in the morning **He came toward them** walking on the sea, and wanted to pass by them.

Mt 14:26When the disciples saw Him walking on the sea, **they were terrified**. "It's a ghost!" they said, and cried out in fear.

27Immediately Jesus spoke to them. "Have courage! It is I. Don't be afraid."

28"Lord, if it's You," Peter answered Him, "command me to come to You on the water."

29a"Come!" He said.

29bAnd climbing out of the boat, **Peter started walking on the water** and came toward Jesus. 30But **when he saw** the strength of **the wind, he was afraid**. And beginning to sink he cried out, "Lord, save me!"

31Immediately Jesus reached out His hand, caught hold of him, and said to him, "You of little faith, why did you doubt?"

Mk 6:51aThen He got into the boat with them, and the wind ceased, Jn 6:21band at once the boat was at the shore where they were heading. Mk 6:51b–52They were completely astounded, 52because they did not understand about the loaves. Instead, their hearts were hardened.

Mt 14:33Then **those in the boat worshiped Him** and said, "Truly You are the Son of God!"

Mk 6:53–56When they had crossed over, **they came to land at Gennesaret** and beached the boat. 54As they got out of the boat, immediately people recognized

---

87. JESUS WALKS ON THE WATER

the wind was against them: This fierce wind was blowing from the west, the direction in which the disciples were rowing.

He came toward them: John's Gospel tells us that "Jesus had not yet come" to the disciples (John 6:17b). They must have been expecting Jesus to join them on their trip back across Lake Galilee to Capernaum. They may have skirted the shore, expecting Him to hail them and come on board.

they were terrified: The disciples were frustrated over their lack of progress against the wind and fearful of the storm. No wonder they were terrified when they saw this figure walking toward them on the water.

Peter started walking on the water: Peter insisted on walking out on the water to meet Jesus. He tended to rush into situations without considering the consequences of his actions. To test his faith—and the staying power of his trust—Jesus encouraged Peter to walk toward Him.

when he saw . . . the wind, he was afraid: As long as Peter's attention was fixed on Jesus, he stayed afloat. But when he was distracted by the power of the storm, his faith failed. Jesus took his hand to keep him from sinking.

those in the boat worshiped Him: This verse shows the disciples in one of their better moments, when they recognized Jesus as the divine Son of God. At times they accepted Him as the Messiah, God's divine messenger. But at other times they were puzzled and confused about who He was.

they came to land at Gennesaret: Gennesaret was a coastal plain south of the city of Capernaum. Since they had sailed for Capernaum, the boat was probably diverted to this area by the storm. Jesus and His disciples apparently passed through several towns in the plain of Gennesaret on their way north to Capernaum. Sick people were laid in the streets so he could touch them as He passed through (Mark 6:53–56).

Him. [55]They hurried throughout that vicinity and began to carry the sick on stretchers to wherever they heard He was. [56]Wherever He would go, into villages, towns, or the country, they laid the sick in the marketplaces and begged Him that they might touch just the tassel of His robe. And everyone who touched it was made well.

88. JESUS' MESSAGE ON THE BREAD OF LIFE

John 6:22–71

[22]The next day, the crowd that had stayed on the other side of the sea knew there had been only one boat. They also knew that Jesus had not boarded the boat with His disciples, but His disciples had gone off alone. [23]Some boats from Tiberias came near the place where they ate the bread after the Lord gave thanks. [24]When the crowd saw that neither Jesus nor His disciples were there, they got into the boats and went to Capernaum, looking for Jesus.

[25]When they found Him on the other side of the sea, they said to Him, "Rabbi, when did You get here?"

[26]Jesus answered, "I assure you: You are looking for Me, not because you saw the signs, but **because you ate the loaves** and were filled. [27]Don't work for the food that perishes but for the food that lasts for eternal life, which the Son of Man will give you, because on Him God the Father has set His seal of approval."

[28]**"What can we do to perform the works of God?"** they asked.

[29]Jesus replied, "This is the work of God: that you believe in the One He has sent."

[30]"Then what sign are You going to do so we may see and believe You?" they asked. "What are You going to perform? [31]**Our fathers ate the manna** in the desert, just as it is written: 'He gave them bread from heaven to eat.'"

---

88. JESUS' MESSAGE ON THE BREAD OF LIFE

because you ate the loaves: Jesus accused the crowd of following Him because of the food He had provided. He warned them not to work for food that spoils but for the kind of food that lasts forever. Jesus claimed that He was the source of this bread of everlasting life, because He had been sent by the Father.

What can we do to perform the works of God? Jesus had come to provide food that would satisfy them forever. This kind of food cannot be attained by working for it; it can only be received as a gift from God (see Isa. 55:1–2). The people misunderstood. They wanted to know what they must do in order to perform the works of God. Jesus told them it was a matter of believing, not working.

Our fathers ate the manna: The crowds asked for a sign, even though they had witnessed Him feeding the five thousand people only the day before. Jesus' reference to food brought to their minds the manna that their forefathers had eaten in the wilderness. Jewish tradition credited Moses with the manna, but Jesus emphasized that God gave the manna. Jewish tradition also expected manna to accompany the Messiah's coming, but Jesus insisted that He was the true life-giving bread from heaven.

The Father and the True Bread

³²Jesus said to them, I assure you: Moses didn't give you the bread from heaven, but My Father gives you the true bread from heaven. ³³For the bread of God is the One who comes down from heaven and gives life to the world."

³⁴Then they said, "Sir, give us this bread always!"

³⁵"**I am the bread of life**," Jesus told them. "No one who comes to Me will ever be hungry, and no one who believes in Me will ever be thirsty again. ³⁶But as I told you, you've seen Me, and yet you do not believe. ³⁷Everyone the Father gives Me will come to Me, and the one who comes to Me I will never cast out. ³⁸For I have come down from heaven, not to do My will, but the will of Him who sent Me. ³⁹This is the will of Him who sent Me: that I should lose none of those He has given Me but should raise them up on the last day. ⁴⁰For this is the will of My Father: that everyone who sees the Son and believes in Him may have eternal life, and I will raise him up on the last day."

⁴¹Therefore **the Jews started complaining** about Him, because He said, "I am the bread that came down from heaven." ⁴²They were saying, "Isn't this Jesus the

---

The "I Am" Statements of Jesus in John's Gospel

Jesus' claim to be the Bread of Life is one of seven "I Am" statements by Him in the Gospel of John. Here's a complete list of these declarations and their theological meanings:

1. *"I am the bread of life" (John 6:35). Jesus offers permanent spiritual sustenance to the believer.*
2. *"I am the light of the world" (John 8:12). Jesus offers guidance and direction to a world in darkness.*
3. *"I am the door of the sheep" (John 10:7). Jesus cares for and protects those who belong to Him.*
4. *"I am the good shepherd" (John 10:11, 14). Jesus is committed to keeping watch over His people.*
5. *"I am the resurrection and the life" (John 11:25). Jesus is Lord of life and the victor over death.*
6. *"I am the way, the truth, and the life" (John 14:6). As the source of all truth about God, Jesus is the only way to the Father.*
7. *"I am the true vine" (John 15:1). Believers are like branches off the main vine. His love flows through us as we bear fruit for the good of His kingdom.*

I am the bread of life: As the Bread of Life, Jesus offers nourishment that satisfies forever. This is in contrast to the manna, which satisfied hunger only temporarily. In order to receive the Bread of Life, people must believe. Although these people had seen what He did, they did not believe.

the Jews started complaining: The religious leaders began to whisper that this Jesus who was making such great claims was a local nobody. They tried to discredit Him by pointing out that He was just the son of a Nazareth carpenter named Joseph.

son of Joseph, whose father and mother we know? How can He now say, 'I have come down from heaven'?"

⁴³Jesus answered them, "Stop complaining among yourselves. ⁴⁴No one can come to Me **unless the Father** who sent Me **draws him**, and I will raise him up on the last day. ⁴⁵It is written in the Prophets: 'And they will all be taught by God.' Everyone who has listened to and learned from the Father comes to Me— ⁴⁶not that anyone has seen the Father except the One who is from God. He has seen the Father.

⁴⁷"I assure you: Anyone who believes has eternal life. ⁴⁸I am the bread of life. ⁴⁹Your fathers ate the manna in the desert, and they died. ⁵⁰This is the bread that comes down from heaven so that anyone may eat of it and not die. ⁵¹I am the living bread that came down from heaven. If anyone eats of this bread he will live forever. The bread that I will give for the life of the world is My flesh."

⁵²At that, the Jews argued among themselves, "How can this man give us His flesh to eat?"

⁵³So Jesus said to them, "I assure you: Unless you **eat the flesh of the Son of Man** and drink His blood, you do not have life in yourselves. ⁵⁴Anyone who eats My flesh and drinks My blood has eternal life, and I will raise him up on the last day, ⁵⁵because My flesh is true food and My blood is true drink. ⁵⁶The one who eats My flesh and drinks My blood lives in Me, and I in him. ⁵⁷Just as the living Father sent Me and I live because of the Father, so the one who feeds on Me will live because of Me. ⁵⁸This is the bread that came down from heaven; it is not like the manna your fathers ate—and they died. The one who eats this bread will live forever."

⁵⁹He said these things while teaching in the synagogue in Capernaum. ⁶⁰Therefore, when many of His disciples heard this, they said, "This teaching is hard! Who can accept it?"

⁶¹Jesus, knowing in Himself that His disciples were complaining about this, asked them, "Does this offend you? ⁶²Then what if you were to observe the Son of Man ascending to where He was before? ⁶³The Spirit is the One who gives life. The flesh doesn't help at all. The words that I have spoken to you are spirit and are life. ⁶⁴But there are some among you who don't believe." (For Jesus knew from the beginning those who would not believe and the one who would betray Him.) ⁶⁵He said, "This is why I told you that no one can come to Me unless it is granted to him by the Father."

---

unless the Father . . . draws him: Jesus ignored the slur and gave the reason for this antagonistic attitude toward Him. Only those who are drawn by the Father come to Jesus and believe in Him. The religious leaders were proud of their superior knowledge of spiritual matters, but they were actually resisting the will of God.

eat the flesh of the Son of Man: With these words, Jesus referred to His atoning death for the sins of the world.

⁶⁶From that moment **many of His disciples turned back** and no longer walked with Him. ⁶⁷Therefore Jesus said to the Twelve, "You don't want to go away too, do you?"

⁶⁸Simon Peter answered, "Lord, to whom should we go? You have the words of eternal life. ⁶⁹And we have come to believe and know that You are the Holy One of God!"

⁷⁰Jesus replied to them, "Didn't I choose you, the Twelve? Yet one of you is the Devil!" ⁷¹He was referring to Judas, Simon Iscariot's son, one of the Twelve, because he was going to betray Him.

89. PHARISEES CRITICIZE JESUS BECAUSE OF UNWASHED HANDS

Matthew 15:1–20; Mark 7:1–23

Mk 7:1–5The Pharisees and some of the scribes who had come from Jerusalem gathered around Him. ²They observed that some of His disciples were eating their bread with **unclean**—that is, unwashed—**hands**. ³(For the Pharisees, in fact all the Jews, will not eat unless they wash their hands ritually, keeping the tradition of the elders. ⁴When they come from the marketplace, they do not eat unless they have washed. And there are many other customs they have received and keep, like the washing of cups, jugs, copper utensils, and dining couches). ⁵Then the Pharisees and the scribes asked Him, "Why don't Your disciples live according to the tradition of the elders, instead of eating bread with ritually unclean hands?"

⁶But He said to them, "Isaiah prophesied correctly about **you hypocrites**, as it is written: 'This people honors Me with their lips, but their heart is far from Me. ⁷They worship Me in vain, teaching as doctrines the commands of men.' ⁸Disregarding the commandment of God, **you keep the tradition of men**."

---

many of His disciples turned back: These concepts were difficult for some of the followers of Jesus. They "turned back and no longer walked with Him" (John 6:66). Were they dissatisfied with the answer He gave to the crowd? Did they become sympathetic with the critics who found His words hard to understand? But Simon Peter made a strong affirmation of faith in Jesus (John 6:68–69).

89. PHARISEES CRITICIZE JESUS BECAUSE OF UNWASHED HANDS

unclean . . . hands: Instead of attacking Jesus directly, the Pharisees and scribes tried to get at Him by condemning His disciples. They criticized them for failing to perform a ceremonial washing of their hands before eating.

you hypocrites: Jesus issued a sharp charge of His own against the religious leaders. He called them hypocrites. This word was used by the Greeks to describe actors who played a part. Jesus accused them of making outward claims of devotion to God while their hearts were actually far from God.

you keep the tradition of men: Jesus referred to the traditions of the elders as human rules, not God's command. He considered these oral laws to be nothing more than the interpretations of human beings. The scribes and Pharisees had substituted human traditions for the Word of God.

[9]He also said to them, "You splendidly disregard God's commandment, so that you may maintain your tradition! [10]For Moses said: 'Honor your father and your mother;' and, 'Whoever speaks evil of father or mother must be put to death.' [11]But you say, 'If a man tells his father or mother, "Whatever benefit you might have received from me is *Corban*"' (that is, a gift committed to the temple), [12]"you no longer let him do anything for his father or mother. [13]You revoke God's word by your tradition that you have handed down. And you do many other similar things."

[14]Summoning the crowd again, He told them, "Listen to Me, all of you, and understand: [15]Nothing that goes into a man from outside can defile him, but **the things that come out of a man are what defile** a man [Mt 15:11 *It's not what goes into the mouth that defiles a man, but what comes out of the mouth, this defiles a man*]. [16]If anyone has ears to hear, he should listen!"

Mt 15:12Then the disciples came up and told Him, "Do You know that the Pharisees took offense when they heard this statement?"

[13]He replied, "Every plant that My heavenly Father didn't plant will be uprooted. [14]Leave them alone! They are blind guides. And if the blind guide the blind, both will fall into a pit."

Mk 7:17–22When He went into the house away from the crowd, the disciples asked Him about the parable. [18]And He said to them, "Are you also as lacking in understanding? Don't you realize that nothing going into a man from the outside can defile him? [19]For it doesn't go into his heart but into the stomach, and is eliminated." (As a result, He made all foods clean.) [20]Then He said, "What comes out of a man—that defiles a man. [21]For from within, out of people's hearts, come evil thoughts, sexual immoralities, thefts, murders, [22]adulteries, greed, evil actions, deceit,

The Traditions of the Elders

The traditions of the elders was the oral interpretation of the first five books of the Old Testament, accumulated and passed on across the generations. These oral interpretations were an attempt to apply the Old Testament law to all of life. The traditions of the elders was considered by the scribes and Pharisees to be as authoritative as the written Scriptures.

Among the oral traditions were requirements about various washings. Because the Jews considered certain foods and certain people unclean, they decided that the safest way to deal with defilement was to wash. Such washings were supposed to remove the defilement caused by touching unclean food or unclean people. It was scandalous to the scribes and Pharisees that Jesus and His disciples did not participate in the ceremonial washing of their hands before eating.

---

the things that come out of a man are what defile: Jesus shattered the Jewish ceremonial system by pointing out that true religion does not consist of outward rituals but inner purity. Real religion shows up in what a person does, not in what he eats or touches. A person is defiled by evil attitudes, because these lead to evil actions.

lewdness, stinginess, blasphemy, pride, and foolishness. ^{Mt 15:20}These are the things that defile a man, but eating with unwashed hands does not defile a man."

90. Jesus Heals the Daughter of a Canaanite Woman

Matthew 15:21–28; Mark 7:24–30

^{Mt 15:21}When Jesus left there, **He withdrew to** the area of **Tyre and Sidon**. ^{Mk 7:24b}He entered a house and did not want anyone to know it, but He could not escape notice. ^{Mt 15:22a}Just then **a Canaanite woman** from that region came, ^{Mk 7:25b}fell at His feet, ^{Mt 15:22b}and kept crying out, "Have mercy on me, Lord, Son of David! My daughter is cruelly tormented by a demon." ^{Mk 7:26}Now the woman was Greek, a Syrophoenician by birth, and she kept asking Him to drive the demon out of her daughter.

^{Mt 15:23}Yet **He did not say a word to her.** So His disciples approached Him and urged Him, "Send her away, because she cries out after us."

²⁴He replied, "I was sent only to the lost sheep of the house of Israel."

²⁵But she came, knelt before Him, and said, "Lord, help me!"

^{Mk 7:27}And He said to her, "Allow the children to be satisfied first, because it isn't right to take the children's bread and throw it to the dogs."

^{Mt 15:27}"Yes, Lord," she said, "yet **even the dogs eat the crumbs** that fall from their masters' table!"

²⁸Then Jesus replied to her, "Woman, your faith is great. Let it be done for you as you want [^{Mk 7:29b}*Because of this reply, you may go. The demon has gone out of your daughter*]." And from that moment her daughter was cured. ^{Mk 7:30}When she went back to her home, she found her child lying on the bed, and the demon was gone.

---

90. Jesus Heals the Daughter of a Canaanite Woman

He withdrew to . . . Tyre and Sidon: In His search for rest, Jesus left the territory ruled by Herod Antipas, the Roman official who had put John the Baptizer to death. He withdrew to Gentile territory in Phoenicia along the coast of the Mediterranean Sea.

a Canaanite woman: This woman was a Gentile and a native of the area. She had heard of Jesus' miracles of healing, and she asked Him to heal her daughter.

He did not say a word to her: Jesus did not respond to the woman's request. To the disciples, this Gentile woman was bothering Jesus. She must have been walking with the group as she repeated her plea. In tune with the feeling of the disciples, Jesus seemed to conclude the matter by declaring His mission to be exclusively to "the lost sheep of the house of Israel."

even the dogs eat the crumbs: But the woman was persistent. She fell at Jesus' feet with the cry, "Lord, help me." He still seemed unmoved as He spoke of not giving the children's bread to dogs. The word He used was "little dogs," puppies, or family pets. If we could have seen the expression on His face as He said this, we might better understand the hopeful reply of the woman. She rose to the occasion, was commended for her faith, and her daughter was healed.

91. Jesus Heals a Deaf Man

Mark 7:31–37

³¹Again, leaving the region of Tyre, He went by way of Sidon to the Sea of Galilee, **through the region of the Decapolis**. ³²And **they brought to Him a deaf man** who also had a speech difficulty, and begged Him to lay His hand on him. ³³So He took him away from the crowd privately. After putting His **fingers** in the man's **ears** and spitting, He touched his **tongue**. ³⁴Then, looking up to heaven, He sighed deeply and said to him, *"Ephphatha!"* (that is, "Be opened!"). ³⁵Immediately his ears were opened, his speech difficulty was removed, and he began to speak clearly. ³⁶Then **He ordered them to tell no one**, but the more He would order them, the more they would proclaim it.

³⁷They were extremely astonished and said, "He has done everything well! He even makes deaf people hear, and people unable to speak, talk!"

The Decapolis

The Decapolis, a distinct region as large as the province of Galilee, was located south of Lake Galilee and east of the Jordan River. Most of the citizens of the Decapolis were of Greek heritage and background. Thus, Jesus was in Gentile territory.

Jesus had visited this Gentile region at least once before. On that occasion He cast several demons out of a demented man (see segment 79, "Jesus Heals a Wild Man among the Tombs," p. 91).

Mark's description of Jesus' trip from Sidon on the coast of the Mediterranean Sea to Lake Galilee "through the region of the Decapolis" shows the Gospel writers were selective in the activities of Jesus that they reported. This was a journey of more than 60 miles on foot, requiring several days even if Jesus had not stopped to minister along the way. But Mark covers this journey in one brief sentence.

---

91. Jesus Heals a Deaf Man

through the region of the Decapolis: Jesus left the region of Tyre, traveled northward toward Sidon, and then made a broad sweep east and south. He remained in Gentile territory, skirting the province of Galilee. The journey would have been long and arduous. He probably used the time of solitude to instruct the Twelve.

they brought to Him a deaf man: Friends of this man must have brought him to Jesus. He was probably a Gentile.

fingers . . . ears . . . tongue: Jesus drew the man away from the crowd before He began a process of healing that was appropriate to the sufferer. First, He put His fingers in the man's ears to emphasize his defective hearing. Then He put saliva on his tongue, indicating that both his hearing and speech were matters of concern. Saliva was regarded as a remedy for some conditions. Then Jesus looked up to heaven and sighed.

Ephphatha! Jesus spoke one word, *Ephphatha*, in the language of everyday Palestinian speech—Aramaic. This command, meaning "be opened," was obeyed immediately by the deaf man's ears and tongue.

He ordered them to tell no one: Jesus avoided the kind of popularity that centered in works of healing. He had an important ministry of teaching to discharge, and curious crowds could hinder this. But He could not restrain the enthusiasm of the crowds. They told everyone about the miracle they had seen.

92. FEEDING OF THE FOUR THOUSAND

Matthew 15:29–38; Mark 8:1–10

Mt 15:29–31Moving on from there, Jesus passed along the Sea of Galilee. He went up on a mountain and sat there, 30and large crowds came to Him, having with them those who were **lame, blind, deformed**, unable to speak, and many others. They put them at His feet, and He healed them. 31So the crowd was amazed when they saw those unable to speak talking, the deformed restored, the lame walking, and the blind seeing. And they gave glory to the God of Israel.

32Now Jesus summoned His disciples and said, "I have compassion on the crowd, because they've already stayed with Me three days and have nothing to eat. I don't want to send them away hungry; otherwise they might collapse on the way, Mk 8:3band some of them have come a long distance."

Mt 15:33The disciples said to Him, "Where could we get enough bread in this desolate place to fill such a crowd?"

34a"How many loaves do you have?" Jesus asked them.

34b"Seven," they said, "and a few small fish."

35After commanding the crowd to sit down on the ground, 36He took the seven loaves and the fish, and He gave thanks, broke them, and kept on giving them to the disciples, and the disciples gave them to the crowds. 37They all ate and were filled. Then they collected the leftover pieces—seven large baskets full. 38Now those who ate were **four thousand men**, besides women and children. Mk 8:9bHe dismissed them.

93. PHARISEES AND SADDUCEES ASK FOR A SIGN

Matthew 15:39–16:4; Mark 8:11–12

Mt 15:39aAfter dismissing the crowds, He Mk 8:10agot into the boat with His disciples Mt 15:39band **went to the region of Magadan** [Mk 8:10b *district of Dalmanutha*]. Mt 16:1aThe Pharisees and Sadducees approached Mk 8:11band began to argue with Him, demanding of Him **a sign from heaven** to test Him.

---

92. FEEDING OF THE FOUR THOUSAND

lame, blind, deformed: Matthew gives us some insight into the prevalence of sickness and disease in Jesus' day. No attempt is made to catalog all the ailments with which people were afflicted. When they brought these poor sufferers to Jesus, they had reached a point of despair.

four thousand men: All four Gospels had already recorded the feeding of the five thousand. This second similar miracle, recorded by Matthew and Mark, seems to have been performed for the benefit of Gentiles (see segment 86, "Feeding of the Five Thousand," p. 103).

93. PHARISEES AND SADDUCEES ASK FOR A SIGN

went to the region of Magadan: Jesus and His disciples apparently crossed over to the western shore of Lake Galilee. The word *Magadan* probably refers to Magdala, a city on the western shore of the lake.

a sign from heaven: The Pharisees and Sadducees refused to accept Jesus' miracles as signs of His messiahship. They had accused Him on other occasions of performing such miracles in the power of Beelzebub (see segment 63, "Jesus

Mt 16:2–3He answered them: "When evening comes you say, 'It will be good weather, because the sky is red.' 3And in the morning, 'Today will be stormy because the sky is red and threatening.' You know how to read the appearance of the sky, but **you can't read the signs of the times**."

Mk 8:12aBut sighing deeply in His spirit, He said, "Why does this generation demand a sign? Mt 16:4An evil and adulterous generation wants a sign, but **no sign will be given** to it except the sign of Jonah." Then He left them and went away.

94. Jesus Warns about the Influence of Pharisees and Sadducees

Matthew 16:5–12; Mark 8:13–21

Mk 8:13Then He left them, got on board the boat again, and went to the other side. Mt 16:5When the disciples reached the other shore, they had forgotten to take bread. Mk 8:14They . . . had only one loaf with them in the boat.

Mt 16:6Then Jesus told them [Mk 8:15a*began to give them strict orders*], "Watch out and **beware of the yeast of the Pharisees** and Sadducees [Mk 8:15b*the yeast of the Pharisees and the yeast of Herod*]."

Mt 16:7And they discussed among themselves, "**We didn't bring any bread!**"

8Aware of this, Jesus said, "You of little faith! Why are you discussing among yourselves that you do not have bread? 9a**Don't you understand yet?** Mk 8:17b–19aIs your heart hardened? 18'Do you have eyes, and not see, and do you have ears, and not hear?' And do you not remember? 19aWhen I broke the five loaves for the five thousand, how many baskets full of pieces of bread did you collect?"

19b"Twelve," they told Him.

Answers the Blasphemous Charge of the Pharisees," p. 80). They asked Jesus for a sign that only God could give to show He was who He claimed to be.

you can't read the signs of the times: Jesus declared that the Pharisees could read the signs that signified a change in the weather. But they refused to believe He was the fulfillment of the Old Testament prophecies about the coming Messiah and servant of God. They had seen His miraculous power with their own eyes, but still they refused to believe.

no sign will be given: Jesus knew it was useless to give new proofs of His messiahship to those who were blind to the proofs that already existed.

94. Jesus Warns about the Influence of Pharisees and Sadducees

beware of the yeast of the Pharisees: Jesus compared the influence of the Pharisees to yeast in bread. Yeast was a symbol of evil to the Jews. Jesus was referring to their legalism and hypocrisy.

We didn't bring any bread! The disciples did not understand Jesus' reference to yeast. They assumed He was referring to some particular type of bread that the Jews considered unclean. Perhaps they also thought Jesus was criticizing them for failing to bring bread for their journey.

Don't you understand yet? After a gentle rebuke of His disciples, Jesus went on to tell them what He was talking about. Notice the contrast in His attitudes toward the Pharisees and the disciples. Both were puzzled by Jesus' teachings. Jesus had only condemnation for the Pharisees because they were deliberately blind about spiritual matters. But for the disciples, who were slow to understand rather than stubborn, He had great patience.

^{20a}"When I broke the seven loaves for the four thousand, how many large baskets full of pieces of bread did you collect?"

^{20b}"Seven," they said.

^{21a}And He said to them, ^{Mt 16:11–12} "Why is it you don't understand that when I told you, 'Beware of the yeast of the Pharisees and Sadducees,' it wasn't about bread?" ¹²Then they understood that He did not tell them to beware of the yeast in bread, but of the teaching of the Pharisees and Sadducees.

Jesus and the Pharisees

As Jesus' popularity grew, His conflict with the Jewish leaders—particularly the Pharisees—intensified. These people considered themselves the guardians of the religious traditions of the Jewish nation. To them Jesus was a dangerous revolutionary who disregarded the law and its requirements and encouraged others to do so.

The zeal of the Pharisees was not a bad thing in itself. They worked hard to overcome the spiritual permissiveness brought on by the Greek and Roman cultures. The word Pharisee means "separated ones," and they wanted to keep their religion pure, free of foreign influence and moral corruption.

But the problem was that their zeal led to legalism and hypocrisy. They allowed the basic laws of God to degenerate into a complicated system of petty rules and requirements. To them these were the tests of a person's religious faith. They majored in minor issues while ignoring the things that really mattered.

Jesus expressed the problem of the Pharisees perfectly in this biting assessment: "Woe to you, scribes and Pharisees, hypocrites! You pay a tenth of mint, dill and cumin, yet you have neglected the more important matters of the law—justice, mercy and faith. These things should have been done without neglecting the others. Blind guides! You strain out a gnat, yet gulp down a camel!" (Matt. 23:23–24).

---

95. JESUS HEALS A BLIND MAN AT BETHSAIDA

Mark 8:22–26

²²Then **they came to Bethsaida**. They brought a blind man to Him and begged Him to touch him. ²³He **took the blind man** by the hand and brought him **out of the village. Spitting on his eyes** and laying His hands on him, He asked him, "Do you see anything?"

---

95. JESUS HEALS A BLIND MAN AT BETHSAIDA

they came to Bethsaida: This was not the village outside Capernaum, but Bethsaida Julias, a town on the east side of the Jordan River, near the spot where it flows into Lake Galilee. Jesus and His disciples were traveling northward toward Caesarea Philippi.

took the blind man . . . out of the village: Perhaps Jesus took the blind man away to avoid the crowd. He did not heal people just to create a spectacle.

Spitting on his eyes: For two other instances when Jesus healed with saliva and the possible meaning, see segment 91, "Jesus Heals a Deaf Man," page 113, and segment 112, "Jesus Heals a Man Blind from Birth," page 135.

²⁴He looked up and said, "I see people—they look to me like trees walking."

²⁵**Again He placed His hands on his eyes**, and he saw distinctly. He was cured and could see everything clearly. ²⁶Then He sent him home, saying, "Don't even go into the village."

96. PETER'S GREAT CONFESSION ABOUT JESUS

Matthew 16:13–20; Mark 8:27–30; Luke 9:18–20

Mt 16:13When Jesus came to the region of **Caesarea Philippi**, He asked His disciples, "**Who do people say** that the Son of Man is?"

¹⁴And they said, "Some say John the Baptist; others, Elijah; still others, Jeremiah or one of the prophets [Lk 9:19b *still others, that one of the ancient prophets has come back*]."

¹⁵"**But** you," He asked them, "**who do you say that I am?**"

¹⁶Simon Peter answered, "You are the Messiah, the Son of the living God! [Lk 9:20b *God's Messiah*]."

¹⁷And Jesus responded, "**Blessed are you, Simon** son of Jonah, because flesh and blood did not reveal this to you, but My Father in heaven. ¹⁸And I also say to you that you are Peter, and on this rock I will build My church, and the **forces of Hades** will not overpower it. ¹⁹I will give you the **keys of the kingdom of**

Again He placed His hands on his eyes: This is the only recorded miracle of Jesus that took place in two stages. He touched the blind man's eyes twice before he could see clearly. Perhaps this emphasized that it took two feedings of the crowds on the part of Jesus to open the blind eyes of the disciples (see segment 86, "Feeding of the Five Thousand," p. 103 and segment 92, "Feeding of the Four Thousand," p. 114).

96. PETER'S GREAT CONFESSION ABOUT JESUS

Caesarea Philippi: This town about 25 miles north of Lake Galilee was named for Herod Philip and for Tiberias Caesar, the emperor of Rome. This region contained a shrine dedicated to the pagan god Pan. Since it was associated with pagan worship, Caesarea Philippi was an impressive location for Jesus to seek an answer from His disciples about His own identity.

Who do people say: Jesus first asked His disciples what others were saying about His identity. They replied that He was being identified as Elijah, John the Baptizer, Jeremiah, or one of the prophets.

But . . . who do you say that I am? Jesus addressed this question to all the disciples, but Peter was the one who answered. He often served as spokesman for the group. Peter's confession shows that he believed that Jesus was the promised Messiah. This was a huge step of faith for the disciples, but unfortunately it was qualified by the prevailing concept of messiahship. Even the disciples clung to the idea that Jesus would be a patriotic leader who would restore Israel's power and prestige.

Blessed are you, Simon: In pronouncing a blessing on Peter, Jesus declared that this faith of Peter's was not a purely human achievement. Peter had not reasoned his way to this conclusion. God had used the words and acts of Jesus to reveal to Peter that Jesus was His Son and the promised Messiah.

forces of Hades: This phrase could be interpreted as "the power of death." Thus, Jesus promised that the power of death would not be able to destroy His church. Jesus was soon to die, and many of His followers would be put to death; but death would not be able to overcome His church.

keys of the kingdom of heaven: The Lord is the One who receives people into His kingdom, but He has entrusted to us the task of pointing people to the open door.

heaven, and whatever you bind on earth will have been bound in heaven, and whatever you loose on earth will have been loosed in heaven."

²⁰And He gave the disciples orders to **tell no one that He was the Messiah.**

Peter: The Foundation of the Church?

Did Jesus promise the apostle Peter that His church would be built on him? What did Jesus mean when He said, "You are Peter, and on this rock I will build My church" (Matt. 16:18)?

A look at this passage in the original Greek language leads us to the correct interpretation. Jesus declared, "You are Peter [Petros]," that is, "a stone." Then Jesus added, "and on this rock [petra]," that is, a "ledge of rock," "I will build My church." He did not call Peter the rock foundation on which His church would be built. Jesus Himself is the foundation of the church (see 1 Cor. 3:11).

Another New Testament passage on the church also gives us additional insights on the meaning of Jesus' statement to Peter. The apostle Paul declared that the church is "built on the foundation of the apostles and prophets, with Christ Jesus Himself as the cornerstone" (Eph. 2:20). Perhaps Jesus was speaking of Peter as a representative of all the apostles. The testimony of the apostles, the unique eyewitnesses of Jesus, in a sense forms the foundation for the church.

---

97. JESUS PREDICTS HIS DEATH AND RESURRECTION

Matthew 16:21–28; Mark 8:31–9:1; Luke 9:21–27

Mt 16:21From then on Jesus began to point out to His disciples that He must go to Jerusalem and **suffer** many things from the elders, chief priests, and scribes, **be killed**, and be raised the third day. Mk 8:32aAnd He was openly talking about this. Mt 16:22Then **Peter** took Him aside and **began to rebuke Him,** "Oh no, Lord! This will never happen to You!"

---

tell no one that He was the Messiah: Jesus knew that many Jews were looking for an earthly king who would lead Israel to defeat the Romans and restore the nation to its former glory. If He were called the Messiah, this would fuel the hope of the people that He was this long-awaited political deliverer. But He had come as a spiritual leader, not a military conqueror. This is why He warned His disciples not to tell others what they knew about Him. After His death and resurrection, He would commission them to tell the whole world (Matt. 28:18–20).

97. JESUS PREDICTS HIS DEATH AND RESURRECTION

suffer . . . be killed: The time had come for a clear statement of the course Jesus would take to fulfill His mission. He spelled out the antagonism and rejection that would lead to His violent death. But this rejection would be countered by divine approval; He would "be raised the third day."

Peter . . . began to rebuke Him: Peter drew Jesus aside and began to scold Him for saying such a thing. This shows that Peter and the other disciples agreed with the popular expectations for an earthly messiah. They thought Jesus had come to be another king like David.

Mk 8:33aBut turning around and looking at His disciples, He rebuked Peter and said, Mt 16:23b**"Get behind Me, Satan!** You are an offense to Me, because you're not thinking about God's concerns, but man's."

Mk 8:34Summoning the crowd along with His disciples, He said to them, "If anyone wants to be My follower, he must deny himself, **take up his cross**, and follow Me. Mt 16:25–26For whoever wants to save his life will lose it, but whoever loses his life because of Me will find it. 26What will it benefit a man if he gains the whole world yet loses his life [Lk 9:25b*loses or forfeits himself*]? Or what will a man give in exchange for his life?

27"For the Son of Man is going to come with His angels in the glory of His Father, and then He will reward each according to what he has done. Mk 8:38For whoever is ashamed of Me and of My words in this adulterous and sinful generation, the Son of Man will also be ashamed of him when He comes in the glory of His Father with the holy angels. Mt 16:28I assure you: There are some of those standing here who will not taste death until they see the Son of Man coming in His kingdom [Lk 9:27b*until they see the kingdom of God*]."

98. JESUS IS TRANSFORMED BEFORE HIS DISCIPLES

Matthew 17:1–8; Mark 9:2–8; Luke 9:28–36

Lk 9:28–31About eight days after these words, He took along **Peter, John, and James**, and went up on the mountain to pray. 29As He was praying, the appearance of His face changed [Mt 17:2b*His face shone like the sun*], and His clothes became dazzling white [Mt 17:2c*became as white as the light*] [Mk 9:3*became dazzling, extremely white, as no launderer on earth could whiten them*]. 30Suddenly, two men were talking with Him—none other than **Moses and Elijah**. 31They appeared in glory and were speaking of His death, which He was about to accomplish in Jerusalem.

Get behind Me, Satan! Jesus condemned Peter with strong words. His attempt to divert Jesus from the way of the cross was a recurrence of the temptations that Jesus had faced at the beginning of His ministry. Satan's approach was to suggest some easier way for Jesus to fulfill His mission (see segment 22, "Jesus Tempted by Satan," p. 30). Peter was doing the same thing.

take up his cross: Jesus had another surprise for the disciples. Not only must He go to the cross, but anyone who followed Him had to take up his own cross. Christ demanded that His followers put God at the center of life and serve God by loving others in His name.

98. JESUS IS TRANSFORMED BEFORE HIS DISCIPLES

Peter, John, and James: The trio of disciples who accompanied Jesus on the mountain were His chosen companions on other significant occasions. Jesus was preparing them for special ministry in the future. Both Peter and James were eventually martyred, but John outlived most of his companions and fellow witnesses and became the author of the Fourth Gospel.

Moses and Elijah: These were two of the most important personalities in the Old Testament. Moses represented the law and Elijah represented the prophets. Thus, the Old Testament bore witness to Jesus in two people whose lives ended uniquely—Moses being buried by God (Deut. 34:5–6) and Elijah ascending to heaven in a whirlwind (2 Kgs. 2:1).

³²Peter and those with him were in a deep sleep, and when they became fully awake, they saw His glory and the two men who were standing with Him. ³³As the two men were departing from Him, Peter said to Jesus, "Master, **it's good for us to be here**! Let us make three tabernacles: one for You, one for Moses, and one for Elijah"—not knowing what he said [Mk 9:6 *because he did not know what he should say, since they were terrified*].

³⁴While he was saying this, **a cloud** appeared and overshadowed them. They became afraid as they entered the cloud. ³⁵Then **a voice** came from the cloud, saying: "This is My Son, the Chosen One; listen to Him!"

³⁶After the voice had spoken, **only Jesus was found** [Mt 17:8b *they saw no one, except Jesus Himself alone*]. They kept silent, and in those days told no one what they had seen.

The Transformation/Transfiguration of Jesus

What happened to Jesus when He was "transformed" or "transfigured" before these three disciples? It's impossible to know because Luke tells us only that His "face changed" and His clothes became "dazzling white."

We do know that Jesus had told His disciples several times that He would be glorified by the Father, received into heaven, and then would return to earth one day in all His glory (Matt. 25:31; Luke 24:26). In His transformation Jesus must have been giving these disciples a preview of His future glory. He probably did this to strengthen and encourage them for the ordeal that lay ahead—His crucifixion and death.

The timing of this event is also significant. Jesus' disciples had just confessed Him as the Messiah—the Christ, God's Son. Before this confession, He could not have revealed Himself to the Twelve in such a spectacular way. They would have been overwhelmed and awestruck, prone to follow Him through emotional reaction rather than by exercise of their free will.

---

it's good for us to be here: Peter was so caught up in this experience that he wanted to make it permanent. He could not ignore the conversation about Jesus' coming death, but he wanted to prevent, or at least postpone, that dreaded event.

a cloud . . . a voice: The descent of a cloud symbolized the presence of God, who acknowledged Jesus as His Son in an audible voice. It was important that all who heard Him speak should pay heed to His words, but particularly so for the three disciples with Jesus. According to the Gospel writers, God spoke aloud three times during the earthly ministry of Jesus. The other two occasions were at Jesus' baptism (Mark 1:11) and during His triumphal entry into Jerusalem (John 12:28).

only Jesus was found: This phrase shows that Jesus is God's one and only Son, superior even to the heroic Old Testament personalities, Moses and Elijah.

99. Jesus Discusses John the Baptizer and Elijah

Matthew 17:9–13; Mark 9:9–13

Mk 9:9–10As they were coming down from the mountain, He **ordered them to tell no one** what they had seen until the Son of Man had risen from the dead. 10They kept this word to themselves, discussing what "rising from the dead" meant.

11Then they began to question Him, "Why do the scribes say that Elijah must come first?"

12"Elijah does come first and restores everything," He replied. "How then is it written about the Son of Man that He must suffer many things and be treated with contempt? Mt 17:12–13 But I tell you: **Elijah has already come**, and they didn't recognize him. On the contrary, they did whatever they pleased to him. In the same way the Son of Man is going to suffer at their hands." 13Then the disciples understood that He spoke to them about John the Baptist.

100. Jesus Casts a Stubborn Demon Out of a Boy

Matthew 17:14–21; Mark 9:14–29; Luke 9:37–42

Mk 9:14–16**When they came to the disciples**, they saw a large crowd around them and **scribes disputing with them**. 15All of a sudden, when the whole crowd saw Him, they were amazed and ran to greet Him. 16Then He asked them, "What are you arguing with them about?"

17Out of the crowd, **one man answered Him**, "Teacher, I brought my son [Lk 9:38b*my only child*] to You. He has a spirit that makes him unable to speak [Mt 17:15a*Lord, . . . have mercy on my son, because he has seizures and suffers severely*]. 18Wherever it seizes him, it throws him down, and he foams at the mouth,

---

99. Jesus Discusses John the Baptizer and Elijah

ordered them to tell no one: Jesus' transformation was so mysterious that those who saw it were not qualified to discuss it with others. Perhaps Jesus thought their descriptions would lead to misunderstandings that would hinder His mission.

Elijah has already come: The three disciples raised a question about the prophet Elijah. Many people believed Elijah would come to prepare the way for the Messiah. Jesus declared that Elijah had already appeared in the person of John the Baptizer. John's role had not been recognized, and he had been executed (Matt. 14:1–12). The same fate awaited Jesus.

100. Jesus Casts a Stubborn Demon Out of a Boy

When they came to the disciples: These were the nine disciples who had been left at the foot of the mountain while Jesus was transformed before Peter, James, and John.

scribes disputing with them: These scribes had caught the apostles in a situation where they were unable to heal. The critics were probably taking advantage of this opportunity to discredit Jesus and His disciples before the people by asking sarcastic questions.

one man answered Him: The father of the boy who was the center of the controversy told Jesus what was going on. His child was deaf and he suffered from epileptic seizures. But he believed these physical ailments were produced by a demon or evil spirit.

grinds his teeth, and becomes rigid. So I asked Your disciples to drive it out, but they couldn't."

[19]He replied to them, "**O, unbelieving generation!** [Mt 17:17a*O unbelieving and rebellious generation*]. How long will I be with you? How long must I put up with you? Bring him to Me [Lk 9:41b*Bring your son here*]." [20]So they brought him to Him. When the spirit saw Him, it immediately convulsed the boy. He fell to the ground and rolled around, foaming at the mouth. [21a]"**How long has this been happening to him?**" Jesus asked his father.

[21b]"From childhood," he said. [22]"And many times it has thrown him into fire or water to destroy him. But **if You can do anything**, have compassion on us and help us."

[23]Then Jesus said to him, "'If You can?' Everything is possible to the one who believes."

[24]Immediately the father of the boy cried out, "**I do believe! Help my unbelief.**"

[25]When Jesus saw that a crowd was rapidly coming together, He rebuked the unclean spirit, saying to it, "You mute and deaf spirit, I command you: come out of him and never enter him again!"

[26]Then it came out, shrieking and convulsing him violently. The boy became like a corpse, so that many said, "He's dead." [27]But Jesus, taking him by the hand, raised him, and he stood up.

[28]After He went into a house, **His disciples asked Him privately**, "Why couldn't we drive it out?"

Mt 17:20"Because of your little faith," He told them. "For I assure you: If you have faith the size of a mustard seed, you will tell this mountain, 'Move from here to there,' and it will move. Nothing will be impossible for you."

O, unbelieving generation! Jesus addressed this rebuke to everyone in the crowd and not particularly to the disciples. Unbelief is contagious. It started with the hostile scribes and then spread to the fickle crowds, finally creating doubt in the disciples.

How long has this been happening to him? Jesus immediately took charge of the situation. After observing one of the boy's seizures, He wanted to know how long these had been happening. The father's response, "From childhood," established the seriousness and permanence of his illness.

if You can do anything: The father had already seen Jesus' disciples fail to heal his son. Perhaps he wondered if there was anything to those stories he had heard about the wonderful miracle worker from Capernaum. Jesus caught the note of doubt in this father's request. He repeated his phrase, "if You can," back to him to encourage a stronger faith.

I do believe! Help my unbelief: This declaration of the father shows that he did have faith in Jesus. He was so anxious to have his son healed that he asked Jesus to give him even more faith. Jesus honored his request by ordering the demon to come out of his son.

His disciples asked Him privately: The disciples later asked Jesus why they were not able to drive the demon out of this boy. He told them they had failed not because of the weakness of Jesus' power—power He had delegated to them as His helpers—but because of their lack of faith. They had not tapped into this source of power (Matt. 17:19–20).

101. Jesus Again Predicts His Death and Resurrection

Matthew 17:22–23; Mark 9:30–32; Luke 9:43–45

Mk 9:30Then they left that place and made their way through Galilee, but He did not want anyone to know it. Lk 9:43–44And they were all astonished at the greatness of God. While everyone was amazed at all the things He was doing, He told His disciples, 44"**Let these words sink in**: the Son of Man is about to be betrayed into the hands of men. Mk 9:31bThey will kill Him, and after He is killed, He will rise three days later."

Lk 9:45But they did not understand this statement; it was concealed from them so that they could not grasp it, and **they were afraid to ask Him about it**.

102. Jesus Produces a Coin to Pay the Temple Tax

Matthew 17:24–27

24When they came to Capernaum, those who collected **the double-drachma tax** approached Peter and said, "Doesn't your Teacher pay the double-drachma tax?"

25a"Yes," he said.

25bWhen he went into the house, Jesus spoke to him first, "What do you think, Simon? From whom do earthly kings collect tariffs or taxes? From their sons or from strangers?"

26a"From strangers," he said.

26b"Then the sons are free," Jesus told him. 27"But, so we won't offend them, go to the sea, cast in a fishhook, and catch the first fish that comes up. When you open its mouth **you'll find a coin**. Take it and give it to them for Me and you."

---

101. Jesus Again Predicts His Death and Resurrection

Let these words sink in: This was the second time Jesus had told His disciples about His upcoming death. He wanted them to be prepared for these events. But they found it hard to believe that He would be captured and killed by His enemies.

they were afraid to ask Him about it: In their fear and uncertainty, the disciples were silent about these predictions. Perhaps they remembered how Jesus had condemned Peter when Peter protested Jesus' first prediction of His death. Or they may have wondered about their own future in the light of these disturbing words.

102. Jesus Produces a Coin to Pay the Temple Tax

the double-drachma tax: The Jewish law required every male to pay this tax annually for the support of the temple in Jerusalem (Exod. 30:12–16). Some Jewish religious officials asked Peter whether Jesus intended to pay the tax. Peter answered these officials on behalf of Jesus with his usual impulsiveness. In discussing the tax with Peter, Jesus implied that He, as Lord of the temple, was exempt from paying temple taxes. But He gave up this privilege to set a good example for others.

you'll find a coin: Jesus told Peter to catch a fish and he would find a coin to pay the tax "for Me and you" in the fish's mouth.

103. JESUS TEACHES ABOUT SERVICE

Matthew 18:1–11; Mark 9:33–50; Luke 9:46–50

Mk 9:33 Then they came to Capernaum. When He was **in the house, He asked them,** "What were you arguing about on the way?"

34 **But they were silent**, because on the way they had been arguing with one another about who was the greatest. 35 Sitting down, He called the Twelve and said to them, "If anyone wants to be first, he must be last of all and **servant of all** [Lk 9:48b *For whoever is least among you all—this one is great*]." 36 Then He took a child, had him stand among them, and taking him in His arms, He said to them, 37 "**Whoever welcomes one little child** such as this in My name welcomes Me. And whoever welcomes Me does not welcome Me, but Him who sent Me. Mt 18:3–4 I assure you," He said, "unless you are converted and become like children, you will never enter the kingdom of heaven. 4 Therefore, whoever humbles himself like this child—this one is the greatest in the kingdom of heaven."

In His Name

Mk 9:38 John said to Him, "Teacher, we saw someone driving out demons in Your name, and we tried to stop him because he wasn't following us."

39 "Don't stop him," said Jesus, "because there is no one who will perform a miracle in My name who can soon afterward speak evil of Me. 40 For whoever is not against us is for us. 41 And whoever gives you a **cup of water** to drink **because of My name**, since you belong to the Messiah—I assure you: He will never lose his reward. 42 But whoever causes the downfall of one of these little ones who believe in Me—it would be better for him if a heavy millstone were

---

103. JESUS TEACHES ABOUT SERVICE

in the house, He asked them: Rather than confronting the disciples in public, Jesus waited until they were inside. He had overheard them arguing as they walked along the road. Just a few days before, Jesus had been transformed before the members of His inner circle of disciples—Peter, James, and John. Perhaps this had brought on the argument among the disciples about which of them was the greatest and most important.

But they were silent: The disciples did not answer Him. They must have realized that their self-seeking was contrary to what Jesus wanted them to do.

servant of all: Jesus insisted that whoever wanted to be first or greatest needed to be willing to be considered last and least. Instead of trying to claim prominence that would lead others to praise and serve them, they should give themselves to the humble service of others.

Whoever welcomes one little child: Jesus took a little child in His arms and held him before His disciples as an object lesson. A child is humble, dependent, and pure in motive and thought. The spirit in which a child looks to his parents presented a dramatic contrast to the self-seeking ambition of the disciples.

cup of water . . . because of My name: Giving a thirsty traveler a cup of water was an act of kindness and hospitality. Jesus declared that the smallest act of righteousness, if performed for the sake of the King and His kingdom, will be honored by the Lord.

hung around his neck and he were thrown into the sea. ^{Mt 18:14}In the same way, it is not the will of your Father in heaven that one of these little ones perish.

^{Mk 9:43–46}"And if your hand causes your downfall, cut it off. It is **better** for you **to enter life maimed** than to have two hands and go to hell—the unquenchable fire, ⁴⁴where 'their worm does not die, and the fire is not quenched.' ⁴⁵And if your foot causes your downfall, cut it off. It is better for you to enter life lame than to have two feet and be thrown into hell—the unquenchable fire, ⁴⁶where 'their worm does not die, and the fire is not quenched.'*

⁴⁷"And if your eye causes your downfall, gouge it out. It is better for you to enter the kingdom of God with one eye than to have two eyes and be thrown into **hell**, ⁴⁸where 'their **worm** does not die, and the **fire** is not quenched.' ⁴⁹For **everyone will be salted with fire**. ⁵⁰Salt is good, but if the salt should lose its flavor, how can you make it salty? Have salt among yourselves and be at peace with one another."

104. JESUS TEACHES ABOUT RECLAMATION AND FORGIVENESS

Matthew 18:15–22

¹⁵"If your brother sins against you, go and rebuke him in private. If he listens to you, you have won your brother. ¹⁶But if he won't listen, take one or two more with you, so that 'by the testimony of two or three witnesses every fact may be established.' ¹⁷If he pays no attention to them, tell the church. But if he doesn't pay attention even to the church, let him be like an unbeliever and a tax collector to you.

¹⁸"I assure you: Whatever you bind on earth will have been bound in heaven, and whatever you loose on earth will have been loosed in heaven. ¹⁹Again, I assure you: If two of you on earth agree about any matter that you pray for, it will be done for you by My Father in heaven. ²⁰For where two or three are gathered together in My name, I am there among them."

The words "the unquenchable fire, where 'their worm does not die, and the fire is not quenched'" in verses 44 and 45 do not appear in some New Testament manuscripts.

---

better . . . to enter life maimed: Jesus was not saying that we should literally cut off parts of our bodies to suppress the desires of the flesh in order to attain heaven. He was using deliberate exaggeration to drive home a point. The judgment of hell, Jesus declared, is so serious that it is better to sacrifice ourselves rather than fall into sin.

hell . . . worm . . . fire: The word translated hell means the "valley of Hinnom." This place just south of Jerusalem was used as a garbage dump. Fires burned continuously on the dump, and worms multiplied throughout the rotting garbage. This is a striking portrait of the eternal destination of those who have not received Jesus Christ as Savior and Lord.

everyone will be salted with fire: Both fire and salt are spoken of in the Bible as purifying agents. Unbelievers will face the judgment of fire as they endure His punishment for their lack of faith. But believers will experience the salt of eternal life, preserved to enjoy the love of God in heaven.

²¹Then Peter came to Him and said, "Lord, how many times could my brother sin against me and I forgive him? **As many as seven times?**"

²²"I tell you, not as many as seven," Jesus said to him, "but **seventy times seven.**"

Jesus' Method for Settling Disputes

Jesus was a realist. He knew that problems among believers were bound to happen. In this passage He outlined a process by which such problems were to be solved.

The first step is for the person who has been wronged to confront his fellow Christian about what he has done. This is exactly the opposite of what generally happens. The wronged person usually pouts and retreats, waiting for the offender to take the first step. The offender may not be aware of the pain he has caused. Only the person who has been hurt is fully aware of his feelings and the severity of the problem. It is his responsibility to communicate this to the wrongdoer.

If this approach fails, the wronged person should take other Christians ("one or two more," Matt. 18:16) with him to talk with the offender. These impartial witnesses will observe the attitudes and interactions of both parties and attempt to bring about a reconciliation.

Finally, the matter should be brought before the assembled church if the first attempts to settle the problem do not work. A dispute between believers is a serious matter. It can undermine the fellowship of the church and destroy its witness in the community. Restoration of broken relationships should be the goal of all actions taken by the believing community.

---

105. JESUS REFUSES TO DESTROY A SAMARITAN VILLAGE

Luke 9:51–56

⁵¹When the days were coming to a close for Him to be taken up, He was determined to journey to Jerusalem. ⁵²He sent messengers ahead of Him, and on the way they **entered a village of the Samaritans** to make preparations for Him.

---

104. JESUS TEACHES ABOUT RECLAMATION AND FORGIVENESS

As many as seven times? The Jewish rabbis taught that nobody should expect to have their offenses against others forgiven more than three times. Peter must have thought he was displaying an exceptional spirit of tolerance by suggesting that a person might be forgiven for offenses "as many as seven times."

seventy times seven: Jesus declared that we should go on forgiving without keeping count. Behind His answer may have been an incident in Genesis 4:23–24 in which Lamech boasted to his wives that he would seek venegance "seventy-seven times" (NIV) against his enemies. By contrast, the followers of Jesus should extend unlimited forgiveness to offenders.

105. JESUS REFUSES TO DESTROY A SAMARITAN VILLAGE

entered a village of the Samaritans: Jesus was traveling to Jerusalem with His disciples for His final Passover observance. He chose to go directly through Samaria, and they rejected Him.

⁵³But they did not welcome Him, because He was determined to journey to Jerusalem. ⁵⁴When the disciples James and John saw this, they said, "Lord, do You want us to **call down fire from heaven** to consume them?"

⁵⁵But He turned and rebuked them, ⁵⁶and they went to another village.

106. The Parable of the Unforgiving Slave

Matthew 18:23–35

²³"For this reason, the kingdom of heaven can be compared to a king who wanted to settle accounts with his slaves. ²⁴When he began to settle accounts, one who owed **ten thousand talents** was brought before him. ²⁵Since he had no way to pay it back, his master commanded that he, his wife, his children, and everything he had be sold to pay the debt.

²⁶"At this, the slave fell down on his face before him and said, 'Be patient with me, and I will pay you everything!' ²⁷Then the **master** of that slave **had compassion**, released him, and **forgave him** the loan.

²⁸"But that slave went out and found **one of his fellow slaves** who owed him **a hundred denarii**. He grabbed him, started choking him, and said, 'Pay what you owe!'

²⁹"At this, his fellow slave fell down and began begging him, 'Be patient with me, and I will pay you back.' ³⁰But he wasn't willing. On the contrary, **he** went and **threw him into prison** until he could pay what was owed. ³¹When the other slaves saw what had taken place, they were deeply distressed and went and reported to their master everything that had happened.

³²"Then, after he had summoned him, his master said to him, 'You wicked slave! I forgave you all that debt because you begged me. ³³Shouldn't you also have had mercy on your fellow slave, as I had mercy on you?' ³⁴And **his master**

---

call down fire from heaven: Two of Jesus' disciples, James and John, wanted to call down fire from heaven to destroy the village, as the prophet Elijah had done on one occasion (2 Kgs. 1:9–12). But Jesus was a Savior and not a destroyer, so He passed on to another village.

106. The Parable of the Unforgiving Slave

ten thousand talents: The "slave" who was guilty of misappropriating this huge amount was probably a court official. The king in the parable decided to reclaim as much of the debt as possible by selling the debtor and his family into slavery.

master . . . had compassion . . . forgave him: The desperate debtor pleaded for the king to be patient. He promised to pay back all he owed. The king knew the debtor could never pay off his debt, so he had compassion on him. He wrote off the enormous liability.

one of his fellow slaves . . . a hundred denarii: The slave who had been shown such generosity displayed an unforgiving attitude toward a colleague who owed him a small sum. One hundred denarii represented about three months' wages for a working man—an amount that could be easily repaid.

he . . . threw him into prison: The second slave's pleas were the same as the earlier pleas of the first slave to the king. Each slave pleaded for patience and promised to repay the debt. But the first slave responded differently to the pleas of his debtor. He sent the man to debtor's prison.

his master . . . handed him over to the jailers: When other members of the king's court heard about this, they made

got angry and **handed him over to the jailers** until he could pay everything that was owed. [35]So **My heavenly Father will also do to you** if each of you does not forgive his brother from his heart."

107. JESUS CHALLENGES HIS FOLLOWERS TO FULL COMMITMENT

Matthew 8:19–22; Luke 9:57–62

[Lk 9:57]As they were traveling on the road someone [[Mt 8:19a]*A scribe*] said to Him, "**I will follow You** wherever You go!"

[58]Jesus told him, "Foxes have dens, and birds of the sky have nests, but the Son of Man has no place to lay His head." [59a]Then He said to another, "Follow Me."

[59b]"Lord," he said, "first let me go to bury my father."

[60]But He told him, "**Let the dead bury their own dead**, but you go and spread the news of the kingdom of God."

[61]Another also said, "I will follow You, Lord, but first **let me go and say goodbye** to those at my house."

[62]But Jesus said to him, "No one who puts his hand to the plow and looks back is fit for the kingdom of God."

108. JESUS HESITATES ABOUT GOING TO JERUSALEM

John 7:1–9

[1]After this Jesus traveled in Galilee, since He did not want to travel in Judea because the Jews were trying to kill Him. [2]The Jewish **Festival of Tabernacles**

---

the details known to the king. He summoned the offender into his presence, gave him a tongue lashing, and had him imprisoned. The unforgiving debtor would not be released "until he could pay everything that was owed"—an unlikely prospect.

My heavenly Father will also do to you: An unforgiving spirit cuts us off from God's forgiveness. By refusing to forgive, we place ourselves among the unforgiven and remain under the judgment of God.

107. JESUS CHALLENGES HIS FOLLOWERS TO FULL COMMITMENT
I will follow You: This man declared that he was willing to follow Jesus anywhere. Perhaps he had been caught up in a surge of enthusiasm to identify himself with Jesus as an amazing miracle worker. But was he ready to share homelessness and poverty with Jesus?

Let the dead bury their own dead: Jesus issued a call to discipleship to another man who wanted to postpone his response until after the death of his father. Family duties took precedence in this follower's life. Jesus reminded him that he must put the kingdom of God first.

let me go and say goodbye: For those who wanted to be Jesus' followers there was no time to waste with long farewells to friends and family. Response to follow Jesus must be immediate and without reservation.

108. JESUS HESITATES ABOUT GOING TO JERUSALEM
Festival of Tabernacles: This festival was the most popular of the three major Jewish celebrations. Observed six months before the Passover, it fell at the end of the harvest.

was near, [3]so **His brothers** said to Him, "Leave here and go to Judea so Your disciples can see Your works that You are doing. [4]For no one does anything in secret while he's seeking public recognition. If You do these things, show Yourself to the world." [5](For not even His brothers believed in Him.)

[6]Jesus told them, "**My time** has not yet arrived, but **your time** is always at hand. [7]The world cannot hate you, but it does hate Me because I testify about it—that its deeds are evil. [8]Go up to the festival yourselves. I'm not going up to the festival yet, because My time has not yet fully come." [9]After He had said these things, He stayed in Galilee.

109. JESUS' DISCUSSION AT THE FESTIVAL OF TABERNACLES

John 7:10–52

[10]When His brothers had gone up to the festival, then **He also went up**, not openly but **secretly**. [11]The Jews were looking for Him at the festival and saying, "Where is He?" [12]And there was a lot of discussion about Him among the crowds. Some were saying, "He's a good man." Others were saying, "No, on the contrary, He's deceiving the people." [13]Still, nobody was talking publicly about Him because they feared the Jews.

[14]When the festival was already half over, Jesus went up **into the temple complex and began to teach**. [15]Then the Jews were amazed and said, "How does He know the Scriptures, since He hasn't been trained?"

[16]Jesus answered them, "**My teaching isn't Mine**, but is from the One who sent Me. [17]If anyone wants to do His will, he will understand whether the teaching is from God or if I am speaking on My own. [18]The one who speaks for himself seeks his own glory. But He who seeks the glory of the One who sent Him is true, and unrighteousness is not in Him. [19]Didn't Moses give you the law? Yet **none of you keeps the law!** Why do you want to kill Me?"

His brothers: Jesus' half brothers—children born to Mary and Joseph after His virgin birth—taunted Him with the suggestion that He should go to Jerusalem for the feast and work His miracles there.

My time . . . your time: Jesus declared that the time for the greatest manifestation of His work—His death and resurrection—had not yet arrived. It was six months before the Passover celebration, when these events would occur. But His brothers, having no mission and message to declare, could go to Jerusalem at any time.

109. JESUS' DISCUSSION AT THE FESTIVAL OF TABERNACLES

He also went up . . . secretly: After his brothers went to the festival, Jesus decided to go. But He went "secretly," without identifying Himself as the Messiah. Six months later, at the Passover celebration, He would declare Himself and His mission "openly," for all the people to see.

into the temple complex and began to teach: Jesus' teaching at the festival produced different reactions. Many believed in Him, but the religious leadership hardened their opposition and tried to seize Him.

My teaching isn't Mine: Jesus rooted His authority in the Father who had sent Him. His teaching was not something He had made up. He taught in accordance with the will and purpose of God.

none of you keeps the law! The Jewish religious leaders cherished the Mosaic Law, but Jesus charged that they failed to keep the law. This was evident because they were plotting to break the law in their attempts to kill Jesus.

²⁰"You have a demon!" the crowd responded. "Who wants to kill You?"

²¹" I did one work, and you are all amazed," Jesus answered. ²²"Consider this: Moses has given you circumcision—not that it comes from Moses but from the fathers—and you circumcise a man on the Sabbath. ²³If a man receives circumcision on the Sabbath so that the law of Moses won't be broken, are you angry at Me because I made a man entirely well on the Sabbath? ²⁴Stop judging according to outward appearances; rather judge according to righteous judgment."

The Identity of the Messiah

²⁵Some of the people of Jerusalem were saying, "Isn't this the man they want to kill? ²⁶Yet, look! He's speaking publicly and they're saying nothing to Him. Can it be true that the authorities know He is the Messiah? ²⁷But **we know where this man is from**. When the Messiah comes, nobody will know where He is from."

²⁸As He was teaching in the temple complex, Jesus cried out, "You know Me and you know where I am from. Yet I have not come on My own, but the One who sent Me is true. You don't know Him; ²⁹I know Him because I am from Him, and He sent Me."

³⁰Therefore they tried to seize Him. Yet no one laid a hand on Him because His hour had not yet come. ³¹However, many from the crowd believed in Him and said, "When the Messiah comes, He won't perform more signs than this man has done, will He?"

³²The Pharisees heard the crowd muttering these things about Him, so the chief priests and the Pharisees sent temple police to arrest Him.

³³Therefore Jesus said, "I am only with you for a short time. Then I'm going to the One who sent Me. ³⁴You will look for Me, and you will not find Me; and where I am, you cannot come."

³⁵Then the Jews said to one another, "Where does He intend to go so we won't find Him? He doesn't intend to go to the Dispersion among the Greeks and teach the Greeks, does He? ³⁶What is this remark He made: 'You will look for Me and you will not find Me; and where I am, you cannot come'?"

The Promise of the Spirit

³⁷On the last and most important day of the festival, Jesus stood up and cried out, "**If anyone is thirsty**, he should come to Me and drink! ³⁸The one who

---

we know where this man is from: The Jewish leaders rejected Jesus' claim to messiahship because of His origin. They knew He was from Nazareth in Galilee. It was inconceivable to them that the Messiah would come from such an insignificant village and that He would appear with no fanfare or spectacular announcement.

If anyone is thirsty: Part of the ritual during the Festival of Tabernacles was the pouring of water, brought by priests

believes in Me, as the Scripture has said, will have streams of living water flow from deep within him." [39]He said this about the Spirit, whom those who believed in Him were going to receive, for the Spirit had not yet been received, because Jesus had not yet been glorified.

[40]When some from the crowd heard these words, they said, "This really is the Prophet!" [41]Others said, "This is the Messiah!" But some said, "Surely the Messiah doesn't come from Galilee, does He? [42]Doesn't the Scripture say that the Messiah comes from David's offspring and from the town of Bethlehem, where David once lived?" [43]So a division occurred among the crowd because of Him. [44]Some of them wanted to seize Him, but no one laid hands on Him.

[45]Then the temple police came to the chief priests and Pharisees, who asked them, "Why haven't you brought Him?"

[46]**The police answered**, "No man ever spoke like this!"

[47]Then the Pharisees responded to them: "Are you fooled too? [48]Have any of the rulers believed in Him? Or any of the Pharisees? [49]But this crowd, which doesn't know the law, is accursed!"

[50]**Nicodemus**—the one who came to Him previously, being one of them— **said to them**, [51]"Our law doesn't judge a man before it hears from him and knows what he's doing, does it?"

[52]**"You aren't from Galilee too**, are you?" they replied. "Search and see: no prophet arises from Galilee."

110. Jesus Forgives a Woman Accused of Adultery

John 7:53–8:11

[7:53]So each one went to his house.

[8:1]But Jesus went to the Mount of Olives. [2]At dawn He went to the temple complex again, and all the people were coming to Him. He sat down and began to teach them.

---

to the temple. It probably was an act of acknowledgment for divine supply, both of water in the wilderness and of rain for recent crops. If there were any among the temple crowds who were spiritually unsatisfied after engaging in all the ceremonial activities of the feast, Jesus declared, let them come to Him. Those who did would have their spiritual thirst satisfied.

The police answered: Finally, the Pharisees and chief priests sent members of the temple guard to arrest Jesus. His growing popularity with the common people prompted the fear that He might lead an uprising against the Romans. But the temple guards returned without their prisoner. Jesus' words had made them powerless.

Nicodemus . . . said to them: Nicodemus had already met with Jesus (see John 3), so he probably knew more about Jesus than any of his fellow Pharisees. He protested against the disregard of the law by those who were seeking to condemn Jesus. It was not legal, said Nicodemus, to judge a person without permitting him to speak in his own defense.

You aren't from Galilee too: This enraged the other Pharisees. They wanted to know whether Nicodemus's opinion was being swayed by local prejudice. Perhaps he was a Galilean, as was Jesus, and, therefore, was coming to His support. By his courage in speaking out, Nicodemus apparently caused the meeting of the enemies of Jesus to break up in frustration; "each one went to his house" (John 7:53).

³Then **the scribes and the Pharisees brought a woman** caught in adultery, making her stand in the center. ⁴"Teacher," they said to Him, "this woman was caught in the act of committing adultery. ⁵In the law Moses commanded us to **stone such women**. So **what do You say?**" ⁶ᵃThey asked this to trap Him, in order that they might have evidence to accuse Him.

⁶ᵇJesus stooped down and started **writing on the ground** with His finger. ⁷When they persisted in questioning Him, He stood up and said to them, "The **one without sin** among you should be the **first to throw a stone** at her."

⁸Then He stooped down again and continued writing on the ground. ⁹When they heard this, they left one by one, starting with the older men. Only He was left, with the woman in the center. ¹⁰When Jesus stood up, He said to her, "Woman, where are they? Has no one condemned you?"

¹¹ᵃ"No one, Lord," she answered.

¹¹ᵇ"**Neither do I condemn you**," said Jesus. "Go, and from now on do not sin any more."*

111. JESUS CLAIMS TO BE THE LIGHT OF THE WORLD

John 8:12–59

¹²Then Jesus spoke to them again: "I am the light of the world. Anyone who follows Me will never walk in the darkness, but will have the light of life."

Verse 53 of John 7 and verses 1–11 of John 8 do not appear in some New Testament manuscripts.

---

110. JESUS FORGIVES A WOMAN ACCUSED OF ADULTERY

the scribes and the Pharisees brought a woman: This woman had probably been brought to the Sanhedrin for trial. But the scribes and Pharisees recognized that her case offered a good opportunity to trap Jesus.

stone such women: Under the Old Testament law, death by stoning was the prescribed method of capital punishment for a person caught in adultery (Deut. 22:22).

what do You say? The hypocritical religious leaders reasoned that Jesus could not set aside the law of Moses and clear the woman without losing the confidence and favor of the people. But if He ordered her to be executed, He would be assuming authority that belonged only to the Roman rulers. Then He would be accused and condemned as one who usurped Roman authority.

writing on the ground: By writing on the ground, Jesus emphasized His authority. He would answer them when He was ready.

one without sin . . . first to throw a stone: In cases of capital punishment under the Old Testament law, the accusers or witnesses were to cast the first stone to begin the execution (Deut. 17:7). Jesus upheld the law, but He introduced a condition that the scribes and Pharisees had not counted on. He declared that only a person who had not had any adulterous thoughts or illicit sexual desire was free to stone the woman. None of them could measure up to this standard.

Neither do I condemn you: Jesus did not come as an earthly judge; neither did He come to condemn, but to save (see Luke 12:14). His refusal to condemn this woman did not mean He approved of her actions. He challenged her to make a revolutionary change in her life. His mercy and forgiveness served as the motivation for this change.

Jesus as the Light of the World

Jesus' claim to be the "light of the world" (John 8:12) is one of His famous "I Am" statements in the Gospel of John. In this situation, Jesus was responding to the Jewish religious leaders who denied that He was the Messiah because He came from Galilee.

The prophet Isaiah had predicted several centuries before that a great light would shine in Galilee, bringing illumination and understanding to all who lived in darkness and death. Jesus declared that this prophecy had been fulfilled in Him. He was the eternal light from God that brought life to sinful humanity: "The people walking in darkness have seen a great light; on those living in the land of the shadow of death a light has dawned" (Isa. 9:2 NIV).

As the light of the world, Jesus symbolizes the presence of God (Exod. 13:21–22), good in contrast to evil (Isa. 5:20), salvation from sin into new life (Matt. 4:16), and guidance for life (Ps. 119:105).

---

¹³So the Pharisees said to Him, "You are testifying about Yourself. Your testimony is not valid."

¹⁴"Even if I testify about Myself," Jesus replied, "My testimony is valid, because I know where I came from and where I'm going. But you don't know where I come from or where I'm going. ¹⁵You judge by human standards. I judge no one. ¹⁶And if I do judge, My judgment is true, because I am not alone, but I and the Father who sent Me judge together. ¹⁷Even in your law it is written that the witness of two men is valid. ¹⁸I am the One who testifies about Myself, and the Father who sent Me testifies about Me."

¹⁹ᵃThen they asked Him, "Where is Your Father?"

¹⁹ᵇ"You know neither Me nor My Father," Jesus answered. "If you knew Me, you would also know My Father." ²⁰He spoke these words by the treasury, while teaching in the temple complex. But no one seized Him, because His hour had not come.

Jesus Predicts His Departure

²¹Then He said to them again, "I'm going away; you will look for Me, and you will die in your sin. Where I'm going, you cannot come."

²²So the Jews said again, "He won't kill Himself, will He, since He says, 'Where I'm going, you cannot come'?"

²³"You are from below," He told them, "I am from above. You are of this world; I am not of this world. ²⁴Therefore I told you that you will die in your sins. For if you do not believe that I am He, you will die in your sins."

^{25a}**"Who are You?"** they questioned.

^{25b}"Precisely what I've been telling you from the very beginning," Jesus told them. ²⁶"I have many things to say and to judge about you, but the One who sent Me is true, and what I have heard from Him—these things I tell the world."

²⁷They did not know He was speaking to them about the Father. ²⁸So Jesus said to them, "When you lift up the Son of Man, then you will know that I am He, and that I do nothing on My own. But just as the Father taught Me, I say these things. ²⁹The One who sent Me is with Me. He has not left Me alone, because I always do what pleases Him."

Truth and Freedom

³⁰As He was saying these things, many believed in Him. ³¹So Jesus said to the Jews who had believed Him, "If you continue in My word, you really are My disciples. ³²You will know the truth, and the truth will set you free."

³³"We are **descendants of Abraham**," they answered Him, "and we have never been enslaved to anyone. How can You say, 'You will become free'?"

³⁴Jesus responded, "I assure you: Everyone who commits sin is a slave of sin. ³⁵A slave does not remain in the household forever, but a son does remain forever. ³⁶Therefore if the Son sets you free, **you really will be free**. ³⁷I know you are descendants of Abraham, but you are trying to kill Me because My word is not welcome among you. ³⁸I speak what I have seen in the presence of the Father, and therefore you do what you have heard from your father."

^{39a}"Our father is Abraham!" they replied.

^{39b}"If you were Abraham's children," Jesus told them, "you would do what Abraham did. ⁴⁰But now **you are trying to kill Me**, a man who has told you the truth that I heard from God. Abraham did not do this! ^{41a}You're doing what your father does."

^{41b}"We weren't born of sexual immorality," they said. "We have one Father—God."

---

111. JESUS CLAIMS TO BE THE LIGHT OF THE WORLD

Who are You? By asking this question, the Pharisees were probably looking for some basis for accusing Jesus of blasphemy. Jesus replied that He had been telling them who He was from the beginning. If they had paid attention, they would have known that Jesus spoke only the truth given to Him by His Father. They would know the truth and truth would set them free.

descendants of Abraham: Except for a brief time of independence, the Jews had been under the control of some foreign nation for centuries. Yet the Pharisees claimed that being physical descendants of Abraham made them free people, no matter what happened.

you really will be free: Jesus clarified what He meant about being set free. He was thinking of the basic slavery that afflicts humanity—slavery to sin. Those who choose to live in sin become enslaved by their sin. As the divine Son of God, only Jesus could set people free from their slavery to sin.

you are trying to kill Me: The Pharisees were children of Abraham by physical lineage, but Jesus accused them of planning to kill Him. He declared that being like Abraham was more important than being descended from Abraham. Their murderous intentions revealed they were actually children of Satan.

⁴²Jesus said to them, "If God were your Father, you would love Me, because I came from God and I am here. For I didn't come on My own, but He sent Me. ⁴³Why don't you understand what I say? Because you cannot listen to My word. ⁴⁴You are of your father the Devil, and you want to carry out your father's desires. He was a murderer from the beginning and has not stood in the truth, because there is no truth in him. When he tells a lie, he speaks from his own nature, because he is a liar and the father of liars. ⁴⁵Yet because I tell the truth, you do not believe Me. ⁴⁶Who among you can convict Me of sin? If I tell the truth, why don't you believe Me? ⁴⁷The one who is from God listens to God's words. This is why you don't listen, because you are not from God."

Jesus and Abraham

⁴⁸The Jews responded to Him, "Aren't we right in saying that You're a Samaritan and have a demon?"

⁴⁹"I do not have a demon," Jesus answered. "On the contrary, I honor My Father and you dishonor Me. ⁵⁰I do not seek My glory; the One who seeks it also judges. ⁵¹I assure you: If anyone keeps My word, he will never see death—ever!"

⁵²Then the Jews said, "Now we know You have a demon. Abraham died and so did the prophets. You say, 'If anyone keeps My word, he will never taste death—ever!' ⁵³Are You greater than our father Abraham who died? Even the prophets died. Who do You pretend to be?"

⁵⁴"If I glorify Myself," Jesus answered, "My glory is nothing. My Father is the One who glorifies Me, of whom you say, 'He is our God.' ⁵⁵You've never known Him, but I know Him. If I were to say I don't know Him, I would be a liar like you. But I do know Him, and I keep His word. ⁵⁶Your father Abraham was overjoyed that he would see My day; he saw it and rejoiced."

⁵⁷The Jews replied, "You aren't 50 years old yet, and You've seen Abraham?"

⁵⁸Jesus said to them, "I assure you: Before Abraham was, I am."

⁵⁹At that, they picked up stones to throw at Him. But Jesus was hidden and went out of the temple complex.

112. Jesus Heals a Man Blind from Birth

John 9:1–41

¹As He was passing by, He saw a man blind from birth. ²His disciples questioned Him: "Rabbi, **who sinned**, this man or his parents, **that he was born blind?**"

---

112. Jesus Heals a Man Blind from Birth

who sinned . . . that he was born blind? The people of Jesus' time believed that health and wealth were the rewards of righteous living and that personal disaster was brought on by sin. The Jews believed that an unborn child could sin and bring punishment on himself later in life.

[3]"Neither this man sinned nor his parents," Jesus answered. "This came about so that **God's works might be displayed** in him. [4]We must do the works of Him who sent Me while it is day. **Night is coming** when no one can work. [5]As long as I am in the world, I am the light of the world."

[6]After He said these things He spit on the ground, made some **mud from the saliva,** and spread the mud on his eyes. [7]"Go," He told him, "wash in the pool of Siloam" (which means "Sent"). So he left, washed, and came back seeing.

[8]His neighbors and those who formerly had seen him as a beggar said, "Isn't this the man who sat begging?" [9a]Some said, "He's the one." "No," others were saying, "but he looks like him."

[9b]He kept saying, "I'm the one!"

[10]Therefore they asked him, "Then how were your eyes opened?"

[11]He answered, "The man called Jesus made mud, spread it on my eyes, and told me, 'Go to Siloam and wash.' So when I went and washed I received my sight."

[12a]"Where is He?" they asked.

[12b]"**I don't know,**" he said.

The Healed Man's Testimony

[13]They brought to the Pharisees the man who used to be blind. [14]The day that Jesus made the mud and opened his eyes was a Sabbath. [15a]So again the Pharisees asked him how he received his sight.

[15b]"He put mud on my eyes," he told them. "I washed and I can see."

[16]Therefore some of the Pharisees said, "This man is not from God, for He doesn't keep the Sabbath!" But others were saying, "How can a sinful man perform such signs?" And there was a division among them.

[17a]Again they asked the blind man, "What do you say about Him, since He opened your eyes?"

[17b]"He's a prophet," he said.

God's works might be displayed: Jesus corrected this erroneous idea. Whatever the reason for the man's affliction, Jesus would make it an opportunity to grant healing and glorify God. He had come into the world to reveal the power and love of His Father.

Night is coming: The growing hostility toward Jesus made Him aware that He had limited time to accomplish His work. He must fulfill His ministry "while it is day," on the Sabbath as well as any other time. Where need existed, He must respond.

mud from the saliva: The method Jesus used in this healing was probably dictated by the ignorance of the blind man concerning his healer. He was not like some people who came seeking help on the basis of what Jesus had done for others. His expectation needed to be stimulated and his faith given opportunity to express itself. The mud from Jesus' saliva lay heavily on the blind man's closed eyelids. Jesus then sent him to the pool of Siloam for healing.

I don't know: The healed man did not know specifically who had healed him. He only knew that his healer was a "man called Jesus." In a few words he told exactly what had happened to him and gave credit to Jesus as his healer. The Pharisees questioned the man about the identity of his healer.

¹⁸The Jews did not believe this about him—that he was blind and received sight—until **they summoned the parents** of the one who had received his sight. ¹⁹They asked them, "Is this your son, whom you say was born blind? How then does he now see?"

²⁰"We know this is our son and that he was born blind," his parents answered. ²¹"But we don't know how he now sees, and we don't know who opened his eyes. Ask him; he's of age. He will speak for himself." ²²His parents said these things because they were afraid of the Jews, since the Jews had already agreed that if anyone confessed Him as Messiah, he would be banned from the synagogue. ²³This is why his parents said, "He's of age; ask him."

²⁴So a second time they summoned the man who had been blind and told him, "Give glory to God. We know that this man is a sinner!"

²⁵He answered, "Whether or not He's a sinner, I don't know. One thing I do know: I was blind, and now I can see!"

²⁶Then they asked him, "What did He do to you? How did He open your eyes?"

²⁷"I already told you," he said, "and you didn't listen. Why do you want to hear it again? You don't want to become His disciples too, do you?"

²⁸They ridiculed him: "You're that man's disciple, but we're Moses' disciples. ²⁹We know that God has spoken to Moses. But this man—we don't know where He's from!"

³⁰"This is an amazing thing," the man told them. "**You don't know where He is from; yet He opened my eyes!** ³¹We know that God doesn't listen to sinners; but if anyone is God-fearing and does His will, He listens to him. ³²Throughout history no one has ever heard of someone opening the eyes of a person born blind. ³³If this man were not from God, He wouldn't be able to do anything."

³⁴"You were born entirely in sin," they replied, "and are you trying to teach us?" Then they threw him out.

³⁵When **Jesus** heard that they had thrown the man out, He **found him** and asked, "Do you believe in the Son of Man?"

³⁶"Who is He, Sir, that I may believe in Him?" he asked in return.

---

they summoned the parents: In their search for grounds to take action against Jesus, the Pharisees questioned the man's parents. Their answers to the Pharisees' questions were deliberately evasive because they were fearful of being "banned from the synagogue."

You don't know where He is from; yet He opened my eyes! The healed beggar was not cowed by the Pharisees' questions. It was odd to him that these leaders knew nothing about a man who had given him sight. His final declaration was, "If this man were not from God, He wouldn't be able to do anything." For this, "they threw him out." This may mean that they ejected him from the temple area, or that they excommunicated him by some official decree.

Jesus . . . found him: Jesus went looking for the man, asked him a pointed question, and then revealed Himself as "the Son of Man." The man responded with an affirmation of faith and an act of worship. He had progressed from "the man called Jesus" (v. 11), to "He's a prophet" (v. 17), to this final declaration of faith, "I believe, Lord."

[37]Jesus answered, "You have both seen Him and He is the One speaking with you."

[38]"I believe, Lord!" he said, and he worshiped Him.

[39]Jesus said, "I came into this world for judgment, in order that those who do not see may see and those who do see may become blind."

[40]Some of the Pharisees who were with Him heard these things and asked Him, "**We aren't blind too, are we?**"

[41]"If you were blind," Jesus told them, "you wouldn't have sin. But now that you say, 'We see'—your sin remains."

113. JESUS CLAIMS TO BE THE GOOD SHEPHERD

John 10:1–21

[1]"I assure you: Anyone who doesn't enter the sheep pen **by the door**, but climbs in some other way, is **a thief and a robber**. [2]The one who enters by the door is the shepherd of the sheep. [3]The doorkeeper opens it for him, and the sheep hear his voice. He **calls his own sheep** by name **and leads them out**. [4]When he has brought all his own outside, he goes ahead of them. The sheep follow him because they recognize his voice. [5]They will never follow a stranger; instead they will run away from him, because they don't recognize the voice of strangers."

[6]Jesus gave them this illustration, but they did not understand what He was telling them.

[7]So Jesus said again, "I assure you: **I am the door of the sheep**. [8]All who came before Me are thieves and robbers, but the sheep didn't listen to them. [9]I am the door. If anyone enters by Me, he will be saved, and will come in and go out and find pasture. [10]A thief comes only to steal and to kill and to destroy. I have come that they may have life and have it in abundance.

We aren't blind too, are we? Through Jesus' ministry, sight was being given to some people while it was being taken away from others. To claim to have spiritual perception, as these religious leaders did, and yet to be unresponsive to truth was to be blind indeed.

113. JESUS CLAIMS TO BE THE GOOD SHEPHERD

by the door . . . a thief and a robber: The first requirement for a true undershepherd is that he has entered into the sheepfold by the door. Those who enter by climbing the walls are thieves and robbers. Jesus was referring to the scribes and Pharisees. He had just seen an example of their lack of compassion in the way they had treated the man born blind (see John 9:1–41).

calls his own sheep . . . and leads them out: A shepherd knew his sheep and had a special call for them. They knew him and recognized his distinctive call. After the doorkeeper allowed the shepherd into the fold, he called his sheep and led them out.

I am the door of the sheep: The door was the only way into the safety of the sheepfold and out into the pasture. Jesus gives eternal life that extends beyond death and abundant life in the here and now.

¹¹"I am the good shepherd. The good shepherd lays down His life for the sheep. ¹²The hired man, since he's not the shepherd and doesn't own the sheep, leaves them and runs away when he sees a wolf coming. The wolf then snatches and scatters them. ¹³This happens because he is a hired man and doesn't care about the sheep.

¹⁴"I am the good shepherd. I know My own sheep, and they know Me, ¹⁵as the Father knows Me, and I know the Father. I lay down My life for the sheep. ¹⁶But I have other sheep that are not of this fold; I must bring them also, and they will listen to My voice. Then there will be one flock, one shepherd. ¹⁷This is why the Father loves Me, because I am laying down My life that I may take it up again. ¹⁸No one takes it from Me, but I lay it down on My own. I have the right to lay it down and I have the right to take it up again. I have received this command from My Father."

¹⁹Again a division took place among the Jews because of these words. ²⁰Many of them were saying, "**He has a demon** and He's crazy! Why do you listen to Him?" ²¹Others were saying, "These aren't the words of someone demon-possessed. Can a demon open the eyes of the blind?"

Jesus as the Good Shepherd

A shepherd taking care of sheep was a familiar scene among the Jews. They knew about the shepherd boy David, one of their national heroes, who had killed a lion and a bear to protect his father's sheep (1 Sam. 17:34–36). They were familiar with the imagery of the Lord as a shepherd of His people in the twenty-third Psalm.

But Jesus introduced something new into the shepherd symbolism when He described Himself as the Good Shepherd: He would give His life for the sheep (John 10:11, 15). In contrast to the "hired man" (John 10:12), who would run away at the first sign of danger, Jesus loved His sheep and would sacrifice His life to keep them safe.

Jesus came into the world to save sinners—to gather straying sheep to Himself through His atoning death. The apostle Peter declared, "You were like sheep going astray, but you have now returned to the shepherd and guardian of your souls" (1 Pet. 2:25).

He has a demon: This was the response of the Pharisees to Jesus' claim that He would be resurrected. But the Good Shepherd knew that dying would not accomplish His task. Only by returning from the grave would He prove to all the world that His sacrifice on our behalf had been accepted by God.

114. Jesus Sends Seventy Followers
on a Preaching Mission

Luke 10:1–24

¹After this the Lord appointed **70 others**, and He sent them ahead of Him **in pairs** to every town and place where He Himself was about to go. ²He told them: "The harvest is abundant, but the workers are few. Therefore, pray to the Lord of the harvest to **send out workers into His harvest**.

³"Now go; I'm sending you out like **lambs among wolves**. ⁴**Don't carry** a money-bag, backpack, or sandals; **don't greet** anyone along the road. ⁵Whatever house you enter, first say, 'Peace to this household.' ⁶If a son of peace is there, your peace will rest on him; but if not, it will return to you. ⁷**Remain in the same house**, eating and drinking what they offer, for the worker is worthy of his wages. Don't be moving from house to house. ⁸Whatever town you enter, and they welcome you, eat the things set before you. ⁹Heal the sick who are there, and tell them, 'The kingdom of God has come near you.'

¹⁰"But whatever town you enter, and they don't welcome you, go out into its streets and say, ¹¹'Even the **dust** of your town that clings to our feet **we wipe off** against you. But know this: the kingdom of God has come near.' ¹²I tell you, on that day it will be more tolerable for Sodom than for that town.

¹³"Woe to you, Chorazin! Woe to you, Bethsaida! For if the miracles that were done in you had been done in Tyre and Sidon, they would have repented long

---

114. Jesus Sends Seventy Followers on a Preaching Mission

70 others . . . in pairs: In Genesis 10, the nations of the world are numbered as 70. Perhaps this is the significance of the 70 by whom Jesus indicated His outreach to the whole world. Before His ascension, Jesus would make His followers His witnesses to the ends of the earth. Sending these messengers out in pairs echoes the words of Deuteronomy 19:15, where truth is established "by the testimony of two or three witnesses" (NIV).

send out workers into His harvest: Jesus knew that 12 plus 70 would not be sufficient for the task. Those who gather the harvest must also pray for more workers to be recruited.

lambs among wolves: Jesus did not hide the high price of discipleship from His followers. In New Testament times, hostility was open and often violent. Today it is often more subtle, but still sometimes violent. Too often Jesus' disciples avoid hostility by compromise.

Don't carry . . . don't greet: Extra baggage would hinder the movement of these messengers. They were to carry no purse for money, no bag for incidentals, and no sandals. Neither were they to engage in courtesies along the road—long greetings typical of that culture. They were not to waste any time in getting on with their mission.

Remain in the same house: Normal courtesies should be observed toward occupants of homes who offered food and shelter. These followers of Jesus must not shop around for better accommodations. Rather, they should accept what was offered.

dust . . . we wipe off: When Jews left Gentile territory, they shook off the dust that clung to their clothes and feet, affirming their separateness. Jesus told the 70 to use this same symbolic action when their message was rejected. He did not promise His followers that everyone would accept their message. These messengers were to make the consequences of rejection clear to those who turned them away.

ago, sitting in sackcloth and ashes! [14]But it will be more tolerable for Tyre and Sidon at the judgment than for you. [15]And you, Capernaum, will you be exalted to heaven? No, you will go down to Hades! [16]Whoever listens to you listens to Me. Whoever rejects you rejects Me. And whoever rejects Me rejects the One who sent Me."

[17]The 70 returned with joy, saying, "Lord, even the demons submit to us in Your name."

[18]He said to them, "I watched Satan fall from heaven like a lightning flash. [19]Look, I have given you the authority to trample on snakes and scorpions and over all the power of the enemy; nothing will ever harm you. [20]However, don't rejoice that the spirits submit to you, but rejoice that your names are written in heaven."

[21]In that same hour He rejoiced in the Holy Spirit and said, "I praise You, Father, Lord of heaven and earth, because You have hidden these things from the wise and the learned and have revealed them to infants. Yes, Father, because this was Your good pleasure. [22]All things have been entrusted to Me by My Father. No one knows who the Son is except the Father, and who the Father is except the Son, and anyone to whom the Son desires to reveal Him."

[23]Then turning to His disciples He said privately, "Blessed are the eyes that see the things you see! [24]For I tell you that many prophets and kings wanted to see the things you see, yet didn't see them; to hear the things you hear, yet didn't hear them."

115. The Parable of the Good Samaritan

Luke 10:25–37

[25]Just then an expert in the law stood up to test Him, saying, "Teacher, **what must I do** to inherit eternal life?"

[26]**"What is written in the law?"** He asked him. "How do you read it?"

[27]He answered: "You shall love the Lord your God with all your heart, with all your soul, with all your strength, and with all your mind; and your neighbor as yourself."

[28]"You've answered correctly," He told him. "Do this and you will live."

[29]But wanting to justify himself, he asked Jesus, "And **who is my neighbor?**"

---

115. The Parable of the Good Samaritan

what must I do: Those who practice a religion of works seek a guaranteed way of obtaining the prize of eternal life. This was also the question of the rich young ruler (Luke 18:18). This matter must have been discussed a great deal among rabbis and other religious teachers.

What is written in the law? The inquirer was a scholar, an expert in the law, so it was appropriate that Jesus should turn the question back to him. The law expert found his answer in Deuteronomy 6:5 and Leviticus 19:18. These passages state the dual duty of love for God and others. Jesus told the expert in the law that he had answered correctly. He had tried keeping the law of God, but he had discovered this was not possible.

who is my neighbor? Jews regarded fellow Jews only as neighbors, drawing a circle around these to the exclusion of all

³⁰Jesus took up the question and said: "A man was going down **from Jerusalem to Jericho** and fell into the hands of robbers. They stripped him, beat him up, and fled, leaving him half dead. ³¹A priest happened to be going down that road. When he saw him, he passed by on the other side. ³²In the same way, a Levite, when he arrived at the place and saw him, passed by on the other side.

³³"**But a Samaritan**, while traveling, came up to him; and when he saw the man, he **had compassion**. ³⁴He went over to him and bandaged his wounds, pouring on oil and wine. Then he put him on his own animal, brought him to an inn, and took care of him. ³⁵The next day he took out two denarii, gave them to the innkeeper, and said, 'Take care of him; and when I come back I'll reimburse you for whatever extra you spend.'

³⁶"**Which of these three** do you think proved to be a neighbor to the man who fell into the hands of the robbers?"

³⁷ª"The one who showed mercy to him," he said.

³⁷ᵇThen Jesus told him, "**Go and do the same.**"

Priests and Levites

Priests and Levites were the professional ministers of Jesus' time who were responsible for conducting worship services in the Jewish temple in Jerusalem. The priests officiated at worship by offering various sacrifices and by leading the people in confession. The Levites, as assistants to the priests, conducted such menial duties as preparing the sacrifices, providing music, and taking care of the temple.

The priest and the Levite in Jesus' parable of the good Samaritan had probably completed their duties at the temple and were on their way home. The priest avoided the wounded man, perhaps supposing him to be dead and wishing to avoid ritual defilement by contact with a dead body. His attitude was one of callous indifference. The Levite showed even greater insensitivity. He satisfied his curiosity by stopping to look at the man but offered no help.

The two are cold examples of religious professionalism. The priest and the Levite were committed to service in the name of God, but they apparently assumed their responsibilities ended when they left the temple.

---

others. If this expert in the law was to keep the law of human kindness, he needed to have a clear definition of exactly who his neighbor was. Jesus responded by telling him a parable.

from Jerusalem to Jericho: The Jerusalem-to-Jericho road was a very steep descent lined with rocks behind which robbers could easily hide. This unfortunate man was the victim of such thieves.

But a Samaritan . . . had compassion: No people were more unneighborly toward one another than Jews and Samaritans. But this kind Samaritan traveler offered first aid to the wounded man, pouring oil and wine on his wounds and wrapping them in bandages. Then the Samaritan took him to the nearest inn and "took care of him." This was a thorough commitment to the wounded man's physical welfare. He paid the immediate expenses and promised to take care of the rest of the bill on his return journey.

Which of these three: Now it was time for Jesus to ask a question. Which one of these three people was neighbor to the wounded traveler? In a technical sense, the priest and Levite who failed to help the traveler were neighbors, assuming they were Jews. But this did not make them neighborly. They put their own interests ahead of another's needs when they

116. JESUS VISITS MARY AND MARTHA IN BETHANY

Luke 10:38–42

[38]While they were traveling, He entered a village, and a woman named **Martha** welcomed Him into her home. [39]She had a sister named **Mary**, who also **sat at the Lord's feet** and was listening to what He said. [40]But Martha was distracted by her many tasks, and she came up and asked, "Lord, don't You care that my sister has left me to serve alone? So **tell her to give me a hand.**"

[41]The Lord answered her, "Martha, Martha, you are worried and upset about many things, [42]but one thing is necessary. **Mary has made the right choice**, and it will not be taken away from her."

117. JESUS TEACHES THE DISCIPLES HOW TO PRAY

Matthew 6:9–13; Luke 11:1–13

[Lk 11:1]He was praying in a certain place, and when He finished, one of His disciples said to Him, "**Lord, teach us to pray**, just as John also taught his disciples."

[2a]He said to them, [Mt 6:9–13]"Therefore, you should pray like this: 'Our Father in heaven, Your name be honored as holy. [10]Your kingdom come. Your will be done on earth as it is in heaven. [11]Give us today our daily bread. [12]And forgive us our debts, as we also have forgiven our debtors [[Lk 11:4]*And forgive us our sins, for we ourselves also forgive everyone in debt to us*]. [13]And do not bring us into temptation, but deliver us from the evil one. For Yours is the kingdom and the power and the glory forever, Amen.'"*

The words "For Yours is the kingdom and the power and the glory forever, Amen" do not appear in some New Testament manuscripts.

"passed by on the other side." Love creates neighbors, sometimes of the most unlikely persons, and it expresses itself in neighborliness toward others.

Go and do the same: This expert in the law wanted eternal life, and he thought he could achieve it by keeping a code of laws. Jesus declared that until his religious performance reached out in compassion to the needy around him, his relationship with God was incomplete.

116. JESUS VISITS MARY AND MARTHA IN BETHANY

Martha . . . Mary: Mary and Martha were among the larger group of Jesus' friends and followers. They lived in the village of Bethany, about two miles southeast of Jerusalem (John 11:18). Martha was probably the older sister.

sat at the Lord's feet: Mary showed her devotion by sitting at Jesus' feet to learn from Him. To "sit at someone's feet" was to study His teachings.

tell her to give me a hand: As a hostess, Martha had more to do than she could accomplish alone. She asked Jesus to tell Mary to help her prepare the meal for their guest.

Mary has made the right choice: Jesus told Martha that only one thing ultimately is necessary—hearing and responding to the word of God. Mary had chosen to spend this precious time learning from Jesus. Martha's hospitality was good, but she was missing the best by failing to sit at Jesus' feet.

117. JESUS TEACHES THE DISCIPLES HOW TO PRAY

Lord, teach us to pray: By His own practice of prayer, Jesus stimulated His disciples to ask Him about how they should pray.

The Model Prayer

Luke 11:2–4 is an abbreviated version of the Model Prayer, more often called the "Lord's Prayer." The full version of this prayer appears in Jesus' Sermon on the Mount in the Gospel of Matthew (Matt. 6:9–13). It is called the "Model Prayer" because Jesus taught it to His disciples as a model to follow in response to their request, "Lord, teach us to pray" (Luke 11:1).

Jesus declared that we should begin our prayers by acknowledging God as our heavenly Father, respecting and honoring His name, and asking for His kingdom to reign on earth. It is also appropriate to ask God to give us "our daily bread"—to provide for our physical needs day by day (Luke 11:2–3).

Our prayers also ought to include our requests for God to forgive our sins. We also need His grace and love to fill our hearts so we can have a forgiving spirit toward others. Finally, we recognize through our prayers that temptation is strong. We need God's strength and guidance on a daily basis to keep us from giving in to temptation (Luke 11:4).

Lk 11:5–8He also said to them: "Suppose one of you has a friend and goes to him at midnight and says to him, 'Friend, **lend me three loaves** of bread, 6because a friend of mine on a journey has come to me, and I don't have anything to offer him.' 7Then he will answer from inside and say, 'Don't bother me! The door is already locked, and my children and I have gone to bed. I can't get up to give you anything.' 8I tell you, even though he won't get up and give him anything because he is his friend, yet **because of his persistence**, he will get up and give him as much as he needs.

9"So I say to you, **keep asking**, and it will be given to you. Keep **searching**, and you will find. Keep **knocking**, and the door will be opened to you. 10For everyone who asks receives, and the one who searches finds, and to the one who knocks, the door will be opened. 11What father among you, if his son asks for a fish, will, instead of a fish, give him a snake? 12Or if he asks for an egg, will **give him a scorpion**? 13If you then, who are evil, know how to give good gifts to your

---

lend me three loaves: Jesus described a traveler who showed up at midnight at a house whose occupants were out of food. There was not enough time for the hosts to bake new bread. The only alternative was to borrow a few loaves from a neighbor.

because of his persistence: At first, the neighbor refused this request for bread. But he finally gave in because of this host's persistence. Jesus was making a contrast between this man's reaction to a midnight request and our heavenly Father's response to His children's prayers. Our heavenly Father may be counted on to answer willingly when we call on Him in prayer for His aid.

keep asking . . . searching . . . knocking: To "ask," to "seek," and to "knock" indicate desire and determination. Our requests are tested by the fervency with which they are presented.

give him a scorpion: Jesus portrayed a child mistaking a snake for a fish. Fathers protect their children against their poor judgment or foolish ideas. They say no when refusal is necessary to safeguard the child. In the same way, God may not give us what we ask for, but we can rest assured He will always act in our best interest.

children, how much more will the heavenly Father give the Holy Spirit to those who ask Him?"

118. Jesus Accused of Healing through Beelzebul

Luke 11:14–28

[14]Now He was driving out a demon that was mute. When the demon came out, the man spoke who had been unable to speak, and the crowds were amazed. [15]But some of them said "He **drives out demons by Beelzebul**, the ruler of the demons!" [16]And others, as a test, were demanding of Him a sign from heaven.

[17]Knowing their thoughts, He told them: "Every kingdom divided against itself is headed for destruction, and a house divided against itself falls. [18]If Satan also is divided against himself, how will his kingdom stand? For you say I drive out demons by Beelzebul. [19]And **if I drive out demons by Beelzebul**, by whom do your sons drive them out? For this reason they will be your judges. [20]**If I drive out demons by the finger of God**, then the kingdom of God has come to you.

[21]"When **a strong man**, fully armed, guards his estate, his possessions are secure. [22]But when **one stronger than he** attacks and overpowers him, he takes from him all his weapons in which he trusted, and divides up his plunder. [23]Anyone who is not with Me is against Me, and anyone who does not gather with Me scatters.

[24]"When an unclean spirit comes out of a man, it roams through waterless places looking for rest, and not finding rest, it then says, 'I'll go back to my house where I came from.' [25]And returning, it finds the house swept and put in order. [26]Then off it goes and brings seven other spirits more evil than itself, and they enter and settle down there. As a result, that man's last condition is worse than the first."

[27]As He was saying these things, a woman from the crowd raised her voice and said to Him, "Blessed is the womb that bore You, and the breasts that nursed You!"

[28]He said, "More blessed still are those who hear the word of God and keep it!"

---

118. Jesus Accused of Healing through Beelzebul

drives out demons by Beelzebul: Beelzebul is a corruption of Baalzebub, the god of the fly. The pagans of Jesus' time named their gods after the pests they were supposed to avert. Jesus' critics could not deny that He had performed a miracle. So they tried to discredit it by claiming that Jesus had performed it through the power of Satan.

if I drive out demons by Beelzebul: Jesus argued that it was against reason and experience that He would cast out demons through the power of Satan. To cast out satanic evil spirits by Satan's power would mean that Satan was divided against himself.

If I drive out demons by the finger of God: The finger of God signifies the power of God. Since Jesus did not cast out demons by Satan, He must cast them out by the power of God. His actions demonstrated the arrival of the kingdom of God.

a strong man . . . one stronger than he: Satan is the strong man, his house the body of the demoniac, and his goods the evil spirit within the man. Jesus had entered his house and robbed him of his goods. Instead of being in league with Satan, He had overpowered Satan. The power of Jesus to cast out the demon was proof of His power over sin and evil.

119. The Sign of Jonah

Luke 11:29–36

²⁹As the crowds were increasing, He began saying: "**This generation** is an evil generation. It **demands a sign**, but **no sign** will be given to it **except the sign of Jonah**. ³⁰For just as Jonah became a sign to the people of Nineveh, so also the Son of Man will be to this generation. ³¹The queen of the south will rise up at the judgment with the men of this generation and condemn them, because she came from the ends of the earth to hear the wisdom of Solomon; and look—something greater than Solomon is here! ³²The men of Nineveh will rise up at the judgment with this generation and condemn it, because they repented at Jonah's proclamation; and look—something greater than Jonah is here!

³³"No one lights a lamp and puts it in the cellar or under a basket, but on a lampstand, so that those who come in may see its light. ³⁴Your eye is the lamp of the body. When your eye is good, your whole body is also full of light. But when it is bad, your body is also full of darkness. ³⁵Take care then, that the light in you is not darkness. ³⁶If therefore your whole body is full of light, with no part of it in darkness, the whole body will be full of light, as when a lamp shines its light on you."

120. Jesus Criticized by a Pharisee and an Expert in the Law

Luke 11:37–54

³⁷As He was speaking, a Pharisee asked Him to dine with him. So He went in and reclined at the table. ³⁸When the Pharisee saw this, he was amazed that He did not first perform the ritual washing before dinner. ³⁹But the Lord said to him: "Now you Pharisees clean the outside of the cup and dish, but **inside you are full of greed and evil**. ⁴⁰Fools! Didn't He who made the outside make the inside too? ⁴¹But give to charity what is within, and then everything is clean for you.

⁴²"But woe to you Pharisees! You **give a tenth** of mint, rue, and **every kind of herb**, and you bypass justice and love for God. These things you should have done without neglecting the others.

---

119. The Sign of Jonah

This generation . . . demands a sign: After Jesus rebuked them, the scribes and Pharisees asked for a sign. They wanted spectacular proof directly from heaven that Jesus was who He claimed to be.

no sign . . . except the sign of Jonah: Jonah was shown to be a true prophet of God because he was rescued from the stomach of a great fish. In the same way, Jesus would give irrefutable proof that He had been sent by God as the Christ, the promised Savior. This would be demonstrated by His resurrection from the dead.

120. Jesus Criticized by a Pharisee and an Expert in the Law

inside you are full of greed and evil: Jesus' words to this Pharisee may seem harsh, since He was an invited guest in his house. But the man's hypocrisy and self-righteous attitude deserved such biting words. Jesus was governed by higher laws than those of conventional politeness.

give a tenth . . . every kind of herb: The Pharisees were so fastidious in giving a tithe to God that they offered a tenth of the seed of small garden herbs. Jesus commended this care about little things. But He criticized the Pharisees because they were careless about important things, such as justice and the love of God.

⁴³"Woe to you Pharisees! You love the **front seat in the synagogues** and greetings in the marketplaces.

⁴⁴"Woe to you! You are **like unmarked graves**; the people who walk over them don't know it."

⁴⁵**One of the experts in the law** answered Him, "Teacher, when You say these things You insult us too."

⁴⁶And He said: "Woe to you experts in the law as well! **You load people with burdens** that are hard to carry, yet you yourselves don't touch these burdens with one of your fingers.

⁴⁷"Woe to you! **You build monuments to the prophets**, and your fathers killed them. ⁴⁸Therefore you are witnesses that you approve the deeds of your fathers, for they killed them, and you build their monuments. ⁴⁹And because of this, the wisdom of God said, 'I will send them prophets and apostles, and some of them they will kill and persecute,' ⁵⁰so that this generation may be held responsible for the blood of all the prophets shed since the foundation of the world, ⁵¹from the blood of Abel to the blood of Zechariah, who perished between the altar and the sanctuary. Yes, I tell you, this generation will be held responsible.

Ritual Washings

The Pharisee was amazed at Jesus because the traditions of the elders required them to wash their hands before eating. These washings were not performed for hygienic purposes but for ceremonial reasons. The Pharisees thought washing their hands was necessary to make them holy and acceptable to God. They avoided contact with the common people because they thought their touch would make them unclean. If they had been in a crowd where their bodies might have brushed against some "unclean" person, they even washed their entire bodies before eating.

Such fastidious ritual washings were not prescribed in the Mosaic Law. They had been added to the original law across the centuries through oral interpretation. But the Pharisees thought these traditions were just as binding as the original law.

---

front seat in the synagogues: Jesus focused on the Pharisees' vanity and love for attention. During the week, they enjoyed being greeted in the marketplace, and on the Sabbath they liked to sit in the seats behind the lectern of the reader in the synagogue. In these seats they faced the congregation and were sure to be noticed.

like unmarked graves: According to the Old Testament law, any person who touched a grave was rendered unclean (Num. 19:16). The Jews whitewashed their graves and tombs once a year to keep people from touching them by accident and being defiled. Jesus compared the Pharisees to unmarked graves that people wouldn't notice until they had touched them. The hypocrisy of the Pharisees concealed their true nature, so that people were corrupted by their influence without being aware of it.

One of the experts in the law: Experts in the law expounded on the oral law or the traditions of the elders. This law expert felt that Jesus was condemning them unfairly as a group along with His harsh criticism of the Pharisees.

You load people with burdens: Jesus had not spoken unfairly of the experts in the law. In fact, He declared that they were just as bad as the Pharisees. They had added hundreds of burdensome rules to the original law in the Hebrew Scriptures. The interpretations and teachings of the experts in the law had become more important than the original law. The legal experts had placed these burdensome rules on the common people, but they refused to be bound by these rules themselves.

You build monuments to the prophets: Jesus accused the Pharisees and teachers of the law of opposing and killing

⁵²"Woe to you experts in the law! **You have taken away the key of knowledge!** You didn't go in yourselves, and you hindered those who were going in."

⁵³When He left there, the scribes and the Pharisees began to oppose Him fiercely and to cross-examine Him about many things; ⁵⁴they were lying in wait for Him to trap Him in something He said.

121. JESUS WARNS ABOUT THE DECEPTION OF THE PHARISEES

Luke 12:1–12

¹In these circumstances, a crowd of many thousands came together, so that they were trampling on one another. He began to say to His disciples first: "Be on your guard against the **yeast of the Pharisees**, which is hypocrisy. ²There is nothing **covered** that won't be **uncovered**; nothing **hidden** that won't be **made known**. ³Therefore whatever you have said in the dark will be heard in the light, and what you have whispered in an ear in private rooms will be proclaimed on the housetops.

⁴"And I say to you, My friends, don't fear those who kill the body, and after that can do nothing more. ⁵But I will show you the One to fear: Fear Him who, after He has killed, has authority to throw into hell. Yes, I say to you, **this is the One to fear!** ⁶Aren't five sparrows sold for two pennies? Yet not one of them is forgotten in God's sight. ⁷But even **the hairs of your head are all counted**. Don't be afraid; you are worth more than many sparrows!

⁸"And I say to you, anyone who acknowledges Me before men, the Son of Man will also acknowledge him before the angels of God; ⁹but whoever denies Me before men will be denied before the angels of God. ¹⁰Anyone who speaks a

the prophets whom God had sent to the Jewish people. They pretended to honor the prophets by building ornate tombs in their honor. But a prophet is honored only when his message is received and obeyed.

You have taken away the key of knowledge! A knowledge of the Scriptures is the key that opens the door to the glories of Christ and His kingdom. The experts in the law had taken away this knowledge by teaching the nonsense of tradition rather than the genuine word of God. They did not open the door for themselves, and they confused others in their efforts to open it.

121. JESUS WARNS ABOUT THE DECEPTION OF THE PHARISEES

yeast of the Pharisees: The yeast of the Pharisees was hypocrisy—pretending to be what one is not, living a life of contempt for others and pride in one's moral superiority and self-righteousness. This type of life, Jesus declared, is like yeast. It gradually permeates a person's life, just as yeast or leaven works its way into the dough in the process of baking bread.

covered . . . uncovered . . . hidden . . . made known: Jesus warned His disciples about the persecution that would come in the future. Many of His followers would try to hide their faith. But this would be in vain. A person could not trust his own family to keep silent about what was said in the secret chambers of the home. Bold speech would be best.

this is the One to fear! The fear of God must be stronger than the fear of humans in such perilous times. Trust in God should cause His followers to speak out.

the hairs of your head are all counted: These words assured Jesus' followers of His constant care, no matter what dangers they might face.

teach you . . . what must be said: A believer might be tempted to hide or cover up his faith. Jesus directed His hearers to rely upon the Holy Spirit for what they needed to say at such times.

word against the Son of Man will be forgiven; but the one who blasphemes against the Holy Spirit will not be forgiven. [11]Whenever they bring you before synagogues and rulers and authorities, don't worry about how you should defend yourselves, or what you should say. [12]For the Holy Spirit will **teach you** at that very hour **what must be said**."

122. The Parable of the Rich Fool

Luke 12:13–21

[13]Someone from the crowd said to Him, "Teacher, tell my brother to **divide the inheritance with me**."

[14]"Friend," He said to him, "**who appointed Me a judge** or arbitrator over you?" [15]And He told them, "Watch out and be on guard against all greed, because one's life is not in the abundance of his possessions."

[16]Then He told them a parable: "A rich man's land was very productive. [17]He **thought to himself**, 'What should I do, since I don't have anywhere to store my crops? [18]I will do this,' he said. 'I'll tear down my barns and build bigger ones, and store all my grain and my goods there. [19]Then I'll say to myself, "You have many goods stored up for many years. Take it easy; eat, drink, and enjoy yourself,"'

[20]"But God said to him, '**You fool!** This very night your life is demanded of you. And the things you have prepared—whose will they be?'

[21]"That's how it is with the one who stores up treasure for himself and is not rich toward God."

123. The Wildflowers and the Ravens

Luke 12:22–34

[22]Then He said to His disciples: "Therefore I tell you, **don't worry** about your life, what you will eat; or about the body, what you will wear. [23]For life is more

---

122. The Parable of the Rich Fool

divide the inheritance with me: In the crowd was a man whose father had died. Apparently, an elder brother had taken possession of everything, disregarding any claim he might have on his father's estate. This man's request of Jesus showed his preoccupation with material concerns.

who appointed Me a judge: Jesus used this opportunity to condemn the view that the material is more important than the spiritual by telling this parable.

thought to himself: Jesus did not condemn the man in His parable because he was wealthy; He condemned his self-centeredness. He gave thought neither to others, nor to God—the source of His abundance.

You fool! This rich man's shortcoming was leaving God out of the picture and assuming he was the master of his own destiny. Jesus reminded His hearers of the uncertainty of life and the foolishness of presuming on the future.

123. The Wildflowers and the Ravens

don't worry: Jesus was speaking to disciples who had left their homes and occupations to follow Him. They did not know how they might get their next meal. He told them not to worry about material needs.

than food and the body more than clothing. ²⁴Consider the **ravens**: they don't sow or reap; they don't have a storeroom or a barn; yet God feeds them. Aren't you worth much more than the birds? ²⁵Can any of you **add a cubit to his height** by worrying? ²⁶If then you're not able to do even a little thing, why worry about the rest?

²⁷"Consider how the **wildflowers** grow: they don't labor or spin thread. Yet I tell you, not even Solomon in all his splendor was adorned like one of these! ²⁸If that's how God clothes the grass, which is in the field today and is thrown into the furnace tomorrow, how much more will He do for you—you of little faith? ²⁹Don't keep striving for **what you should eat and** what you should **drink**, and do not be anxious. ³⁰For the Gentile world eagerly seeks all these things, and your Father knows that you need them.

³¹"But seek His kingdom, and these things will be provided for you. ³²Don't be afraid, little flock, because your Father delights to give you the kingdom. ³³Sell your possessions and give to the poor. Make money bags for yourselves that won't grow old, an inexhaustible treasure in heaven, where no thief comes near and no moth destroys. ³⁴For where your treasure is, there your heart will be also."

124. Jesus Discusses His Second Coming

Luke 12:35–48

³⁵"Be ready for service and **have your lamps lit**. ³⁶You must be like people waiting for their master to return from the wedding banquet so that when he comes and knocks, they can open the door for him at once. ³⁷Blessed are those slaves whom **the master** will find alert when he comes. I assure you: He will get ready, have them recline at the table, then come and serve them. ³⁸If he comes in the middle of the night, or even near dawn, and finds them alert, blessed are those slaves.

³⁹"But know this: if the homeowner had known at what hour **the thief** was coming, he would not have let his house be broken into. ⁴⁰You also be ready, because the Son of Man is coming at an hour that you do not expect."

---

ravens . . . wildflowers: The God who provides for ravens and wildflowers can surely be trusted to take care of His children. God's human creatures are more important than birds or flowers.

add a cubit to his height: Jesus was probably referring to age, not height. Worrying about how long we are going to live only adds to the possibility of death. Jesus was appealing to common sense by this illustration of the futility of worry.

what you should eat and . . . drink: When believers worry about food and clothing, we are acting no different than the people of the world. When we make God's interests our own and are more concerned about the needs of others than our own needs, worry will have no place in our lives.

124. Jesus Discusses His Second Coming

have your lamps lit: Jesus used this analogy to show that His followers should be ready at all times for His return. This lamp illustration reminds us of His parable of the virgins, five of whom were ready for the appearance of the groom and five of whom were unprepared (see segment 172, "The Parable of the Ten Virgins," p. 202).

the master . . . the thief: To some people the coming of Jesus will be like that of a master whom they have served faith-

⁴¹"Lord," Peter asked, "are You telling this parable **to us or to everyone?**"

⁴²The Lord said: "Who then is **the faithful and sensible manager** whom his master will put in charge of his household servants to give them their alloted food at the proper time? ⁴³Blessed is that slave whom his master, when he comes, will find at work. ⁴⁴I tell you the truth: he will put him in charge of all his possessions.

⁴⁵"But if that slave says in his heart, 'My master is delaying his coming,' and starts to beat the male and female slaves, and to eat and drink and get drunk, ⁴⁶that slave's master will come on a day he does not expect him, and at an hour he does not know. He will cut him to pieces and assign him a place with the unbelievers. ⁴⁷And that slave who knew his master's will, and didn't prepare himself or do it, will be severely beaten.

⁴⁸"But the one who did not know, and did things deserving of blows, will be beaten lightly. Much will be required of everyone who has been given much. And even more will be expected of the one who has been entrusted with more."

125. Jesus Predicts His Death by Crucifixion

Luke 12:49–59

⁴⁹"I came to bring **fire** on the earth, and how I wish it were already set ablaze! ⁵⁰But I have **a baptism** to be baptized with, and how it consumes Me until it is finished! ⁵¹Do you think that I came here to give peace to the earth? No, I tell you, but rather division! ⁵²From now on, five in one household will be divided: three against two, and two against three. ⁵³'They will be divided, father against son, son against father, mother against daughter, daughter against mother, mother-in-law against her daughter-in-law, and daughter-in-law against mother-in-law.'"

⁵⁴He also said to the crowds: "When you see **a cloud** rising in the west, right away you say, 'A storm is coming,' and so it does. ⁵⁵And when **the south wind** is blowing, you say, 'It's going to be a scorcher!' and it is. ⁵⁶Hypocrites! You know how to interpret the appearance of the earth and the sky, but why don't you know how to interpret this time?

---

fully. But to those who are not ready, His coming will seem like that of a plunderer who comes in suddenly and robs them of all their possessions.

to us or to everyone? Peter wanted to know if Jesus' instructions applied only to the apostles or to all His followers.

the faithful and sensible manager: Jesus' answer shows that He was especially encouraging the disciples to be watchful. A manager is distinct from the household. He is responsible for the management of the entire household. But Jesus did not exclude any of His followers from His exhortation to watchfulness.

125. Jesus Predicts His Death by Crucifixion

fire . . . a baptism: "Fire" represents the divisions caused by the ministry of Jesus. His "baptism" is His suffering and death that were drawing closer every day.

a cloud . . . the south wind: Jesus was criticizing the spiritual blindness of the people. They could interpret weather signs, but they could not see what God was doing in their midst in the person of His Son.

⁵⁷"Why don't you judge for yourselves what is right? ⁵⁸As you are going with your adversary to the ruler, **make an effort to settle with him** on the way. Then he won't drag you before the judge, the judge hand you over to the bailiff, and the bailiff throw you into prison. ⁵⁹I tell you, you will never get out of there until you have paid the last cent."

126. The Parable of the Barren Fig Tree

Two Useless Fig Trees

In this parable Jesus compared the nation of Israel to a fruitless fig tree. Later, he pronounced a curse against a fig tree, declaring that it would never bear fruit again (see segment 158, "Jesus Curses a Fig Tree and Cleanses the Temple," p. 185). To Jesus, both trees demonstrated Israel's lack of faith. He was clearly revealed to the Jewish nation as the Messiah, but they refused to believe.

Luke 13:1–9

¹At that time, some people came and reported to Him about the Galileans whose blood Pilate had mixed with their sacrifices. ²And He responded to them, "Do you think that these Galileans were more sinful than all Galileans because they suffered these things? ³No, I tell you; but unless you repent, you will all perish as well! ⁴Or those eighteen that the tower in Siloam fell on and killed—do you think they were **more sinful than all** the people **who live in Jerusalem?** ⁵No, I tell you; but unless you repent, you will all perish as well!"

⁶And **He told this parable**: "A man had a fig tree that was planted in his vineyard. He came looking for fruit on it and found none. ⁷He told the vineyard worker, 'Listen, for three years I have come looking for fruit on this fig tree and haven't found any. Cut it down! Why should it even waste the soil?'

⁸"But he replied to him, 'Sir, leave it this year also, until I dig around it and fertilize it. ⁹Perhaps it will bear fruit next year, but if not, you can cut it down.'

---

make an effort to settle with him: Jesus compared the people to a guilty man who was about to be taken to court by his accuser. He could settle the matter if he acted quickly. Otherwise, he would be taken before the judge, convicted, and thrown into prison. Jesus declared that the people faced God's certain judgment, but they still had time to repent.

126. The Parable of the Barren Fig Tree

more sinful than all . . . who live in Jerusalem? The people of Jesus' time generally believed that persons who were struck by disaster were being punished by God because of their sin. This is probably why these people mentioned the Galileans who had been murdered by Pilate. But Jesus rejected this false premise. He warned the people who brought this report that they themselves would perish unless they repented. Those Galileans were not greater sinners than they were.

He told this parable: Jesus compared Israel to a fig tree. God had given the Jewish people every opportunity to bear fruit, but they were still unfruitful. But God would give them a final chance through the ministry of Jesus. If they persisted in their unbelief and sin, they would be cut down from their privileged position as the chosen people of God.

127. Jesus Heals a Woman with a Crooked Back

Luke 13:10–17

[10]As He was teaching in one of the synagogues on the Sabbath, [11]a woman was there who had been **disabled by a spirit** for over 18 years. She was bent over and could not straighten up at all. [12]When Jesus saw her, He called out to her, "Woman, you are free of your disability." [13]Then He laid His hands on her, and instantly she was restored and began to glorify God.

[14]But the **leader of the synagogue, indignant** because Jesus had healed on the Sabbath, responded by telling the crowd, "There are six days when work should be done; therefore come on those days and be healed, and not on the Sabbath day."

[15]But the Lord answered him and said, "Hypocrites! Doesn't each one of you untie his ox or donkey from the manger on the Sabbath, and lead it to water? [16]And this woman, a daughter of Abraham, whom Satan has bound for 18 years—shouldn't she be **untied from this bondage on the Sabbath day?**"

[17]When He had said these things, all His adversaries were humiliated, but the whole crowd was rejoicing over all the glorious things He was doing.

128. Jesus Claims to Be One with God

John 10:22–42

[22]Then the Festival of Dedication took place in Jerusalem; and it was winter. [23]Jesus was walking in the temple complex in Solomon's Colonnade. [24]Then the Jews surrounded Him and asked, "How long are you going to keep us in suspense? If You are the Messiah, tell us plainly."

[25]"**I did tell you** and you don't believe," Jesus answered them. "The works that I do in My Father's name testify about Me. [26]But you don't believe because

---

127. Jesus Heals a Woman with a Crooked Back

disabled by a spirit: The word *spirit* indicates that the curvature of the spine that afflicted this woman was attributed to demons. Jesus agreed with this assessment after He healed her when He declared that Satan had bound her "for 18 years."

leader of the synagogue, indignant: The ruler of the synagogue reprimanded the worshipers for this action, apparently because some were there in hopes of being healed. This was also a criticism of Jesus for healing on the Sabbath.

untied from this bondage on the Sabbath day? Jesus responded to this criticism by declaring that a person was more important than an animal. Even the Pharisees in their interpretation of the law allowed a person to untie an ox on the Sabbath and lead it to water. Was it not appropriate for this woman to be set free from her disability on the Sabbath?

128. Jesus Claims to Be One with God

I did tell you: Jesus was the Messiah predicted in the Old Testament, but He was not the type of Messiah the Jewish people expected. He was a spiritual deliverer, not a military leader. He had demonstrated repeatedly that He was the Son of God but the Pharisees and other Jewish religious leaders had refused to accept Him as such.

The Festival of Dedication

John 10:22 is the only place in the Bible where the Festival of Dedication is mentioned. Jesus was in Jerusalem for this festival, which commemorated the restoration and purification of the Jewish temple in 164 B.C. after it had been desecrated by the Syrian ruler Antiochus Epiphanes. Known today as Hanukkah, this festival is still celebrated by the Jewish people.

Since the Festival of Dedication commemorated a time of national deliverance for the Jews, the religious leaders considered it an opportune time to tempt Jesus to declare Himself to be the Messiah. They wanted Him to tell them clearly whether He would deliver them from oppression by the Romans. This was the popular expectation of what the Messiah would do. They wanted Jesus to make an open declaration that might be used as an accusation against Him.

---

you are not My sheep. ²⁷My sheep hear My voice, I know them, and they follow Me. ²⁸I give them eternal life, and they will never perish—ever! No one will snatch them out of My hand. ²⁹My Father, who has given them to Me, is greater than all. No one is able to snatch them out of the Father's hand. ³⁰The Father and I are one."

³¹Again the Jews picked up rocks to stone Him.

³²Jesus replied, "I have shown you many good works from the Father. For which of these works are you stoning Me?"

³³"We aren't stoning You for a good work," the Jews answered, "but for blasphemy, and because You—being a man—make Yourself God."

³⁴Jesus answered them, "Isn't it written in your law, 'I said, you are gods'? ³⁵If He called those to whom the Word of God came 'gods'—and the Scripture cannot be broken—³⁶do you say, 'You are blaspheming,' to the One the Father set apart and sent into the world, because I said 'I am the Son of God'? ³⁷If I am not doing My Father's works, don't believe Me. ³⁸But if I am doing them and you don't believe Me, **believe the works**. This way you will know and understand that the Father is in Me and I in the Father." ³⁹Then they were trying again to seize Him, yet He eluded their grasp.

⁴⁰So He departed again across the Jordan to the place where John first was baptizing, and He remained there. ⁴¹Many came to Him and said, "John never did a sign, but everything John said about this man was true." ⁴²And many believed in Him there.

---

you are not My sheep: Jesus declared that the religious leaders did not believe He was the Messiah because they did not belong to Him. Their failure to be His sheep was evidence of their unbelief.

believe the works: The religious leaders attempted to stone Jesus for what they considered blasphemy—claiming to be God. If you don't believe what I say, Jesus declared, then consider what I do. Surely His work of healing and performing miracles should have convinced them He was doing God's work as God's divine representative. But this appeal fell on deaf ears as they attempted to arrest Him.

129. The Narrow Way of Salvation

Luke 13:22–30

²²He went through one town and village after another, teaching and making His way to Jerusalem. ²³ᵃ"Lord," someone asked Him, "**are there few being saved?**"

²³ᵇHe said to them, ²⁴"Make every effort to **enter through the narrow door**, because I tell you, many will try to enter and won't be able ²⁵once the home-owner gets up and shuts the door. Then you will stand outside and knock on the door, saying, 'Lord, open up for us!' He will answer you, '**I don't know you** or where you're from.'

²⁶"Then you will say, 'We ate and drank in Your presence, and You taught in our streets!' ²⁷But He will say, 'I tell you, I don't know you or where you're from. Get away from Me, all you workers of unrighteousness!' ²⁸There will be weeping and gnashing of teeth in that place, when you see Abraham, Isaac, Jacob, and all the prophets in the kingdom of God, but yourselves thrown out. ²⁹They will come from east and west, from north and south, and recline at the table in the kingdom of God. ³⁰Note this: some are **last** who will be **first**, and some are **first** who will be **last**."

130. Jesus Is Warned about Herod

Luke 13:31–33

³¹At that time some Pharisees came and told Him, "Go, get out of here! **Herod wants to kill You!**"

---

129. The Narrow Way of Salvation

are there few being saved? The Jews took great pride in their status as God's chosen people. They extended their exclusive spirit even to the world to come. They believed that none but the chosen race would experience the glories of the afterlife. The person who asked this question probably wanted Jesus to commit Himself to this narrow Jewish spirit.

enter through the narrow door: Jesus pointed out that the doorway to eternal life is very narrow. Only those who strive with all their might to enter in by this narrow door will be saved. Many of the Jews particularly who thought they had the exclusive right to enter God's kingdom would be excluded.

I don't know you: When the door to eternal life has been shut and the time of grace is past, Jesus declared, many people would try to obtain entry but in vain. It would then be too late.

last ... first ... first ... last: The Jews thought they had the first place in God's kingdom secured. But Jesus declared that the first in His kingdom would be those who came to Him in faith. (For more teachings of Jesus on the "first/last" theme, see segment 149, "Jesus and the Rich Young Ruler," p. 174, and segment 150, "The Parable of the Vineyard Workers," p. 175.)

130. Jesus Is Warned about Herod

Herod wants to kill You! Jesus was in Perea—the region east of the Jordan River—where Herod Antipas had jurisdiction. The Pharisees who came to Jesus had little authority in this part of Palestine. Perhaps they were trying to frighten Jesus into the southern section of Palestine known as Judea. Here Jesus would be subject to their authority and the power of the Sanhedrin.

³²And He said to them, "Go tell that fox, 'Look! I'm driving out demons and performing healings today and tomorrow, and on the third day **I will complete My work**.' ³³Yet I must travel today, tomorrow, and the next day, because it is not possible for **a prophet to perish outside of Jerusalem!**"

131. JESUS EXPRESSES HIS SORROW OVER JERUSALEM

Matthew 23:37–39; Luke 13:34–35

Lk 13:34–35"**O Jerusalem! Jerusalem!** The city who kills the prophets and stones those who are sent to her! How often I wanted to gather your children together, as a hen gathers her chicks under her wings, **but you were not willing!** ³⁵See! Your house is abandoned to you. And I tell you, you will not see Me until the time comes when you say, 'Blessed is He who comes in the name of the Lord!'"

132. JESUS HEALS A MAN WHOSE BODY WAS SWOLLEN WITH FLUID

Luke 14:1–6

¹One Sabbath, when He went to eat at the house of **one of the leading Pharisees**, they were watching Him closely. ²There in front of Him was a man whose body was swollen with fluid. ³In response, Jesus asked the law experts and the Pharisees, "**Is it lawful to heal on the Sabbath** or not?" ⁴ªBut they kept silent.

I will complete My work: Jesus ordered the Pharisees to tell Herod that, in spite of all his threats, He would continue to release people from their physical and spiritual misery until His work in that region was complete.

a prophet to perish outside of Jerusalem! Jesus would choose the time when He would leave Herod's jurisdiction to go to Jerusalem—the traditional place for prophets to be killed.

131. JESUS EXPRESSES HIS SORROW OVER JERUSALEM

O Jerusalem! Jerusalem! Since Jerusalem was the religious center of the Jewish nation, Jesus may have been speaking metaphorically. Practically the entire nation, represented by Jerusalem, had rejected His message and refused to accept Him as God's Son.

but you were not willing! No matter how much Jesus loved people and called them to faith and commitment, He would not force them to follow Him.

132. JESUS HEALS A MAN WHOSE BODY WAS SWOLLEN WITH FLUID

one of the leading Pharisees: This man was a leader or prominent member of the Pharisees, perhaps a ruler of a local synagogue.

Is it lawful to heal on the Sabbath: Among the spectators of this Sabbath feast was a man with excess fluid in his body. Knowing the extreme views on the Sabbath held by Pharisees, Jesus asked whether it would be in order for Him to heal the man. The silence that attended this question was as good as a resounding no. But Jesus healed the man. Then He followed up with another question. Would not these Pharisees go to the aid of one of their animals that had fallen into a pit on the Sabbath?

⁴ᵇHe took the man, healed him, and sent him away. ⁵And to them, He said, "Which of you whose son or ox falls into a well, will not immediately pull him out on the Sabbath day?" ⁶To this they could find no answer.

133. Jesus Teaches about Humility

Luke 14:7–14

⁷He told a parable to those who were invited, when He noticed how they would **choose the best places for themselves**: ⁸"When you are invited by someone to a wedding banquet, don't recline at the best place, because a more distinguished person than you may have been invited by your host. ⁹The one who invited both of you may come and say to you, 'Give your place to this man,' and then in humiliation, you will proceed to take the lowest place.

¹⁰"But when you are invited, go and recline in the lowest place, so that when the one who invited you comes, he will say to you, 'Friend, move up higher.' **You will then be honored** in the presence of all the other guests. ¹¹For everyone who exalts himself will be humbled, and the one who humbles himself will be exalted."

¹²He also said to the one who had invited Him, "When you give a lunch or a dinner, don't invite your friends, your brothers, your relatives, or your rich neighbors, because they might invite you back, and you would be repaid. ¹³On the contrary, when you host a banquet, **invite those who are poor**, maimed, lame, or blind. ¹⁴And you will be blessed, because they cannot repay you; for you will be repaid at the resurrection of the righteous."

134. The Parable of the Large Banquet

Luke 14:15–24

¹⁵When one of those who reclined at the table with Him heard these things, he said to Him, "**Blessed is the one** who will eat bread in the kingdom of God!"

---

133. Jesus Teaches about Humility

choose the best places for themselves: The highest honor at a banquet was the seat next to the host. Jesus noticed a competitive spirit among the guests in the Pharisee's home as they competed for the best seats.

You will then be honored: Jesus told these people that the better course was to be seated at a distance from the host. Then they might be honored as the host said, "Friend, move up higher."

invite those who are poor: From the time of Moses, hospitality toward outsiders was urged upon God's people. The Festival of Pentecost and the Festival of Tabernacles were to be shared with the poor and helpless (Deut. 16:9–15). But Jesus extended this rule beyond religious festivals. Instead of always inviting friends and family to special meals, places at a table should be provided for the underprivileged—those who would never be able to repay the favor.

134. The Parable of the Large Banquet

Blessed is the one: Jesus' talk about whom to invite to a feast made at least one of His fellow guests uncomfortable. He tried to turn the conversation away from the present to the distant future. Jesus responded with a parable on the need to respond to God's gracious invitation.

¹⁶Then He told him: "A man was giving a large banquet and invited many. ¹⁷At the time of the banquet, he sent his slave to tell those who were invited, 'Come, because everything is now ready.'

¹⁸"But without exception they **all began to make excuses**. The first one said to him, 'I have bought a field, and I must go out and see it. I ask you to excuse me.'

¹⁹"Another said, 'I have bought five yoke of oxen, and I'm going to try them out. I ask you to excuse me.'

²⁰"And another said, 'I just got married, and therefore I'm unable to come.'

²¹"So the slave came back and reported these things to his master. Then in anger, the master of the house told his slave, 'Go out quickly **into the streets and alleys** of the city, and bring in here the poor, maimed, blind, and lame!'

²²"'Master,' the slave said, 'what you ordered has been done, and there's still room.'

²³"Then the master told the slave, 'Go out into the highways and lanes and make them come in, so that my house may be filled. ²⁴For I tell you, not one of those men who were invited will enjoy my banquet!'"

A Parable of Exclusion and Inclusion

Jesus' listeners would have been blind not to recognize the history of Israel in this parable. God had planned "a large banquet," an opportunity for fellowship between Himself and the Jewish people. The invitation was issued at Sinai, when a covenant relationship was established between God and His people. But they treated this covenant with contempt and abused its conditions. Many in Israel turned from the Lord to worship pagan idols.

But God continued to send His servants, the prophets, to invite the nation and its leaders to return to Him to enjoy the blessings He had promised if they were obedient. In Jesus' time, the religious leaders rejected Him and His message. Yet there was room in the heart of God for others. He sent His servants into the Gentile world to offer them the joys of His eternal kingdom. The favored were excluded by their rejection, while the pagan Gentiles were included because of their willingness to hear and obey.

God's intention from the beginning when He called Abraham was to include all people in His invitation. No one is excluded except those who refuse to accept His invitation.

---

all began to make excuses: The guests invited to a banquet began immediately to excuse themselves. The newly married man probably had the best reason for declining the host's invitation. The Old Testament law excused a man from business or military service for one year after he was married (Deut. 24:5). But the other two were almost ridiculous in the excuses they used. All three declared they had more important things to do. This was an insulting reply to a generous host.

into the streets and alleys: The reaction of the host was to seek other guests from among the disabled and distressed. These were the "street people" of Jesus' day. What the upper crust of society had rejected, the poor and afflicted were invited to enjoy.

135. THE COST OF FOLLOWING JESUS

Luke 14:25–35

^{25}Now great crowds were traveling with Him. So He turned and said to them: ^{26}"If anyone comes to Me and does not **hate his own father and mother**, wife and children, brothers and sisters—yes, and even his own life—he cannot be My disciple. ^{27}Whoever does not **bear his own cross** and come after Me cannot be My disciple.

^{28}"For which of you, wanting to build a tower, doesn't first sit down and calculate the cost, to see if he has enough to complete it? ^{29}Otherwise, after he has laid the foundation, and cannot finish it, all the onlookers will begin to make fun of him, ^{30}saying, 'This man **started to build and wasn't able to finish**.'

^{31}"Or what king, going to war against another king, will not first sit down and decide if he is able with ten thousand to oppose the one who comes against him with twenty thousand? ^{32}If not, while the other is still far off, he sends a delegation and asks for terms of peace. ^{33}In the same way, therefore, every one of you who does not say goodbye to all his possessions cannot be My disciple.

^{34}"Now, salt is good, but **if salt should lose its taste**, how will it be made salty? ^{35}It isn't fit for the soil or for the manure pile; they throw it out. Anyone who has ears to hear should listen!"

136. THE PARABLE OF THE LOST SHEEP

Matthew 18:12–14; Luke 15:1–7

$^{Lk\ 15:1-2}$All the tax collectors and sinners were drawing near to listen to Him. ^{2}And the Pharisees and scribes were complaining, "This man welcomes sinners and eats with them!"

^{3}So He told them this parable: ^{4}"What man among you, who has a hundred sheep and loses one of them, does not leave the ninety-nine in the open field and **go after the lost one** until he finds it? ^{5}When he has found it, he joyfully puts it

---

135. THE COST OF FOLLOWING JESUS

hate his own father and mother: Jesus wanted to encourage whole-hearted discipleship. All other loyalties—even to members of one's own family—were to be secondary to the loyalty and affection He demanded of them.

bear his own cross: Jesus declared that the person who followed Him must be willing to deny himself and to renounce all ambition and self-interest and even to die for His sake. To bear a cross meant to be willing to die the death of a martyr for the cause of Christ.

started to build and wasn't able to finish: A person should count the cost before enlisting as a follower of Christ. Discipleship carries a high cost, and those who follow Christ must be willing to pay the price.

if salt should lose its taste: A follower who was unwilling to sacrifice everything for Christ's sake was of no value—as worthless as salt that had lost its taste and been thrown away.

136. THE PARABLE OF THE LOST SHEEP

go after the lost one: A concerned shepherd would search for one lost sheep until he found it. Jesus was explaining His attitude toward tax collectors and sinners. He saw these people through the eyes of the One from whom they had gone

Jesus' Association with Sinners

To the scribes and Pharisees, Jesus could not associate with sinners without becoming tainted with their sins. They were "unclean" people who passed on their sin and corruption to others. The Pharisees shunned such people, hoping to keep themselves clean and morally pure.

Jesus' attitude toward tax collectors and sinners explains why they were attracted to Him. Rather than avoiding them, He treated them with respect and compassion. Eating with someone is an act of friendship and fellowship. Jesus did not hesitate to eat with tax collectors and sinners. He showed by His actions the desire of God to welcome all repentant sinners—even those considered unworthy outcasts by the self-righteous Pharisees.

---

on his shoulders, ⁶and coming home, he calls his friends and neighbors together, saying to them, 'Rejoice with me, because I have found my lost sheep!' ⁷I tell you, in the same way, there will be more **joy in heaven** over one sinner who repents than over ninety-nine righteous people who don't need repentance."

137. THE PARABLE OF THE LOST COIN

Luke 15:8–10

⁸"Or what woman who has ten silver coins, if she loses one coin, does not light a lamp, sweep the house, and **search carefully until she finds it**? ⁹When she finds it, she calls her women friends and neighbors together, saying, 'Rejoice with me, because I have found the silver coin I lost!' ¹⁰I tell you, in the same way, there is **joy in the presence of God's angels** over one sinner who repents."

---

astray. He went after sinners and associated with them wherever He could find them.

joy in heaven: The Pharisees might not rejoice over repentant sinners whom Jesus sought, but heaven rings with joy over one repentant sinner.

137. THE PARABLE OF THE LOST COIN

search carefully until she finds it: This woman had managed to save an amount equal to about ten days' wages. Losing one of these coins was a great loss to her. She did what the shepherd did about his lost sheep—she searched for it until she found it.

joy in the presence of God's angels: God is like the woman who calls in her friends and neighbors to rejoice with her over her lost coin. God calls the angels of heaven to rejoice with Him over one lost sinner who repents.

138. The Parable of the Lost Son

Luke 15:11–32

[11]He also said: "A man had two sons. [12]The younger of them said to his father, '**Father, give me the share** of the estate I have coming to me.' So he distributed the assets to them. [13]Not many days later, the younger son gathered together all he had and traveled to a distant country, where he squandered his estate in foolish living. [14]After he had spent everything, a severe famine struck that country, and he had nothing. [15]Then he went to work for one of the citizens of that country, who sent him into his fields to **feed pigs**. [16]He longed to eat his fill from the carob pods the pigs were eating, and no one would give him any.

[17]"But when he came to his senses, he said, 'How many of my father's hired hands have more than enough food, and here I am dying of hunger! [18]I'll get up, go to my father, and say to him, "**Father, I have sinned** against heaven and in your sight. [19]I'm no longer worthy to be called your son. Make me like one of your hired hands."'

[20]"So he got up and went to his father. But while the son was still a long way off, **his father saw him and** was filled with compassion. He **ran**, threw his arms around his neck, and kissed him. [21]The son said to him, 'Father, I have sinned against heaven and in your sight. I'm no longer worthy to be called your son.'

[22]"But the father told his slaves, 'Quick! Bring out the **best robe** and put it on him; put a **ring** on his finger and **sandals** on his feet. [23]Then bring the fatted calf and slaughter it, and let's celebrate with a feast, [24]because this son of mine was dead and is alive again; he was lost and is found!' So they began to celebrate.

[25]"Now his **older son** was in the field; as he came near the house, he heard music and dancing. [26]So he summoned one of the servants and asked what these things meant. [27]'Your brother is here,' he told him, 'and your father has slaughtered the fatted calf because he has him back safe and sound.'

---

138. The Parable of the Lost Son

Father, give me the share: An estate generally was not divided between sons until the death of the father. But in this case, the younger son requested his share immediately.

feed pigs: Money proved to be this son's downfall. He squandered his inheritance in "foolish living." When his money gave out, he hired himself out to a keeper of pigs. To Jesus' Jewish listeners, this would be the lowest point to which a person could fall—working for a Gentile, feeding pigs, and satisfying his hunger from their feeding trough.

Father, I have sinned: Thoughts of home and a loving father motivated the son to think about a new start. His father's hired hands fared better than he. As he thought about the mistake he had made and the sins he had committed, he felt deep remorse. He must retrace his steps, acknowledge his guilt, and be prepared for the consequences.

his father saw him and . . . ran: The father was waiting expectantly for his wayward son. From the day the boy left home, he had kept watch for him. The son's words of regret and repentance were stifled by his father's warm embrace.

best robe . . . ring . . . sandals: The father ignored his son's suggestion that he should be treated like a household servant. Nothing was too good or too expensive for this lost son who had returned home at last. It was as though a person mourned as dead had been raised to life again.

older son . . . became angry: When the father and his household "began to celebrate," there was one absentee—the older son. He showed his annoyance over the homecoming party by staying away. Proud of his record as an obedient

²⁸"Then he **became angry** and didn't want to go in. So his father came out and pleaded with him. ²⁹But he replied to his father, 'Look, I have been slaving many years for you, and I have never disobeyed your orders; yet you never gave me a young goat so I could celebrate with my friends. ³⁰But when this son of yours came, who has devoured your assets with prostitutes, you slaughtered the fatted calf for him.'

³¹"'Son,' he said to him, '**you are always with me**, and everything I have is yours. ³²But we had to celebrate and rejoice, because this brother of yours was dead and is alive again; he was lost and is found.'"

139. THE PARABLE OF THE DISHONEST MANAGER

Luke 16:1–18

¹He also said to the disciples: "There was a rich man who received an accusation that his manager was squandering his possessions. ²So he called the manager in and asked, 'What is this I hear about you? **Give an account of your management**, because you can no longer be my manager.'

³"Then the manager said to himself, 'What should I do since my master is taking the management away from me? I'm not strong enough to dig; I'm ashamed to beg. ⁴I know what I'll do so that when I'm removed from management, people will welcome me into their homes.'

⁵"So he **summoned** each one of **his master's debtors**. 'How much do you owe my master?' he asked the first one.

⁶ᵃ"'A hundred measures of oil,' he said.

⁶ᵇ"'Take your invoice,' he told him, 'sit down quickly, and write fifty.'

⁷ᵃ"Next he asked another, 'How much do you owe?'

⁷ᵇ"'A hundred measures of wheat,' he said.

⁷ᶜ"'Take your invoice,' he told him, 'and write eighty.'

---

son, he was disgruntled over his brother's return. Compare this attitude with the critics of Jesus—the scribes and Pharisees—who were strict observers of the Mosaic Law. In their righteous pride, they passed judgment on those people who did not conform to their hypocritical standards.

you are always with me: The father issued a gentle rebuke to the older son. He had a place in his heart for both sons. Only by our own action can we exclude ourselves from God's love. This comes about through our pride and self-righteousness.

139. THE PARABLE OF THE DISHONEST MANAGER

Give an account of your management: This manager was the caretaker of the rich man's estate. He was accused of mismanaging his employer's property. The rich man prepared to fire the manager and told him to turn over the records of all his transactions.

summoned . . . his master's debtors: The manager hit upon a plan to assure his future after his employment with the rich man was terminated. He called in his employer's debtors one by one and reduced their debts, assuming they would return the favors at a later time.

master praised the unrighteous manager: The rich man in Jesus' parable commended the manager for his shrewd actions. It may have been a reluctant commendation, as if to say, "What a clever and scheming scoundrel he is!"

[8]"The **master praised the unrighteous manager** because he had acted astutely. For the sons of this age are **more astute than the sons of light** in dealing with their own people. [9]And I tell you, make friends for yourselves by means of the money of unrighteousness, so that when it fails, they may welcome you into eternal dwellings. [10]Whoever is faithful in very little is also faithful in much; and whoever is unrighteous in very little is also unrighteous in much. [11]So if you have not been faithful with the unrighteous money, who will trust you with what is genuine? [12]And if you have not been faithful with what belongs to someone else, who will give you what is your own?

[13]"No servant can be the slave of two masters, since either he will hate one and love the other, or he will be devoted to one and despise the other. You can't be slaves to both God and money."

[14]The Pharisees, who were lovers of money, were listening to all these things and scoffing at Him. [15]And He told them, "You are the ones who justify yourselves in the sight of others, but God knows your hearts. For what is highly admired by people is revolting in God's sight.

[16]"The Law and the Prophets were until John; since then, the good news of the kingdom of God has been proclaimed, and everyone is strongly urged to enter it. [17]But it is easier for heaven and earth to pass away than for one stroke of a letter in the law to drop out.

[18]"Everyone who divorces his wife and marries another woman commits adultery, and everyone who marries a woman divorced from her husband commits adultery."

A Commendation for Dishonesty?

Many people are disturbed by this parable because Jesus seems to be commending a scheming manger for his dishonesty. But notice that Jesus didn't commend the man. The manager was praised for his shrewdness by the rich man, his employer (v. 8a). Jesus' observations on the manager's actions begin with the second part of verse 8.

After his employer praised the man, Jesus observed that believers—the sons of light—can learn a lesson from this schemer. He showed initiative and foresight in planning for the future. Followers of Jesus should do the same.

140. The Parable of the Rich Man and Lazarus

Luke 16:19–31

[19]"There was **a rich man** who would dress in purple and fine linen, feasting lavishly every day. [20]But at his gate was left a poor man named **Lazarus, covered**

---

more astute than the sons of light: The dishonest manager realized he was about to be dismissed, so he took decisive action to prepare for it. Likewise, death is a certainty for everyone. We should prepare properly for the eternity that follows our earthly existence.

140. The Parable of the Rich Man and Lazarus

a rich man: This man is often called *Dives,* the Latin term for "rich man." From his description, it is clear that he lived a life of luxury and indulgence.

with sores. [21]He longed to be filled with what fell from the rich man's table, but instead the dogs would come and lick his sores.

[22]"One day the poor man died and was carried away by the angels to **Abraham's side.** The rich man also died and was buried. [23]And being in torment in **Hades,** he looked up and saw Abraham a long way off, with Lazarus at his side. [24]'Father Abraham!' he called out, 'Have mercy on me and **send Lazarus to** dip the tip of his finger in water and **cool my tongue,** because I am in agony in this flame!'

[25]"'Son,' Abraham said, 'remember that during your life you received your good things, just as Lazarus received bad things; but now he is comforted here, while you are in agony. [26]Besides all this, **a great chasm** has been fixed between us and you, so that those who want to pass over from here to you cannot; neither can those from there cross over to us.'

[27]"'Father,' he said, 'then I beg you to send him to my father's house— [28]because I have five brothers—to warn them, so they won't also come to this place of torment.'

[29]"But Abraham said, 'They have Moses and the prophets; they should listen to them.'

[30]"'No, father Abraham,' he said. 'But if someone from the dead goes to them, they will repent.'

[31]"But he told him, 'If they don't listen to Moses and the prophets, they will not be persuaded if someone rises from the dead.'"

141. JESUS TEACHES ABOUT FAITH AND SERVICE

Luke 17:1–10

[1]He said to His disciples, "Offenses will certainly come, but woe to him through whom they come! [2]It would be better for him if a millstone were hung

---

Lazarus, covered with sores: In contrast to the rich man's expensive clothing ("purple and fine linen," v. 19), Lazarus was covered with sores. He lived on table scraps instead of rich banquet foods. He limited his desire to crumbs from the rich man's table. This suggests his freedom from envy and worldly lust. The point of the parable is that the rich man gave Lazarus nothing. The rich man was surrounded by attentive servants, while Lazarus was the companion of dogs, the scavengers of the streets.

Abraham's side . . . Hades: After they died, the rich man and Lazarus went to different places. Lazarus was received at Abraham's side—a symbol of heaven. But the rich man went to Hades. This was the Greek name for the abode of the dead. Jesus used the word to refer to a place where the wicked spent their days in pain and torment.

send Lazarus to . . . cool my tongue: Notice the situations of the rich man and Lazarus were now reversed. In their earthly existence, Lazarus lived off scraps from the rich man's table. Now in the afterlife, the rich man asked for Lazarus to cool his tongue with a finger dipped in water.

a great chasm: A great chasm or gap separated the rich man and Lazarus in the afterlife. This was a continuation of the distance between the two in their earthly existence. A life dedicated to material values and lived in isolation from human need separates a person from God. We show that we have left God out of our lives when we fail to show compassion for others.

around his neck and he were thrown into the sea than for him to **cause one of these little ones to stumble**. ³Be on your guard. **If your brother sins, rebuke him**; and if he repents, forgive him. ⁴And if he sins against you seven times in a day, and comes back to you seven times, saying, 'I repent,' you must forgive him."

⁵The apostles said to the Lord, "Increase our faith."

⁶"If you have **faith the size of a mustard seed**," the Lord said, "you could say to this mulberry tree, 'Be uprooted and planted in the sea,' and it would obey you.

⁷"Which one of you having a slave plowing or tending sheep, would say to him when he comes in from the field, 'Come at once and sit down to eat'? ⁸Instead, would he not tell him, 'Prepare something for me to eat, get ready, and serve me while I eat and drink; later you may eat and drink'? ⁹Does he thank that slave because he did what was commanded? ¹⁰In the same way, when you have done all that you were commanded, you should say, 'We are good-for-nothing slaves; **we've only done our duty.**'"

142. JESUS RAISES LAZARUS FROM THE DEAD

John 11:1–44

¹Now a man was sick, Lazarus, from Bethany, the village of Mary and her sister Martha. ²Mary was the one who anointed the Lord with fragrant oil and wiped His feet with her hair, and it was her brother Lazarus who was sick. ³So the sisters sent a message to Him: "**Lord, the one You love is sick.**"

⁴When Jesus heard it, He said, "**This sickness** will not end in death, but **is for the glory of God**, so that the Son of God may be glorified through it." ⁵(Jesus

---

141. JESUS TEACHES ABOUT FAITH AND SERVICE

cause one of these little ones to stumble: "Little ones" are persons of immature faith as well as children. Christians should serve as good examples and role models for others.

If your brother sins, rebuke him: The word *brother* shows the close ties that exist between members of the family of faith. Christians are encouraged to rebuke fellow Christians who have sinned against them and to be just as quick to extend forgiveness.

faith the size of a mustard seed: The mustard seed was known for its tiny size. Jesus declared that the least amount of faith will open up miracle-working possibilities. (For another reference of Jesus to the mustard seed, see segment 72, "The Parable of the Mustard Seed and the Parable of the Yeast," p. 87.)

we've only done our duty: Our service for God should not make us feel that God owes us something. God has called and equipped His disciples for service. When we serve Him by serving others, we are doing nothing extraordinary and spectacular; we are only performing the work that God has called us to do.

142. JESUS RAISES LAZARUS FROM THE DEAD

Lord, the one You love is sick: Jesus was a close friend of Mary and Martha and their brother Lazarus. He must have retreated on occasion to their home in Bethany for needed rest and relaxation. When Lazarus fell ill, they appealed to Him for help.

This sickness . . . is for the glory of God: The message from Bethany took a day to reach Jesus. By this time Lazarus

loved Martha, her sister, and Lazarus.) ⁶So when He heard that he was sick, He stayed two more days in the place where He was. ⁷Then after that, He said to the disciples, "Let's go to Judea again."

⁸"Rabbi," the disciples told Him, "just now the Jews tried to stone You, and You're going there again?"

⁹"Aren't there twelve hours in a day?" Jesus answered. "If anyone walks during the day, he doesn't stumble, because he sees the light of this world. ¹⁰If anyone walks during the night, he does stumble, because the light is not in him." ¹¹He said this, and then He told them, "Our friend Lazarus has fallen asleep, but I'm on My way to wake him up."

¹²Then the disciples said to Him, "Lord, if he has fallen asleep, he will get well."

¹³Jesus, however, was speaking about his death, but they thought He was speaking about natural sleep. ¹⁴So Jesus then told them plainly, "Lazarus has died. ¹⁵I'm glad for you that I wasn't there, so that you may believe. But let's go to him."

¹⁶Then Thomas (called "Twin") said to his fellow disciples, "Let's go so that we may die with Him."

The Resurrection and the Life

¹⁷When Jesus arrived, He found that Lazarus had already been in the tomb four days. ¹⁸Bethany was near Jerusalem (about two miles away). ¹⁹Many of the Jews had come to Martha and Mary to comfort them about their brother. ²⁰As soon as Martha heard that Jesus was coming, she went to meet Him. But Mary remained seated in the house.

²¹Then Martha said to Jesus, "Lord, if You had been here, **my brother wouldn't have died**. ²²Yet even now I know that whatever You ask from God, God will give You."

²³"Your brother will rise again," Jesus told her.

²⁴Martha said, "I know that he will rise again in the resurrection at the last day."

²⁵Jesus said to her, "I am the resurrection and the life. The one who believes in Me, even if he dies, will live. ²⁶**Everyone who** lives and **believes in Me will never die**—ever. Do you believe this?"

---

had died. The two days' delay, plus another day to make the journey to Bethany, amounted to four days. But Jesus had already determined the course He would take. In the miracle of raising Lazarus, God would be glorified.

my brother wouldn't have died: Martha went out to meet Jesus when she heard He was coming. She blurted out what had probably been said repeatedly during the days of waiting: If Jesus had been there, He would have healed their brother and he would not have died. She followed this up with a statement of faith in Jesus' power to help, even though Lazarus was dead.

Everyone who . . . believes in Me will never die: This claim of Jesus went far beyond Martha's thinking or that of any of her contemporaries. Jesus was about to restore Lazarus to life, but His power exceeded this because He offered everlasting life to all who would believe in Him.

[27]"Yes, Lord," she told Him, "I believe You are the Messiah, the Son of God, who was to come into the world."

[28]Having said this, she went back and called her sister Mary, saying in private, "The Teacher is here and is calling for you."

[29]As soon as she heard this, she got up quickly and went to Him. [30]Jesus had not yet come into the village, but was still in the place where Martha had met Him. [31]The Jews who were with her in the house consoling her saw that Mary got up quickly and went out. So they followed her, supposing that she was going to the tomb to cry there.

[32]When **Mary came to where Jesus was** and saw Him, she fell at His feet and told Him, "Lord, if You had been here, my brother would not have died!"

[33]When Jesus saw her crying, and the Jews who had come with her crying, He was angry in His spirit and deeply moved. [34a]"Where have you put him?" He asked.

[34b]"Lord," they told Him, "come and see."

[35]**Jesus wept**.

[36]So the Jews said, "See how He loved him!" [37]But some of them said, "Couldn't He who opened the blind man's eyes also have kept this man from dying?"

[38]Then Jesus, angry in Himself again, came to the tomb. It was a cave, and a stone was lying against it. [39a]"Remove the stone," Jesus said.

[39b]Martha, the dead man's sister, told Him, "Lord, he already stinks. It's been four days."

[40]Jesus said to her, "Did I not tell you that if you believed you would see the glory of God?"

The Raising of Lazarus and the Resurrection of Jesus

It is natural to seek some link between the raising of Lazarus and the resurrection of Jesus. But it is important to recognize the distinct differences between the two. Lazarus was resuscitated, or restored to life, only to experience death a second time as human frailty returned him to the grave. Jesus was resurrected, brought back from the dead to die no more, thus becoming "the firstfruits of those who have fallen asleep" (1 Cor. 15:20). Lazarus was only a sign of the resurrection, but Jesus was the reality itself. Lazarus was released from the tomb with the help of others. Jesus needed no such human help (John 20:1). Lazarus appeared bound in grave-clothes, but Jesus left these behind (John 20:6–7). Lazarus was restored to his family, while Jesus ascended to His Father (John 20:17).

Mary came to where Jesus was: Mary also came out to meet Jesus, sobbing the same words as her sister.

Jesus wept: The sight of Mary and other mourners weeping affected Jesus so deeply that He mingled His tears with theirs. Perhaps He also wept over the consequences of the Fall, which ended the bliss of Eden and brought death into the world.

⁴¹So they removed the stone. Then Jesus raised His eyes and said, "Father, I thank You that You heard Me. ⁴²I know that You always hear Me, but because of the crowd standing here I said this, so they may believe You sent Me." ⁴³After He said this, He shouted with a loud voice, "**Lazarus, come out!**" ⁴⁴The dead man came out bound hand and foot with linen strips and with his face wrapped in a cloth. Jesus said to them, "Loose him and let him go."

143. THE SANHEDRIN'S PLOT AGAINST JESUS

John 11:45–54

⁴⁵Therefore many of the Jews who came to Mary and saw what He did believed in Him. ⁴⁶But some of them went to the Pharisees and told them what Jesus had done.

⁴⁷So the chief priests and the Pharisees convened the Sanhedrin and said, "What are we going to do since this man does many signs? ⁴⁸If we let Him continue in this way, everybody will believe in Him! Then the Romans will come and remove both our place and our nation."

⁴⁹One of them, Caiaphas, who was high priest that year, said to them, "You know nothing at all! ⁵⁰You're not considering that it is to your advantage that **one man should die** for the people rather than the whole nation perish." ⁵¹He did not say this on his own; but being high priest that year he prophesied that Jesus was going to die for the nation, ⁵²and not for the nation only, but also to unite the scattered children of God. ⁵³So from that day on they plotted to kill Him. ⁵⁴Therefore Jesus no longer walked openly among the Jews, but **departed** from there to the countryside near the wilderness, **to a town called Ephraim**. And He stayed there with the disciples.

Lazarus, come out! Jesus called out to Lazarus in a loud voice. Lazarus emerged from the tomb with the linen burial strips still wrapped around his body and the burial cloth covering his face. Jesus directed the bystanders to unwrap him and set him free. This was a dramatic demonstration of Jesus' power over death and the grave.

143. THE SANHEDRIN'S PLOT AGAINST JESUS

one man should die: Caiaphas, the high priest of the Jews, argued that it would be better for Jesus to die than for the entire nation to come under Rome's displeasure. This was a political statement. The Sanhedrin was worried that the public acclaim Jesus was receiving would cause a civil disturbance, leading the Romans to take action against the Jews. It would be better for them to put Jesus to death than to risk a riot that might wipe out the entire nation.

departed . . . to a town called Ephraim: Jesus retreated to Ephraim, about 18 miles from Jerusalem, to avoid confrontation with His enemies. He wanted to wait until the Passover celebration with its parallels to His coming redemptive death before the final clash with His enemies.

The Jewish Sanhedrin

Jesus' raising of Lazarus near Jerusalem caused such a sensation among the people that Jesus' enemies decided it was time for official action. They called a meeting of the Sanhedrin, the highest Jewish court in the land. This group, consisting of 70 members plus the Jewish high priest, exercised authority over the religious life of the Jewish people. The Romans were the ultimate authority in Palestine, but they generally let the Jews take care of their own religious matters.

From the time of this meeting of the Sanhedrin, Jesus was a marked man. His enemies were determined to arrest Him and to orchestrate His execution. They knew they would have to make a civil case against Him and get Him convicted by the Roman officials. Rome refused to allow groups such as the Sanhedrin in their subject provinces to pronounce and carry out the death penalty.

---

144. Jesus Heals Ten Lepers on His Way to Jerusalem

Luke 17:11–19

¹¹While traveling to Jerusalem, He **passed between Samaria and Galilee**. ¹²As He entered a village, **ten men with leprosy** met Him. They stood at a distance ¹³and raised their voices, saying, "**Jesus, Master**, have mercy on us!"

¹⁴When He saw them, He told them, "Go and show yourselves to the priests." And while they were going, **they were cleansed**.

¹⁵But one of them, seeing that he was healed, returned and, with a loud voice, gave glory to God. ¹⁶He fell on his face at His feet, thanking Him. And he was a Samaritan.

¹⁷Then Jesus said, "Were not ten cleansed? Where are the nine? ¹⁸**Didn't any return** to give glory to God **except this foreigner?**" ¹⁹And He told him, "Get up and go on your way. Your faith has made you well."

---

144. Jesus Heals Ten Lepers on His Way to Jerusalem

passed between Samaria and Galilee: On other occasions, Jesus had traveled through Samaria. But this time He followed the normal Jewish practice of avoiding Samaria.

ten men with leprosy: These men, nine of them Jews and one a Samaritan, had formed their own fellowship of suffering. In their common need, they forgot their racial animosities. (For another instance of Jesus' encounter with leprosy, see segment 44, "A Leper Healed," p. 54.)

Jesus, Master: These lepers were required by law to keep away from people, so they hailed Him from a distance.

they were cleansed: Jesus told them to go to a priest for official confirmation of their healing. Under Jewish law, a priest had to certify that a person was free of leprosy before he could resume contact with others.

Didn't any return . . . except this foreigner? Jesus expressed disappointment that a foreigner, a non-Jew, was the only person to express his thanks for healing. This anticipated the rejection of Jesus by His own people and the embracing of His gospel by Gentiles.

145. JESUS TEACHES ABOUT THE ADVENT OF THE KINGDOM

Luke 17:20–37

20Being asked by the Pharisees when the kingdom of God will come, He answered them, "The kingdom of God is **not coming with something observable**; 21no one will say, 'Look here!' or 'There!' For you see, **the kingdom of God is among you**."

22Then He told the disciples: "The days are coming when you will long to see one of the days of the Son of Man, but you won't see it. 23They will say to you, 'Look there!' or 'Look here!' Don't follow or run after them. 24For as the **lightning** flashes from horizon to horizon and **lights up the sky**, so the Son of Man will be in His day. 25But first He must suffer many things and be rejected by this generation.

Kingdom of God/Kingdom of Heaven

The kingdom of God was one of the most consistent themes in the preaching ministry of Jesus. He was referring to God's rule of grace in the world, a period that had been foretold for centuries by the prophets of the Old Testament.

John the Baptizer announced that this kingdom had "come near" in the person of Jesus (Matt. 3:2). Jesus affirmed that the kingdom of God began with His public ministry (Mark 1:15). He emphasized that He was the full embodiment of God's kingdom. This was demonstrated particularly through His healing miracles (Matt. 12:28).

Another related phrase that Jesus used often was "kingdom of heaven." This phrase appears particularly in Matthew's Gospel. A careful analysis of all His statements about the "kingdom of God" and the "kingdom of heaven" reveals that He used these phrases interchangeably.

Jesus also taught that the kingdom of God has both a present and a future dimension. He referred to both these realities in this passage from Luke (17:20–37). God's kingdom was present already in His person, but this kingdom would be realized perfectly when He returned in glory at the end of the age.

---

145. JESUS TEACHES ABOUT THE ADVENT OF THE KINGDOM

not coming with something observable: By this time in His public ministry, Jesus had been teaching about the kingdom of God for more than three years. The Pharisees asked Jesus to tell them how they would know when the kingdom was arriving. He pointed out there were no "observable" signs that would signal the date of its arrival.

the kingdom of God is among you: Jesus then declared that the kingdom of God was there among them. Jesus Himself was the demonstration of the power of God's rule. People were looking for the kingdom of God "out there" in some spectacular display. They should look in their midst to see the revelation of the kingdom in the person of Christ.

lightning . . . lights up the sky: Jesus switched from talking about the kingdom of God as a present reality to describe His second coming as a future event. He declared that His return would be as clear and unmistakable as a flash of lightning in the darkness. But His return would be preceded by His death and resurrection and ascension to the Father.

²⁶"Just as it was **in the days of Noah**, so it will be in the days of the Son of Man: ²⁷people went on eating, drinking, marrying and giving in marriage until the day Noah boarded the ark, and the flood came and destroyed them all. ²⁸It will be the same as it was in the days of Lot: people went on eating, drinking, buying, selling, planting, building; ²⁹but on the day Lot left Sodom, fire and sulfur rained from heaven and destroyed them all. ³⁰It will be like that on the day the Son of Man is revealed.

³¹"On that day, a man on the housetop, whose belongings are in the house, must not come down to get them. And likewise the man who is in the field must not turn back. ³²Remember Lot's wife! ³³Whoever tries to make his life secure will lose it, and whoever loses his life will preserve it. ³⁴I tell you, on that night two will be in one bed: one will be taken and the other will be left. ³⁵Two women will be grinding grain together: one will be taken and the other left."³⁶Two will be in a field: one will be taken, and the other will be left.*

³⁷ª"Where, Lord?" they asked Him.

³⁷ᵇHe said to them, "Where the corpse is, there also the vultures will be gathered."

146. PARABLES ON PRAYER: THE PERSISTENT WIDOW AND THE PROUD PHARISEE

Luke 18:1–14

¹He then told them a parable on the need for them to pray always and not become discouraged: ²"There was **a judge** in one town **who didn't fear God** or respect man. ³And **a widow** in that town **kept coming to him**, saying, 'Give me justice against my adversary.'

⁴"For a while he was unwilling; but later he said to himself, 'Even though I don't fear God or respect man, ⁵yet because this widow keeps pestering me, **I will give her justice**, so she doesn't wear me out by her persistent coming.'"

⁶Then the Lord said, "Listen to what the unjust judge says. ⁷Will not God grant justice to His elect who cry out to Him day and night? Will He delay to help them? ⁸I tell you that He will swiftly grant them justice. Nevertheless, when the Son of Man comes, will He find that faith on earth?"

Verse 36 of Luke 17 is not included in some New Testament manuscripts.

---

in the days of Noah: Jesus used the example of Noah and the great flood to illustrate the suddenness of His return. His coming will be as unexpected for many people as the flood was for the people of Noah's generation.

146. PARABLES ON PRAYER: THE PERSISTENT WIDOW AND THE PROUD PHARISEE

a judge . . . who didn't fear God: This judge was not a model of honesty and impartiality. By Old Testament standards, he was everything a judge should not be (Exod. 23:6–8; Deut. 16:18–20).

a widow . . . kept coming to him: Widows in the ancient world were generally dependent on others for survival. This judge was doing nothing to help her, but she kept coming back repeatedly, urging him to hear her case.

I will give her justice: Finally, the judge rendered a favorable judgment in the woman's behalf. God is so much more than a human judge. If we place our prayers before Him in faith and trust, He will hear and answer.

⁹He also told this parable to some who trusted in themselves that they were righteous and looked down on everyone else: ¹⁰"Two men went up to the temple complex to pray, one **a Pharisee** and the other **a tax collector.** ¹¹The Pharisee took his stand and was praying like this: 'God, I thank You that **I'm not like other people**—greedy, unrighteous, adulterers, or even like this tax collector. ¹²I fast twice a week; I give a tenth of everything I get.'

¹³"But the tax collector, standing far off, would not even raise his eyes to heaven, but kept striking his chest and saying, 'O God, turn your wrath from **me—a sinner'** ¹⁴I tell you, **this one went down** to his house **justified** rather than the other; because everyone who exalts himself will be humbled, but the one who humbles himself will be exalted."

147. Jesus Discusses Divorce and Remarriage

Matthew 19:1–12; Mark 10:1–12

Mt 19:1–3When Jesus had finished this instruction, He departed from Galilee and went to the region of Judea across the Jordan. ²Large crowds followed Him, and He healed them there. ³Some **Pharisees approached Him to test Him.** They asked, "Is it lawful for a man to **divorce his wife on any grounds?**"

Mk 10:3He replied to them, "What did Moses command you?"

⁴They said, "Moses permitted us to write divorce papers and send her away."

Mt 19:8, 4b–6He told them, "Moses permitted you to divorce your wives because of the **hardness of your hearts.** But it was not like that from the beginning.

---

a Pharisee . . . a tax collector: These two men represented the extremes in Jewish life. The Pharisee was committed to observing every detail of the law, while the tax collector was indifferent toward its rituals. As they prayed, the Pharisee stood aloof from other worshipers, while the tax collector took his position at a distance in a deep sense of unworthiness.

I'm not like other people: The Pharisee looked out of the corner of his eye at the tax collector, adding words of thanks that he was not like him. The Pharisee also claimed that he fasted and prayed religiously. Behind this excessive zeal was his belief that acceptance with God depended on one's good works.

me—a sinner: The tax collector had no list of good works that he could present to God. But something had happened to give him an overwhelming sense of his unworthiness. He admitted he was a sinner and threw himself on God's mercy.

this one went down . . . justified: Jesus said the tax collector rather than the Pharisee would go home forgiven. Sin acknowledged and forsaken brings acceptance with God.

147. Jesus Discusses Divorce and Remarriage

Pharisees approached Him to test Him: Jesus' enemies asked a question to trap Him. Perhaps they wanted to force Jesus to say something negative about the Mosaic Law on divorce.

divorce his wife on any grounds? The debate among Jewish scholars revolved around the meaning of an obscure Hebrew phrase in Deuteronomy 24:1, translated "something indecent." One famous rabbi, Shammai, understood Deuteronomy 24:1 to mean that adultery was the only grounds for divorce. Another respected rabbi, Hillel, interpreted the phrase more broadly to refer to just about anything a wife did that displeased her husband.

hardness of your hearts: Jesus emphasized that divorce was not a commandment; instead, it was a concession to human sinfulness. The reason for Deuteronomy 24:1 was not because God wanted divorce or commanded it; it was because He recognized that some provision was needed in light of the hardness of human hearts.

⁴ᵇHaven't you read . . . that He who created them in the beginning 'made them **male and female**' ⁵and He also said: 'For this reason a man will leave his father and mother and be joined to his wife, and the two will become one flesh'? ⁶So they are no longer two, but one flesh. Therefore what God has joined together, **man must not separate**.

ᴹᵗ ¹⁹:⁹"And I tell you, whoever divorces his wife, except for sexual immorality, **and marries another, commits adultery**."

¹⁰His disciples said to Him, "If the relationship of a man with his wife is like this, it's better not to marry!"

¹¹But He told them, "Not everyone can accept this saying, but only those to whom it has been given. ¹²For there are eunuchs who were born that way from their mother's womb, there are eunuchs who were made by men, and there are eunuchs who have made themselves that way because of the kingdom of heaven. Let anyone accept this who can."

148. Jesus Welcomes Little Children

Matthew 19:13–15; Mark 10:13–16; Luke 18:15–17

ᴹᵏ ¹⁰:¹³⁻¹⁵Some people were **bringing little children** [ᴸᵏ ¹⁸:¹⁵*infants*] to Him so He might touch them [ᴹᵗ ¹⁹:¹³ᵇ*might put His hands on them and pray*]. But His disciples rebuked them. ¹⁴When Jesus saw it, He was indignant and said to them, "Let the little children come to Me; don't stop them [ᴹᵗ ¹⁹:¹⁴ᵇ*Leave the children alone, and don't try to keep them from coming to Me*], for **the kingdom of God belongs to such as these**. ¹⁵I assure you: Whoever does not welcome the kingdom of God like a little child will never enter it."

¹⁶After taking them in His arms, He laid His hands on them and blessed them.

---

male and female: Jesus referred the Pharisees to some inspired words from the first two chapters of Genesis. These verses revealed aspects of God's good creation before sin marred the situation. God created woman because it was not good for man to be alone. Thus, God created Eve and joined Adam and Eve as husband and wife for companionship, intimacy, and procreation.

man must not separate: God's intention for this "one-flesh" union is that it be a lifetime relationship based on a total commitment to each other. Such commitment involves total trust and trustworthiness.

and marries another, commits adultery: Jesus was speaking of situations in which a husband or a wife initiated a divorce in order to marry someone else. If anyone tries to make adultery legal and respectable by getting a divorce, the person is still guilty of adultery in the eyes of God.

148. Jesus Welcomes Little Children

bringing little children: Parents brought their children to Jesus so He could bless them. But His disciples tried to keep them away. Perhaps they thought Jesus was too busy conducting "adult" business.

the kingdom of God belongs to such as these: Jesus welcomed the children and used them to illustrate an important lesson. Children are trusting and dependent. These are traits that everyone needs to enter God's kingdom.

149. JESUS AND THE RICH YOUNG RULER

Matthew 19:16–30; Mark 10:17–31; Luke 18:18–30

Mk 10:17As He was going out on the road, a man [Lk 18:18*a ruler*] ran up, knelt down before Him, and asked Him, "Good Teacher, **what must I do** [Mt 19:16b*what good must I do*] to inherit eternal life?"

Mt 19:17"Why do you ask Me about what is good?" He said to him. "There is only One who is good. If you want to enter into life, **keep the commandments**."

18a"Which ones?" he asked Him.

18bJesus answered, "You shall not murder; You shall not commit adultery; You shall not steal; You shall not bear false witness; 19honor your father and your mother; and you shall love your neighbor as yourself."

Mk 10:20He said to Him, "Teacher, I have kept all these from my youth. Mt 19:20bWhat do I still lack?"

Mk 10:21Then, looking at him, Jesus loved him and said to him, "You lack one thing [Mt 19:21a*If you want to be perfect*]: **Go, sell all you have** and give to the poor, and you will have treasure in heaven. Then come, follow Me."

Mt 19:22When the young man heard that command, he went away grieving, because he had many possessions [Lk 18:23b*he was very rich*].

Mk 10:23–25Jesus looked around and said to His disciples, "How hard it is for those who have wealth to enter the kingdom of God!" 24But the disciples were **astonished at His words**. Again Jesus said to them, "Children, how hard it is to enter the kingdom of God! 25It is easier for a camel to go through the eye of a needle than for a rich person to enter the kingdom of God."

"Who Can Be Saved?"

26But they were even more astonished [Mt 19:25*utterly astonished*], saying to one another, "Then who can be saved?"

27Looking at them, Jesus said, "With men it is impossible, but not with God, because all things are possible with God."

---

149. JESUS AND THE RICH YOUNG RULER

what must I do: This man was probably a member of the administrative board of a synagogue. He was an eager, questing person who was willing to listen to anyone who would help him gain top marks in life's final examination. He thought Jesus would know the secret of spiritual achievement.

keep the commandments: Keeping the commandments is precisely what the rich young ruler had been doing. But living a decent, orthodox life had brought him no spiritual assurance.

Go, sell all you have: Jesus knew the young man's problem, and He prescribed the needed solution. This man's religion had cost him little. If he wanted eternal life, he must be willing to let go of what he valued most.

astonished at His words: The disciples shared the prevailing belief that possessions were a sign of divine approval and blessing. If a rich person could not be saved, what chance did a poor man have?

Eye of a Needle

Jesus' statement about a camel going through "the eye of a needle" is a good example of hyperbole—a figure of speech or exaggerated statement not to be taken literally. We do the same thing today when we make some bizarre statement—for example, "It's raining cats and dogs!"—to empasize a point.

Jesus used this graphic word picture to show the power of possessions. People of means tend to trust in their riches rather than throw themselves upon the love and mercy of God.

Here are some other examples of Jesus' use of hyperbole in the Gospels:

The Phraisees in their attention to the most minute details of the law tended to "strain out a gnat, yet gulp down a camel" (Matt. 23:24).

Believers are admonished to refrain from judging others—to remove the "log" from our own eyes before taking the "speck" out of another's eye (Matt. 7:3–5).

The disciple of Jesus must "hate his own father and mother, wife and children, brothers and sisters" (Luke 14:26).

If a believer's eye leads to temptation, it is better to "gouge it out" than to fall into sin (Mark 9:47).

---

²⁸Peter began to tell Him, "Look, we have left everything and followed You. ᴹᵗ ¹⁹:²⁷ᵇSo **what will there be for us?**"

²⁸Jesus said to them, "**I assure you**: In the Messianic Age, when the Son of Man sits on His glorious throne, you who have followed Me will also sit on twelve thrones, judging the twelve tribes of Israel. ᴹᵏ ¹⁰:²⁹ᵇ⁻³¹There is no one who has left house, brothers or sisters, mother or father, children, or fields because of Me and the gospel, ³⁰who will not receive a hundred times more, now at this time—houses, brothers and sisters, mothers and children, and fields, with persecutions—and eternal life in the age to come. ³¹But many who are first will be last, and the last first."

150. THE PARABLE OF THE VINEYARD WORKERS

Matthew 20:1–16

¹"For the kingdom of heaven is like a landowner who went out **early in the morning** to hire workers for his vineyard. ²After agreeing with the workers on one denarius for the day, he sent them into his vineyard. ³When he went out

---

what will there be for us? Peter thought of himself and his fellow disciples. They had "left everything" to follow Christ. Peter wanted to know what he and the other disciples would receive in return for their sacrifice.

I assure you: Jesus gave a promise to all who practice self-denial for His sake. Christian discipleship brings immediate rewards and a prospect of everlasting life in the future.

150. THE PARABLE OF THE VINEYARD WORKERS

early in the morning: During harvest season, vineyard owners hired extra workers to pick grapes. This man went early

about nine in the morning, he saw **others** standing in the marketplace **doing nothing**. ⁴To those men he said, 'You also go to my vineyard and I'll give you whatever is right.' So off they went. ⁵About noon and at three, he went out again and did the same thing. ⁶Then about five he went and found others standing around, and said to them, 'Why have you been standing here all day doing nothing?'

⁷ᵃ"Because no one hired us,' they said to him.

⁷ᵇ"You also go to my vineyard,' he told them. ⁸When evening came, the owner of the vineyard told his foreman, 'Call the workers and **give them their pay**, starting with the last and ending with the first.'

⁹"When those who were hired about five came, they each received one denarius. ¹⁰So when the first ones came, they assumed they would get more, but they also received a denarius each. ¹¹When they received it, **they began to complain** to the landowner: ¹²'These last men put in one hour, and you made them equal to us who bore the burden of the day and the burning heat!'

¹³"He replied to one of them, 'Friend, I'm doing you no wrong. Didn't you agree with me on a denarius? ¹⁴Take what's yours and go. I want to give this last man the same as I gave you. ¹⁵Don't I have the right to do what I want with my business? Are you jealous because I'm generous'?

¹⁶"So the **last will be first**, and the first last."

151. JESUS AGAIN DISCUSSES HIS DEATH AND RESURRECTION

Matthew 20:17–19; Mark 10:32–34; Luke 18:31–34

Mk 10:32They were on the road, going up to Jerusalem, and Jesus was walking ahead of them. They were astonished, but those who followed Him were afraid.

---

to the marketplace where such workers gathered in hope of being hired for the day. He enlisted several laborers and promised to pay them one denarius, a coin equal to pay for one day's work. The workers agreed and began working in the vineyard.

others . . . doing nothing: The vineyard owner returned for more workers four other times during the day. He did not promise to pay these groups a denarius, as he had the first group. Instead, he told them he would pay them what was right.

give them their pay: Paying these workers at the end of each day was customary. The vineyard owner told the foreman to begin paying the last group first and to pay everyone one denarius.

they began to complain: The early workers were angry at the vineyard owner. They complained because he gave so generously to the late workers. In a human situation, the early workers' grievance was predictable and probably justified. Extra work deserves extra pay. But in our relationship with God, we would be in trouble if God gave us what we deserved. We can be glad that He relates to us with mercy and grace.

last will be first: This parable grew out of the disciples' reaction to a man who said no to the claims of Jesus (see segment 149, "Jesus and the Rich Young Ruler," p. 174). Their egos were inflated by the realization that, in contrast, they had agreed to follow Him. But they needed to realize that others would follow them—at 9:00, 12:00, and 3:00. These people would be equally valuable to the cause of Christ, and God would honor them in His own gracious fashion.

And **taking the Twelve aside** again [Mt 20:17 *aside privately*], He began to tell them the things that would happen to Him.

Mk 10:33a"Listen! We are going up to Jerusalem. Lk 18:31bEverything that is written through the prophets about the Son of Man will be accomplished. Mk 10:33b–34The **Son of Man will be handed over** to the chief priests and the scribes, and they will condemn Him to death. Then they will hand Him over to the Gentiles, 34and they will mock Him, spit on Him, flog Him, and kill Him, and He will rise after three days."

Lk 18:34**They understood none of these things**. This saying was hidden from them, and they did not grasp what was said.

152. James and John Ask for Prominent Places in Jesus' Kingdom

Matthew 20:20–28; Mark 10:35–45

Mk 10:35Then **James and John**, the sons of Zebedee, approached Him and said, "Teacher, we want You to do something for us if we ask You" [Mt 20:20 *Then the mother of Zebedee's sons approached Him with her sons. She knelt down to ask Him for something*].

36"What do you want Me to do for you?" He asked them.

37"Grant us," they answered Him, "that we may sit at **Your right** and at **Your left** in Your glory [Mt 20:21b*Promise . . . that these two sons of mine may sit, one on Your right and the other on Your left, in Your kingdom*]."

38But Jesus said to them, "You don't know what you're asking. Are you able to drink the **cup** I drink, or to be baptized with the **baptism** I am baptized with?"

---

151. Jesus Again Discusses His Death and Resurrection

taking the Twelve aside: Jesus separated His disciples from the larger group of His followers on the way to celebrate the Passover Festival. His more casual followers did not need to hear what He was about to reveal about His death. This might encourage them to resist His arrest, resulting in riot and bloodshed.

Son of Man will be handed over: This prediction of His death was the most detailed description Jesus had given. He would be delivered to the chief priests and scribes, then to the "Gentiles" (Roman authorities). The phrase "handed over" implies that He would be betrayed. He also described His shameful treatment—being mocked, spat upon, and flogged. Jesus also stated clearly that He would be resurrected after three days.

They understood none of these things: The Twelve had seen Jesus work great miracles. They could not believe that a person of such awesome authority and power would be humiliated and executed like a common criminal.

152. James and John Ask for Prominent Places in Jesus' Kingdom

James and John: These two brothers came privately to Jesus and asked Him to give them whatever they asked for. In Matthew's account, their mother approached Jesus on their behalf (Matt. 20:20). Jesus wisely asked them what they wanted.

Your right . . . Your left: Places at the right hand and left hand of a king were places of first and second prominence in the kingdom. James and John were thinking Jesus would become a powerful earthly king like David. Such a ruler would need loyal aides to work with him.

cup . . . baptism: Jesus told James and John they had no idea what they were asking for. He asked if they could drink

^{39a}**"We are able,"** they told Him.

^{39b}But Jesus said to them, "You will drink the cup I drink, and you will be baptized with the baptism I am baptized with. ⁴⁰But to sit at My right or left is not Mine to give, but it is for those for whom it has been prepared [^{Mt 20:23b}*those for whom it has been prepared by My Father*]." ⁴¹When the **other ten disciples heard this**, they began to be indignant with James and John [^{Mt 20:24b}*became indignant with the two brothers*].

⁴²And **Jesus called them over** and said to them, "You know that those who are regarded as rulers of the Gentiles dominate them, and their men of high positions exercise power over them. ⁴³But it must not be like that among you. On the contrary, whoever wants to become great among you must be your servant, ⁴⁴and whoever wants to be first among you must be a slave to all. ⁴⁵For **even the Son of Man** did not come to be served, but to serve, and to give His life—a ransom for many."

153. JESUS HEALS BLIND BARTIMAEUS

Matthew 20:29–34; Mark 10:46–52; Luke 18:35–43

^{Mk 10:46}They came to Jericho. And as He was leaving Jericho, and along with His disciples and a large crowd, **Bartimaeus** (the son of Timaeus), **a blind beggar**, was sitting by the road. ^{Lk 18:36–37}Hearing a crowd passing by, he inquired what this meant. ³⁷"Jesus the Nazarene is passing by," they told him.

^{Mk 10:47–48}When he heard that it was Jesus the Nazarene, he began to cry out, "Son of David, Jesus, have mercy on me!" ⁴⁸Many **people told him to keep quiet**, but he was crying out all the more, "Have mercy on me, Son of David!"

---

from the cup He was to drink or to be baptized with the baptism with which He was to be baptized. Jesus' cup was the agony of His suffering and death for the sins of the world. Jesus also referred to His death as a baptism (Luke 12:50).

We are able: The brothers said they could meet the test. Jesus recognized the ironic truth of their glib claim. They would later follow Jesus in the way of the cross. James was the first of the Twelve to be put to death (Acts 12:1–2). John became an exile on the island of Patmos (Rev. 1:9). But Jesus pointed out that places at His right hand and left hand were not His to give.

other ten disciples heard this: The other disciples learned about the selfish request of James and John. They were outraged because these brothers were trying to get what each disciple wanted for himself.

Jesus called them over: Jesus patiently taught the disciples about true greatness by contrasting how the world defined greatness with His view. The person considered the greatest in the first-century world was the Roman emperor because he exercised authority over everyone else in his kingdom. But this was not Jesus' view of greatness. The greatest in God's kingdom are those who serve others, not those who are served.

even the Son of Man: Jesus Himself was the ultimate example of service. No one deserved to be served more than the divine Son of Man, but His life and ministry were acts of self-giving service to others.

153. JESUS HEALS BLIND BARTIMAEUS

Bartimaeus . . . a blind beggar: A blind man named Bartimaeus sat by the road, begging alms from the passing throng. (Matthew reports there were two unidentified blind men; Matt. 20:30a; Luke records one unnamed blind man; Luke 18:35a). He must have overheard the people talking about this miracle worker named Jesus among the crowd.

people told him to keep quiet: Why did the crowd try to silence this blind beggar? Perhaps his cries were loud and

⁴⁹ᵃJesus stopped and said, "Call him."

⁴⁹ᵇSo they called the blind man and said to him, "Have courage! Get up; He's calling for you." ⁵⁰He threw off his coat, jumped up, and came to Jesus.

⁵¹ᵃThen Jesus answered him, "What do you want Me to do for you?"

⁵¹ᵇ*"Rabbouni,"* the blind man told Him, "I want to see!"

Lk 18:42–43"Receive your sight!" Jesus told him. "Your faith has healed you." ⁴³Instantly he could see, and he began to follow Him, glorifying God. All the people, when they saw it, gave praise to God.

154. Jesus Talks with Zacchaeus

Luke 19:1–10

¹He entered Jericho and was passing through. ²There was a man named **Zacchaeus** who was a **chief tax collector**, and he was rich. ³He was trying to see who Jesus was, but he was not able, in the crowd, because he was a short man. ⁴So running ahead, **he climbed up a sycamore tree** to see Jesus, since He was about to pass that way. ⁵When Jesus came to the place, He looked up and said to him, "Zacchaeus, hurry and come down, because today **I must stay at your house**."

⁶So he quickly came down, and welcomed Him joyfully. ⁷All who saw it began to complain, "He's gone to lodge with a sinful man!"

The City of Jericho

Jericho was about 25 miles northeast of Jerusalem. Jesus was passing through the city with His disciples and other followers as they made their way to the Holy City for observance of the Jewish Passover. Mark tells us that Jesus healed this blind man, Bartimaeus, as He passed through. Luke records Jesus' encounter with the tax collector, Zacchaeus, on a brief stopover in Jericho (see segment 154, "Jesus Talks with Zacchaeus," p. 179).

The Jericho that Jesus passed through is known as New Testament Jericho. This city was built south of the site of Old Testament Jericho, the ancient Canaanite city that Joshua and the invading Israelites destroyed (see Josh. 6:1–21).

---

bothersome. Some people might have resented Jesus being called the Messiah. Perhaps others, believing Jesus was about to be crowned king, thought He should quit paying attention to beggars and assume the dignities of royalty. But Bartimaeus cried out even louder. His persistence was rewarded when Jesus declared, "Your faith has healed you."

154. Jesus Talks with Zacchaeus

Zacchaeus . . . chief tax collector: Jericho was on an important highway used by merchants and traders. Their goods were subject to taxation. As the main tax agent, Zacchaeus probably farmed out this work to other tax collectors. This system was subject to abuse. The statement "and he was rich" suggests that Zacchaeus benefited financially from inflated tax revenues.

he climbed up a sycamore tree: Because he was a short man, Zacchaeus climbed a sycamore tree to get a good view of the road along which Jesus would pass.

I must stay at your house: Zacchaeus would have been content with a glimpse of Jesus as He passed by. But the celebrated teacher asked to be a guest in Zacchaeus's home! Among all the citizens of Jericho, this hated tax collector was the one whom Jesus selected for this honor.

The Minas and the Talents

There are similarities between this parable and the parable of the talents (see segment 173, "The Parable of the Talents," p. 203). But the differences are more impressive than the similarities, indicating they should be considered two distinct accounts. In the Matthew passage on the talents, varying amounts—all of which are large sums—are entrusted to the slaves. These represent opportunities granted according to individual abilities. But in this parable, each slave receives the same amount, one mina, a sum equal to about four months' wages—a comparatively small sum of money.

Both parables teach that all we have actually belongs to God. We are held accountable for how we use and manage the resources that God has entrusted to our care.

⁸But Zacchaeus stood there and said to the Lord, "Look, I'll give half of my possessions to the poor, Lord! And **if I have extorted** anything from anyone, I'll pay back four times as much!" ⁹"Today salvation has come to this house," Jesus told him, "because **he too is a son of Abraham**. ¹⁰For the Son of Man has come to seek and to save the lost."

155. THE PARABLE OF THE MINAS

Luke 19:11–27

¹¹As they were listening to this, He went on to tell a parable, because He was near Jerusalem, and they thought the kingdom of God was going to appear right away.

¹²Therefore He said: "A nobleman traveled to a far country to receive for himself authority to be king, and then return; ¹³and having called ten of his slaves, he gave them ten minas and told them, 'Do business until I come back.'

¹⁴"But his subjects hated him and sent a delegation after him, saying, 'We don't want this man to rule over us!'

¹⁵"At his return, having received the authority to be king, he summoned those slaves to whom he had given the money so that he could find out how much they had made in business.

---

if I have extorted: The word *if* did not express any doubt by Zacchaeus that he had cheated people. His statement should be understood as, "From those I have cheated, I will give back four times as much." This went far beyond what the law required (Num. 5:7). As evidence of his change of heart, he promised to give half of his possessions to the poor.

he too is a son of Abraham: Because he was a tax collector, Zacchaeus had been excommunicated from the religious practices of his people. Jesus reinstated him. Now he could enjoy the blessings and privileges of the covenant.

155. THE PARABLE OF THE MINAS

The first . . . The second: Ten of the king's slaves were given responsibilities, but only three were called to account. These are probably representative of all ten. One slave reported that his one mina had gained ten more, another five. Both slaves recognized they were trustees of what had been put in their charge, and they worked hard to have something to show their master on his return. They were rewarded generously with increased responsibilities.

Master, here is your mina: The third slave failed to increase the mina he was given. He explained his failure by drawing a false picture of his master, claiming this caused him to do nothing. The mina he had received was given to the slave who made ten because he would be likely to put the extra mina to maximum use.

¹⁶**The first** came forward and said, 'Master, your mina has earned ten more minas.'

¹⁷"'Well done, good slave!' he told him. 'Because you have been faithful in a very small matter, have authority over ten towns.'

¹⁸"**The second** came and said, 'Master, your mina has made five minas.'

¹⁹"So he said to him, 'You will be over five towns.'

²⁰"And another came and said, '**Master, here is your mina.** I have kept it hidden away in a cloth ²¹because I was afraid of you, for you're a tough man: you collect what you didn't deposit and reap what you didn't sow.'

²²"He told him, 'I will judge you by what you have said, you evil slave! If you knew I was a tough man, collecting what I didn't deposit and reaping what I didn't sow, ²³why didn't you put my money in the bank? And when I returned, I would have collected it with interest!' ²⁴So he said to those standing there, 'Take the mina away from him and give it to the one who has ten minas.'

²⁵"But they said to him, 'Master, he has ten minas.'

²⁶"'I tell you, that to everyone who has, more will be given; and from the one who does not have, even what he does have will be taken away. ²⁷But bring here these enemies of mine, who did not want me to rule over them, and slaughter them in my presence.'"

Jesus arrived in Bethany, a village outside Jerusalem, on Friday, just before the celebration of the Jewish Passover began. He was arrested by the Jewish authorities late Thursday night, just one week later, then crucified the next day (Friday) and resurrected on Sunday.

These seven days before His arrest were busy days for Jesus. He issued a direct challenge to the religious leaders by riding into Jerusalem on a donkey and accepting the proclamation of the crowds that He was the Messiah.

Mary of Bethany poured a bottle of expensive oil on His head. He interpreted this as an advance anointing of His body in preparation for His death. He also instituted the Memorial Supper with His disciples as they observed the Jewish Passover meal together. During this meal, Jesus also indicated that one of His own disciples, Judas, would betray Him to His enemies. He shocked His disciples by predicting that all of them would abandon Him and deny Him in His hour of need.

156. The Sanhedrin Plots against Jesus and Lazarus

John 11:55–12:1, 9–11

Jn 11:55–56 Now the Jewish Passover was near, and before the Passover **many** went up to Jerusalem **from the country** to purify themselves. 56 They were looking for Jesus, and asking one another as they stood in the temple complex: "What do you think? He won't come to the festival, will He?"

57 The chief priests and the Pharisees had given orders that if anyone knew where He was, he should report it so they could arrest Him.

Jn 12:1, 9–11 Six days before the Passover, Jesus came to Bethany where Lazarus was, whom Jesus had raised from the dead. . . . 9 Then a large crowd of the Jews learned that He was there. **They came** not only because of Jesus, but **also to see Lazarus** whom He had raised from the dead. 10 Therefore the chief priests decided to kill Lazarus too, 11 because he was the reason many of the Jews were deserting them and believing in Jesus.

---

156. The Sanhedrin Plots against Jesus and Lazarus

many . . . from the country: As the Jewish Passover approached, news of the raising of Lazarus spread like a wildfire throughout Palestine. Many pilgrims "from the country," not residents of Jerusalem, were excited at the prospect of seeing Jesus. Others, "the chief priests and the Pharisees," made plans for His arrest as soon as He arrived in Jerusalem.

They came . . . also to see Lazarus: Lazarus had become a tourist attraction. Even among those who were in Jerusalem hoping to see Jesus, excitement was aroused by the presence of Lazarus. The religious leaders were worried by the popular demonstrations. They could not deny Jesus' miracles, but they feared the consequences of His soaring popularity.

157. Jesus' Triumphal Entry into Jerusalem

The Mount of Olives

The Mount of Olives was one of a series of gently sloping hills east of Jerusalem that offered a panoramic view of the Holy City. It took its name from the olive groves that grew on the hill. Jesus began His triumphal entry from this prominent overlook just outside the city walls.

After entering Jerusalem and cleansing the temple, Jesus retreated to the Mount of Olives, where He delivered His great Olivet Discourse to the disciples. The Garden of Gethsemane, where He agonized in prayer before His betrayal, was also located on the Mount of Olives.

Matthew 21:1–11; Mark 11:1–11; Luke 19:28–44; John 12:12–19

Lk 19:28-31When He had said these things, He went on ahead, going up to Jerusalem. 29As He approached Bethphage and Bethany, at the place called the Mount of Olives, He **sent two of the disciples** 30and said, "Go into the village ahead of you. As you enter it, you will find a young donkey tied there, on which no one has ever sat. Untie it and bring it here [Mt 21:2b*you will find a donkey tied there, and a colt with her. Untie them and bring them to Me*]. 31And if anyone asks you, 'Why are you untying it?' say this: 'The Lord needs it' [Mt 21:3*them*] [Mk 11:3b*The Lord needs it and will send it back here right away*]."

Mk 11:4So they went and found a young donkey outside in the street, tied by a door. They untied it. Lk 19:33As they were untying the young donkey, its owners said to them, "Why are you untying the donkey?" Mk 11:6-7Then they answered them just as Jesus had said, so they let them go. 7And they brought the donkey [Mt 21:7a*the donkey and the colt*] to Jesus and threw their robes on it, and

He sat on it. Mt 21:4-5This took place so that what was spoken through the prophet might be fulfilled: 5"Tell the Daughter of Zion, 'See, your King is coming to you, gentle, and mounted on a donkey, even on a colt, the foal of a beast of burden.'"

Jn 12:16His disciples did not understand these things at first. However when Jesus was glorified, then they remembered that these things had been written about Him and that they had done these things to Him.

Lk 19:36aAs He was going along, Mk 11:8many **people spread their robes on the road**, and others spread leafy branches [Jn 12:13*palm branches*] cut from the fields.

---

157. Jesus' Triumphal Entry into Jerusalem

sent two of the disciples: As Jesus prepared to enter Jerusalem for the final time, He gave instructions to two disciples. They were to enter a village (probably Bethphage), find a female donkey and her colt, and bring them to Jesus. He told the disciples what to say if anyone questioned what they were doing.

He sat on it: According to Matthew, Jesus' riding into Jerusalem on a donkey fulfilled Zechariah 9:9 (see Matt. 21:4–5). He did not enter Jerusalem as a military and political king, riding a white horse and dressed as a king and warrior. He entered as a Servant-King. But the people saw Him as a political king, their kind of king, one worthy of being called Son of David, the great warrior king of their glorious past.

people spread their robes on the road: Jesus entered Jerusalem during Passover season (Matt. 26:2), a time when

Lk 19:37–38Now He came near the path down the Mount of Olives, and the whole crowd of the disciples began to praise God joyfully with a loud voice for all the miracles they had seen: 38"Blessed is the King [Jn 12:13bBlessed is . . . the King of Israel] [Mk 11:10aBlessed is the coming kingdom of our father David] [Mt 21:9aHosanna to the son of David] who comes in the name of the Lord. Peace in heaven and glory in the highest heaven!"

39And some of the Pharisees from the crowd told Him, "Teacher, rebuke Your disciples."

40He answered, "I tell you, if they were to keep silent, the stones would cry out!"

Mt 21:10–11When He entered Jerusalem, Lk 19:41bHe wept over it, Mt 21:10b[and] the whole city was shaken, saying, "**Who is this?**" 11And the crowds kept saying, "This is the prophet Jesus from Nazareth in Galilee."

Jn 12:19Then the Pharisees said to one another, "You see? You've accomplished nothing. Look—the world has gone after Him!"

Mk 11:11And He went into . . . the temple complex. After looking around at everything, since the hour was already late, He went out to Bethany with the Twelve.

158. JESUS CURSES A FIG TREE AND CLEANSES THE TEMPLE

Matthew 21:12–19; Mark 11:12–19; Luke 19:45–48

Mk 11:12–14The next day, when they came out from Bethany, He was hungry. 13After seeing in the distance a fig tree with leaves, He went to find out if there was anything on it. When He came to it, He found nothing but leaves, because it was not the season for figs. 14And He said to it, "May no one ever eat fruit from you again! [Mt 21:19bMay no fruit ever come from you again]." And His disciples heard it.

15They came to Jerusalem, and He went into the temple complex and began to throw out **those buying and selling in the temple**. He overturned the **money**

---

expectations of the Messiah ran high. At this most famous of Jewish festivals, the city was crowded with Jews from many places. The crowds placed their robes in front of Him and put branches from trees on the road, paying Jesus great honor. **Who is this?** This question must have come from different people than those who cheered Jesus. Perhaps the questioners were citizens of Jerusalem while the cheering crowds were pilgrims from far and near, many from Galilee. Those from Galilee, the region where Jesus was well-known, answered, "This is the prophet Jesus from Nazareth in Galilee" (Matt. 21:11b). This linked His humble background with the expectations of Israel for a coming Messiah.

158. JESUS CURSES A FIG TREE AND CLEANSES THE TEMPLE
those buying and selling in the temple: Jews who came to worship in the temple needed animals to offer as sacrifices. Many worshipers traveled great distances to reach Jerusalem, and the animals had to be declared unblemished by the priests. Booths were set up in the outer court of the Gentiles, where travelers could buy sacrificial animals guaranteed to pass inspection by the priests. The chief priests, who ran the temple, probably received a percentage of these sales.
money changers' tables: Jews also needed Jewish coins with which to pay the temple tax. Tables were set up where Jews

changers' tables and the seats of those who were selling doves, [16]and would not permit anyone to carry goods through the temple complex. [17]Then He began to teach them: "Is it not written, 'My house will be called a house of prayer for all nations'? But you have made it a 'den of thieves'!"

[Mt 21:14–16a]The blind and the lame came to Him in the temple complex, and He healed them. [15]When **the chief priests and the scribes** saw the wonders that He did, and the children in the temple complex cheering, "Hosanna to the Son of David!" they were indignant [16a]and said to Him, "Do You hear what these children are saying?" [Mk 11:18a]Then . . . [they] . . . started looking for a way to destroy Him. For they were afraid of Him, [Lk 19:48a]but they could not find a way to do it, because all the people were spellbound by what they heard.

[Mt 21:17]Then He left them, went out of the city to Bethany, and spent the night there.

159. GREEKS ASK TO SEE JESUS

John 12:20–50

[20]Now among those who went up to worship at the festival were **some Greeks**. [21]So they came to Philip, who was from Bethsaida in Galilee, and requested of him, "Sir, we want to see Jesus."

[22]Philip went and told Andrew; then Andrew and Philip went and told Jesus. [23]Jesus replied to them, "**The hour has come** for the Son of Man to be glorified.

[24]"I assure you: Unless a grain of wheat **falls into the ground and dies**, it remains by itself. But if it dies, it produces a large crop. [25]The one who loves his life will lose it, and the one who hates his life in this world will keep it for eternal

---

could exchange foreign money for Jewish coins. Jesus didn't accept selling animals and exchanging money as legitimate enterprises in the temple, even in the large outer court. When He entered the temple, He turned over the tables of those who were selling in the temple. Jesus explained His actions by quoting Isaiah 56:7 and Jeremiah 7:11.

the chief priests and the scribes: Watching Jesus were two groups of religious leaders: the chief priests and the scribes. The scribes had been hostile toward Jesus from near the beginning of His ministry because He seemed to disregard their interpretations of the law. Most of the chief priests were Sadducees, who had not paid much attention to Jesus until He cleansed the temple. When He did that, He struck a blow at the source of their power and wealth. Now these two powerful groups joined forces against Jesus.

159. GREEKS ASK TO SEE JESUS

some Greeks: During the Passover Festival, a group of Greeks—probably God-fearing Gentiles—had come to Jerusalem to worship. They told Philip they wanted to see Jesus. Philip passed this word to Andrew, and the two of them informed Jesus.

The hour has come: This incident was a moving experience for Jesus. He declared that His time to be glorified had arrived. "His hour" referred to the climax of His mission through suffering and death. In these inquiring Gentiles He saw a future ingathering of persons of all races who would respond to His gospel.

falls into the ground and dies: Jesus compared His approaching death to planting a seed. The seed has to die in order to bring the harvest. Only by choosing to give up His life could Jesus make possible a rich harvest of believers—including many from among the Gentiles.

life. ²⁶If anyone serves Me, he must follow Me. Where I am, there My servant also will be. If anyone serves Me, the Father will honor him.

²⁷"Now My soul is troubled. What should I say—'Father, **save Me from this hour**'? But that is why I came to this hour. ²⁸ᵃFather, glorify Your name!"

²⁸ᵇThen **a voice came from heaven**: "I have glorified it, and I will glorify it again!"

²⁹The crowd standing there heard it and said it was thunder. Others said, "An angel has spoken to Him!"

³⁰Jesus responded, "This voice came, not for Me, but for you. ³¹Now is the judgment of this world. Now the ruler of this world will be cast out. ³²As for Me, **if I am lifted up** from the earth I will draw all people to Myself." ³³He said this to signify what kind of death He was about to die.

³⁴Then the crowd replied to Him, "We have heard from the law that the Messiah would remain forever. So how can You say, 'The Son of Man must be lifted up'? Who is this Son of Man?"

³⁵Jesus answered, "The light will be with you only a little longer. Walk **while you have the light**, so that darkness doesn't overtake you. The one who walks in darkness doesn't know where he's going. ³⁶While you have the light, believe in the light, so that you may become sons of light." Jesus said this, then went away and hid from them.

Isaiah's Prophecies Fulfilled

³⁷Even though He had performed so many signs in their presence, they did not believe in Him. ³⁸But this was to fulfill the word of Isaiah the prophet, who said: "Lord, who has believed our report? And to whom has the arm of the Lord been revealed?"

³⁹This is why they were unable to believe, because Isaiah also said: ⁴⁰"He has blinded their eyes and hardened their hearts, so that they would not see with their eyes or understand with their hearts, and be converted, and I would heal them." ⁴¹Isaiah said these things because he saw His glory and spoke about Him.

---

save Me from this hour: Just as in the Gethsemane prayer, Jesus dreaded the terrible price He must pay by His suffering and death. He considered asking the Father to save Him from this hour, but He rejected that notion and recommitted Himself to the cross.

a voice came from heaven: A voice from heaven confirmed Jesus' commitment to the way of the cross. At the beginning of His ministry (Matt. 3:17), at His transformation (Luke 9:35), and now toward the close of His ministry, Jesus was fortified by words of approval and encouragement from His Father.

if I am lifted up: Instead of speaking of suffering, Jesus gave a victory speech. By the course He was taking, Satan would suffer defeat. As Jesus was lifted up on the cross to die, all kinds of people would be drawn to Him. "Lifted up" also implies being resurrected from the grave and later being taken into heaven.

while you have the light: Jesus compared the time to the fading light just before dark. The night was about to fall with the end of His ministry. While they could still see the light, they should believe.

⁴²Nevertheless, many did believe in Him even among the rulers, but because of the Pharisees they did not confess Him, so they would not be banned from the synagogue. ⁴³For they loved praise from men more than praise from God.

⁴⁴Then Jesus cried out, "The one who believes in Me believes not in Me, but in Him who sent Me. ⁴⁵And the one who sees Me sees Him who sent Me. ⁴⁶I have come as a light into the world, so that everyone who believes in Me would not remain in darkness. ⁴⁷If anyone hears My words and doesn't keep them, I do not judge him; for I did not come to judge the world, but to save the world. ⁴⁸**The one who rejects Me** and doesn't accept My sayings has this as his judge: the word I have spoken will judge him on the last day. ⁴⁹For I have not spoken on My own, but the Father Himself who sent Me has given Me a command as to what I should say and what I should speak. ⁵⁰I know that His command is eternal life. So the things that I speak, I speak just as the Father has told Me."

160. THE MESSAGE OF THE WITHERED FIG TREE

Matthew 21:19–22; Mark 11:20–26

Mk 11:20–21Early in the morning, as they were passing by, they saw **the fig tree withered** from the roots up. ²¹Then Peter remembered and said to Him, "Rabbi, look! The fig tree that You cursed is withered" [Mt 21:20 *When the disciples saw it, they were amazed and said, "How did the fig tree wither so quickly?"*].

²²Jesus replied to them, "Have faith in God. ²³I assure you: If anyone says to this mountain, 'Be lifted up and thrown into the sea,' and does not doubt in his heart, but believes that what he says will happen, it will be done for him. ²⁴Therefore, I tell you, all the things you pray and ask for—**believe** that you have received them, **and you will have them**. ²⁵And whenever you stand praying, **if you have anything against anyone, forgive him**, so that your Father in heaven may also forgive you your wrongdoing. ²⁶But if you don't forgive, neither will your Father in heaven forgive your wrongdoing."*

---

* *Verse 26 of Mark 11 does not appear in some New Testament manuscripts.*

The one who rejects Me: As His public ministry drew to a close, Jesus issued a final invitation for people to believe in Him and in the Father who sent Him. He warned that those who rejected Him would face certain judgment.

160. THE MESSAGE OF THE WITHERED FIG TREE

the fig tree withered: This was the fig tree that Jesus had condemned because of its unfruitfulness just the day before. The dead tree represented the Jewish nation that abounded in the leaves of religious profession but was actually barren of real fruit.

believe . . . and you will have them: Jesus also used this occasion to teach His disciples a lesson in effective prayer. The key to answered prayer is faith and trust. By faith the followers of Jesus could achieve the impossible through the power of prayer.

if you have anything against anyone, forgive him: Because He had just performed a miracle of judgment, Jesus wanted His disciples to understand that they must not exercise their miraculous gifts with a vengeful, unforgiving spirit. Mountain-moving faith must be accompanied by forgiving love.

Events of Jesus' Final Week

The last week of Jesus' earthly life was only a small portion of His three-and-one-half-year ministry. But each of the Gospel writers devoted several chapters to these closing events. His suffering, death, and resurrection were obviously the crowning achievement of His work as God's Son.

Here's a brief summary of the main events of this final week—from Palm Sunday to Resurrection Sunday—reported by the Gospel writers:

Sunday
- *Jesus' triumphal entry into Jerusalem*

Monday
- *Jesus cleanses the temple and curses a fig tree*

Tuesday
- *Jesus predicts the destruction of Jerusalem and His return*
- *Mary of Bethany anoints Jesus*
- *Judas arranges to betray Jesus to the Jewish authorities*

Thursday Evening
- *Jesus eats the Passover meal with His disciples*
- *Jesus institutes the Memorial Supper*
- *Jesus' agonizing prayer in the Garden of Gethsemane*

Friday
- *Jesus betrayed by Judas and delivered to His enemies*
- *Trial of Jesus before the Jewish Sanhedrin*
- *Peter's denial of Jesus*
- *Trial of Jesus before the Roman officials Pilate and Herod*
- *Crucifixion and death of Jesus*
- *Jesus' burial in Joseph's tomb*

Sunday
- *Jesus is resurrected from the dead*

---

161. THE SANHEDRIN QUESTIONS JESUS' AUTHORITY

Matthew 21:23–27; Mark 11:27–33; Luke 20:1–8

Mt 21:23When He entered the temple complex, the chief priests and the elders of the people came up to Him as He was teaching and said, "**By what authority** are You doing these things? Who gave You this authority?"

---

161. THE SANHEDRIN QUESTIONS JESUS' AUTHORITY

By what authority: The religious leaders demanded that Jesus reveal the source of His authority for cleansing the temple, since the operation of the temple was their responsibility. They probably hoped that Jesus would make an admission to give them grounds to arrest Him.

[24]Jesus answered them, "I will also ask you one question, and if you answer it for Me, then I will tell you by what authority I do these things. [25a]**Where did John's baptism come from?** From heaven or from men?"

[25b]They began to argue among themselves, "If we say, 'From heaven,' He will say to us, 'Then why didn't you believe him?' [26]But if we say, 'From men,' we're afraid of the crowd [[Lk 20:6a]*all the people will stone us*], because everyone thought that John was a prophet." [27a]So they answered Jesus, "We don't know."

[27b]And He said to them, "Neither will I tell you by what authority I do these things."

162. The Parable of the Two Vineyard Workers

Matthew 21:28–32

[28]"But what do you think? **A man had two sons**. He went to the first and said, 'My son, go, work in the vineyard today.'

[29]"He answered, 'I don't want to!' Yet later he changed his mind and went. [30a]Then the man went to the other and said the same thing.

[30b]"'I will, sir,' he answered. But he didn't go.

[31a]"Which of the two did his father's will?"

[31b]"The first," they said.

[31c]Jesus said to them, "I assure you: Tax collectors and prostitutes are entering the kingdom of God before you! [32]For John came to you in the way of righteousness, and you didn't believe him. Tax collectors and prostitutes did believe him, but you, when you saw it, didn't change your mind later to believe him.

163. The Parable of the Vineyard Owner

Matthew 21:33–46; Mark 12:1–12; Luke 20:9–19

[Lk 20:9a]Then He began to tell the people this parable: [Mt 21:33b]There was a man, **a landowner, who planted a vineyard**, put a fence around it, dug a winepress in

---

Where did John's baptism come from? Jesus put His questioners in a quandary by asking about the authority of John the Baptizer. If they acknowledged John's authority, why did they not accept his witness to Jesus? If they denied it, this would offend the common people, who admired John. They would not answer Jesus' question, so He refused to declare His source of authority to them.

162. The Parable of the Two Vineyard Workers

A man had two sons: In this parable, the Jewish religious leaders are represented by the son who promised to work in the vineyard but didn't follow through. These leaders had promised to do God's will, but they refused to believe John the Baptizer, who called them to repentance and pointed to Jesus as the Messiah. The son who refused at first to work in the vineyard but then did so represents the sinners. They were far from God's kingdom at first, but they believed John the Baptizer and repented. Thus, they were actually the people who had done God's will and followed His commands.

163. The Parable of the Vineyard Owner

a landowner, who planted a vineyard: The vineyard in this parable was the nation of Israel, God's chosen people. The

it, and built a watchtower. **He leased it to tenant farmers** and went away ^{Lk} ^{20:9b}for a long time.

^{Mt 21:34a}When the grape harvest drew near, ^{Mk 12:2b–5}**he sent a slave** to the farmers so that he might collect some of the fruit of the vineyard from the farmers. ³But they took him, beat him, and sent him away empty-handed. ⁴And again he sent another slave to them, and they hit him on the head and treated him shamefully. ⁵Then he sent another, and that one they killed. He also sent **many others**; they beat some and they killed some.

^{Lk 20:13}"Then the owner of the vineyard said, 'What should I do? **I will send my beloved son**. Perhaps they will respect him.'

^{Mt 21:38}"But when the tenant farmers saw the son, they said among themselves, 'This is the heir. Come, let's kill him and seize his inheritance ^{Lk 20:14b}so that the inheritance may be ours.' ^{Mt 21:39–40}So they seized him and threw him out of the vineyard, and killed him. ⁴⁰Therefore, when the owner of the vineyard comes, what will he do to those farmers?"

⁴¹"He will destroy those terrible men in a terrible way," they told Him, "and lease his vineyard to other farmers who will give him his produce at the harvest."

⁴²Jesus said to them, "Have you never read in the Scriptures: 'The stone that the builders rejected, this has become the cornerstone. This cornerstone came from the Lord and is wonderful in our eyes'? ⁴³Therefore I tell you, **the kingdom of God will be taken away from you** and given to a nation producing its fruit. ⁴⁴Whoever falls on this stone will be broken to pieces; but on whomever it falls, it will grind him to powder!"

⁴⁵When the chief priests and the Pharisees heard His parables, they knew He was speaking about them. ⁴⁶Although they were looking for **a way to arrest**

---

landowner planted the vineyard, put a fence around it, dug a place for the winepress, and built a watchtower. This signifies God's action in delivering Israel and in making a covenant with them. God had done everything possible to help them fulfill their intended purpose.

He leased it to tenant farmers: The owner hired tenants to tend his vineyard. They were responsible for protecting it and cultivating it. These tenant farmers represented the leaders of Israel.

he sent a slave . . . many others: When the harvest season came, the vineyard owner sent his servants to collect his part of the harvest. But the tenants rejected, beat, and even killed some of these servants. The servants represent God's prophets. God had repeatedly sent prophets to call His people back to the covenant. Instead of obeying God's word through the prophets, Israel had rejected the prophets and their message. In some cases they even killed God's prophets.

I will send my beloved son: Why would the owner of the vineyard think these evil tenants would respect his son when they had mistreated his servants so badly? The intention of Jesus was to force His listeners to consider God's purpose in sending His Son into the world. But the tenants showed no respect for the owner's son. They killed him and dumped his body out of the vineyard. This may reflect the shameful way Jesus was executed outside the city walls of Jerusalem (Heb. 13:11–13).

the kingdom of God will be taken away from you: This parable teaches that the Jewish leaders rejected the Son and that God turned to others who would accept Him. During the first century, Christianity became increasingly a Gentile rather than a Jewish religion. Gentiles became the majority, while the chosen people of the Old Testament increasingly rejected Christ.

a way to arrest Him: The reaction of the religious leaders proves the truth of Jesus' parable. They became more determined to arrest Him. The only thing that restrained them was Jesus' popularity with the people. They finally left without arresting Him.

Him, they feared the crowds, because they regarded Him as a prophet. ^{Mk 12:12b}So they left Him and went away.

164. THE PARABLE OF THE WEDDING BANQUET

Matthew 22:1–14

¹Once more Jesus spoke to them in parables: ²"The kingdom of heaven may be compared to a king who gave a wedding banquet for his son. ³He sent out his slaves to summon those invited to the banquet, but they didn't want to come. ⁴Again, he sent out other slaves, and said, 'Tell those who are invited, "Look, I've prepared my dinner; my oxen and fatted cattle have been slaughtered, and everything is ready. Come to the wedding banquet."'

⁵"But **they paid no attention** and went away, one to his own farm, another to his business. ⁶And the others seized his slaves and killed them. ⁷The king was enraged, so he sent out his troops, destroyed those murderers, and burned down their city.

⁸"Then he told his slaves, 'The banquet is ready, but those who were invited were not worthy. ⁹Therefore, go to where the roads exit the city and **invite everyone you find** to the banquet.' ¹⁰So those slaves went out on the roads and gathered everyone they found, both evil and good. The wedding banquet was filled with guests. ¹¹But when the king came in to view the guests, he saw a man there who was not dressed for a wedding. ¹²So he said to him, 'Friend, how did you get in here without wedding clothes?' The man was speechless.

¹³"Then the king told the attendants, 'Tie him up hand and foot, and **throw him into the outer darkness**, where there will be weeping and gnashing of teeth.'

¹⁴"For **many are invited, but few are chosen**."

165. JESUS QUESTIONED ABOUT PAYING TAXES TO CAESAR

Matthew 22:15–22; Mark 12:13–17; Luke 20:20–26

^{Lk 20:20}They [^{Mt 22:15}*the **Pharisees***] watched closely and sent spies who pretended to be righteous, so they could catch Him in what He said, to hand Him over to the

---

164. THE PARABLE OF THE WEDDING BANQUET

they paid no attention: This parable teaches that the Jews who have rejected the Messiah will be turned away from the messianic feast, while Gentiles will be brought in to take their place. The Jewish nation was invited to the blessings of the kingdom of heaven, but they scorned the invitation. As a result, God's judgment will fall upon them.

invite everyone you find: The king who gave this wedding banquet commanded that the wedding room should be filled with people gathered from the streets. These people represent the Gentiles.

throw him into the outer darkness: But the salvation of the Gentiles is not to be a universal experience. One of the guests was not properly dressed, so he was cast out. A place at the messianic feast of the kingdom of God can be enjoyed only when a guest is properly dressed in the wedding garment that God Himself provides.

many are invited, but few are chosen: Many people receive God's invitation to the messianic banquet, but only a few accept the blessings that He provides.

165. JESUS QUESTIONED ABOUT PAYING TAXES TO CAESAR

Pharisees . . . Herodians: In an attempt to trap Jesus, the Jewish religious leaders sent representatives of two opposing

governor's rule and authority. ^{Mt 22:16–17}They sent their disciples to Him, with the **Herodians**. "Teacher," they said, "we know that You are truthful and teach the way of God in truth. You defer to no one, for You don't show partiality. ¹⁷Tell us, therefore, what You think. **Is it lawful to pay taxes to Caesar** or not?"

¹⁸But perceiving their malice [^{Mk 12:15}*hyposcrisy*] [^{Lk 20:23}*craftiness*], Jesus said, "Why are you testing Me, hypocrites? ¹⁹Show Me the coin used for the tax [^{Mk 12:15b}*Bring Me a denarius to look at*]." So **they brought Him a denarius**. ²⁰"Whose image and inscription is this?" He asked them.

^{21a}"Caesar's," they said to Him.

^{21b}Then He said to them, "Therefore, give back to Caesar the **things that are Caesar's**, and to God the **things that are God's**."

^{Lk 20:26a}They were not able to catch Him in what He said in public, and ^{Mt 22:22b}they left Him and went away, ^{Lk 20:26b}[and] became silent.

166. THE SADDUCEES QUESTION JESUS ABOUT THE RESURRECTION

Matthew 22:23–33; Mark 12:18–27; Luke 20:27–40

^{Mt 22:23–28}The same day some Sadducees, who say there is no resurrection, came up to Him and questioned Him: ²⁴"Teacher, Moses said, 'if a man dies, having no children, his brother is to marry his wife and raise up offspring for his brother.' ²⁵Now there were seven brothers among us. The first got married and died. Having no offspring, he left his wife to his brother. ²⁶The same happened to the second also, and the third, and so to all seven. ²⁷Then last of all the woman died. ²⁸Therefore, in the resurrection, **whose wife will she be** of the seven? For they all had married her."

---

parties—the Pharisees, who hated Roman rule, and the Herodians, who supported it. Perhaps they believed no matter how Jesus answered, He was bound to alienate one of these groups.

Is it lawful to pay taxes to Caesar: This question was designed to trap Jesus. If He said yes, the nationalistic Pharisees would say to the crowds, "He is no prophet of God because He is not loyal to our nation." If He said no, the Herodians would report Him to the civil authorities as a dangerous revolutionary who encouraged rebellion against Rome.

they brought Him a denarius: Jesus was more than a match for their trickery. He asked the Pharisees and Herodians to show Him a coin they used to pay taxes. The denarius was a silver coin stamped with the image of the Roman emperor. It showed clearly the sovereignty of Rome throughout the land.

things that are Caesar's . . . things that are God's: Jesus confounded His critics by suggesting that if the tax money carried Caesar's name and image, it obviously belonged to him and should be given to him. They were obligated to pay taxes to him as long as he continued to be their emperor. But some things belonged to God alone, and these should be rendered only to Him. For Jesus the relationship of the individual to God outweighed all other considerations. We owe our ultimate devotion to our Creator.

166. THE SADDUCEES QUESTION JESUS ABOUT THE RESURRECTION

whose wife will she be: The Sadducees posed a hypothetical case of a woman who married seven brothers in succession. The Jewish law of levirate marriage specified that the brother of a deceased man should marry his widow to produce sons to carry on the family name. The Sadducees wanted to know which brother's wife she would be in the afterlife. Jesus explained that there will be no marriage in the next life.

²⁹Jesus answered them, "You are deceived, because you don't know the Scriptures or the power of God. ᴸᵏ ²⁰:³⁴ᵇ⁻³⁸ The children of this age marry and are given in marriage. ³⁵But those who are counted worthy to take part in that age, and the resurrection from the dead, neither marry nor are given in marriage. ³⁶For they cannot die any more, because they are like angels and are children of God, since they are children of the resurrection. ³⁷But **even Moses indicated** in the passage about the burning bush **that the dead are raised**, where he calls the Lord 'the God of Abraham and the God of Isaac and the God of Jacob.' ³⁸He is not God of the dead but of the living, because all are living to Him."

³⁹Some of the scribes answered, "Teacher, You have spoken well." ⁴⁰And they no longer dared to ask Him anything. ᴹᵗ ²²:³³And when the crowds heard this, they were astonished at His teaching.

167. JESUS DISCUSSES THE GREATEST COMMANDMENT

Matthew 22:34–40; Mark 12:28–34

ᴹᵗ ²²:³⁴When the Pharisees heard that He had silenced the Sadducees, they came together in the same place. ᴹᵏ ¹²:²⁸One of the scribes approached. When he heard them debating and saw that Jesus answered them well, he asked Him,

---

The Sadducees

Although they were not as numerous as the Pharisees, the Sadducees were a powerful and influential group in Jesus' day. They were from the upper echelon of Jewish society. Many of them were prosperous merchants and businessmen. Their ranks also included the high priests and the most influential members of the priesthood (Acts 5:17).

The Sadducees accepted only the first five books of the Old Testament as authoritative. They did not believe in the resurrection because it was not supported, so they claimed, by these five books. As antisupernaturalists, they also denied the existence of angels and spirits (Mark 12:18–27). These beliefs may have been motivated by their power and status in Jewish society. Since they did not believe in the resurrection and life after death, they did not have to worry about rewards or punishments in the afterlife.

The Sadducees probably argued with the leaders of other Jewish groups and condemned their beliefs. In this situation they hoped to undermine Jesus by making Him look ridiculous.

---

even Moses indicated . . . that the dead are raised: Jesus went on to quote a passage from Exodus, a book that the Sadducees accepted as authoritative, to show that they were wrong in their denial of the resurrection (see Exod. 3:6). In this passage Moses called God "the God of Abraham, the God of Isaac and the God of Jacob" (NIV) many years after the death of the patriarchs. If the patriarchs were not immortal, God would not have been called their God because He is the God of the living, not the dead. It followed logically that though they had died, the patriarchs would receive the resurrection life at the end of the age.

167. JESUS DISCUSSES THE GREATEST COMMANDMENT
Which commandment is the most important: Jesus responded to the question of a scribe by quoting the *Shema* from

"**Which commandment is the most important** of all? [^{Mt 22:36} *Which command-ment in the law is the greatest?*]"

²⁹"This is the most important [^{Mt 22:38}*greatest and most important command-ment*]," Jesus answered: "'Hear, O Israel! The Lord our God is one Lord. ³⁰And you shall love the Lord your God with all your heart, with all your soul, with all your mind, and with all your strength.' ³¹The second is: 'You shall **love your neighbor as yourself.**' There is no other commandment greater than these. ^{Mt 22:39b}All the Law and the Prophets depend on these two commandments."

^{Mk 12:32–33}Then the scribe said to Him, "**Well said, Teacher!** You have spoken in truth that He is one, and there is no one else except Him. ³³And to love Him with all the heart, with all the understanding, and with all the strength, and to love one's neighbor as oneself, is far more important than all the burnt offerings and sacrifices."

³⁴When Jesus saw that he answered intelligently, He said to him, "You are **not far from the kingdom of God.**" And no one dared to question Him any longer.

168. Jesus Discusses the Deity of the Davidic Messiah

Matthew 22:41–46; Mark 12:35–37; Luke 20:41–44

^{Mt 22:41}While the Pharisees were together, Jesus questioned them, ^{Mk 12:35a}as He taught in the temple complex, ^{Mt 22:42a}"What do you think about the **Messiah? Whose Son is He?**"

^{42b}"David's," they told Him.

^{43a}He asked them, "How is it then that David ^{Lk 20:42a}in the Book of Psalms ^{Mt 22:43b–45}inspired by the Spirit, calls Him 'Lord': ⁴⁴'The Lord said to my Lord, "Sit at My right hand until I put Your enemies under Your feet"'? ⁴⁵If, then, David calls Him 'Lord,' how is He his Son?"

Deuteronomy 6:4–9. All Jews accept these verses as the supreme confession of their faith. The words "heart . . . soul . . . mind . . . strength" indicate that the total person must be involved in love for God.

love your neighbor as yourself: Jesus went on to say that the commandment to love others (Lev. 19:18) was just as important as the first. Professed devotion to God is worth nothing unless it is accompanied by just and compassionate treatment of others.

Well said, Teacher! The scribe accepted Jesus' answer, and he also affirmed the superiority of love over ritual sacrifices. He took his stand with the most revolutionary teaching of the prophets (Mic. 6:6–8) and anticipated such New Testament teaching as Hebrews 10:1–6.

not far from the kingdom of God: Jesus declared that this scribe was ready to enter God's kingdom since he had accepted divinely revealed truth.

168. Jesus Discusses the Deity of the Davidic Messiah

Messiah? Whose Son is He? The Passover season brought Jews from all parts of Palestine to Jerusalem, where they met in patriotic fervor. Hopes ran high that this festive season would bring the manifestation of the Messiah. Quoting Psalm 110:1, Jesus asked why David referred to the Messiah as "Lord" if the Messiah was to be David's son, or descendant. Jesus rejected the idea of the Messiah as only a human descendant of David and affirmed His superiority as God's Son.

⁴⁶No one was able to answer Him at all, and from that day no one dared to question Him any more. ^{Mk 12:37b}And the large crowd was listening to Him with delight.

169. Jesus Condemns the Scribes and Pharisees

Matthew 23:1–36; Mark 12:38–40; Luke 20:45–47

^{Mt 23:1}Then Jesus spoke to the crowds and to His disciples: ^{Lk 20:46}"Beware of the scribes, who want to go around in long robes, and who love greetings in the marketplaces, the front seats in the synagogues, and the places of honor at banquets. ^{Mt 23:2–3}**The scribes and the Pharisees** are **seated in the chair of Moses**. ³Therefore do and observe whatever they tell you. But don't do what they do, because they don't do what they say.

⁴"They tie up **heavy loads that are hard to carry** and put them on people's shoulders, but they themselves aren't willing to lift a finger to move them. ⁵They do everything to be observed by others: They enlarge their **phylacteries** and lengthen their **tassels**. ⁶They love the place of honor at banquets, the front seats in the synagogues, ⁷greetings in the marketplaces, and to be called 'Rabbi' by people. ⁸But as for you, do not be called 'Rabbi,' because you have one Teacher, and you are all brothers.

One Father and One Master

⁹"Do not call anyone on earth your father, because you have one Father, who is in heaven. ¹⁰And do not be called masters either, because you have one Master, the Messiah. ¹¹The greatest among you will be your servant. ¹²Whoever exalts himself will be humbled, and whoever humbles himself will be exalted.

Jesus claimed to be the Messiah as well as the Son of God. This was in agreement with Old Testament prophecies (see Ps. 2:7, 12).

169. Jesus Condemns the Scribes and Pharisees

The scribes and the Pharisees: Jesus had spoken harshly of the scribes and Pharisees before (see segment 120, "Jesus Criticized by a Pharisee and an Expert in the Law," p. 146, and segment 121, "Jesus Warns about the Deception of the Pharisees," p. 148). But His language in this passage is particularly critical and biting. As His time on earth drew to a close, He wanted to make sure His followers were aware of the pitfalls of their approach to religion.

seated in the chair of Moses: This was the chair in the synagogue from which the meaning of the Law of Moses was expounded. Although the Pharisees occupied this chair, their teachings were not to be followed by His disciples.

heavy loads that are hard to carry: The Pharisees multiplied rules and regulations about every detail of the law. This increased the burden on the common people, who did not have the time or resources to observe all their petty regulations.

phylacteries . . . tassels: Phylacteries were verses of Scripture encased in tiny boxes that were worn on the arm and forehead. The Pharisees made their phylacteries larger than usual to appear more religious than other people. They also lengthened the fringes on their robes to give the same impression.

¹³"But **woe to you**, scribes and Pharisees, hypocrites! You lock up the kingdom of heaven from people. For you don't go in, and you don't allow those entering to go in.

¹⁴"Woe to you, scribes and Pharisees, hypocrites! You devour widows' houses, and make long prayers just for show. This is why you will receive a harsher punishment.*

¹⁵"Woe to you, scribes and Pharisees, hypocrites! You travel over land and sea to make one convert, and when he becomes one, you make him twice as fit for hell as you are!

¹⁶"Woe to you, blind guides, who say, 'Whoever takes an oath by the sanctuary, it is nothing. But whoever takes an oath by the gold of the sanctuary is bound by his oath.' ¹⁷Blind fools! For which is greater, the gold or the sanctuary that sanctified the gold? ¹⁸Also, 'Whoever takes an oath by the altar, it is nothing. But whoever takes an oath by the gift that is on it is bound by his oath.' ¹⁹Blind people! For which is greater, the gift or the altar that sanctifies the gift?

²⁰"Therefore the one who takes an oath by the altar takes an oath by it and by everything on it. ²¹The one who takes an oath by the sanctuary takes an oath by it and by Him who dwells in it. ²²And the one who takes an oath by heaven takes an oath by God's throne and by Him who sits on it.

²³"Woe to you, scribes and Pharisees, hypocrites! You pay a tenth of mint, dill and cumin, yet you have neglected the more important matters of the law—justice, mercy and faith. These things should have been done without neglecting the others. ²⁴Blind guides! You strain out a gnat, yet gulp down a camel!

²⁵"Woe to you, scribes and Pharisees, hypocrites! You clean the outside of the cup and dish, but inside they are full of greed and self-indulgence! ²⁶Blind Pharisee! First clean the inside of the cup, so the outside of it may also become clean.

²⁷"Woe to you, scribes and Pharisees, hypocrites! You are like whitewashed tombs, which appear beautiful on the outside, but inside are full of dead men's bones and every impurity. ²⁸In the same way, on the outside you seem righteous to people, but inside you are full of hypocrisy and lawlessness.

²⁹"Woe to you, scribes and Pharisees, hypocrites! You build the tombs of the prophets and decorate the monuments of the righteous, ³⁰and you say, 'If we had lived in the days of our fathers, we wouldn't have taken part with them in shedding the prophets' blood.' ³¹You therefore testify against yourselves that you are

---

* Verse 14 of Matthew 23 does not appear in some New Testament manuscripts.

---

woe to you: Verses 13–29 of Matthew 23 contain eight statements of woe issued by Jesus against the Pharisees. The theme of these "woes" is hypocrisy. The Pharisees pretended to be pious and superrighteous, but they were actually "full of dead men's bones and every impurity" (v. 27).

sons of those who murdered the prophets. ³²Fill up, then, the measure of your fathers' sins!

³³"Snakes! Brood of vipers! How can you escape being condemned to hell? ³⁴This is why I am sending you prophets, sages, and scribes. Some of them **you will kill and crucify**, and some of them you will flog in your synagogues and hound from town to town. ³⁵So all the righteous blood shed on the earth will be charged to you, from the blood of righteous Abel to the blood of Zechariah, son of Berechiah, whom you murdered between the sanctuary and the altar. ³⁶I assure you: All these things will come on this generation!"

170. A SACRIFICIAL OFFERING BY A POOR WIDOW

Mark 12:41–44; Luke 21:1–4

Mk 12:41–44Sitting across from **the temple treasury**, He watched how the crowd dropped money into the treasury. Many rich people were putting in **large sums**. ⁴²And a poor widow came and dropped in **two tiny coins** worth very little. ⁴³Summoning His disciples, He said to them, "I assure you: This poor widow has put in more than all those giving to the temple treasury. ⁴⁴For they all gave out of their surplus, but she out of her poverty has put in everything she possessed—all she had to live on."

171. JESUS' GREAT PROPHETIC DISCOURSE

Matthew 24:1–51; Mark 13:1–37; Luke 21:5–38

Mt 24:1As Jesus left and was going out of the temple complex, His disciples came up and called His attention to the **temple buildings**, Lk 21:5bhow it was adorned with beautiful stones and gifts dedicated to God.

---

you will kill and crucify: Jesus ended His denunciation of the Pharisees by accusing them of murdering the prophets whom God had sent to them throughout Jewish history. He realized they harbored the same sort of hate against Him; He was destined to become their next victim.

170. A SACRIFICIAL OFFERING BY A POOR WIDOW

the temple treasury: Offering boxes for voluntary contributions were scattered throughout the Jewish temple in Jerusalem. The money collected was used for the operation and maintenance of the temple. Jesus watched the people as they dropped their offerings into one of these boxes.

large sums . . . two tiny coins: The contributions made by many of the wealthy people did not impress Jesus. He knew these gifts represented no sacrifice. What they gave was little in comparison with what they had. But this poor widow gave all she had to live on. Her small gift counted far more in His sight than the larger donations of others.

171. JESUS' GREAT PROPHETIC DISCOURSE

temple buildings: As Jesus and His disciples were leaving the temple, one of the disciples expressed pride in the beautiful temple buildings. Although the Jewish people had little regard for Herod the Great, they took pride in the temple that Herod began to build about 20 B.C. It was still under construction in Jesus' day (John 2:20) and was not completed until A.D. 64. Some of the stones were white marble, and portions of the temple were plated with gold.

Mt 24:2–3aThen He replied to them, "Do you not see all these things? I assure you: Not one **stone** will be left here on another that will not be **thrown down!**" 3aWhile He was sitting on the Mount of Olives, Mk 13:3aacross from the temple complex, Mt 24:3bthe disciples [Mk 13:3b *Peter, James, John, and Andrew*] approached Him privately and said, "Tell us, when will these things happen? And what is the sign of Your coming and of the end of the age [Mk 13:4b *when all these things are about to take place*]?"

4Then Jesus replied to them: "Watch out that no one deceives you. 5For **many will come in My name**, saying, 'I am the Messiah,' and they will deceive many. 6You are going to hear of **wars and rumors of wars.** See that you are not alarmed, because these things must take place, but the end is not yet. 7For nation will rise up against nation, and kingdom against kingdom. There will be famines and earthquakes in various places. Lk 21:11band there will be terrifying sights and great signs from heaven. Mt 24:8All these events are the beginning of birth pains. Mk 3:23And you must watch! I have told you everything in advance.

Persecutions Predicted

Mt 24:9"Then they will hand you over to persecution, and they will kill you. You will be hated by all nations because of My name [Lk 21:12b *they will lay their hands on you and persecute you. They will hand you over to the synagogues and prisons, and you will be brought before kings and governors because of My name*]. Lk 21:13–15It will lead to an opportunity for you to witness. 14Therefore make up your minds not to prepare your defense ahead of time, 15for I will give you such words and a wisdom that none of your adversaries will be able to resist or contradict.

Mt 24:10"Then many will take offense, betray one another and hate one another. Lk 21:16–19You will even be betrayed by parents, brothers, relatives, and friends; and they will kill some of you. 17And you will be hated by all because of My name. 18But not a hair of your head will be lost. 19By your endurance gain your lives. Mt 24:11–14Many false prophets will rise up and deceive many. 12And because lawlessness will multiply, the love of many will grow cold. 13But the one who endures to the end, this one will be delivered. 14This good news of the kingdom will be pro-

---

stone . . . thrown down: Jesus told the disciples that this beautiful temple would be destroyed. The prediction of Jesus came true during the Jewish-Roman War. The Roman army laid siege to Jerusalem and finally captured it after a long struggle. In A.D. 70 they burned the temple.

many will come in My name: Jesus warned His disciples against being deceived by false messiahs. He stated that many people would claim to be acting in His name and would deceive many people. Some messianic figures appeared before A.D. 70, and many have appeared since.

wars and rumors of wars: Jesus warned His disciples not to assume that every disaster meant that the end of the age was at hand. False messiahs, wars and natural disasters, persecution and betrayal, false prophets, great evil, and apostasy are only the beginning of troubles to be expected by believers. During those times Christians are to remain faithful and take the good news to all nations.

claimed in all the world as a testimony to all nations. And then the end will come.

[15]"So when you see 'the abomination that causes desolation' spoken of by the prophet Daniel, standing in the holy place" (let the reader understand) [Lk 21:20 *But when you see Jerusalem surrounded by armies, then know that its desolation has come near*], [16]"then those in Judea must flee to the mountains! Lk 21:21b Those inside the city must leave it, and those who are in the country must not enter it. Mt 24:17-18 A man on the housetop must not come down to get things out of his house. [18]And a man in the field must not go back to get his clothes.

[19]"Woe to pregnant women and nursing mothers in those days Lk 21:23b for there will be great distress in the land and wrath against this people. Mt 24:20-22 Pray that your escape may not be in winter or on a Sabbath. [21]For at that time there will be great tribulation, the kind that hasn't taken place since the beginning of the

---

Twin Themes of the Olivet Discourse

Jesus' long exhortation in Matthew 24–25 is often called the "Prophetic Discourse," the "Eschatological Discourse," or the "Olivet Discourse." Proclaimed to His disciples on the Mount of Olives, it is one of His longest speeches in the Gospels, continuing without interruption across these two chapters for more than 90 verses.

In this long discourse, Jesus was responding to two separate questions from His disciples. They wanted to know when the temple in Jerusalem would be destroyed. They also asked about the signs that would indicate the end of the age (Matt. 24:3). The Olivet Discourse is difficult for interpreters because Jesus intermingled His answer to these two questions.

Most interpreters believe Jesus dealt with the question about the destruction of the temple in Matthew 24:4–25, ending with the phrase, "Take note: I have told you in advance." This prophecy was fulfilled in A.D. 70, when the city of Jerusalem was destroyed by the Roman army. The remainder of the discourse (Matt. 24:26–25:46) deals with the end of the age and the second coming of Christ.

The disciples assumed the Jewish temple was eternal and that it would last until the end of the age. Jesus corrected this misunderstanding. In spite of all the woes leading up to its destruction, He declared, this would not mark the end of the age. They must continue to remain watchful for His return.

---

the abomination that causes desolation: This phrase is a quotation from the Book of Daniel. The prophet Daniel had predicted "the abomination that causes desolation" (Dan. 12:11 NIV). Most interpreters believe this prophecy was fulfilled in 168 B.C., when the Syrian ruler Antiochus Epiphanes sacrificed a pig on the holy altar in the Jewish temple in Jerusalem. Jesus was probably referring to a second "abomination of desolation" that He predicted would occur in Jerusalem. Some interpreters think this was the appearance of Roman soldiers in the Holy City in A.D. 70 (see Luke 21:20).

world until now, and never will again! [22]Unless those days were cut short, no one would survive. But because of the elect those days will be cut short.

[23]"If anyone tells you then, 'Look, here is the Messiah!' or, 'Over here!' do not believe it! [24]False messiahs and false prophets will arise and perform great signs and wonders to lead astray, if possible, even the elect. [25]Take note: I have told you in advance. [26]So if they tell you, 'Look, he's in the wilderness!' don't go out; 'Look, he's in the inner rooms!' do not believe it. [27]For as the lightning comes from the east and flashes as far as the west, so will be the coming of the Son of Man. [28]Wherever the carcass is, there the vultures will gather.

The Coming of the Son of Man

[29a]"Immediately after the tribulation of those days, 'The **sun** will be darkened, and the **moon** will not shed her light; the **stars** will fall from the sky, [Lk 21:25b-26a]and there will be anguish on the earth among nations, bewildered by the roaring sea and waves. [26a]People will faint from fear and expectation of the things that are coming on the world, [Mt 24:29b]and the celestial powers will be shaken.'

[30]"Then the sign of the Son of Man will appear in the sky, and then all the tribes of the land will mourn; and they will see the Son of Man coming on the clouds of heaven with power and great glory. [Lk 21:28]But when these things begin to take place, stand up and lift up your heads, because your redemption is near! [Mt 24:31]He will send out His angels with a loud trumpet, and they will gather His elect from the four winds, from one end of the sky to the other [[Mk 13:27b]*from the end of the earth to the end of the sky*].

[32]"Now from the fig tree learn this parable: As soon as its branch becomes tender and sprouts leaves, you know that summer is near. [33]In the same way, when you see all these things, know that He is near—at the door [[Lk 21:31b]*know that the kingdom of God is near*]! [34]I assure you: This generation will certainly not pass away until all these things take place. [35]Heaven and earth will pass away, but My words will never pass away.

[36]"Now concerning that day and hour **no one knows**—neither the angels in heaven, nor the Son—except the Father only. [37]As the days of Noah were, so the coming of the Son of Man will be. [38]For in those days before the Flood they were eating and drinking, marrying and giving in marriage, until the day Noah boarded the ark. [39]They didn't know until the flood came and swept them all away. So this is the way the coming of the Son of Man will be: [40]Then two men

---

sun . . . moon . . . stars: With these words Jesus described His second coming and the spectacular signs that would show when His return was near. The sun and moon would grow dark and stars would fall from the heavens. Then the "sign of the Son of Man" would appear (v. 30a). Some interpreters believe this sign will be the appearance of Jesus Himself.

no one knows: No one but God knows the time of Christ's coming. As in the time of Noah, people will be going about their usual tasks and will be caught unprepared for Christ's coming. Believers should be ready for this event at all times.

will be in the field: one will be taken and one left. ⁴¹Two women will be grinding at the mill: one will be taken and one left. ⁴²Therefore be alert, since you don't know what day your Lord is coming.

⁴³"But know this: If the homeowner had known what time the thief was coming, he would have stayed alert and not let his house be broken into. ⁴⁴This is why you also should get ready, because the Son of Man is coming at an hour you do not expect. ⁴⁵Who then is a faithful and sensible slave, whom his master has put in charge of his household, to give them food at the proper time? ⁴⁶Blessed is that slave whom his master, when he comes, will find working. ⁴⁷I assure you: He will put him in charge of all his possessions.

An Unexpected Return

⁴⁸"But if that wicked slave says in his heart, 'My master is delayed,' ⁴⁹and starts to beat his fellow slaves, and eats and drinks with drunkards, ⁵⁰that slave's master will come on a day he does not expect and at a time he does not know. ⁵¹He will cut him to pieces and assign him a place with the hypocrites. In that place there will be weeping and gnashing of teeth.

Lk 21:34–36"Be on your guard, that your minds are not dulled from carousing, drunkenness, and worries of life, and that day come on you unexpectedly ³⁵like a trap. For it will come on all who live on the face of the whole earth. ³⁶But be alert at all times, praying that you may have strength to escape all these things that are going to take place, and to stand before the Son of Man.

Mk 13:34–37"It is like a man on a journey, who left his house, gave authority to his slaves, gave each one his work, and commanded the doorkeeper to be alert. ³⁵Therefore be alert, since you don't know when the master of the house is coming—whether in the evening, or at midnight, or at the crowing of the rooster, or early in the morning. ³⁶Otherwise, he might come suddenly and find you sleeping. ³⁷And what I say to you, I say to everyone: Be alert!"

Lk 21:37–38During the day, He was teaching in the temple complex, but in the evening He would go out and spend the night on what is called the Mount of Olives. ³⁸Then all the people would come early in the morning to hear Him in the temple complex.

172. The Parable of the Ten Virgins

Matthew 25:1–13

¹"Then the kingdom of heaven will be like **ten virgins** who took their lamps and went out to **meet the groom**. ²Five of them were **foolish** and five were **sensible**. ³When the foolish took their lamps, they didn't take oil with them. ⁴But the sensible ones took oil in their flasks with their lamps. ⁵Since the groom was delayed, they all became drowsy and fell asleep.

⁶"In the middle of the night there was a shout: '**Here's the groom!** Come out to meet him.'

⁷"Then all those virgins got up and trimmed their lamps. ⁸But the foolish ones said to the sensible ones, '**Give us some of your oil**, because our lamps are going out.'

⁹"The sensible ones answered, 'No, there won't be enough for us and for you. Go instead to those who sell, and buy oil for yourselves.'

¹⁰"When they had gone to buy some, the groom arrived. Then **those who were ready went in** with him to the wedding banquet, and the door was shut.

¹¹"Later the rest of the virgins also came and said, 'Master, master, open up for us!'

¹²"But he replied, 'I assure you: I do not know you!'

¹³"Therefore be alert, because you don't know either the day or the hour."

173. THE PARABLE OF THE TALENTS

Matthew 25:14–30

¹⁴"For it is just like a man going on a journey. He called his own slaves and turned over his possessions to them. ¹⁵To one he gave **five talents**; to another, **two**; and to another, **one**—to each according to his own ability. Then he went on a journey. Immediately ¹⁶the man who had received five talents went, put them to work, and earned five more. ¹⁷In the same way the man with two earned two more. ¹⁸But the man who had received one talent went off, dug a hole in the ground, and hid his master's money.

---

172. THE PARABLE OF THE TEN VIRGINS

ten virgins . . . meet the groom: In weddings of New Testament times, the groom went to the bride's home to conduct her to his own house, where the ceremony took place. But the language of this parable suggests that the bride and her maidens were already at her future home. The groom had left the house, and the time of his return was not known. A reception was planned for him when he returned.

foolish . . . sensible: Because of uncertainty about the groom's return, the wise maidens had gathered a reserve of oil for their small lamps. The foolish maidens made no such provision. As the groom's absence grew longer, the young women went to sleep.

Here's the groom! The groom came back at midnight. As soon as he was sighted, all the women checked their lamps.

Give us some of your oil: When the five foolish women found their oil supply was exhausted, they asked their companions to share with them. They refused. Readiness is a commodity that cannot be shared. Every person must do it for himself.

those who were ready went in: The foolish virgins went to the store to buy oil. While they were gone, the festivities began, and the door of the house was shut. This is a solemn warning against casual attitudes toward the groom's return. We must always be ready for Christ's return.

173. THE PARABLE OF THE TALENTS

five talents . . . two . . . one: Before traveling to a distant country, a man entrusted five talents to one of his slaves, two to another, and one to a third slave. A talent was the largest measure of weight, used to measure precious metals such as gold or silver. While their master was away, they were expected to handle his possessions in a trustworthy manner.

[19]"After a long time **the master of those slaves came** and settled accounts with them. [20]The man who had received five talents approached, presented five more talents, and said, 'Master, you gave me five talents. Look, **I've earned five more** talents.'

[21]"His master said to him, 'Well done, good and faithful slave! You were faithful over a few things; I will put you in charge of many things. Enter your master's joy!'

[22]"Then the man with two talents also approached. He said, 'Master, you gave me two talents. Look, **I've earned two more** talents.'

[23]"His master said to him, 'Well done, good and faithful slave! You were faithful over a few things; I will put you in charge of many things. Enter your master's joy!'

[24]"Then the man who had received one talent also approached and said, 'Master, I know you. You're a difficult man, reaping where you haven't sown and gathering where you haven't scattered seed. [25]So **I was afraid and** went off and **hid your talent** in the ground. Look, you have what is yours.'

[26]"But his master replied to him, 'You evil, lazy slave! If you knew that I reap where I haven't sown and gather where I haven't scattered, [27]then you should have deposited my money with the bankers. And when I returned I would have received **my money back with interest.**

[28]"'So take the talent from him and give it to the one who has ten talents. [29]For to everyone who has, more will be given, and he will have more than enough. But from the one who does not have, even what he has will be taken away from him. [30]And throw this good-for-nothing slave into the outer darkness. In that place there will be weeping and gnashing of teeth.'"

---

the master of those slaves came: The return of the master after a long time represents the future return of Jesus. The reckoning with the slaves was a time of settling accounts.

I've earned five more: The slave with five talents was commended for doubling his master's money and was rewarded with greater responsibilities.

I've earned two more: The master's words to the second slave are almost the same as to the first slave because he had also doubled his talents. He was rewarded on the basis of what his master had entrusted to him.

I was afraid and . . . hid your talent: The third slave explained that he had dug a hole and buried his master's talent, failing to increase its value. He thought his master was the kind of man who harvested what he did not plant. His primary feeling toward his master was fear.

my money back with interest: The master replied that if the slave had really believed he was a harsh, demanding person, he should have put the money in the bank at the safest level of risk. At least the talent would have earned some interest. What we do with what God has entrusted to us determines whether we are judged faithful or unfaithful by the Lord.

174. THE SHEEP AND THE GOATS

Matthew 25:31–46

[31]"When the Son of Man comes in His glory, and all the angels with Him, then He will sit on the throne of His glory. [32]All the nations will be gathered before Him, and **He will separate them one from another**, just as a shepherd separates **the sheep from the goats**. [33]He will put the sheep on His right, and the goats on the left. [34]Then the King will say to those on His right, 'Come, you who are blessed by My Father, inherit the kingdom prepared for you from the foundation of the world: [35]For I was **hungry** and you gave Me something to eat; I was **thirsty** and you gave Me something to drink; I was a stranger and you took Me in; [36]I was naked and you clothed Me; I was sick and you took care of Me; I was **in prison** and you visited Me.'

[37]"Then the righteous will answer Him, 'Lord, when did we see You hungry and feed You, or thirsty and give You something to drink? [38]When did we see You a stranger and take You in, or without clothes and clothe You? [39]When did we see You sick, or in prison, and visit You?'

[40]"And the King will answer them, 'I assure you: Whatever you did for one of the least of these brothers of Mine, you did for Me.' [41]Then He will also say to those on the left, 'Depart from Me, you who are cursed, into the eternal fire prepared for the Devil and his angels! [42]For I was hungry and you gave Me nothing to eat; I was thirsty and you gave Me nothing to drink; [43]I was a stranger and you didn't take Me in; I was naked and you didn't clothe Me, sick and in prison and you didn't take care of Me.'

[44]"Then they too will answer, 'Lord, when did we see You hungry, or thirsty, or a stranger, or without clothes, or sick, or in prison, and not help You?'

[45]"Then He will answer them, 'I assure you: Whatever you did not do for one of the least of these, you did not do for Me either.'

[46]"And they will go away into eternal punishment, but the righteous into eternal life."

---

174. THE SHEEP AND THE GOATS

He will separate them one from another: Jesus ended His Olivet Discourse with a vivid picture of judgment. It portrays what the second coming of Jesus will mean in terms of the ultimate separation of people.

the sheep from the goats: Shepherds of the Middle East allowed sheep and goats to graze together during the day, and they separated them at night. This custom demonstrates the present mixture and final separation of righteous and unrighteous people.

hungry . . . thirsty . . . in prison: All these conditions would apply to loyal disciples—hunger, thirst, imprisonment, deprivation of all sorts. Those who came to their aid and ministered to their needs would be considered as ministering to Christ Himself, thus entering into an eternal reward. Servants like this are deserving of reward, since they were not aware they were doing anything that merited praise. Their deeds were the natural expression of their transformed natures as disciples of Christ.

175. THE SANHEDRIN CONTINUES ITS PLOT AGAINST JESUS

Matthew 26:1–5; Mark 14:1–2; Luke 22:1–2

Lk 22:1The Festival of Unleavened Bread, which is called Passover, was drawing near. Mt 26:1–2When Jesus had finished saying all this, He told His disciples, 2"You know that the Passover takes place after two days, and the Son of Man will be **handed over to be crucified**."

Mk 14:1b–2The chief priests and the scribes Mt 26:3band the elders of the people assembled in the palace of the high priest, who was called Caiaphas, Mk 14:1b–2were looking for a way to arrest Him by deceit and kill Him. 2 "**Not during the festival**," they said, "or there may be rioting among the people."

176. MARY OF BETHANY ANOINTS JESUS

Matthew 26:6–13; Mark 14:3–9; John 12:2–8

Mk 14:3aWhile He was in Bethany at the house of Simon the leper, Jn 12:2they gave a dinner for Him there; Martha was serving them, and Lazarus was one of those reclining at the table with Him. Mk 14:3b**A woman** came with an alabaster jar of **pure and expensive** fragrant oil of **nard**. She broke the jar and poured it on His head [Jn 12:3 *Then Mary took a pound of fragrant oil—pure and expensive nard— anointed Jesus' feet, and wiped His feet with her hair. So the house was filled with the fragrance of the oil*].

Mk 14:4–5But some [Mt 26:8*the disciples*] were expressing indignation to one another: "Why has this fragrant oil been wasted? 5For this oil might have been **sold for** more than **three hundred denarii** and given to the poor" [Jn 12:4–6 *Then one of His disciples, Judas Iscariot (who was about to betray Him), said,* 5 *"Why*

---

175. THE SANHEDRIN CONTINUES ITS PLOT AGAINST JESUS

handed over to be crucified: Jesus knew His death was drawing near. He warned His disciples about this, just as He had done several times before.

Not during the festival: The Jewish leaders decided not to kill Jesus until after the Passover Festival, since the crowds would not tolerate His being harmed (Mark 14:2). But God overruled their decision; it was His will that the Lamb of God be sacrificed during the Passover. Judas's treachery enabled the Jewish leaders to seize Jesus without interference from the people.

176. MARY OF BETHANY ANOINTS JESUS

A woman: Mark does not give the name of this woman who anointed Jesus (Mark 14:3). Neither does Matthew (Matt. 26:7a). But the Gospel of John clearly identifies her as Mary of Bethany, the sister of Martha and Lazarus (John 12:2–3).

pure and expensive . . . nard: Nard was an expensive ointment or perfume. Mary anointed the feet of Jesus with an entire pound of this ointment. (For another similar anointing of Jesus during His Galilean ministry, see segment 60, "Jesus Anointed by a Sinful Woman," p. 78.) According to John's account, Mary wiped Jesus' feet with her hair (John 12:3). The crowning glory of a woman was her long hair (1 Cor. 11:15). It was unthinkable for a woman of Mary's reputation to use her hair to wipe someone's feet. The act showed her humility, love, and devotion.

sold for . . . three hundred denarii: Jesus' disciples declared that Mary was wasteful and callous toward the poor. If the expensive ointment had been sold, the money could have fed many poor people. Three hundred denarii were about a year's

wasn't this fragrant oil sold for three hundred denarii and given to the poor?" ⁶*He didn't say this because he cared about the poor, but because he was a thief. He was in charge of the money bag and would steal part of what was put in it].* And they began to scold her.

⁶Then Jesus said, "**Leave her alone.** Why are you bothering her? She has done a noble thing for Me. ⁷You always have the poor with you, and you can do good for them whenever you want, but you do not always have Me. ⁸She has done what she could; she has anointed My body in advance for burial. ⁹I assure you: Wherever the gospel is proclaimed in the whole world, what this woman has done will also be told in memory of her."

Why Did Judas Betray Jesus?

The New Testament never gives a clear answer to the question of why Judas betrayed Jesus. Several theories have been proposed. Most of the theories agree about two things: (1) Judas wanted Jesus to set up an earthly kingdom, and (2) Judas was convinced that Jesus would not do so, but would sacrifice His life.

One theory says that Judas betrayed Jesus because he hoped to force Jesus to use His power and bring in an earthly kingdom. Another theory is that when Judas became convinced that Jesus was determined to throw away His life, he decided to salvage for himself what he could. This theory emphasizes the selfishness in Judas's question, "What are you willing to give me if I hand Him over to you?" (Matt. 26:15). Perhaps the best reason is stated by Luke: "Satan entered Judas" (Luke 22:3a).

---

177. Judas Plans to Betray Jesus

Matthew 26:14–16; Mark 14:10–11; Luke 22:3–6

Lk 22:3–4Then Satan entered Judas, called Iscariot, who was numbered among the Twelve. ⁴He went away and discussed with the chief priests and temple police **how he could hand Him over** to them Mt 26:15aand said, "What are you willing to

---

salary for a laborer. According to John's account, these words of criticism were spoken only by Judas (John 12:4–5).

Leave her alone: Jesus pointed out that Mary's act showed an empathy about His coming death and burial. He had tried to tell His followers about His future suffering, but they had not understood. Mary had anointed Him as if for burial. Her act meant a great deal to Jesus because it showed that at least one of His friends realized what He was going through.

177. Judas Plans to Betray Jesus

how he could hand Him over: Judas took the initiative to betray Jesus. The high priest and the other plotters were probably surprised that one of Jesus' disciples would offer to betray Him, but they quickly accepted Judas's offer. They made a deal with him for thirty pieces of silver, the price of a slave (Exod. 21:32). From that time on, Judas was alert for an opportunity to betray Jesus.

give me if I hand Him over to you?" [Mk 14:11a]And when they heard this, [Lk 22:5a]they were glad, and [Mt 26:15b–16]weighed out thirty pieces of silver for him. [16]And from that time he started looking for a good opportunity to betray Him [Lk 22:6b]when the crowd was not present.

178. PREPARATIONS MADE
FOR THE MEMORIAL SUPPER

Matthew 26:17–19; Mark 14:12–16; Luke 22:7–13

[Mt 26:17a]On the first day of **Unleavened Bread**, [Lk 22:7b]on which the **Passover** lamb had to be sacrificed, [Mt 26:17b]the disciples came to Jesus and asked, "Where do You want us to prepare the Passover so You may eat it?"

[Lk 22:10–11a]"Listen," He said to them, "when you've entered the city, **a man carrying a water jug** will meet you. Follow him into the house that he enters. [11a]Tell the owner of the house, [Mt 26:18b]'My time is near. [Lk 22:11b]Where is the guest room, where I may eat the Passover with My disciples?' [Mk 14:15]He will show you a large room upstairs, furnished and ready. **Make the preparations** for us there."

[Mk 14:16]So the disciples went out, entered the city, and found it just as He had told them, and they prepared the Passover.

179. JESUS WASHES THE DISCIPLES' FEET

John 13:1–20

[1]Before the Passover Festival, Jesus knew that His hour had come to depart from this world to the Father. **Having loved His own** who were in the world, He loved them to the end.

---

178. PREPARATIONS MADE FOR THE MEMORIAL SUPPER

Unleavened Bread . . . Passover: Originally, the Passover and the Feast of Unleavened Bread were separate observances, one following the other. But over time the two had become one. Together, these celebrations lasted eight days. The Passover commemorated the deliverance of the Jewish people from Egyptian bondage (see Exod. 12). The meal centered around the slaughtered lamb whose blood gave protection to Hebrew households.

a man carrying a water jug: Jesus had probably made arrangements with this man for the use of his house as a place where He and His disciples could partake of the Passover meal. Since carrying water was considered women's work, the disciples would recognize this man immediately when they entered the city.

Make the preparations: The disciples would follow procedure in having the lamb for their meal slaughtered in the temple and then carried to the meeting place.

179. JESUS WASHES THE DISCIPLES' FEET

Having loved His own: Jesus had loved His disciples while He was in the world. As He prepared to take His leave, He loved these who would remain in the world to continue His work.

²Now by the time of supper, the Devil had already put it into the heart of Judas, Simon Iscariot's son, to betray Him. ³Jesus knew that the Father had given everything into His hands, that He had come from God, and that He was going back to God. ⁴So He got up from supper, laid aside His robe, took a towel, and tied it around Himself. ⁵Next, He poured water into a basin and **began to wash His disciples' feet** and to dry them with the towel tied around Him.

⁶He came to Simon Peter, who asked Him, **"Lord, are You going to wash my feet?"**

⁷Jesus answered him, "What I'm doing you don't understand now, but **afterward you will know."**

⁸ᵃ"You will never wash my feet—ever!" Peter said.

⁸ᵇJesus replied, "If I don't wash you, **you have no part with Me**."

⁹Simon Peter said to Him, **"Lord, not only my feet**, but also my hands and my head."

¹⁰"One who has bathed," Jesus told him, "doesn't need to wash anything except his feet, but he is completely clean. **You are clean**, but not all of you." ¹¹For He knew who would betray Him. This is why He said, **"You are not all clean**."

The Ritual of Footwashing

Footwashing, an expression of hospitality extended to guests, was necessary in first-century Palestine. The roads were dusty, and the people wore sandals. When people entered a house, dust needed to be washed from their feet for comfort and cleanliness. A good host provided for the washing of his guests' feet. If the household had slaves or servants, this was the job of the lowest slave. In a poorer home the children or the wife were expected to wash the feet of the guests.

---

began to wash His disciples' feet: The disciples were probably surprised to see Jesus get up, remove His robe, and tie a towel around His waist. Then He got a basin of water and began to wash the disciples' feet. Why had none of the disciples performed this humble service for Jesus and the others? Each probably would have been glad to do it for Him, but none was willing to do it for the other disciples.

Lord, are You going to wash my feet? Apparently no one spoke until Jesus came to Peter. All the disciples were probably embarrassed that He was performing a task they should have done. This is why Peter asked Jesus if He intended to wash his feet.

afterward you will know: Jesus knew that Peter and the others had not accepted His role as Suffering Servant. This is why Peter did not understand this act of humble service that pointed to the cross. But after His resurrection, Peter and the others would understand that Jesus had acted in accordance with the Scriptures and the will of God.

you have no part with Me: Peter declared that he would not allow Jesus to wash his feet. Jesus replied that if he refused to allow Jesus to minister to him in this way, he would show that he did not belong to the Lord. Peter needed to learn that every proud spirit must submit to Christ.

Lord, not only my feet: Again, Peter overstated his feelings. If he needed his feet washed to belong to Jesus, he asked Him to wash his hands and his head as well.

You are clean: Jesus pointed out that Peter didn't need a bath, only a foot-washing. He had already had a bath. Jesus was probably comparing Peter's cleansing from sin to a bath. Peter had already committed himself to discipleship; he did not need to renew this commitment.

You are not all clean: Jesus may have been referring to Judas with these words. Judas had not been through the total cleansing of spirit that Peter and the other disciples had experienced. Perhaps Jesus was trying to turn the traitor away from his chosen course and to spare him the shame toward which he was headed.

¹²When Jesus had washed their feet and put on His robe, He reclined again and said to them, "**Do you know what I have done** for you? ¹³You call Me Teacher and Lord. This is well said, for I am. ¹⁴So if I, your Lord and Teacher, have washed your feet, you also ought to wash one another's feet. ¹⁵For I have given you an example that you also should do just as I have done for you.

¹⁶"I assure you: A slave is not greater than his master, and a messenger is not greater than the one who sent him. ¹⁷If you know these things, you are blessed if you do them. ¹⁸I'm not speaking about all of you; I know those I have chosen. But the Scripture must be fulfilled: 'The one who eats My bread has raised his heel against Me.'

¹⁹"I am telling you now before it happens, so that when it does happen you will believe that I am He. ²⁰I assure you: The one who receives whomever I send receives Me, and the one who receives Me receives Him who sent Me."

180. JESUS IDENTIFIES JUDAS AS THE BETRAYER

Matthew 26:20–25; Mark 14:17–21; Luke 22:21–23; John 13:21–30

Mk 14:17–18aWhen evening came, He arrived with the Twelve. 18aWhile they were reclining and eating, Jn 13:21aHe was troubled in His spirit and testified, "I assure you: **One of you**—Mk 14:18bone who is eating with Me—Jn 13:21b**will betray Me!** Lk 22:21But look, the hand of the one betraying Me is at the table with Me!"

Jn 13:22The disciples started looking at one another—at a loss as to which one He was speaking about. Mt 26:22Deeply distressed, each one began to say to Him, "Surely not I, Lord?" [Lk 22:23 *So they began to argue among themselves which of them it could be who was going to do this thing.*]

Jn 13:23–25One of His disciples, whom Jesus loved, was reclining close beside Jesus. ²⁴Simon Peter motioned to him to find out who it was He was talking about. ²⁵So he leaned back against Jesus and asked Him, "Lord, who is it?"

Mk 14:20–21He said to them, "It is one of the Twelve—the one who is dipping bread with Me in the bowl [Jn 13:26a *He's the one I give the piece of bread to after I have dipped it*]. ²¹For the Son of Man will go just as it is written about Him, but

---

Do you know what I have done: Jesus taught by many methods. In this situation, He asked the disciples if they understood His actions. If He was willing to wash their feet, they ought to be willing to wash one another's feet.

180. JESUS IDENTIFIES JUDAS AS THE BETRAYER

One of you . . . will betray Me! The Passover meal was in progress when Jesus made the startling announcement that there was a traitor among the Twelve. Amazed at His statement, they questioned their own loyalty, each unwilling to attribute such treachery to the others.

Surely not I, Rabbi? Judas showed cold hypocrisy in making essentially the same statement as the others. He knew he was the betrayer, and he was beginning to realize that Jesus knew it too. Jesus replied, "You have said it yourself" (Matt. 26:25b). Jesus was aware of the plot against Him and of Judas's plans to betray Him, but He did not retreat and run. He moved deliberately toward His mission and purpose.

woe to that man by whom the Son of Man is betrayed! It would have been better for that man if he had not been born."

Jn 13:26b–27When He had dipped the bread, He gave it to Judas, Simon Iscariot's son. 27After Judas ate the piece of bread, Satan entered him. Therefore Jesus told him, "What you're doing, do quickly."

28None of those reclining at the table knew why He told him this. 29Since Judas kept the money bag, some thought that Jesus was telling him, "Buy what we need for the festival," or that he should give something to the poor.

Mt 26:25aThen Judas, His betrayer, replied, "**Surely not I, Rabbi?**"

25b"You have said it yourself," He told him.

Jn 13:30After receiving the piece of bread, he went out immediately. And it was night.

181. JESUS PREDICTS THAT HIS DISCIPLES WILL DENY HIM

Matthew 26:31–35; Mark 14:27–31; Luke 22:31–38; John 13:31–38

Mt 26:31–32Then Jesus said to them, "Tonight all of you will fall because of Me, for it is written: 'I will strike the shepherd, and the sheep of the flock will be scattered.' 32But after I have been resurrected, I will go ahead of you to Galilee. Lk 22:31–32"Simon, Simon, look out! **Satan has asked to sift you like wheat.** 32**But I have prayed for you**, that your faith may not fail. And you, when you have turned back, **strengthen your brothers**."

Lk 22:33"Lord," he told Him, "I'm ready to go with You to prison and to death!"

Jn 13:36bJesus answered, "Where I am going you cannot follow Me now; but you will follow later."

Jn 13:37"Lord," Peter asked, "why can't I follow You now? I will lay down my life for You!"

Jn 13:38aJesus replied, "Will you lay down your life for Me?"

Mt 26:33Peter told Him, "Even if everyone falls because of You, I will never fall!"

34"I assure you," Jesus said to him, "tonight—[Mk 14:30b*today, this very night*] before the rooster crows [Mk 14:30b*before the rooster crows twice*]—you will deny Me three times!"

---

181. JESUS PREDICTS THAT HIS DISCIPLES WILL DENY HIM

Satan has asked to sift you like wheat: Jesus pointed out that through the events that were at hand—His capture and crucifixion—Satan would make a last desperate attempt to weaken and frustrate His followers, particularly Peter. He would try to sift Peter and the other disciples like wheat and to blow them away like chaff before the wind, just as he had done with Judas.

But I have prayed for you: But Jesus had prayed that His disciples' faith would not fail during these critical times. He had prayed especially for Peter, the leader of the group. Jesus acted as their advocate and intercessor.

strengthen your brothers: Jesus declared that Peter would suffer a temporary lapse. The rooster that signaled the break of day would not crow that very night (crow twice, according to Mark's account; Mark 14:30b) before Peter had denied Him three times. But after he had been restored to usefulness, he was to strengthen the other disciples in their faith and loyalty to Christ.

Mk 14:31But he kept insisting, "If I have to die with You, I will never deny You!" And they all said the same thing.

Lk 22:35aHe also said to them, "When I sent you out without money-bag, backpack, or sandals, did you lack anything?"

35b"Not a thing," they said.

36Then He said to them, "But now, whoever has a money-bag should take it, and also a backpack. And whoever doesn't have a sword should sell his robe and buy one. 37For I tell you, what is written must be fulfilled in Me: 'And He was counted among the outlaws.' Yes, what is written about Me is coming to its fulfillment."

38a"Lord," they said, "look, here are two swords."

38b"Enough of that!" He told them.

182. JESUS TEACHES ABOUT TRUE GREATNESS

Luke 22:24–30

24Then **a dispute also arose among them** about who should be considered the greatest. 25But He said to them, "The kings of the Gentiles dominate them, and those who have authority over them are called 'Benefactors.' 26But it must not be like that among you. On the contrary, whoever is greatest among you must become like the youngest, and whoever leads, like the one serving. 27For who is greater, the one at the table or the one serving? Isn't it the one at the table? But I am among you as the One who serves.

28"You are the ones who stood by Me in My trials. 29I grant you a kingdom, just as My Father granted one to Me, 30so that you may eat and drink at My table in My kingdom. And you will sit on thrones judging the 12 tribes of Israel."

183. JESUS INSTITUTES THE MEMORIAL SUPPER

Matthew 26:26–30; Mark 14:22–26; Luke 22:14–20

Lk 22:14–15When the hour came, He reclined at the table, and the apostles with Him. 15Then He said to them, "I have fervently desired to eat this Passover with you before I suffer." Mk 14:22As they were eating, He took bread, blessed and broke it, gave it to them, and said, "Take it; this is My body Lk 22:19bwhich is given for you. **Do this in remembrance of Me.**"

---

182. JESUS TEACHES ABOUT TRUE GREATNESS

a dispute also arose among them: Just before sharing in the Memorial Supper, Jesus' disciples began to argue about who was the greatest and who would fill the most important places in His kingdom. Jesus condemned this petty spirit and reminded His disciples that true greatness consisted of sacrificial service to others. They were not to seek earthly glory and worldly power as their reward but heavenly joy and a holy calling in His eternal kingdom.

183. JESUS INSTITUTES THE MEMORIAL SUPPER

Do this in remembrance of Me: Jesus used the word *remembrance* as a refrain after partaking of both the bread and the

Mk 14:23a Then he took a cup [Lk 22:20a *In the same way He also took the cup after supper*], and after giving thanks, He gave it to them. Mk 14:23b So they all drank from it. Mk 14:24 He said to them, "This is **My blood of the covenant**, which is shed for many Mt 26:28b for the forgiveness of sins. Mk 14:25 I assure you: I will no longer drink of the fruit of the vine until that day when I drink it new in the kingdom of God [Mt 26:29b *drink it new in my Father's kingdom with you*]."

184. JESUS' FAREWELL TO HIS DISCIPLES

John 14:1–16:33

14:1 "**Your heart must not be troubled**. Believe in God; believe also in Me. ²In My Father's house are many dwelling places; if not, I would have told you. **I am going away to prepare a place for you**. ³If I go away and prepare a place for you, I will come back and receive you to Myself, so that where I am you may be also. ⁴You know the way where I am going."

⁵"Lord," Thomas said, "**we don't know where You're going**. How can we know the way?"

⁶Jesus told him, "I am the way, the truth, and the life. No one comes to the Father except through Me. ⁷If you know Me, you will also know My Father. From now on you do know Him and have seen Him."

⁸"Lord," said Philip, "**show us the Father**, and that's enough for us."

⁹Jesus said to him, "Have I been among you all this time without you knowing Me, Philip? The one who has seen Me has seen the Father. How can you say, 'Show us the Father'? ¹⁰Don't you believe that I am in the Father and the Father is in Me? The words I speak to you I do not speak on My own. The Father who

---

cup. The central purpose of the Lord's Supper is to bring the sacrifice of Christ sharply to our minds.

My blood of the covenant: The prophet Jeremiah predicted a new covenant that would replace the old covenant (Jer. 31:31–34). Jesus laid down His life to make that new covenant a reality. At the Last Supper He spoke of His blood of the new covenant. Hebrews 9:12–28 gives a more detailed description of how Christ's blood sealed God's new covenant with believers. The apostle Paul also describes the Last Supper of Jesus with His disciples in 1 Corinthians 11:23–25.

184. JESUS' FAREWELL TO HIS DISCIPLES

Your heart must not be troubled: The disciples needed this reassurance from Jesus because He had been speaking of troubling things: there was a traitor in their midst; Jesus would soon leave them; and they would not be able to find Him or follow Him.

I am going away to prepare a place for you: Jesus was going away to prepare an adequate place with room for all the disciples—indeed, for *all* disciples. He would welcome them to this place and remain there with them.

we don't know where You're going: Thomas protested that he and the other disciples did not know where Jesus was going; how would they find the way? In His reply Jesus professed to be the *way* to God, the *truth* about God, and the source of *life* from God. These great gospel truths apply to salvation now and security in the afterlife.

show us the Father: Philip did not understand these words of Jesus. He asked to be shown the Father; then he would be satisfied. Jesus reminded Philip of the three years or so that he had been a disciple. Philip was one of the first whom Jesus enlisted (John 1:43). Had he learned nothing from this time spent with Jesus? Then Jesus declared, "The one who has seen Me has seen the Father." His words carried the authority of God Himself.

lives in Me does His works. ¹¹Believe Me that I am in the Father and the Father is in Me. Otherwise, believe because of the works themselves.

¹²"I assure you: The one who believes in Me will also do the works that I do. And he will do even **greater works than these**, because I am going to the Father. ¹³Whatever you ask in My name, I will do it, so that the Father may be glorified in the Son. ¹⁴If you ask Me anything in My name, **I will do it**.

Another Counselor Promised

¹⁵"If you love Me, you will keep My commandments; ¹⁶and I also will ask the Father, and He will give you another Counselor to be with you forever. ¹⁷He is the Spirit of truth, whom the world is unable to receive because it doesn't see Him or know Him. But you do know Him, because He remains with you and will be in you. ¹⁸**I will not leave you as orphans**; I am coming to you.

¹⁹"In a little while the world will see Me no longer, but you will see Me. Because I live, you will live too. ²⁰In that day you will know that I am in My Father, you are in Me, and I am in you. ²¹The one who has My commandments and keeps them is the one who loves Me. And the one who loves Me will be loved by My Father. I also will love him and will reveal Myself to him."

²²Judas (not Iscariot) said to Him, "Lord, how is it You're going to reveal Yourself to us and not to the world?"

²³Jesus answered, "If anyone loves Me, he will keep My word. My Father will love him, and We will come to him and make Our home with him. ²⁴The one who doesn't love Me will not keep My words. The word that you hear is not Mine, but is from the Father who sent Me.

²⁵"I have spoken these things to you while I remain with you. ²⁶But the Counselor, **the Holy Spirit**, whom the Father will send in My name, **will teach you all things** and remind you of everything I have told you.

²⁷"**Peace I leave with you**. My peace I give to you. I do not give to you as the world gives. Your heart must not be troubled or fearful. ²⁸You have heard Me tell

---

greater works than these: Jesus was talking about works that were not greater in quality—but quantity. After His death and resurrection, His followers were to take His gospel to all parts of the Roman Empire. This geographical expansion meant that a great many more people would be reached with the gospel message.

I will do it: Jesus claimed that, after His return to the Father, He would continue to work in the world through the agency of His followers. As in the days of His flesh, His purpose would be "that the Father may be glorified in the Son."

I will not leave you as orphans: Although Jesus was going away, He promised His disciples they would not be left alone because He would come to them. Jesus was thinking of His return from the grave to be with them.

the Holy Spirit: This title emphasizes the presence of the holy God. Although the Spirit of God deals with believers in intimate ways as the Counselor, He is still the presence of the holy God within us. The Spirit would continue the work of God in Christ.

will teach you all things: During Jesus' life, the disciples often did not understand Him and His mission. After His resurrection, He began to open their minds to the Scriptures (Luke 24:44–45). The Spirit would continue that work.

Peace I leave with you: Peace, joy, and faith are part of Jesus' legacy to His disciples. He warned the disciples of the dark times ahead as He did battle with Satan, the prince of this world.

you, 'I am going away and I am coming to you.' If you loved Me, you would have rejoiced that I am going to the Father, because the Father is greater than I. ²⁹I have told you now before it happens, so that when it does happen you may believe. ³⁰I will not talk with you much longer, because the ruler of the world is coming. He has no power over Me. ³¹ᵃOn the contrary, I am going away so that the world may know that I love the Father. Just as the Father commanded Me, so I do.

³¹ᵇ"Get up; **let's leave this place**.

ᴶⁿ ¹⁵:¹"**I am the true vine**, and My Father is the vineyard keeper. ²Every branch in Me that does not produce fruit He removes, and He prunes every branch that produces fruit so that it will produce more fruit. ³You are already clean because of the word I have spoken to you. ⁴Remain in Me, and I in you. Just as a branch is unable to produce fruit by itself unless it remains on the vine, so neither can you unless you remain in Me.

⁵"I am the vine; you are the branches. The one who remains in Me and I in him produces much fruit, because you can do nothing without Me. ⁶If anyone does not remain in Me, he is thrown aside like a branch and he withers. They gather them, throw them into the fire, and they are burned. ⁷**If you remain in Me** and My words remain in you, ask whatever you want and it will be done for you. ⁸My Father is glorified by this: that you produce much fruit and prove to be My disciples.

⁹"Just as the Father has loved Me, I also have loved you. Remain in My love. ¹⁰If you **keep My commandments** you will remain in My love, just as I have kept My Father's commandments and remain in His love.

¹¹"I have spoken these things to you so that My joy may be in you and your joy may be complete. ¹²This is My commandment: that you love one another just as I have loved you. ¹³No one has greater love than this, that someone would lay down his life for his friends. ¹⁴You are My friends, if you do what I command you. ¹⁵I do not call you slaves any more, because a slave doesn't know what his master is doing. I have called you friends, because I have made known to you everything I have heard from My Father. ¹⁶You did not choose Me, but I chose you. I appointed you that you should go out and produce fruit, and that your

---

let's leave this place: Jesus cautioned the disciples to be aware of the crisis at hand. They would be tested by the things that would happen to Him.

I am the true vine: The vine was a symbol of Israel. The Old Testament pronounced judgment on Israel as an unfruitful vine (Isa. 5:2; Jer. 2:21). By contrast, Jesus is the True Vine. He is the One in whom God's purpose for Israel was fulfilled.

If you remain in Me: To remain in Christ means to maintain a personal relationship with Him—to make a full commitment to Him in love and loyalty. This is a continuing bond between Master and disciple.

keep My commandments: Abiding in Christ's love means obeying His commandments—especially His commandment to love one another (John 13:34–35; 15:12, 17).

fruit should remain, so that whatever you ask the Father in My name, He will give you. ¹⁷This is what I command you: that you **love one another**.

¹⁸"If the world hates you, understand that it hated Me before it hated you. ¹⁹If you were of the world, the world would love you as its own. However, because you are not of the world, but I have chosen you out of the world, this is why the world hates you. ²⁰Remember the word I spoke to you: 'A slave is not greater than his master.' If they persecuted Me, **they will also persecute you**. If they kept My word, they will also keep yours. ²¹But they will do all these things to you on account of My name, because they don't know the One who sent Me. ²²If I had not come and spoken to them, they would not have sin. Now they have no excuse for their sin. ²³The one who hates Me also hates My Father. ²⁴If I had not done the works among them that no one else has done, they would not have sin. Now they have seen and hated both Me and My Father. ²⁵But this happened so that the statement written in their law might be fulfilled: 'They hated me for no reason.'

²⁶"When the Counselor comes, whom I will send to you from the Father—the Spirit of truth who proceeds from the Father—He will testify about Me. ²⁷You also will testify, because you have been with Me from the beginning.

^Jn 16:1"I have told you these things to keep you from stumbling. ²They will ban you from the synagogues. In fact, a time is coming when anyone who kills you will think he is offering service to God. ³They will do these things because they haven't known the Father or Me. ⁴But I have told you these things so that when their time comes you may remember I told them to you. I didn't tell you these things from the beginning, because I was with you.

The Counselor's Ministry

⁵"But now I am going away to Him who sent Me, and not one of you asks Me, 'Where are You going?' ⁶Yet, because I have spoken these things to you, sorrow has filled your heart. ⁷Nevertheless, I am telling you the truth. It is **for your benefit** that I go away, because if I don't go away the Counselor will not come to you. If I go, I will send Him to you. ⁸When He comes, He will **convict** the world **about sin**, righteousness, and judgment: ⁹about sin, because they do not

---

love one another: Once before, Jesus had told His disciples to love one another (John 13:34). He repeated it here for emphasis, since He had just told them to abide in His love. If we love the Father, we will also love our brothers and sisters in the Lord.

they will also persecute you: Jesus was direct and honest with His disciples about what to expect as His followers. They would be condemned and criticized just as He had been, because "a slave is not greater than his master" (v. 20b). He wanted them to be prepared for these future hardships.

for your benefit: Jesus assured His disciples they would be better off when He went away. After He left, the Counselor would come to comfort and encourage them.

convict . . . about sin: One of the roles of the Holy Spirit on behalf of believers is to serve as an Advocate, or defense

believe in Me; [10]about righteousness, because I am going to the Father and you will no longer see Me; [11]and about judgment, because the ruler of this world has been judged.

[12]"I still have many things to tell you, but you can't bear them now. [13]When the Spirit of truth comes, He will guide you into all the truth. For He will not speak on His own, but He will speak whatever He hears. He will also declare to you what is to come. [14]**He will glorify Me**, because He will take from what is Mine and declare it to you. [15]Everything the Father has is Mine. This is why I told you that He takes from what is Mine and will declare it to you.

[16]"A little while and you will no longer see Me; again a little while and you will see Me."

[17]Therefore some of His disciples said to one another, "What is this He tells us: 'A little while and you will not see Me; again a little while and you will see Me'; and, 'because I am going to the Father'?" [18]They said, "What is this He is saying, 'A little while'? We don't know what He's talking about!"

[19]Jesus knew they wanted to question Him, so **He said to them**, "Are you asking one another about what I said, 'A little while and you will not see Me; again a little while and you will see Me'?

Counselor and Spirit of Truth

As Jesus prepared for His death, resurrection, and ascension, He promised to ask the Father to send the Holy Spirit to His disciples. He described the third person of the Trinity with two significant phrases.

He spoke of the Spirit as "another Counselor." The word Counselor *translates the Greek word* parakletos. *This title for the Spirit is found only in the Gospel of John (John 14:16, 26; 15:26; 16:7). The word conveys the idea of someone called alongside to help. The word* another *means "another of the same kind." Thus, the Counselor would continue to provide the kind of help that Jesus Himself provided while He was with His disciples.*

Jesus also referred to the Counselor as "the Spirit of truth." The Spirit of truth represents the One who is "the way, the truth, and the life" (John 14:6). He also speaks truth (John 15:26). The world neither sees nor knows the Spirit of truth, but true followers of Jesus know Him because He abides within each of us.

---

attorney. But He serves as prosecutor toward unbelievers. The Spirit produces an inner conviction of sin in general and of the sin of rejecting Christ in particular.

He will glorify Me: The Holy Spirit does not call attention to Himself. Instead, the Spirit guides believers to live in ways that are consistent with the life, death, and resurrection of Jesus Christ. When people are led by the Spirit, they point others to Jesus Christ by their words and deeds.

He said to them: Jesus had talked to the disciples many times about His coming death and resurrection. They had not been able to understand because they still thought of Him as a political deliverer. Now He talked plainly about the future rejoicing of His enemies and the sorrow of His friends. But He assured them that their sorrow would be turned to joy.

²⁰"I assure you: You will weep and wail, but the world will rejoice. You will become sorrowful, but your sorrow will turn to joy. ²¹When a woman is in labor she has pain because her time has come. But **when she has given birth** to a child, she no longer remembers the suffering because of the joy that a person has been born into the world. ²²So you also have sorrow now. But I will see you again. Your hearts will rejoice, and no one will rob you of your joy. ²³ªIn that day you will not ask Me anything.

²³ᵇ"I assure you: Anything you ask the Father in My name, He will give you. ²⁴Until now you have asked for nothing in My name. Ask and you will receive, that your joy may be complete.

²⁵"I have spoken these things to you in figures of speech. A time is coming when I will no longer speak to you in figures, but I will tell you plainly about the Father. ²⁶In that day you will ask in My name. I am not telling you that I will make requests to the Father on your behalf. ²⁷For the Father Himself loves you, because you have loved Me and have believed that I came from God. ²⁸I came from the Father and have come into the world. Again, I am leaving the world and going to the Father."

²⁹"Ah!" His disciples said. "Now You're speaking plainly and not using any figurative language. ³⁰Now we know that You know everything and don't need anyone to question You. By this we believe that You came from God."

³¹Jesus responded to them, "Do you now believe? ³²Look: An hour is coming, and has come, when you will be scattered each to his own home, and you will leave Me alone. Yet I am not alone, because the Father is with Me. ³³I have told you these things so that in Me you may have peace. In the world you have suffering. But take courage! I have conquered the world."

185. JESUS' INTERCESSORY PRAYER FOR HIS DISCIPLES

John 17:1–26

¹Jesus spoke these things, then raised His eyes to heaven, and said: "Father, the hour has come. **Glorify Your Son** so that the Son may glorify You, ²just as You gave Him authority over all flesh; so that He may give **eternal life** to all You have

---

when she has given birth: A mother's pain in giving birth is followed by great joy as she embraces her child. So it would be with the disciples. The tragedy of the cross would be followed by events that would bring them great joy.

185. JESUS' INTERCESSORY PRAYER FOR HIS DISCIPLES

Glorify Your Son: Jesus spoke of the cross as a time when He would glorify God and in turn be glorified. He looked beyond the suffering of the crucifixion to the outcome of His atoning death. In light of His resurrection, the world would see the cross as the revelation of the love of God.

eternal life: Eternal life is knowing God and Jesus Christ. This is not a knowledge about God, but personal acquaintance with God. Eternal life is more than what begins after a Christian dies and goes to heaven. It begins when a person comes to know the Lord.

given Him. ³This is eternal life: that they may know You, the only true God, and the One You have sent—Jesus Christ. ⁴I have glorified You on the earth by completing the work You gave Me to do. ⁵Now, Father, glorify Me in Your presence with that glory I had with You before the world existed.

Jesus Prays for His Disciples

⁶"**I have revealed Your name** to the men You gave Me from the world. They were Yours, You gave them to Me, and they have kept Your word. ⁷Now they know that all things You have given to Me are from You, ⁸because the words which You gave to Me, I have given to them. They have received them and have known for certain that I came from You. They have believed that You sent Me. ⁹I pray for them. I am not praying for the world, but for those You have given Me, because they are Yours.

¹⁰"All My things are Yours, and Yours are Mine, and I have been glorified in them. ¹¹I am no longer in the world, but they are in the world, and I am coming to You. Holy Father, **protect them by Your name** that You have given Me, so that they may be one just as We are. ¹²While I was with them I was protecting them by Your name that You have given me. I guarded them and not one of them is lost, except the son of destruction, that the Scripture may be fulfilled.

¹³"Now I am coming to You, and I speak these things in the world so that they may have My joy completed in them. ¹⁴I have given them Your word. The world hated them because they are not of the world, just as I am not of the world. ¹⁵I am not praying that You take them out of the world, but that You protect them from the evil one. ¹⁶They are not of the world, just as I am not of the world.

Jesus' High Priestly Prayer

The seventeenth chapter of John's Gospel contains the longest recorded prayer of Jesus. It is often called His "high priestly" prayer because He assumed the role of the high priest in making intercession for the people and offering a sacrifice on their behalf. Soon He would make the ultimate sacrifice for His people—His own death on the cross.

In this prayer, Jesus prayed for Himself (vv. 1–5), His disciples (vv. 6–19), and future believers (vv. 20–26). As He faced His suffering and death, He reviewed His life and ministry, rejoiced in His experiences with His followers, and looked forward to the unity and love that God and the redeemed will share in eternity.

I have revealed Your name: Jesus had revealed the Father's name to the disciples, and they had kept God's word. They had recognized the words of Jesus as God's words because they believed Jesus had been sent by the Father.

protect them by Your name: Jesus prayed that God would protect the disciples in His absence. He had guarded them while He was with them, having lost only Judas, as the Scriptures predicted. Now that He was leaving, Jesus asked the Father to watch over the disciples. They would continue the work He had begun.

[17]**Sanctify them by the truth**; Your word is truth. [18]Just as You sent Me into the world, **I also have sent them into the world**. [19]I sanctify Myself for them, so they also may be sanctified by the truth.

[20]"I pray not only for these, but also for **those who believe in Me** through their message. [21]**May they all be one**, just as You, Father, are in Me and I am in You. May they also be one in Us, so that the world may believe You sent Me. [22]I have given them the glory that You have given to Me. May they be one just as We are one. [23]I am in them and You are in Me. May they be made completely one, so that the world may know You sent Me and that You have loved them just as You have loved Me.

[24]"Father, I desire those You have given Me to be with Me where I am. Then they may see My glory, which You have given Me because You loved Me before the world's foundation. [25]Righteous Father! The world has not known You. However, I have known You, and these have known that You sent Me. [26]I made Your name known to them and will make it known, so that the love with which You have loved Me may be in them, and that I may be in them."

186. Jesus' Agony in the Garden of Gethsemane

Matthew 26:36–46; Mark 14:26, 32–42; Luke 22:39–46

Mt 26:36a–37a Then Jesus came with them to **a place called Gethsemane**, and He told the disciples, "Sit here **while I go over there and pray**." [37a]Taking along

---

Sanctify them by the truth: The word of God was the message and person of God that Jesus had proclaimed to the disciples. God and His word are true. Jesus Himself had set the example and provided the power for the disciples to be set apart for God's purposes.

I also have sent them into the world: Jesus had been sent into the world on a divine mission. After Jesus completed His mission, He entrusted to the disciples the carrying on of this mission to its next stage—sharing the good news with the lost world.

those who believe in Me: Jesus also prayed for future generations of believers. The way these future believers hear the word is through the words of the apostles. He commissioned the apostles to bear witness to Him. As the apostles began to die, they and others began to write down what the apostles had said about Jesus. Although the apostles are dead, modern believers read about their witness to Jesus in the New Testament.

May they all be one: Jesus prayed that future believers would have a oneness of spirit. This unity is similar to the oneness that exists between Father and Son. This involves a oneness of each of us with God in Christ, and it also includes a unity of spirit with fellow believers. The purpose of this oneness is that the world might believe.

186. Jesus' Agony in the Garden of Gethsemane

a place called Gethsemane: Gethsemane was probably a private property to which Jesus had access and to which He retreated when in Jerusalem. The word *Gethsemane* is Aramaic and means "oil press." Olives may have been processed on this site at one time.

while I go over there and pray: As the hour of trial and temptation came upon Jesus, He fortified Himself through prayer. He also encouraged His disciples to pray. He knew His arrest would involve them in temptations that they would not be able to resist without the strength of God's presence.

Peter, Mk 14:33a**James, and John,** Mt 26:37b–38the two sons of Zebedee, He began to be sorrowful [Mk 14:33*horrified*] and deeply distressed. 38Then He said to them, **"My soul is swallowed up in sorrow**—to the point of death. Remain here and stay awake with Me."

Mk 14:35–36Then He went a little farther, fell to the ground, and began to pray that if it were possible, the hour might pass from Him. 36And He said, "Abba, Father! **All things are possible for You.** Take this cup away from Me. Nevertheless, not what I will, but what You will." Lk 22:43–44Then an angel from heaven appeared to Him, strengthening Him. 44Being in anguish, He prayed more fervently, and His sweat became like drops of blood falling to the ground.*

Mt 26:40aThen He came to **the disciples** and found them **sleeping.** Mk 14:37b"Simon, are you sleeping?" He asked Peter. Mt 26:40b–43"Couldn't you stay awake with Me one hour? 41Stay awake and pray, so that you won't enter into temptation. The spirit is willing, but the flesh is weak." 42Again, a second time, He went away and prayed, "My Father, if this cannot pass unless I drink it, Your will be done." 43And He came again and found them sleeping, because they could not keep their eyes open. Mk 14:40bThey did not know what to say to Him.

Mt 26:44–45aAfter leaving them, He went away again and prayed a third time, saying the same thing once more. 45aThen He came to the disciples and said to them, "Are you still sleeping and resting? Mk 14:41bEnough! Mt 26:45b–46Look, the time is near. The Son of Man is being betrayed into the hands of sinners. 46**Get up; let's go!** See—My betrayer is near."

Verses 43 and 44 of Luke 22 do not appear in some New Testament manuscripts.

Peter, James, and John: While seeking aid from His heavenly Father in this critical hour, Jesus also needed human companionship and support. All the disciples except Judas were with Him. The three disciples most capable of sympathizing with Him were stationed nearer to Him than the others.

My soul is swallowed up in sorrow: The distress of Jesus as He faced the ordeal of the cross shows His true humanity. He drew back from pain as we do.

All things are possible for You: From the time Jesus entered the garden until He died on the cross, the human in Him was strong. He endured these trials as a man with human emotions. His prayer to the Father in this experience was the cry of His humanity. But He mastered His emotions and submitted to the will of the Father.

the disciples . . . sleeping: Allowing their human emotions to control them, the disciples failed to stay awake during this crucial period. Throughout the rest of their lives they would need the exhortation of Jesus, as we do, "Stay awake and pray."

Get up; let's go! Aware that His enemies were closing in on Him, Jesus made no attempt to escape. He summoned His disciples to get up and go with Him to meet His enemies. Although He was the apparent victim, He was in charge of the situation.

Jesus was arrested on Thursday night when Judas led the Jewish authorities to the Garden of Gethsemane, where Jesus had been agonizing in prayer over His approaching death. After a religious trial for blasphemy before the Jewish Sanhedrin, He was turned over to the Roman authorities. The Sanhedrin convinced Pilate, the Roman governor of Judea, to execute Jesus because of their claim that He was a dangerous revolutionary who threatened the authority of Rome.

Jesus was crucified on Friday morning, then placed in the tomb of Joseph of Arimathea before the beginning of the Jewish Sabbath on Friday afternoon.

187. Jesus Betrayed and Arrested

Matthew 26:47–56; Mark 14:43–52; Luke 22:47–53; John 18:1–12

Jn 18:1–2After Jesus had said these things, He went out with His disciples across the Kidron ravine, where there was a garden into which He and His disciples entered. ²Judas, who betrayed Him, also knew the place, because Jesus often met there with His disciples. Mt 26:47While He was still speaking, **Judas**, one of the Twelve, suddenly arrived. With him was **a large mob** [Jn 18:3a*a detachment of soldiers and some temple police*], with swords and clubs [Jn 18:3b*with lanterns, torches, and weapons*], who were sent by the chief priests and elders of the people.

Mt 26:48His betrayer had given them a sign [Mk 14:44*signal*]: "The one I kiss, He's the one; arrest Him Mk 14:44band get Him securely away." Mt 26:49So he went right up to Jesus and said, "Greetings, Rabbi!"—and **kissed Him.**

Mt. 26:50a"Friend," Jesus asked him, "why have you come? [Lk 22:48b*Judas, are you betraying the Son of Man with a kiss?*]"

Mt. 26:50bThen they came up, took hold of Jesus, and arrested Him. Lk 22:49When those around Him saw what was going to happen, they asked, "Lord, should we strike with the sword?" Jn 18:10Then Simon Peter, who had a sword, drew it, struck the high priest's slave, and cut off his right ear. (The slave's name was Malchus.)

Mt 26:52Then Jesus told him, "**Put your sword back in place** because all who take up a sword will perish by a sword. Jn 18:11bShould I not drink the cup that the Father has given Me? Mt 26:53–54Or do you think that I cannot call on My Father, and He will provide Me at once with more than twelve legions of angels? ⁵⁴How,

---

187. Jesus Betrayed and Arrested

Judas . . . a large mob: Judas led into Gethsemane a mixed group of Roman soldiers and temple guards. There must have been several armed men, possibly reflecting fear of a popular uprising on Jesus' behalf.

kissed Him: According to Matthew's account, Judas had agreed to identify Jesus by kissing Him, a normal greeting between friends. Jesus responded by addressing him as "Friend," suggesting a last attempt to redeem Judas.

Put your sword back in place: Peter drew a sword, probably short enough to be hidden in his robe, and took a swing at the high priest's slave. Malchus dodged and lost only an ear. According to Luke, this severed ear was restored by Jesus.

then, would the Scriptures be fulfilled that say it must happen this way?" Lk 22:51bAnd touching his ear, He healed him.

Lk 22:52aThen Jesus said to the chief priests, temple police, and the elders who had come for Him, Mt 26:55b"Have you come out with swords and clubs, as if I were a criminal, to capture Me? Every day I used to sit, teaching in the temple complex, and you didn't arrest Me. Lk 22:53bBut this is your hour—and the dominion of darkness. Mt 26:56aBut all this has happened so that the prophetic Scriptures would be fulfilled."

Jn 18:12Then the detachment of soldiers, the captain, and the Jewish temple police arrested Jesus and tied Him up. Mt 26:56bThen all the disciples deserted Him and ran away. Mk 14:51–52Now a certain young man, having a linen cloth wrapped around his naked body, was following Him. And they caught hold of him. 52But he left the linen cloth behind and ran away naked.

188. HEARING BEFORE ANNAS

John 18:12–14, 19–23

12Then the detachment of soldiers, the captain, and the Jewish temple police arrested Jesus and tied Him up. 13First **they led Him to Annas**, for he was the father-in-law of Caiaphas, who was high priest that year. 14Caiaphas was the one who had advised the Jews that it was advantageous that one man should die for the people. . . . 19The high priest **questioned Jesus about His disciples** and about His teaching.

20"I have spoken openly to the world," Jesus answered him. "I have always taught in the synagogue and in the temple complex, where all the Jews congregate, and I haven't spoken anything in secret. 21**Why do you question Me?** Question those who heard what I told them. Look, they know what I said."

22When He had said these things, one of the temple police standing by slapped Jesus, saying, "Is this the way you answer the high priest?"

23"If I have spoken wrongly," Jesus answered him, "give evidence about the wrong; but if rightly, **why do you hit Me?**"

---

188. HEARING BEFORE ANNAS

they led Him to Annas: Annas, to whose house Jesus was taken, was a corrupt religious leader. According to historians of this era, he had a financial interest in the trading that went on in the temple area. When Jesus cleansed the temple, He acted against this official. Annas appears to have been the power behind the office of high priest, reaping its benefits without discharging its duties.

questioned Jesus about His disciples: Annas questioned Jesus on the enlistment, training, and purpose of His followers. Some were from Galilee in the north—a region notorious as a hotbed of insurrection. He wanted to link Jesus with rebellion and establish a strong case against Him.

Why do you question Me? Jesus declined to be made a witness against Himself. He had taught openly in synagogues and the temple. Let those who had heard Him come forward and testify about His message.

why do you hit Me? An aide to the high priest struck Jesus, accusing Him of being disrespectful. Jesus responded by declaring that if He had said anything wrong, witness should have been borne to this instead of resorting to this act of anger. He had admitted no wrong, so why the violent blow?

189. JESUS APPEARS BEFORE CAIAPHAS

Matthew 26:57–68; Mark 14:53–65; Luke 22:54, 63–65; John 18:24

Mt 26:57–58Those who had arrested Jesus **led Him away to Caiaphas** the high priest, where the scribes and the elders had convened. 58Meanwhile, Peter was following Him at a distance right to the high priest's courtyard. He went in and was sitting with the temple police to see the outcome, Mk 14:54bwarming himself by the fire.

Mt 26:59–61aThe chief priests and **the whole Sanhedrin** were looking for false testimony against Jesus so they could put Him to death. 60But they could not find any, even though **many false witnesses** came forward [Mk 14:56b*For many were giving false testimony against Him, but the testimonies did not agree*]. Finally, two

---

Caiaphas the High Priest

The high priest was the most powerful and influential religious leader among the Jews. He served as president and convener of the Sanhedrin, the highest ruling body of the Jewish nation.

Aaron was the first high priest (Exod. 28–29), and He served a strictly religious function. But the high priesthood evolved over the centuries into a political office held by those who could garner the favor of the Jewish elders or the ruling civil authorities. Caiaphas had been appointed high priest in A.D. 18 by the Roman procurator, Valerius Gratus. Caiaphas apparently succeeded his father-in-law Annas in this position (see Luke 3:2).

Some time before Jesus was arrested and dragged before the Sanhedrin, Caiaphas had determined that Jesus must die for blasphemy and sedition in order to pacify the Roman authorities (see segment 143, "The Sanhedrin's Plot against Jesus," p. 168). This shows that he was an underhanded schemer who put political expediency above truth and honesty.

Archaeologists working just outside Jerusalem have discovered an ornate tomb that bears the name of a "Caiaphas." Perhaps this is the burial place of the very Caiaphas before whom Jesus appeared.

---

189. JESUS APPEARS BEFORE CAIAPHAS

led Him away to Caiaphas: Jesus was probably sent by Annas from one wing of the building to another. With these two unscrupulous men, Annas and Caiaphas, united in determination to put Jesus away, there was no chance for a fair trial. The appearance before Annas may have been for the purpose of allowing time for Caiaphas to assemble the Sanhedrin, before which the final part of His religious trial took place.

the whole Sanhedrin: The word *Sanhedrin* indicates the supreme court. This Jewish court's powers had been limited by the Romans. It could recommend sentence of death, but could not carry it out. This is why Jesus was later brought before the Roman procurator, Pilate.

many false witnesses: The Sanhedrin assembled hurriedly during the night. After a frantic search, the Sanhedrin found

who came forward ⁶¹ᵃstated, ᴹᵏ ¹⁴:⁵⁸⁻⁵⁹**"We heard Him say**, 'I will demolish this sanctuary made by hands, and in three days I will build another not made by hands.'" ⁵⁹But not even on this did their testimony agree.

ᴹᵗ ²⁶:⁶²⁻⁶³The high priest then stood up and said to Him, "Don't You have an answer to what these men are testifying against You?" ⁶³**But Jesus kept silent**. Then the high priest said to Him, "By the living God **I place You under oath**: tell us if You are the Messiah, the Son of God!"

⁶⁴**"You have said it yourself** [ᴹᵏ ¹⁴:⁶²ᵃ*I am*]," Jesus told him. "But I tell you, in the future you will see 'the Son of Man seated at the right hand' of the Power, and 'coming on the clouds of heaven.'"

⁶⁵Then the high priest tore his robes and said, "He has blasphemed! Why do we still need witnesses? Look, now you've heard the blasphemy! ⁶⁶ᵃWhat is your decision?"

⁶⁶ᵇThey answered, "He deserves death!"

ᴹᵏ ¹⁴:⁶⁵Then **some began to spit on Him**, to blindfold Him, and to beat Him, saying, "Prophesy!" Even the temple police took Him and slapped Him. ᴸᵏ ²²:⁶⁵And they were saying many other blasphemous things against Him.

190. PETER DENIES JESUS

Matthew 26:58, 69–75; Mark 14:54, 66–72; Luke 22:54–62; John 18:15–18, 25–27

ᴶⁿ ¹⁸:¹⁵⁻¹⁷ᵃMeanwhile **Simon Peter** was following Jesus, as was another disciple. That disciple was an acquaintance of the high priest; so he went with Jesus into **the high priest's courtyard**. ¹⁶But Peter remained standing outside by the door.

---

two people willing to testify against Jesus. But their testimony was based on misunderstanding of Jesus' words and carried little weight.

We heard Him say: The words Jesus was accused of saying are recorded in John 2:19, "Destroy this sanctuary, and I will raise it up in three days." The writer of the Gospel of John felt it necessary to add this comment: "But he was speaking about the sanctuary of His body" (John 2:21). The temple became almost an object of worship as time passed. Any threat against the temple came to be regarded as a threat against God Himself, hence the seriousness of the charge against Jesus.

But Jesus kept silent: Jesus did not respond to this false accusation, probably because He knew the minds of His enemies were made up. Nothing He might say to defend Himself would change the course of events.

I place You under oath: The high priest questioned Jesus directly about whether He was the Messiah, the Son of God. By declaring, "I place You under oath," the high priest was putting Jesus under oath to tell the truth.

You have said it yourself: Jesus' answer was the equivalent of an affirmative reply. Then, to the people planning to put Him to death, Jesus told of His return in power, coming in the clouds. He whom they were about to crucify would be vindicated in future glory.

some began to spit on Him: For the moment, Jesus was in the hands of evil, abusive people. They mocked and ridiculed Him. He submitted to this treatment, even though He had the power to strike them down.

190. PETER DENIES JESUS

Simon Peter . . . the high priest's courtyard: In Matthew's account of the arrest of Jesus, we are told that "all the disciples deserted him and ran away" (Matt. 26:56b). Two of that number, Peter and John, reconsidered their action. Peter is

So the other disciple, the one known to the high priest, went out and spoke to the girl who kept the door, and brought Peter in. ^{17a}Then **the slave-girl who kept the door** said to Peter, "You aren't one of this man's disciples too, are you?"

^{Mt 26:70}But he denied it in front of everyone: "I don't know what you're talking about!"

^{Jn 18:18, 25a}Now the slaves and the temple police had made a charcoal fire, because it was cold. ^{25a}Now Simon Peter was standing and warming himself. They said to him, "You aren't one of His disciples too, are you?" ^{Mk 14:66b–67b}One of the high priest's servants . . . ^{67b}said, "You also were with that Nazarene, Jesus." ^{Jn 18:25b}**He denied it** and said, "I [was] not!"

^{Mk 14:70b}After a little while those standing there said to Peter again, "You certainly are one of them, since you're a Galilean also!" ^{Jn 18:26}One of the high priest's slaves, a relative of the man whose ear Peter had cut off, said, "Didn't I see you with Him in the garden?" ^{Mt 26:71}When he had gone out to the gateway, another woman saw him and told those who were there, "This man was with Jesus the Nazarene!"

^{Mk 14:71}Then he [Peter] started to curse and to swear with an oath, "**I don't know this man** you're talking about [^{Lk 22:60b} *Man, I don't know what you're talking about*]!" ^{Lk 22:60b–62}Immediately, while he was still speaking, a rooster crowed [^{Mk 14:72a}*a rooster crowed a second time*]. ⁶¹Then the Lord turned and looked at Peter. So Peter remembered the word of the Lord, how He had said to him, "Before the rooster crows today [^{Mk 14:72b}*Before the rooster crows twice*], you will deny Me three times." ⁶²And he went outside and wept bitterly.

191. JESUS CONDEMNED BY THE SANHEDRIN

Matthew 27:1–2; Mark 15:1; Luke 22:66–23:1

^{Lk 22:66–67a}**When daylight came**, the elders of the people, both the chief priests and the scribes, convened [^{Mt 27:1b}*plotted against Jesus to put Him to death*] and

---

named, while John's identity is concealed by the phrase "another disciple" (John 18:15). These two disciples entered the courtyard of the high priest, probably hoping to hear what was happening to Jesus, who had been taken into the high priest's house.

the slave-girl who kept the door: John was apparently known to the personnel of the palace, so he had no difficulty getting Peter admitted to the courtyard. But the girl on duty at the gate was suspicious of Peter. His denial gained him admittance, but she must have passed on her suspicion to others.

He denied it: Peter stood among the high priest's servants, warming himself at the fire. For a second time he was questioned on his relationship to Jesus, and again he denied all knowledge of Him.

I don't know this man: Finally, Peter was betrayed by his Galilean accent. But, added to this, someone recognized him. A kinsman of Malchus, whose ear Peter had cut off, linked accent with face and asked, "Didn't I see you with Him in the garden?" Peter vehemently denied his discipleship. Then the rooster crowed (crowed a second time, according to Mark 14:72a). An unheeded warning from Jesus had brought Peter into the depths of shame.

191. JESUS CONDEMNED BY THE SANHEDRIN
When daylight came: Some members of the Sanhedrin had already questioned Jesus on an informal basis the night

brought Him before their Sanhedrin. [67a]They said, "**If You are the Messiah, tell us.**"

[67b]But He said to them, "If I do tell you, you will not believe. [68]And if I ask you, you will not answer. [69]But from now on, **the Son of Man** will be seated at the right hand of the Power of God."

[70]They all asked, "Are You, then, the Son of God?" And He said to them, "You say that I am."

[71]"Why do we need any more testimony," they said, "since we've heard it ourselves from His mouth?" [Lk 23:1]Then their whole assembly rose up. [Mt 27:2]After tying Him up, they led Him away and **handed Him over to Pilate**, the governor.

Jesus' Court Appearances

A careful study of the four Gospels reveals six different phases in Jesus' trial before the Jewish leaders and the Roman authorities. Here's a brief summary of these appearances:

Before the Jewish Religious Leaders

1. Preliminary hearing before Annas, father-in-law of the high priest Caiaphas (John 18:12–24).

2. Hearing before Caiaphas the high priest and other leaders (Matt. 26:57–67; Mark 14:53–65).

3. Official trial and condemnation before the full Sanhedrin (Matt. 27:1–2; Mark 15:1; Luke 22:66–71).

Before the Roman Authorities

4. First appearance before Pilate, Roman governor of Judea (Matt. 27:11–14; Mark 15:2-5; Luke 23:1–5; John 18:28–37).

5. Hearing before Herod Antipas, Roman governor of Galilee and Perea (Luke 23:6–12).

6. Second appearance before Pilate, who pronounces the death sentence (Matt. 27:15–26; Mark 15:6–15; Luke 23:13–25; John 18:38–19:16).

---

before. But the Sanhedrin could not conduct a trial involving a capital offense at night, so the full court was assembled at daybreak to legalize their conviction.

If You are the Messiah, tell us: The Sanhedrin tried to force Jesus to admit He was the Messiah. His admission would give them grounds for accusing Him before Pilate, the Roman governor.

the Son of Man: Refusing to answer their question on their terms, Jesus referred to Himself as the Son of Man—the title for Himself that He had used throughout His ministry. He was not afraid of whatever punishment they might deliver.

handed Him over to Pilate: With Jesus' admission that He was the Son of God, the Sanhedrin had the evidence they wanted. To them He was guilty of blasphemy—claiming to be God—an offense punishable by death under the Jewish law. But the Sanhedrin did not have the authority to impose the death penalty. This would have to be pronounced by the Roman authorities, so they delivered Jesus to Pontius Pilate, the Roman provincial governor of Judea.

192. JUDAS ISCARIOT COMMITS SUICIDE

Matthew 27:3–10

³Then **Judas**, His betrayer, seeing that He had been condemned, **was full of remorse** and returned the thirty pieces of silver to the chief priests and to the elders. ⁴ᵃ"I have sinned by betraying innocent blood," he said.

⁴ᵇ"**What's that to us?**" they said. "See to it yourself!"

⁵So he threw the silver into the sanctuary and departed. Then he went and hanged himself.

⁶The chief priests took the silver and said, "It's not lawful to put it into the temple treasury, since it is blood money." ⁷So they conferred together and bought the potter's field with it as a burial place for foreigners. ⁸Therefore that field has been called "Blood Field" to this day. ⁹Then what was spoken through the prophet Jeremiah was fulfilled: "They took the thirty pieces of silver, the price of Him whose price was set by the sons of Israel, ¹⁰and they gave them for the potter's field, as the Lord directed me."

193. JESUS' FIRST HEARING BEFORE PILATE

Matthew 27:2, 11–14; Mark 15:1–5; Luke 23:2–5; John 18:28–38

Jn 18:28-29Then they took Jesus from Caiaphas to the governor's headquarters. It was early morning. They did not enter the headquarters themselves; otherwise they would be defiled and unable to eat the Passover. ²⁹Then **Pilate came out to them** and said, "What charge do you bring against this man?"

³⁰They answered him, "If this man weren't a criminal, we wouldn't have handed Him over to you."

³¹ᵃSo Pilate told them, "**Take Him yourselves and judge Him** according to your law."

---

192. JUDAS ISCARIOT COMMITS SUICIDE

Judas . . . was full of remorse: After the Sanhedrin condemned Jesus and sent Him to Pilate, Judas recognized the horror of what he had done. He had betrayed an innocent man. Judas realized the blood of the innocent Jesus would be on his hands.

What's that to us? But the religious leaders shared none of Judas's regrets. When he told them he had sinned by betraying innocent blood, they replied, "What do we care? Keep your regrets to yourself." Judas responded to his guilt by hanging himself. His suicide is also mentioned in Acts 1:17–20.

193. JESUS' FIRST HEARING BEFORE PILATE

Pilate came out to them: Pilate met the Jewish religious leaders apart from his headquarters out of respect for their religious scruples. He wanted to avoid any conflict with these leaders. He probably feared that unfavorable reports on his conduct might be sent to Rome.

Take Him yourselves and judge Him: Pilate assumed that Jesus' offense had something to do with Jewish law and that He should be judged and punished by the Sanhedrin. But the response of the religious leaders showed that the verdict had already been given and the sentence pronounced. Nothing less than Jesus' death would satisfy His accusers.

31b"It's not legal for us to put anyone to death," the Jews declared. 32They said this so that Jesus' words might be fulfilled signifying what sort of death He was going to die.

33Then Pilate went back into the headquarters, summoned Jesus, and said to Him, "**Are You the King of the Jews?**"

34Jesus answered, "Are you asking this on your own, or have others told you about Me?"

35"I'm not a Jew, am I?" Pilate replied. "Your own nation and the chief priests handed You over to me. What have You done?"

A Spiritual Kingdom

36"My kingdom is not of this world," said Jesus. "If My kingdom were of this world, My servants would fight, so that I wouldn't be handed over to the Jews. As it is, My kingdom does not have its origin here."

37a"You are a king then?" Pilate asked.

37b"You say that I'm a king," Jesus replied. "I was born for this, and I have come into the world for this: to testify to the truth. Everyone who is of the truth listens to My voice."

38a"**What is truth?**" said Pilate.

38bAfter he had said this, he went out to the Jews again and told them, "I find no grounds for charging Him.

Lk 23:2They began to accuse Him, saying, "We found this man subverting our nation, opposing payment of taxes to Caesar, and saying that He Himself is the Messiah, a King." Mk 15:3And the chief priests began to accuse Him of many things.

Mt 27:13-14Then Pilate said to Him, "Don't You hear how much they are testifying against You?" 14But He didn't answer him on even one charge, so that the governor was greatly amazed.

Lk 23:5But they kept insisting, "He stirs up the people, teaching throughout all Judea, from Galilee where He started even to here."

Are You the King of the Jews? This charge against Jesus could involve a challenge to the authority of Rome, so Pilate asked a direct question about Jesus' kingship. Jesus accepted the role of king but explained the nature of His kingship. It involved no threat to Pilate or Caesar, since it was "not of this world." Had it been otherwise, His followers would have resisted the plotting of His enemies, exchanging violence for violence.

What is truth? Pilate's question, "You are a king then?" was met by an answer that put the responsibility on Pilate to decide. This Roman governor was used to emperors who came and went, some holding power for only brief periods. But Jesus came into the world to promote a kingdom of truth. Pilate was surrounded by insincerity and duplicity. What was he to believe? He returned to the crowd and declared that he found no fault in Jesus. This enraged the crowd and made them even more determined to see Jesus executed.

194. Pilate Sends Jesus to Herod Antipas

Luke 23:6–10

⁶When **Pilate** heard this, he asked if the man was a Galilean. ⁷Finding that He was under Herod's jurisdiction, he **sent Him to Herod**, who was also in Jerusalem during those days. ⁸**Herod was very glad to see Jesus**; for a long time he had wanted to see Him, because he had heard about Him and was hoping to see some miracle performed by Him. ⁹So he kept asking Him questions, but Jesus did not answer him. ¹⁰The chief priests and the scribes stood by, vehemently accusing Him.

195. Herod Sends Jesus Back to Pilate

Luke 23:11–12

¹¹Then **Herod**, with his soldiers, treated Him with contempt, **mocked Him**, dressed Him in a brilliant robe, and sent Him back to Pilate. ¹²That very day Herod and Pilate became friends. Previously, they had been hostile toward each other.

196. Jesus Condemned to Die

Matthew 27:15–26; Mark 15:6–15; Luke 23:13–25; John 18:39–19:16

Mt 27:19While he [Pilate] was sitting on the judge's bench, his wife sent word to him, "Have nothing to do with that righteous man, for today I've suffered terribly in a dream because of Him!"

Lk 23:13–16Pilate called together the chief priests, the leaders, and the people, ¹⁴and said to them, "You have brought me this man as one who subverts the people. But in fact, after examining Him in your presence, I have found no grounds to charge this man with those things you accuse Him of. ¹⁵Neither has Herod,

---

194. Pilate Sends Jesus to Herod Antipas

Pilate . . . sent Him to Herod: Pilate learned that Jesus was from Galilee and that Herod Antipas, the Roman governor of this region, was in Jerusalem for the Passover celebration. He saw this as an opportunity to shift responsibility for Jesus' fate from himself to Herod.

Herod was very glad to see Jesus: Herod Antipas was the Roman official who had ordered the execution of John the Baptizer (see Mark 6:17–29). For a long time Herod had wanted to meet Jesus because he had a superstitious curiosity about Him and His miracles (Luke 9:7–9). But Jesus refused to perform for Herod's entertainment.

195. Herod Sends Jesus Back to Pilate

Herod . . . mocked Him: Disappointed at Jesus' silence, Herod insulted and humiliated Him. Herod had Jesus dressed in a brilliant robe to make a mockery of His claim to be a king and the Son of God. Then he sent Jesus back to Pilate without ruling on His guilt or innocence.

because he sent Him back to us. Clearly, He has done nothing to deserve death. [16]Therefore I will have Him whipped and release Him."

Mt 27:15-18At the festival it was the **governor's custom to release** to the crowd **one prisoner**, whom they wanted. [16]At that time they had a notorious prisoner called Barabbas. [17]So when they had gathered together, Pilate said to them, "Whom do you want me to release for you—Barabbas, or Jesus who is called Messiah?" [18]For he knew they had handed Him over because of envy.

Mt 27:20-21The chief priests and the elders, however, persuaded the crowds to ask for Barabbas and to execute Jesus. [21]The governor asked them, "Which of the two do you want me to release for you?" Lk 23:18-19Then they all cried out together, "Take this man away! Release Barabbas to us!" [19](He had been thrown into prison for a rebellion that had taken place in the city, and for murder.)

Mt 27:22aPilate asked them, "What should I do then with Jesus, who is called Messiah?"

[22b]They all answered, "Crucify Him!"

[23a]Then he said, "Why? What has He done wrong?"

[23b]But they kept shouting, "Crucify Him!" all the more.

Jn 19:1-3Then Pilate took Jesus and had him flogged. [2]The soldiers also twisted a crown out of thorns, put it on His head, and threw a purple robe around Him. [3]And they repeatedly came up to Him and said, "Hail, king of the Jews!" and were slapping His face.

The Flogging of Jesus

Luke's Gospel reports Pilate's promise to the crowd to have Jesus whipped or flogged. All the other Gospel writers report the actual flogging (Matt. 27:26; Mark 15:15; John 19:1).

A flogging victim was beaten severely on the bare upper body with a whip. The leather thongs of such a whip had pieces of bone or metal attached to make it cut the flesh more effectively. As many as thirty or forty blows might be administered in such a beating.

The pain from this punishment was so severe that prisoners often passed out during the ordeal. The flesh was generally cut deeply by the blows, leading to loss of blood and dehydration. Jesus apparently was so weakened by His punishment that He was not able to carry the bar of His cross all the way to the crucifixion site (see Luke 23:26).

---

196. JESUS CONDEMNED TO DIE

governor's custom to release . . . one prisoner: Pilate, struggling for a reason to release Jesus, recalled a custom intended to curry favor with an oppressed country. The Roman governor often released a prisoner during the Passover season. Pilate offered to release either Jesus or Barabbas—a prisoner charged with rebellion and murder. The people chose Barabbas.

⁴Pilate went outside again and said to them, "Look, I'm bringing Him outside to you to let you know I find no grounds for charging Him."

⁵Then Jesus came out wearing the crown of thorns and the purple robe. Pilate said to them, "Here is the man!"

⁶ᵃWhen the chief priests and the temple police saw Him, they shouted, "Crucify! Crucify!"

⁶ᵇPilate responded, "Take Him and crucify Him yourselves, for I find no grounds for charging Him."

⁷"We have a law," the Jews replied to him, "and according to that law He must die, because He made Himself the Son of God."

⁸When Pilate heard this statement, he was more afraid than ever. ⁹He went back into the headquarters and asked Jesus, "Where are You from?" But Jesus did not give him an answer. ¹⁰So Pilate said to Him, "You're not talking to me? Don't You know that I have the authority to release You and the authority to crucify You?"

Authority from Above

¹¹"You would have no authority over Me at all," Jesus answered him, "if it hadn't been given you from above. This is why the one who handed Me over to you has the greater sin."

¹²From that moment **Pilate made every effort to release Him**. But the Jews shouted, "If you release this man, you are not Caesar's friend. Anyone who makes himself a king opposes Caesar!"

¹³When Pilate heard these words, he brought Jesus outside. He sat down on the judge's bench in a place called the Stone Pavement (but in Hebrew Gabbatha). ¹⁴It was the preparation day for the Passover, and it was about six in the morning. Then he told the Jews, "Here is your king!"

¹⁵ᵃBut they shouted, "Take Him away! Take Him away! **Crucify Him!**"

¹⁵ᵇPilate said to them, "Should I crucify your king?"

¹⁵ᶜ"We have no king but Caesar!" the chief priests answered.

ᴹᵗ ²⁷:²⁴⁻²⁵When Pilate saw that he was getting nowhere, but that a riot was starting instead, he took some water, washed his hands in front of the crowd, and said, "I am innocent of this man's blood. See to it yourselves!" ²⁵All the people answered, "His blood be on us and on our children!"

Pilate made every effort to release Him: Pilate's mind was in turmoil because he was convinced of Jesus' innocence. But every avenue of escape was blocked by the determination of the accusers to put Jesus to death. Finally, the religious leaders told Pilate that Jesus' release would prove he was not "Caesar's friend." He gave in to the demands of the crowd.
Crucify Him! The people who had hailed Jesus as king a few days before now clamored for His death. He had not lived up to their expectations of the Messiah—a military hero who would deliver their nation from the rule of Rome. Because of their disillusionment and disappointment, the leaders of the Sanhedrin found it easy to incite the mob to demand Jesus' death.

Jn 19:16So then, because of them, he **handed Him over to be crucified**. Therefore they took Jesus away.

197. JESUS MOCKED BY THE SOLDIERS

Matthew 27:27–31; Mark 15:16–20

Mt 27:27-30'Then the governor's **soldiers** took Jesus into headquarters and gathered the whole company around Him. 28They stripped Him and dressed Him in a scarlet robe [Mk 15:17*purple robe*]. 29They twisted a crown out of thorns, put it on His head, and placed a reed in His right hand. And they **knelt down before Him** and mocked Him: "Hail, King of the Jews!" 30Then they spit at Him, took the reed, and kept hitting Him on the head. Mk 15:20When they had mocked Him, they stripped Him of the purple robe, put His clothes on Him, and led Him out to crucify Him.

198. SIMON CARRIES THE CROSS TO THE CRUCIFIXION SITE

Matthew 27:32; Mark 15:21; Luke 23:26–31

Lk 23:26aAs they led Him away, they seized **Simon, a Cyrenian,** Mk 15:21bthe father of Alexander and Rufus, Lk 23:26b–27and laid the cross on him to carry behind Jesus. 27A great multitude of the people followed Him, including women who were mourning and lamenting Him.

28But turning to them, Jesus said, "Daughters of Jerusalem, do not weep for Me, but **weep for yourselves and your children.** 29Look, the days are coming when they will say, 'Blessed are the barren, the wombs that never bore, and the breasts that never nursed!' 30Then they will begin 'to say to the mountains, "Fall

---

handed Him over to be crucified: Pilate surrendered to the demands of the religious leaders after washing his hands—a meaningless gesture of denied responsibility. He knew Jesus was innocent, but he abandoned Him to die.

197. JESUS MOCKED BY THE SOLDIERS

soldiers . . . knelt down before Him: The Roman soldiers charged with carrying out the crucifixion of Jesus caught the spirit of the jeering crowd. As they led Jesus away, they insulted Him by dressing Him in a purple robe to mock His claim to be a king. They placed a crown of thorns on His head, spat in His face, struck Him with a reed, and bowed before Him in mock worship.

198. SIMON CARRIES THE CROSS TO THE CRUCIFIXION SITE

Simon, a Cyrenian: Crucifixion victims were forced to carry the cross bar to which their hands were attached to the execution site. Weakened by the flogging, Jesus was not able to carry the cross bar all the way to the crucifixion site. The Roman soldiers pressed a bystander into service to carry the beam. This man, Simon from Cyrene in North Africa, was probably in Jerusalem for the Passover Festival. Mark adds that this Simon was the father of Alexander and Rufus. This father and two sons must have been well known to Mark and the readers of his Gospel (see Rom. 16:13).

weep for yourselves and your children: Jesus addressed these prophetic words to a group of women who followed the crowd to the crucifixion site. He was probably referring to the fall of Jerusalem in A.D. 70, about 35 years after His crucifixion. In their rejection of God's redemption, the Jewish nation had set their course toward the confrontation with Rome that would result in widespread slaughter and destruction.

on us!" and to the hills, "Cover us!"' ³¹For if they do these things when the wood is green, what will happen when it is dry?"

199. JESUS IS CRUCIFIED

Matthew 27:33–37; Mark 15:22–26; Luke 23:32–34; John 19:17–24

Lk 23:33aWhen they arrived at the place called **The Skull** [Jn 19:17 *Skull Place, which in Hebrew is called Golgotha*], they crucified Him there. Mt 27:34They gave Him wine mixed with gall to drink. But when He tasted it, He would not drink it. Mk 15:25Now it was nine in the morning when they crucified Him. Mt 27:36Then they sat down and were guarding Him there. Jn 19:19Pilate also had a sign lettered and put on the cross [Mt 27:37a*above His head they put up the charge against Him in writing*]. The inscription was: "JESUS THE NAZARENE **THE KING OF THE JEWS**."

Jn 19:20–21Many of the Jews read this sign, because the place where Jesus was crucified was near the city, and it was written in Hebrew, Latin, and Greek. ²¹So the chief priests of the Jews said to Pilate, "Don't write, 'The King of the Jews,' but that he said, 'I am the King of the Jews.'"

²²Pilate replied, "What I have written, I have written."

²³When the soldiers crucified Jesus, they took His clothes and divided them into four parts, a part for each soldier. They also took the tunic, which was seamless, woven in one piece from the top. ²⁴So they said to one another, "Let's **not tear it, but toss for it**, to see who gets it." They did this to fulfill the Scripture that says: "They divided My clothes among themselves, and for My clothing they cast lots." And this is what the soldiers did.

Lk 23:34aThen Jesus said, "Father, forgive them, because they do not know what they are doing."*

---

* This part of verse 34 in Luke 23 does not appear in some New Testament manuscripts.

---

199. JESUS IS CRUCIFIED

The Skull: All we know about the place where Jesus was crucified is that it was outside the gate of Jerusalem (Heb. 13:12). It may have been a hill shaped like a skull, or it may have had this name because of the skulls of previous victims left exposed on the site.

THE KING OF THE JEWS: A notice proclaiming to spectators the nature of the crime committed was generally posted on a cross. This also served as a warning to any who might be tempted to challenge the authority of Rome. Pilate had the words "JESUS THE NAZARENE THE KING OF THE JEWS" placed above Jesus' head. That cross of shame was to become the symbol of divine love to all nations of the earth.

not tear it, but toss for it: Gambling for the victim's clothing was a common procedure carried out by soldiers who were hardened by the cruelty of crucifixion. The most desirable item was Jesus' seamless robe. Thus, Psalm 22:18 was fulfilled: "They divide my garments among them and cast lots for my clothing" (NIV).

The Cruelty of Crucifixion

The Roman cross consisted of an upright post implanted in the ground and a cross beam that the accused was required to carry. On reaching the place of execution, the victim was nailed or tied to the cross beam before it was raised into position against the post.

Crucifixion was so horrible that the Romans used it only for slaves and the lowest types of criminals. Citizens of the Roman Empire were never crucified. This method of capital punishment was designed not only to kill but also to torture and humiliate. Criminals were crucified naked, adding physical and mental humiliation to the ordeal. Death generally came slowly through loss of blood and exhaustion. Some victims survived on a cross for days in excruciating pain. But Jesus died within a few hours after being placed on the cross.

The New Testament does not dwell on the horror of what Jesus suffered, perhaps because in bearing human sin, He suffered so much more than crucifixion.

---

200. JESUS' MOTHER AND OTHER WOMEN AT THE CROSS

Matthew 27:55–56; Mark 15:40–41; Luke 23:49; John 19:25–27

Mt 27:55Many women were there, looking on from a distance, who had followed Jesus from Galilee and ministered to Him. Jn 19:25–27**Standing by the cross** of Jesus were His mother, His mother's sister, Mary the wife of Clopas, and Mary Magdalene. 26When Jesus saw His mother and the disciple He loved standing there, He said to His mother, "**Woman, here is your son.**" 27Then He said to the disciple, "Here is your mother." And from that hour the disciple took her into his home.

201. JESUS MOCKED BY THE CROWD

Matthew 27:39–43; Mark 15:29–32; Luke 23:35–38

Lk 23:35aThe people stood watching, and even the leaders kept scoffing [Mk 15:29a*yelling insults at Him*], Mk 15:29a–30shaking their heads and saying, "Ha! The

---

200. JESUS' MOTHER AND OTHER WOMEN AT THE CROSS

Standing by the cross: Four women who loved Jesus stood near the cross. They were His mother Mary; her sister, generally thought to be Salome, the mother of James and John; Mary the wife of Clopas; and Mary Magdalene, the woman out of whom Jesus had cast seven demons (Luke 8:2). Neither Matthew nor Mark include Jesus' mother in the list of women at the cross (Matt. 27:55; Mark 15:40). Apparently most of Jesus' disciples had fled in fear of the Jewish and Roman authorities when Jesus was sentenced to die. But these women were faithful followers to the end.

Woman, here is your son: In His final hour, Jesus commended His mother to the care of the "disciple He loved," generally thought to be the apostle John. Throughout the Gospel of John, this apostle referred to himself as "the disciple whom Jesus loved" (John 13:23; 21:7, 20).

One who would demolish the sanctuary and build it in three days, ³⁰**save Yourself** by coming down from the cross!"

Lk 23:36The soldiers also mocked Him. They came offering Him sour wine. Mt 27:41–43In the same way the chief priests, with the scribes and elders, mocked Him and said, ⁴²"He saved others, but He cannot save Himself! He is the King of Israel! Let Him come down now from the cross, and we will believe in Him. ⁴³**He has put His trust in God**; let God rescue Him now—if He wants Him! For He said, 'I am God's Son.'"

202. TWO CRIMINALS ARE CRUCIFIED WITH JESUS

Matthew 27:38, 44; Mark 15:27–28; Luke 23:39–43

Mt 27:38Then **two criminals** were crucified with Him, one on the right and one on the left. Mk 15:28So the Scripture was fulfilled that says: "And He was counted among outlaws."* Lk 23:39Then one of the criminals hanging there began to yell insults at Him [Mt 27:44*the criminals who were crucified with Him kept taunting Him*]: "Aren't You the Messiah? Save Yourself and us!"

Lk 23:40But the other answered, rebuking him: "Don't you even fear God, since you are undergoing the same punishment? ⁴¹We are punished justly, because we're getting back what we deserve for the things we did, but this man has done nothing wrong." ⁴²Then he said, "Jesus, **remember me** when You come into Your kingdom!"

⁴³And He said to him, "I assure you: **Today you will be with Me** in paradise."

Verse 28 of Mark 15 does not appear in some New Testament manuscripts.

---

201. JESUS MOCKED BY THE CROWD

save Yourself: The crowds taunted Jesus to come down from the cross, using the same words that Satan had used in the wilderness temptations (Matt. 4:3). They taunted Jesus, "Since you are the Son of God, save yourself." When Jesus was arrested, He said He could have summoned more than twelve legions of angels to rescue Him (Matt. 26:53–54). Instead, He voluntarily gave Himself as a sin sacrifice into the hands of His enemies.

He has put His trust in God: The religious leaders also taunted Jesus about His professed trust in God, whom He claimed was His Father. He trusted God, but where was God, they mocked, that He allowed His Son to die in this terrible way?

202. TWO CRIMINALS ARE CRUCIFIED WITH JESUS

two criminals: The thieves crucified with Jesus were probably robbers and insurrectionists like Barabbas. Mark points out that Jesus' crucifixion with these outcasts was a fulfillment of a messianic prophecy in Isaiah: "He . . . was numbered with the transgressors" (Isa. 53:12 NIV). One thief joined in the mockery of the crowd against Jesus, while the other recognized that Jesus was suffering a great injustice. According to Matthew's account, both of these criminals joined in the taunting of Jesus (Matt. 27:38, 44). But Luke tells us that one criminal condemned the other for his mocking and turned to Jesus in earnest faith.

remember me: Even Jesus' closest followers believed all was lost when they saw Him dying on the cross. But this dying thief believed in Jesus, even in that desperate hour. He probably understood little of Jesus' mission. But he must have realized that Jesus was the promised Messiah whose kingdom was coming. He asked Jesus to remember him when He brought in this kingdom.

Today you will be with Me: Jesus assured the repentant criminal that He would not only remember him one day at His second coming, but that he would also be with Jesus in paradise that very day.

203. SUPERNATURAL EVENTS SURROUNDING JESUS' DEATH

Matthew 27:45–54; Mark 15:33–39; Luke 23:44–48; John 19:28–30

Mt 27:45-49From noon until three in the afternoon **darkness came over the whole land**. [46]At about three in the afternoon Jesus cried out with a loud voice, *"Elí, Elí, lemá sabachtháni?"* that is, **"My God, My God**, why have You forsaken Me?"* [47]When some of those standing there heard this, they said, "He's calling for Elijah! . . ." [49]But the rest said, "Let us see if Elijah comes to save Him!"

Jn 19:28-30After this, when Jesus knew that everything was now accomplished, that the Scripture might be fulfilled, He said, "I'm thirsty!" [29]A vessel full of sour wine was sitting there; so they fixed a sponge full of sour wine on hyssop and held it up to His mouth. [30]When **Jesus** had received the sour wine, He said, "It is finished!" [Lk 23:46a*And Jesus called out with a loud voice, "Father, 'into your hands I entrust My spirit'"*]. Then bowing His head, He **yielded up His spirit**.

Mt 27:51-53Suddenly, **the curtain of the sanctuary** was split in two from top to bottom; **the earth quaked** and the rocks were split. [52]The tombs also were opened and many **bodies of the saints** who had gone to their rest **were raised**.

Jesus' Seven Last Words from the Cross
1. *"Father, forgive them, because they do not know what they are doing"* (Luke 23:34).
2. *"I assure you: Today you will be with Me in paradise"* (Luke 23:43).
3. *"Woman here is your son . . . Here is your mother"* (John 19:26–27).
4. *"My God, My God, why have You forsaken Me?"* (Matt. 27:46; Mark 15:34).
5. *"I'm thirsty"* (John 19:28).
6. *"It is finished!"* (John 19:30).
7. *"Father, 'into Your hands I entrust My spirit'"* (Luke 23:46).

---

203. SUPERNATURAL EVENTS SURROUNDING JESUS' DEATH

darkness came over the whole land: Some think this darkness was a sign of evil's attempt to destroy the Son of God. Others believe the darkness was a sign of God's judgment on evil. Still others think God used the darkness to cloak the terrible sufferings of the Savior.

My God, My God: Toward the end of the three hours of darkness, Jesus cried out in words that some bystanders misunderstood. Others knew Aramaic and were near enough to recognize His cry as the words of Psalm 22:1. The psalmist's sense of being forsaken by God was echoed in the cry of Jesus from the cross. His cry was a cry and a prayer. All efforts to understand these words of Jesus fall short of unlocking the full mystery of His atoning death.

Jesus . . . yielded up His Spirit: Jesus uttered "It is finished" just before He died (John 19:30). This was a cry of victory because Jesus had finished His mission by giving His life for the sins of the world.

the curtain of the sanctuary: This curtain closed off the holy of holies, representing the presence of God, from the rest of the temple in Jerusalem. Only the high priest could enter this sacred area of the temple with the proper sacrifices for himself and the people's sins. When Jesus died (according to Luke, just before Jesus died; Luke 23:44b), this curtain was torn from top to bottom—as if by the hand of God. This symbolized the opening up of a way to God through Christ.

⁵³And they came out of the tombs after His resurrection, entered the holy city, and appeared to many.

⁵⁴When the centurion and those with him, who were guarding Jesus, saw the earthquake and the things that had happened, they were terrified and said, "**This man really was God's Son** [Lk 23:47b *This man really was righteous*]."

Lk 23:48All the crowds that had gathered for this spectacle, when they saw what had taken place, went home, striking their chests.

204. SOLDIERS PIERCE THE SIDE OF JESUS

John 19:31–37

³¹Since it was the preparation day, the Jews did not want the bodies to remain on the cross on the Sabbath (for that Sabbath was a special day). They requested that Pilate have the men's legs broken and that their bodies be taken away. ³²So the soldiers came and broke the legs of the first man and of the other one who had been crucified with Him.

³³When they came to Jesus, **they did not break His legs** since they saw that He was already dead. ³⁴But one of the soldiers pierced His side with a spear, and at once blood and water came out. ³⁵He who saw this has testified so that you also may believe. His testimony is true, and he knows he is telling the truth. ³⁶For these things happened so that the Scripture may be fulfilled: "Not one of His bones will be broken." ³⁷Also, another Scripture says: "They will look at the One they pierced."

---

the earth quaked: Later Jewish sources mention an earthquake about 40 years before the fall of Jerusalem in A.D. 70. This may have been the earthquake that occurred at Jesus' death.

bodies of the saints . . . were raised: Many graves were opened—perhaps by the earthquake. Later after Jesus had been raised from the dead, the resurrected bodies of dead believers appeared to many people. This miracle shows that Old Testament believers would share in the new covenant salvation.

This man really was God's Son: The Roman centurion who uttered those words was apparently in command of the soldiers who crucified Jesus. He had been near enough to the cross to see and hear what took place. His confession foreshadowed the millions of Gentiles who would eventually acclaim Jesus as the Son of God.

204. SOLDIERS PIERCE THE SIDE OF JESUS

they did not break His legs: The Jews did not allow bodies to hang on crosses on the Sabbath day. As an act of mercy, soldiers would break the legs of the condemned to hasten their deaths. They broke the legs of the two criminals crucified with Jesus but discovered that Jesus was already dead. To make certain that Jesus was dead, a soldier jabbed His side with a spear. What happened to Jesus was no accident of history, but the fulfillment of a plan, born in the mind and heart of God, and foretold by the Scriptures.

205. JESUS BURIED IN JOSEPH'S TOMB

Matthew 27:57–60; Mark 15:42–46; Luke 23:50–54; John 19:38–42

Mk 15:42When it was already evening, because it was Preparation Day (that is, the day before the Sabbath), Jn 19:38a**Joseph of Arimathea** [Mt 27:57a*a rich man from Arimathea named Joseph*], Lk 23:50aa good and righteous man, Mk 15:43ba prominent member of the Sanhedrin who was himself looking forward to the kingdom of God, Lk 23:51awho had not agreed with their plan and action, Jn 19:38aa disciple of Jesus—but secretly because of his fear of the Jews—asked Pilate that he might remove Jesus' body.

Mk 15:44–45Pilate was surprised that He was already dead. Summoning the centurion, he asked him whether He had already died. 45When he found out from the centurion, he granted the corpse to Joseph, Jn 19:38bso he came and took His body away.

Jn 19:39–40**Nicodemus** (who had previously come to Him at night) also came, bringing a mixture of about 75 pounds of **myrrh and aloes**. 40Then they took Jesus' body and wrapped it in linen cloths with the aromatic spices, according to the burial custom of the Jews.

41There was a garden in the place where He was crucified. And in the garden was **a new tomb** in which no one had yet been placed. 42So because of the Jewish preparation day, since the tomb was nearby, they placed Jesus there. Mt 27:60bHe left after rolling a great stone against the entrance of the tomb.

206. WOMEN MOURN AT THE GUARDED TOMB

Matthew 27:61–66; Mark 15:47; Luke 23:55–56

Mk 15:47aNow **Mary Magdalene** and **Mary** the mother of Joses Lk 23:55–56[and] **the women** who had come with Him from Galilee followed along and observed the

---

205. JESUS BURIED IN JOSEPH'S TOMB

Joseph of Arimathea . . . Nicodemus: Joseph of Arimathaea was a member of the Sanhedrin. According to Luke, he did not vote to execute Jesus with the other members of this body (Luke 23:50–51). The Gospel of John describes him as "a disciple of Jesus, but secretly because of his fear of the Jews." But the death of Jesus compelled Joseph to shake off his fears and ask Pilate for the crucified body so he could bury it with dignity. In this act of love he was joined by Nicodemus, the Pharisee with whom Jesus had discussed the new birth at the beginning of His ministry (John 3:1–21).

myrrh and aloes: The Jews used spices to anoint the bodies of the dead. Some of these spices were very expensive. Nicodemus provided 75 pounds of myrrh and aloes to anoint Jesus' body.

a new tomb: Joseph provided a tomb—new, unused, and in a garden—for the burial of Jesus' body. He had probably purchased it for use by himself or the members of his family.

206. WOMEN MOURN AT THE GUARDED TOMB

Mary Magdalene . . . Mary . . .the women: Joseph and Nicodemus had prepared Jesus' body for burial with aromatic spices and perfumes. But the women who followed Jesus were not satisfied until they had added their own tribute of love. According to Luke's Gospel, they prepared "spices and perfumes" to anoint Jesus' body on the day following the Jewish Sabbath (Luke 23:56).

tomb and how His body was placed. ⁵⁶Then they returned and prepared spices and perfumes. And they rested on the Sabbath according to the commandment.

Mt 27:62–64The next day, which followed the Preparation Day, the chief priests and the Pharisees gathered before Pilate ⁶³and said, "Sir, we remember that while this deceiver was still alive, He said, 'After three days I will rise again.' ⁶⁴Therefore give orders that the tomb be made secure until the third day. Otherwise, His disciples may come, steal Him, and tell the people, 'He has been raised from the dead.' Then the last deception will be worse than the first."

⁶⁵"You have a guard of soldiers," Pilate told them. "Go and make it as secure as you know how." ⁶⁶Then they went and **made the tomb secure** by sealing the stone and setting the guard.

---

made the tomb secure: The religious leaders asked Pilate to seal the tomb and post guards. They wanted to be sure the disciples did not steal the body of Jesus and then claim He had been raised from the dead. After Pilate gave permission, the religious leaders posted guards.

VIII. Resurrection, Post-Resurrection Appearances, and Ascension

Jesus was resurrected early Sunday morning, just as He had predicted—on "the third day" (Matt. 16:21). These were not three full days but one full day—Saturday—and part of the day on which He was buried (Friday) and part of the day on which He was resurrected (Sunday).

Jesus did not ascend to His Father immediately after He was resurrected. For 40 days He appeared to His disciples and other believers (see Acts 1:3). He did this to convince them He was alive and to strengthen them for the task He had trained and commissioned them to do. It was now their job to proclaim the gospel of the kingdom of God to all people and to nurture the infant church to His glory.

207. Jesus Is Resurrected

Matthew 28:2–4

²Suddenly there was a violent earthquake, because an angel of the Lord descended from heaven and approached the tomb. He **rolled back the stone** and was sitting on it. ³His appearance was like lightning, and his robe was as white as snow. ⁴The guards were so shaken from fear of him that they became like dead men.

208. Women Visit the Tomb to Anoint Jesus' Body

Matthew 28:1; Mark 16:1–4; Luke 24:1–2

Mk 16:1aWhen the Sabbath was over, Mt 28:1aas the first day of the week was dawning, Mk 16:1b–4Mary Magdalene, Mary the mother of James, and Salome bought spices, so that they might go and anoint Him. . . ³And they were saying to one another, "**Who will roll away the stone** from the entrance to the tomb for us?" ⁴Looking up, they observed that the stone—which was very large—had been rolled away.

---

207. Jesus Is Resurrected

rolled back the stone: None of the Gospels describe the actual resurrection of Jesus, but Matthew 28:2 tells how the angel of the Lord rolled away the stone from the tomb opening.

208. Women Visit the Tomb to Anoint Jesus' Body

Who will roll away the stone: These women brought spices to anoint Jesus' body. They knew they would have to ask someone to roll the heavy stone away from the tomb opening. They were surprised to find it already moved.

The Women at Jesus' Tomb

These three women were probably the same ones who witnessed the crucifixion of Jesus. Mary Magdalene was one of Jesus' most loyal followers after He cast seven demons out of her. She was one of the women who ministered to Jesus in Galilee (Luke 8:2–3). We don't know for sure who Mary the mother of James was; she may have been the wife of Cleopas (John 19:25) or the mother of James the son of Alphaeus. Salome was probably the mother of James and John, the sons of Zebedee (Matt. 27:56). Matthew's account of the visit of the women to the tomb does not mention Salome (Matt. 28:1).

The role of these women is especially significant in light of the fact that they lived in a male-oriented society. Although only one of the twelve disciples—John—was at the crucifixion (John 19:25–27), these women were present. They were the first people to come to the empty tomb, the first to learn Jesus was alive, the first to see Him alive, and the first to tell the good news of His resurrection.

---

209. WOMEN DISCOVER THE EMPTY TOMB

Matthew 28:5–8; Mark 16:5–8; Luke 24:3–8; John 20:1–2

Lk 24:3–4**They went in** but did not find the body of the Lord Jesus [Jn 20:1 *On the first day of the week Mary Magdalene came to the tomb early, while it was still dark. She saw that the stone had been removed from the tomb*]. 4While they were perplexed about this, suddenly two men stood by them in dazzling clothes [Mk 16:5b *they saw a young man dressed in a long white robe sitting on the right side*].

Lk 24:5aSo the women were terrified and bowed down to the ground. Mk 16:6a"Don't be alarmed," he told them. "You are looking for Jesus the Nazarene, who was crucified. Mt 28:6He is not here! For **He has been resurrected**, just as He said. Come and see the place where He lay. Lk 24:6b–8Remember how He spoke to you when He was still in Galilee, 7saying, 'The Son of Man must be betrayed

---

209. WOMEN DISCOVER THE EMPTY TOMB

They went in: All the Gospels report the discovery of the empty tomb by the women who followed Jesus. But the details of this discovery vary from Gospel to Gospel. John builds his resurrection story around Mary Magdalene (John 20:1–18). Jesus had delivered her from possession by seven demons (Luke 8:2). When the women entered the tomb (according to the Gospel of John, only Mary Magdalene came to the tomb; John 20:1a), they saw two men clothed in white—obviously angels (Luke 24:3–4; Mark's account mentions only one man; Mark 16:5a). Although they were terrified, the angels reassured them.

He has been resurrected: The angels told the women the tomb was empty because Jesus had been raised from the dead. According to the Gospel of Luke, the angels reminded the women that Jesus had predicted not only His crucifixion but also His resurrection (Luke 24:6b–7). Why did none of Jesus' followers expect Jesus to be raised from the dead? The women had not gone to the tomb to see the risen Lord, but to anoint His body. The most likely reason why they were not expecting His resurrection is that they had not really expected Him to suffer and die. When Jesus predicted His suffering, death, and resurrection, the minds of His followers never got past the first part of this prediction.

into the hands of sinful men, be crucified, and rise on the third day'?" [8]And they remembered His words.

[Mk 16:7a]"But **go** [[Mt 28:7]*go quickly*], **tell His disciples** and Peter, [Mt 28:7b–8]'He has been raised from the dead. In fact, He is going ahead of you to Galilee; you will see Him there.' Listen, I have told you." [8]So, **departing quickly from the tomb** with fear and great joy [[Mk 16:8a]*So they went out and started running from the tomb, because trembling and astonishment had gripped them*], they ran to tell His disciples the news [[Mk 16:8b]*they said nothing to anyone, since they were afraid*].

210. PETER AND JOHN HURRY TO THE TOMB

Luke 24:9–12; John 20:3–10

[Lk 24:9–11]Returning from the tomb, they reported all these things to the Eleven and to all the rest. [10]Mary Magdalene, Joanna, Mary the mother of James, and the other women with them were telling the apostles these things. [11]But these words seemed like nonsense to them, and they did not believe the women.

[Jn 20:3–5]At that, Peter and the other disciple went out, heading for the tomb. [4]The two were running together, but **the other disciple outran Peter** and got to the tomb first. [5]Stooping down, he **saw the linen cloths** lying there, yet he **did not go in**.

[6]Then, following him, **Simon Peter** came also. He **entered the tomb** and saw the linen cloths lying there. [7]The wrapping that had been on His head was not lying with the linen cloths but folded up in a separate place by itself. [8]**The other disciple**, who had reached the tomb first, then entered the tomb, **saw, and**

---

go, tell His disciples: Then the angels told the women to go and tell the disciples that Jesus had been raised from the dead. Like a shepherd going ahead of his sheep, Jesus was preceding them to Galilee; they would see Him there.

departing quickly from the tomb: The women quickly obeyed the angels. Their fears were not gone, but these were now overshadowed by their joy. They ran to tell the disciples the joyful news.

210. PETER AND JOHN HURRY TO THE TOMB

the other disciple outran Peter: When Peter and John heard the news from the women about Jesus' resurrection, they rushed to the tomb. (According to Luke 24:12, only Peter went to the tomb.) "The other disciple" was probably John, author of the Gospel of John. John reported that he outran Peter, who was probably the older of the two. John was the first disciple to look inside the tomb and to establish that Jesus was not there.

saw the linen cloths . . . did not go in: John did not enter the tomb, since he saw that only "the linen cloths" were inside. This was an important observation, since it provided evidence against the future rumor that the body of Jesus had been stolen from the grave. Grave robbers were active in those times. If thieves had plundered the grave, they would certainly have taken the grave clothes.

Simon Peter . . . entered the tomb: When Peter reached the tomb, he rushed in ahead of John. What he saw confirmed that the tomb had not been rifled by thieves. The grave clothes were lying there in neat and orderly fashion, indicating that something supernatural had taken place. In the moment of resurrection, Jesus' body had passed through His shroud, just as it later passed through closed doors (John 20:19). Even the wrappings around the head of Jesus had been folded and placed neatly in a separate place.

believed. [9]For they still did not understand the Scripture that He must rise from the dead. [10]Then the disciples went home again.

211. Jesus Appears to Mary Magdalene

Mark 16:9–11; John 20:11–18

[Jn 20:11–13a]But **Mary stood outside** facing the tomb, **crying**. As she was crying, she stooped to look into the tomb. [12]She saw two angels in white sitting there, one at the head and one at the feet, where Jesus' body had been lying. [13a]They said to her, "Woman, why are you crying?"

[13b]"Because they've taken away my Lord," she told them, "and I don't know where they've put Him." [14]Having said this, she turned around and saw Jesus standing there, though she did not know it was Jesus.

[15a]"Woman," Jesus said to her, "why are you crying? Who is it you are looking for?"

[15b]Supposing He was the gardener, she replied, "Sir, if you've removed Him, **tell me where you've put Him**, and I will take Him away."

[16a]"**Mary!**" Jesus said.

[16b]Turning around, she said to Him in Hebrew, "***Rabbouni!***"—which means "Teacher."

[17]"**Don't cling to Me**," Jesus told her, "for I have not yet ascended to the Father. But **go to My brothers** and tell them that I am ascending to My Father and your Father—to My God and your God."

[18]Mary Magdalene went and announced to the disciples, "I have seen the Lord!" And she told them what He had said to her.

The other disciple . . . saw, and believed: What Peter only *saw* caused John to *believe*. John, who wrote his Gospel to generate belief in Jesus (see John 21:24), set an example by his own reaction to the proofs that resurrection had taken place.

211. Jesus Appears to Mary Magdalene

Mary stood outside . . . crying: After inspecting the empty tomb, Peter and John went home (John 20:10). But Mary lingered at the tomb, not sharing John's understanding of what had happened but unwilling to tear herself away. On looking into the tomb, perhaps to convince herself that it was empty, she saw two angelic figures. Questioned by them about her tears, she repeated her belief that someone had removed the body of Jesus.

tell me where you've put Him: When Mary saw Jesus, she did not recognize Him at first. Instead, she thought the person she saw through her tears was the gardener. She even asked if he had taken the body. Her one thought was to retrieve the body of Jesus.

Mary! . . . Rabbouni! Mary's deep devotion was rewarded by the sound of her name, spoken with a tenderness that was unmistakably Jesus'. Mary replied with a term of respect that went beyond the word *rabbi. Rabbouni* (Aramaic for "teacher") meant "my Lord or Master."

Don't cling to Me: When Mary reached out to Jesus, He directed her not to touch Him. Perhaps He was trying to prepare Mary for a time when she would have to relate to Him by something other than the physical senses. It was necessary that all His followers grow accustomed to the lack of His physical presence.

go to My brothers: Jesus instructed Mary to take a message of hope, joy, and reassurance to the disciples.

212. Jesus Sends the Women to Tell the Disciples

Matthew 28:8–10

⁸So, departing quickly from the tomb with fear and great joy, they ran to tell His disciples the news. ⁹Just then **Jesus met them** and said, "Rejoice!" They came up, took hold of His feet, and worshiped Him. ¹⁰Then Jesus told them, "Do not be afraid. Go and tell My brothers to leave for Galilee, and they will see Me there."

Jesus' Appearances After His Resurrection

After His resurrection, Jesus made several appearances to His 11 disciples as well as to other followers. According to the Book of Acts, these appearances occurred across a period of 40 days before His ascension to the Father (see Acts 1:3).

Through these appearances Jesus gave His followers "convincing proofs" (Acts 1:3) that He was alive. Here's a list of Jesus' post-resurrection appearances recorded by the Gospel writers:

- *To Mary Magdalene at the empty tomb in Jerusalem (Mark 16:9; John 20:11–18).*
- *To other women at the empty tomb (Matt. 28:1–10).*
- *To two followers on their way to Emmaus (Mark 16:12–13; Luke 24:13–32).*
- *To Peter, apparently in Jerusalem (Luke 24:33–35).*
- *To ten of His disciples in Jerusalem, Thomas absent (Luke 24:36–43; John 20:19–25).*
- *To the eleven disciples in Jerusalem, Thomas present (John 20:26–29).*
- *To His disciples at Lake Galilee (John 21:1–14).*
- *To His disciples at His ascension near Jerusalem (Mark 16:19–20; Luke 24:44–53).*

The apostle Paul also mentioned three appearances of Jesus not recorded by the Gospel writers. These appearances were to five hundred believers, to James and all the apostles, and to Paul himself (1 Cor. 15:6–8). The Book of Acts also mentions the post-resurrection appearances of Jesus (Acts 1:3).

---

212. Jesus Sends the Women to Tell the Disciples

Jesus met them: No one in the first century would have made up a story in which women were the first to see the angels, meet the risen Lord, and tell others. This is one of many evidences that the New Testament is true. Jesus told these women not to be afraid. He also reinforced the earlier command of the angels to go and tell the disciples that He would appear to them in Galilee.

213. Soldiers Bribed by the Sanhedrin

Matthew 28:11–15

¹¹As they were on their way, some of the guard came into the city and reported to the chief priests everything that had happened. ¹²After the priests had assembled with the elders and agreed on a plan, they **gave the soldiers a large sum of money** ¹³and told them, "Say this, 'His disciples came during the night and stole Him while we were sleeping.' ¹⁴If this reaches the governor's ears, we will deal with him and keep you out of trouble."

¹⁵So they took the money and did as they were instructed. And this story has been spread among Jewish people to this day.

214. Jesus Appears to Two Followers at Emmaus

Luke 24:13–32

¹³Now **that same day two of them** were on their way to a village called Emmaus, which was about seven miles from Jerusalem. ¹⁴Together they were discussing everything that had taken place. ¹⁵And while they were discussing and arguing, **Jesus** Himself came near and **began to walk along with them**. ¹⁶But they were prevented from recognizing Him. ¹⁷Then He asked them, "What is this dispute that you're having with each other as you are walking?" And they stopped walking and looked discouraged.

¹⁸The one named Cleopas answered Him, "Are You **the only visitor** in Jerusalem **who doesn't know** the things that happened there in these days?"

¹⁹ᵃ"What things?" He asked them.

¹⁹ᵇSo they said to Him, "The things concerning Jesus the Nazarene, who was a Prophet powerful in action and speech before God and all the people, ²⁰and how our chief priests and leaders handed Him over to be sentenced to death, and they

---

213. Soldiers Bribed by the Sanhedrin

gave the soldiers a large sum of money: Some of the terrified guards reported to the chief priests what had happened at the tomb of Jesus. The religious leaders bribed the guards to say that the disciples had stolen the body of Jesus while they slept. The guards accepted the bribe. Thus began the first of many ways of trying to explain away the resurrection of Jesus.

214. Jesus Appears to Two Followers at Emmaus

that same day two of them: On the day when Jesus was resurrected, two of His followers were walking on the road from Jerusalem to Emmaus, a distance of about seven miles. The two men were not apostles; they were from the larger group of Jesus' disciples.

Jesus . . . began to walk along with them: As they were concentrating on their conversation with each other, Jesus joined them as they walked. These two followers didn't recognize Him. They were not expecting Him to be raised from the dead, and His resurrection body must have been different.

the only visitor . . . who doesn't know: Jesus used questions to get their thoughts out into the open. Their words give insight into what the followers of Jesus believed during the time between His death and their awareness of His resurrection. They still remembered the ministry of Jesus. They spoke of His power to others.

crucified Him. [21]But we were hoping that He was **the One** who was about **to redeem Israel**. Besides all this, it's the third day since these things happened. [22]Moreover, some women from our group astounded us. They arrived early at the tomb, [23]and when they didn't find His body, they came and reported that they had seen a vision of angels who said He was alive. [24]**Some** of those who were with us **went to the tomb** and found it just as the women had said, but they didn't see Him."

[25]He said to them, "O **how unwise and slow you are** to believe in your hearts all that the prophets have spoken! [26]Didn't the Messiah have to suffer these things and enter into His glory?" [27]Then beginning with Moses and all the Prophets, He interpreted for them in all the Scriptures the things concerning Himself.

[28]They came near the village where they were going, and He gave the impression that He was going farther. [29]But they urged Him: "Stay with us, because it's almost evening, and now the day is almost over." So He went in to stay with them.

[30]It was as He reclined at the table with them that He took the bread, blessed and broke it, and gave it to them. [31]Then their eyes were opened, and they recognized Him; but He disappeared from their sight. [32]So they said to each other, "Weren't our hearts ablaze within us while He was talking with us on the road and explaining the Scriptures to us?"

215. SIMON PETER SEES JESUS

Luke 24:33–35

[33]That very hour they got up and returned to Jerusalem, and found the Eleven and those with them gathered together, [34]who said, "**The Lord has** certainly **been raised, and has appeared to Simon!**" [35]Then they began to describe what had happened on the road, and how He was made known to them in the breaking of the bread.

---

the One . . . to redeem Israel: What these men couldn't understand was why Jesus, who had such power, was condemned and crucified. They were looking for a Messiah who would use His power to redeem Israel from the yoke of Rome and restore the glory days of King David. When they saw evidences of divine power in the ministry of Jesus, they had hoped He was this expected Messiah.

Some . . . went to the tomb: These two followers of Jesus had not believed the women's report of angels who announced that Jesus was alive. Even when some of the men went and found the tomb empty, they still did not believe that Jesus was alive.

how unwise and slow you are: Jesus rebuked these two believers for failing to realize what the Scriptures taught about the suffering and glory of the Messiah. Isaiah 52:13–53:12 tells of the suffering and victory of the Servant. He entered into His victory through His suffering and death for our sins. This was probably one of the passages that Jesus used to emphasize this truth to the two on the Emmaus Road.

215. SIMON PETER SEES JESUS

The Lord has . . . appeared to Simon! The apostle Paul also mentions this event in 1 Corinthians 15:5, but none of the Gospels contain any details about this appearance to Peter.

216. Jesus Appears to His Disciples, but Thomas Is Absent

Luke 24:36–43; John 20:19–25

Jn 20:19In the evening of that first day of the week, **the disciples** were gathered together **with the doors locked** because of their fear of the Jews. Then **Jesus** came, **stood among them**, and said to them, "Peace to you!"

Lk 24:37–40But they were startled and terrified, and thought they were seeing a ghost. 38"Why are you troubled?" He asked them. "And why do doubts arise in your hearts? 39Look at My hands and My feet, that it is I Myself! Touch Me and see, because a ghost does not have flesh and bones as you can see I have." 40Having said this, He showed them His hands and feet.

41But while they still could not believe for joy, and they were amazed, He asked them, "Do you have anything here to eat?" 42So they gave Him a piece of a broiled fish, 43and He took it and ate in their presence. Jn 20:20bSo the disciples rejoiced when they saw the Lord.

21Jesus said to them again, "Peace to you! Just as the Father has sent Me, I also send you." 22After saying this, **He breathed on them** and said, "Receive the Holy Spirit. 23If you forgive the sins of any, they are forgiven them; if you retain the sins of any, they are retained."

24But one of the Twelve, **Thomas** (called "Twin"), **was not with them** when Jesus came. 25So the other disciples kept telling him, "We have seen the Lord!" But he said to them, "If I don't see the mark of the nails in His hands, put my finger into the mark of the nails, and put my hand into His side, **I will never believe!**"

---

216. Jesus Appears to His Disciples, but Thomas Is Absent

the disciples . . . with the doors locked: This event happened on the evening of that first Sunday—the day when Jesus was raised from the dead. Why were the disciples still hiding behind locked doors? Had not Mary Magdalene brought them the good news that Jesus was resurrected? They were not yet convinced that He was alive.

Jesus . . . stood among them: During the 40 days before His ascension, Jesus was not with His followers on a continuous basis—at least not in the flesh. Instead, from time to time, He would suddenly appear. He was trying to help them develop an awareness of His presence in a different form—His resurrection body. One of Jesus' goals for these 40 days was to convince the disciples of the reality of His resurrection. According to Luke, He showed them His hands and side (Luke 24:38–41).

He breathed on them: Jesus empowered His followers to fulfill their mission. In Jesus' instructions to His followers on the night before His death, He had promised to send them the Holy Spirit. His breathing on them on this resurrection night signified the coming of the Spirit's power, which would take place on the day of Pentecost (Acts 2).

Thomas . . . was not with them: We don't know why Thomas was not with the other disciples on this night. Perhaps the death of Jesus had left him in dark despair. Because of his earlier statement about dying with Jesus (see John 11:16), Thomas may have felt guilty about deserting Jesus when He was arrested. During the week following Jesus' appearance on Sunday night, perhaps the other disciples found Thomas to tell him they had seen the Lord.

I will never believe! We tend to single out Thomas for his doubt, forgetting that the other disciples also had not believed when others told them. Thomas was not the only doubter, but he did state his conditions for believing in the sharpest way. His doubts and the doubts of the other disciples prove they were not expecting Jesus to be raised from the dead. Luke's account of this event does not mention the absence of Thomas. Luke also reports that Jesus ate in the presence of the disciples to prove He was not a ghost (Luke 24:41–43).

217. JESUS APPEARS TO THOMAS AND THE OTHER DISCIPLES

John 20:26–29

²⁶**After eight days** His disciples were indoors again, and Thomas was with them. Even though the doors were locked, Jesus came and stood among them. He said, "Peace to you!"

²⁷Then He said to Thomas, "Put your finger here and observe My hands. Reach out your hand and put it into My side. **Don't be an unbeliever** but a believer."

²⁸Thomas responded to Him, "**My Lord and my God!**"

²⁹Jesus said, "Because **you have seen Me**, you have believed. **Blessed are those who believe without seeing.**"

218. A MIRACULOUS CATCH OF FISH AT LAKE GALILEE

John 21:1–14

¹After this, Jesus revealed Himself again to His disciples by the **Sea of Tiberias**. He revealed Himself in this way:

²Simon Peter, Thomas (called "Twin"), Nathanael from Cana of Galilee, Zebedee's sons, and two others of His disciples were together.

³ᵃ"**I'm going fishing**," Simon Peter said to them.

³ᵇ"We're coming with you," they told him. They went out and got into the boat; but that night they caught nothing.

---

217. JESUS APPEARS TO THOMAS AND THE OTHER DISCIPLES

After eight days: Eight days later Thomas was with the other disciples. We should at least give him credit for putting himself where he might have his doubts removed.

Don't be an unbeliever: Jesus' words to Thomas show He was aware of what Thomas had said eight days before.

My Lord and my God! Did Thomas actually touch the nail prints or thrust his hand into Jesus' side? The Bible doesn't say, but the words of Thomas imply that he didn't need to do that when he actually saw Jesus. Thomas could have touched Jesus, because His body was real. But Thomas was so awed by this encounter that he fell down and worshiped Jesus.

you have seen Me: The testimony of Thomas and the other apostles to Jesus' resurrection was based on the fact that they saw Him alive. All of them had to be convinced. Their message of His resurrection was not something they dreamed up. It was a realization to which Jesus brought them in spite of their doubts.

Blessed are those who believe without seeing: Later generations of believers would base their faith on the testimony of those who had seen the Lord for themselves. We are among those who have not seen Jesus in the flesh; yet we are believers. We believe because we accept as truth the testimony of the first witnesses as recorded in the inspired Word of God.

218. A MIRACULOUS CATCH OF FISH AT LAKE GALILEE

Sea of Tiberias: This name was given to Lake Galilee in the second half of the first century in honor of the Roman emperor Tiberias.

I'm going fishing: These fishermen who had left their nets to follow Jesus were suddenly left with nothing to do. It was natural for them to return to their former occupation.

⁴When daybreak came, Jesus stood on the shore. However, the disciples did not know that it was Jesus.

⁵ᵃ"Men," Jesus called to them, "you don't have any fish, do you?"

⁵ᵇ"No," they answered.

⁶"Cast the net on the right side of the boat," He told them, "and you'll find some." So they did, and they were unable to haul it in because of the large number of fish. ⁷ᵃTherefore the disciple whom Jesus loved said to Peter, "It's the Lord!"

⁷ᵇWhen Simon Peter heard that it was the Lord, he tied his outer garment around him (for he was stripped) and plunged into the sea. ⁸But since they were not far from land (about a hundred yards away), the other disciples came in the boat, dragging the net full of fish. ⁹When they got out on land, they saw **a charcoal fire** there, **with fish** lying on it, and bread.

¹⁰"Bring some of the fish you've just caught," Jesus told them. ¹¹So Simon Peter got up and hauled the net ashore, full of large fish—153 of them. Even though there were so many, the net was not torn.

¹²"Come and have breakfast," Jesus told them. **None of the disciples dared ask Him**, "Who are You?" because they knew it was the Lord. ¹³Jesus came, took the bread, and gave it to them. He did the same with the fish.

¹⁴This was now the third time Jesus appeared to the disciples after He was raised from the dead.

219. JESUS REINSTATES PETER

John 21:15–19

¹⁵ᵃWhen they had eaten breakfast, Jesus asked Simon Peter, "**Simon**, son of John, **do you love Me** more than these?"

¹⁵ᵇ"Yes, Lord," he said to Him, "You know that I love You."

---

a charcoal fire . . . with fish: Jesus was waiting for these fishermen beside a fire on which fish were already cooking. He invited the disciples to add some of the fish they had caught. Before doing so they counted the catch—153 fish. Speculative theories have been built around this number. But perhaps these disciples wanted the exact number for future reference.

None of the disciples dared ask Him: Was there something different about Jesus' appearance that caused the disciples not to ask Him any questions? If so, there was no difference in His loving concern. Here was their Master once again filling the role of a servant as He handed out the food.

219. JESUS REINSTATES PETER

Simon . . . do you love Me: With these questions, Jesus invited Peter to make a commitment of absolute devotion to Him. Jesus asked this three times. This was the number of times Peter had denied Jesus (Matt. 26:69–75). That Jesus used different words in His questions may be significant. The first two times Jesus used a form of *agape* (self-giving love) to which Peter replied, "I love You," using *phileo*, the Greek word for "brotherly love." In the third question, Jesus used Peter's word, and it may have been this that grieved Peter. On the other hand, the third question, matching Peter's third denial, may have been the cause of his distress.

[15c]**"Feed My lambs,"** He told him.

[16a]A second time He asked him, "Simon, son of John, do you love Me?"

[16b]"Yes, Lord," he said to Him, "You know that I love You."

[16c]"Shepherd My sheep," He told him.

[17a]He asked him the third time, "Simon, son of John, do you love Me?"

[17b]Peter was grieved that He asked him the third time, "Do you love Me?" He said, "Lord, You know everything! You know that I love You."

[17c]**"Feed My sheep,"** Jesus said. [18]"I assure you: When you were young, you would tie your belt and walk wherever you wanted. But when you grow old, **you will stretch out your hands** and someone else will tie you and carry you where you don't want to go." [19]He said this to signify by what kind of death he would glorify God. After saying this, He told him, "Follow Me!"

220. JESUS AND PETER DISCUSS THE FUTURE OF THE APOSTLE JOHN

John 21:20–24

[20]So Peter turned around and saw the disciple Jesus loved following them. That disciple was the one who had leaned back against Jesus at the supper and asked, "Lord, who is the one that's going to betray You?" [21]When Peter saw him, he said to Jesus, "Lord—what about him?"

[22]"If I want him to remain until I come," Jesus answered, **"what is that to you?** As for you, follow Me."

[23]So this report spread to the brothers that this disciple would not die. Yet Jesus did not tell him that he would not die, but, "If I want him to remain until I come, what is that to you?"

[24]This is **the disciple who testifies to these things** and who wrote them down. We know that his testimony is true.

Feed My lambs . . . Feed My sheep: Another significance in this account is Jesus' reference to His followers as "lambs" and "sheep." Was Jesus telling Peter to be shepherd to young and old or to new believers as well as established believers? He was certainly assigning this disciple an important ministry in the church—a charge that Peter carried out faithfully in the years to come. Peter was repentant, forgiven, and restored. In the early chapters of Acts, he became a courageous follower of Jesus and leader of the church.

you will stretch out your hands: This phrase may refer to the manner of Peter's death—crucifixion. There is no biblical mention of this, but opinion was strong in the early Christian centuries that this is how Peter died. In spite of this grim prospect, Jesus said to Peter, "Follow Me"—and this Peter did for the rest of his life.

220. JESUS AND PETER DISCUSS THE FUTURE OF THE APOSTLE JOHN

what is that to you? Perhaps the shock of Jesus' disclosure about Peter's future suffering caused him to ask what would happen to John ("the disciple Jesus loved," v. 20). Would John also face a martyr's death? Jesus told Peter that the destiny of others was not his concern. He must concentrate on his own discipleship.

the disciple who testifies to these things: The apostle John, the author of the Gospel of John, added his own comments to this narrative. He wanted the readers of his Gospel to know that he had actually witnessed the things he wrote about. The phrase "these things" probably refers to his entire Gospel account.

221. JESUS COMMISSIONS HIS DISCIPLES TO CONTINUE HIS WORK

Matthew 28:16–20; Mark 16:15–18

Mt 28:16–20The **eleven disciples** traveled to Galilee, to the mountain where Jesus had directed them. 17When they saw Him, they worshiped, but some doubted. 18Then Jesus came near and said to them, "**All authority** has been given to Me in heaven and on earth. 19**Go**, therefore, and make disciples of all nations [Mk 16:15b *Go into all the world and preach the gospel to the whole creation*], **baptizing** them in the name of the Father and of the Son and of the Holy Spirit, 20**teaching** them to observe everything I have commanded you. And remember, **I am with you always**, to the end of the age.

Jesus' Great Commission

This passage from Matthew is called the Great Commission, because it is the fullest statement of His commission for world missions and evangelism. As followers of Christ, we are to be on mission for Him in our local communities as well as the remote corners of the globe.

All the Gospels and the Book of Acts have some form of a commission spoken by Jesus (see Mark 16:15; Luke 24:47–48; John 20:21; Acts 1:8).

Mk 16:16–18"Whoever believes and is baptized will be saved, but whoever does not believe will be condemned. 17And these signs will accompany those who believe: In My name they will drive out demons; they will speak with new tongues; 18they will pick up snakes; if they should drink anything deadly, it will never harm them; they will lay hands on the sick, and they will get well."*

222. JESUS ASCENDS TO HIS FATHER

Luke 24:44–53

44Then He told them, "These are My words that I spoke to you while I was still with you, that everything written about Me in the

---

*verses 9–20 of Mark 16 do not appear in some New Testament manuscripts.

---

221. JESUS COMMISSIONS HIS DISCIPLES TO CONTINUE HIS WORK

eleven disciples: Matthew mentions only the eleven disciples, but some interpreters think other believers also could have heard the Great Commission. Jesus certainly did not intend to confine this mission to the apostles.

All authority: The risen Lord now had authority over all things as a result of the successful completion of His mission. As Lord of all the earth, Jesus issued a command that encompasses all people.

Go . . . baptizing . . . teaching: "Go" is translated as a command. It may also mean, "As you go." Sometimes we are called to go to certain places or people. Always we are to bear witness for Christ as we go about our daily tasks. "Baptizing" assumes that those being baptized are people who have heard the good news and have trusted Jesus as Lord and Savior. "Teaching" reminds us that new believers need to be instructed about Jesus and His teachings on how His followers are to live. Believers are considered discipled when they live in obedience to God's will.

I am with you always: To those who obey this Great Commission, Jesus promises His abiding presence until the end time arrives and His kingdom comes in all its glory. By His Spirit, the risen Lord is leading the way for us to make disciples of all nations. Our obedience in fulfilling the Great Commission bears testimony to our belief in His resurrection. The Great Commission is also mentioned in Acts 1:8.

Law of Moses, the Prophets, and the Psalms must be fulfilled." ⁴⁵Then **He opened their minds** to understand the Scriptures. ⁴⁶He also said to them, "This is what is written: the Messiah would suffer and rise from the dead the third day, ⁴⁷and repentance for forgiveness of sins would be proclaimed in His name to all the nations, beginning at Jerusalem. ⁴⁸You are witnesses of these things. ⁴⁹And look, **I am sending you what My Father promised**. As for you, stay in the city until you are empowered from on high."

⁵⁰Then He led them out as far as Bethany, and lifting up His hands He blessed them. ⁵¹And while He was blessing them, He left them and was carried up into heaven. ⁵²After worshiping Him, they returned to Jerusalem with great joy. ⁵³And they were continually in the temple complex blessing God.

223. JOHN'S STATEMENT OF PURPOSE AND CONCLUSION FOR HIS GOSPEL

John 20:30–31; 21:25

ᴶⁿ ²⁰:³⁰⁻³¹Jesus performed many other signs in the presence of His disciples that are not written in this book. ³¹But these are written so **that you may believe** Jesus is the Messiah, the Son of God, and by believing you may have life in His name.

ᴶⁿ ²¹:²⁵And there are also many other things that Jesus did, which, if they were written one by one, I suppose not even the world itself could contain the books that would be written.

---

222. JESUS ASCENDS TO HIS FATHER

He opened their minds: Earlier, Jesus had explained the Scriptures to the two believers on the road to Emmaus. Now he opened the Scriptures to the entire group of His followers. He emphasized that He had been sent to preach the message of repentance and forgiveness for all people. The key to understanding the Scriptures and God's purpose, He pointed out, was to recognize that God had intended all along to declare the good news of salvation to all nations.

I am sending you what My Father promised: With these words, Jesus referred to Joel 2:28–32 (see Acts 2:14–20). The presence and power of the risen Lord would equip the disciples for their disciple-making mission to the world.

223. JOHN'S STATEMENT OF PURPOSE AND CONCLUSION FOR HIS GOSPEL

that you may believe: The selective process followed by all Gospel writers is plainly stated by John. From a wealth of material he chose to record those sayings and actions of Jesus that would further his purpose—to generate belief in Jesus as Son of God and Savior. He wanted people to know the joy that Jesus promised: "I have come that they may have life and have it in abundance" (John 10:10).

A SYSTEMATIC READING PLAN

You may want to use the *Simplified Harmony of the Gospels* individually or with your family as a handy Bible-reading guide. The following plan will take you through the life and ministry of Jesus in about four months if you read from it every day. For example, on day 1 you would read segments 1 and 2 in the book ("Luke's Preface and Dedication," and "John's Introduction"). Some longer segments in the book are broken into two or three separate units in this plan to equalize the daily reading times.

This plan can also be adapted for Lent or Easter readings. Begin with day 86, segment 156, "The Sanhedrin Plots against Jesus and Lazarus," and read on consecutive days through the rest of the plan.

DAY	SEGMENT	DAY	SEGMENT
1	1, 2	27	54 (Matthew 5:1–48)
2	3	28	54 (Matthew 6:1–34)
3	4, 5	29	54 (Matthew 7:1–29)
4	6, 7	30	55, 56
5	8, 9	31	57, 58
6	10	32	59, 60
7	11, 12	33	61, 62, 63
8	13, 14	34	64, 65
9	15, 16	35	66, 67, 68
10	17, 18, 19	36	69, 70, 71, 72
11	20	37	73, 74, 75, 76, 77
12	21, 22	38	78, 79
13	23	39	80
14	24	40	81, 82
15	25, 26	41	83
16	27	42	84, 85
17	28	43	86, 87
18	29, 30, 31, 32	44	88 (John 6:22–40)
19	33	45	88 (John 6:41–71)
20	34, 35	46	89
21	36, 37	47	90, 91
22	38, 39, 40	48	92, 93
23	41, 42, 43, 44	49	94, 95, 96
24	45, 46, 47	50	97, 98, 99
25	48, 49	51	100, 101
26	50, 51, 52, 53	52	102, 103

DAY	SEGMENT
53	104, 105
54	106, 107
55	108, 109 (John 7:11–27)
56	109 (John 7:28–53)
57	110
58	111 (John 8:12–29)
59	111 (John 8:30–59)
60	112
61	113
62	114
63	115
64	116, 117
65	118, 119
66	120, 121
67	122, 123
68	124, 125
69	126, 127
70	128, 129
71	130, 131, 132, 133
72	134, 135
73	136, 137, 138
74	139
75	140, 141
76	142
77	143, 144
78	145
79	146
80	147, 148
81	149
82	150
83	151, 152
84	153, 154
85	155
86	156
87	157, 158
88	159
89	160, 161

DAY	SEGMENT
90	162, 163
91	164, 165
92	166, 167, 168
93	169
94	170, 171 (Matthew 24:1–28)
95	171 (Matthew 24:28–56)
96	172
97	173
98	174
99	175, 176, 177, 178
100	179
101	180, 181
102	182, 183
103	184 (John 14:1–31)
104	184 (John 15:1–27)
105	184 (John 16:1–33)
106	185
107	186
108	187
109	188, 189
110	190, 191
111	192, 193
112	194, 195, 196
113	197, 198, 199
114	200, 201, 202
115	203, 204
116	205, 206
117	207, 208, 209
118	210, 211
119	212, 213
120	214
121	215, 216, 217
122	218
123	219
124	220, 221
125	222, 223

MATTHEW SCRIPTURE INDEX

1:1–17, **12**
1:18–25, **14**
1:25, **19**
2:1–12, **21**
2:13–15, **22**
2:16–18, **23**
2:19–23, **23**
3:1–12, **27**
3:13–17, **29**
4:1–11, **30**
4:12, **42**
4:13–16, **49**
4:17, **47**
4:18–22, **50**
4:23–25, **53**
5:1–7:29, **64**
6:9–13, **143**
8:1–4, **54**
8:5–13, **73**
8:14–15, **52**
8:16–17, **52**
8:18, 23–27, **90**
8:19–22, **128**
8:28–34, **91**
9:1–8, **54**
9:9–13, **56**
9:14–17, **57**
9:18–26, **93**
9:27–38, **95**
10:1, 5–42, **97**
10:2–4, **63**
11:1–19, **75**
11:20–24, 77
11:25–30, **78**
12:1–8, **60**

12:9–14, **61**
12:15–21, **62**
12:22–24, **80**
12:25–37, **80**
12:38–45, **82**
12:46–50, **82**
13:1–9, **84**
13:10–17, **85**
13:18–23, **86**
13:24–30, **87**
13:31–35, **87**
13:36–43, **88**
13:44, **89**
13:45–46, **89**
13:47–51, **89**
13:52, **90**
13:53–58, **96**
14:1–5, **41**
14:6–12, **100**
14:13–21, **103**
14:22–36, **105**
15:1–20, **110**
15:21–28, **112**
15:29–38, **114**
15:39–16:4, **114**
16:5–12, **115**
16:13–20, **117**
16:21–28, **118**
17:1–8, **119**
17:9–13, **121**
17:14–21, **121**
17:22–23, **123**
17:24–27, **123**
18:1–11, **124**
18:12–14, **159**
18:15–22, **125**
18:23–35, **127**
19:1–12, **172**

19:13–15, **173**
19:16–30, **174**
20:1–16, **175**
20:17–19, **176**
20:20–28, **177**
20:29–34, **178**
21:1–11, **184**
21:12–19, **185**
21:19–22, **188**
21:23–27, **189**
21:28–32, **190**
21:33–46, **190**
22:1–14, **192**
22:15–22, **192**
22:23–33, **193**
22:34–40, **194**
22:41–46, **195**
23:1–36, **196**
23:37–39, **156**
24:1–51, **198**
25:1–13, **202**
25:14–30, **203**
25:31–46, **205**
26:1–5, **206**
26:6–13, **206**
26:14–16, **207**
26:17–19, **208**
26:20–25, **210**
26:26–30, **212**
26:31–35, **211**
26:36–46, **220**
26:47–56, **223**
26:57–68, **225**
26:58, 69–75, **226**
27:1–2, **227**
27:2, 11–14, **229**
27:3–10, **229**
27:15–26, **231**

27:27–31, **234**
27:32, **234**
27:33–37, **235**
27:38, 44, **237**
27:39–43, **236**
27:45–54, **238**
27:55–56, **236**
27:57–60, **240**
27:61–66, **240**
28:1, **243**
28:2–4, **243**
28:5–8, **244**
28:8–10, **247**
28:11–15, **248**
28:16–20, **254**

Mark
Scripture Index

1:1–8, **27**
1:9–11, **29**
1:12–13, **30**
1:14, **42**
1:14–15, **47**
1:16–20, **50**
1:21–26, **51**
1:22, 27–28, **52**
1:29–31, **52**
1:32–34, **52**
1:35–39, **53**
1:40–45, **54**
2:1–12, **54**
2:13–17, **56**
2:18–22, **57**
2:23–28, **60**
3:1–6, **61**
3:7–12, **62**
3:13–19, **63**
3:20–30, **80**
3:31–35, **82**
4:1–9, **84**

4:10, 13–20, **86**
4:11–12, **85**
4:21–25, **86**
4:26–29, **87**
4:30–34, **87**
4:35–41, **90**
5:1–20, **91**
5:21–43, **93**
6:1–6, **96**
6:7–13, **97**
6:14–16, **101**
6:17–20, **41**
6:17–29, **100**
6:30–44, **103**
6:45–56, **105**
7:1–23, **110**
7:24–30, **112**
7:31–37, **113**
8:1–10, **114**
8:11–12, **114**
8:13–21, **115**
8:22–26, **116**
8:27–30, **117**
8:31–9:1, **118**
9:2–8, **119**
9:9–13, **121**
9:14–29, **121**
9:30–32, **123**
9:33–50, **124**
10:1–12, **172**
10:13–16, **173**
10:17–31, **174**
10:32–34, **176**
10:35–45, **177**
10:46–52, **178**
11:1–11, **184**
11:12–19, **185**
11:20–26, **188**
11:27–33, **189**
12:1–12, **190**
12:13–17, **192**
12:18–27, **193**

12:28–34, **194**
12:35–37, **195**
12:38–40, **196**
12:41–44, **198**
13:1–37, **198**
14:1–2, **206**
14:3–9, **206**
14:10–11, **207**
14:12–16, **208**
14:17–21, **210**
14:22–26, **212**
14:26, 32–42, **220**
14:27–31, **211**
14:43–52, **223**
14:53–65, **225**
14:54, 66–72, **226**
15:1, **227**
15:1–5, **229**
15:6–15, **231**
15:16–20, **234**
15:21, **234**
15:22–26, **235**
15:27–28, **237**
15:29–32, **236**
15:33–39, **238**
15:40–41, **236**
15:42–46, **240**
15:47, **240**
16:1–4, **243**
16:5–8, **244**
16:9–11, **246**
16:15–18, **254**

Luke
Scripture Index

1:1–4, **5**
1:5–25, **7**
1:26–38, **9**
1:39–56, **10**
1:57–66, **11**

1:67–80, **11**

2:1–7, **17**

2:8–20, **18**

2:21, **19**

2:22–38, **19**

2:39–40, **23**

2:41–52, **24**

3:1–18, **27**

3:19–20, **41**

3:21–23, **29**

3:23–38, **13**

4:1–13, **30**

4:14–15, **42**

4:16–21, **48**

4:22–31, **49**

4:31–35, **51**

4:32, 36–37, **52**

4:38–39, **52**

4:40–41, **52**

4:42–44, **53**

5:1–11, **50**

5:12–16, **54**

5:17–26, **54**

5:27–32, **56**

5:33–39, **57**

6:1–5, **60**

6:6–11, **61**

6:12–16, **63**

6:17–49, **64**

7:1–10, **73**

7:11–17, **74**

7:18–35, **75**

7:36–50, **78**

8:1–3, **80**

8:4–8, **84**

8:9–15, **86**

8:10, **85**

8:16–18, **86**

8:19–21, **82**

8:22–25, **90**

8:26–39, **91**

8:40–56, **93**

9:1–6, **97**

9:7–9, **101**

9:10–17, **103**

9:18–20, **117**

9:21–27, **118**

9:28–36, **119**

9:37–42, **121**

9:43–45, **123**

9:46–50, **124**

9:51–56, **126**

9:57–62, **128**

10:1–24, **140**

10:25–37, **141**

10:38–42, **143**

11:1–13, **143**

11:14–28, **145**

11:29–36, **146**

11:37–54, **146**

12:1–12, **148**

12:13–21, **149**

12:22–34, **149**

12:35–48, **150**

12:49–59, **151**

13:1–9, **152**

13:10–17, **153**

13:18–21, **87**

13:22–30, **155**

13:31–33, **155**

13:34–35, **156**

14:1–6, **156**

14:7–14, **157**

14:15–24, **157**

14:25–35, **159**

15:1–7, **159**

15:8–10, **160**

15:11–32, **161**

16:1–18, **162**

16:19–31, **163**

17:1–10, **164**

17:11–19, **169**

17:20–37, **170**

18:1–14, **171**

18:15–17, **173**

18:18–30, **174**

18:31–34, **176**

18:35–43, **178**

19:1–10, **179**

19:11–27, **180**

19:28–44, **184**

19:45–48, **185**

20:1–8, **189**

20:9–19, **190**

20:20–26, **192**

20:27–40, **193**

20:41–44, **195**

20:45–47, **196**

21:1–4, **198**

21:5–38, **198**

22:1–2, **206**

22:3–6, **207**

22:7–13, **208**

22:14–20, **212**

22:21–23, **210**

22:24–30, **212**

22:31–38, **211**

22:39–46, **220**

22:47–53, **223**

22:54, 63–65, **225**

22:54–62, **226**

22:66–23:1, **227**

23:2–5, **229**

23:6–10, **231**

23:11–12, **231**

23:13–25, **231**

23:26–31, **234**

23:32–34, **235**

23:35–38, **236**

23:39–43, **237**

23:44–48, **238**

23:49, **236**

23:50–54, **240**

23:55–56, **240**

24:1–2, **243**

24:3–8, **244**

24:9–12, **245**
24:13–32, **248**
24:33–35, **249**
24:36–43, **250**
24:44–53, **254**

JOHN
SCRIPTURE INDEX

1:1–18, **5**
1:19–34, **31**
1:35–51, **32**
2:1–11, **34**
2:12, **36**
2:13–25, **36**
3:1–21, **38**
3:22–24, **40**
3:25–36, **40**
4:1–4, **42**
4:5–44, **42**
4:45, **47**
4:46–54, **47**

5:1–15, **57**
5:16–47, **58**
6:1–15, **103**
6:16–21, **105**
6:22–71, **107**
7:1–9, **128**
7:10–52, **129**
7:53–8:11, **131**
8:12–59, **132**
9:1–41, **135**
10:1–21, **138**
10:22–42, **153**
11:1–44, **165**
11:45–54, **168**
11:55–12:1, 9–11, **183**
12:2–8, **206**
12:12–19, **184**
12:20–50, **186**
13:1–20, **208**
13:21–30, **210**
13:31–38, **211**
14:1–16:33, **213**
17:1–26, **218**

18:1–12, **223**
18:12–14, 19–23, **224**
18:15–18, 25–27, **226**
18:24, **225**
18:28–38, **229**
18:39–19:16, **231**
19:17–24, **235**
19:25–27, **236**
19:28–30, **238**
19:31–37, **239**
19:38–42, **240**
20:1–2, **244**
20:3–10, **245**
20:11–18, **246**
20:19–25, **250**
20:26–29, **251**
20:30–31, **255**
21:1–14, **251**
21:15–19, **252**
21:20–24, **253**
21:25, **255**

Abilene, 27

Aenon, 40

Alexander, 234

Andrew (apostle), 33, 50, 52, 63–64, 77, 90, 104, 199

Anna (prophetess), 20

Annas (high priest), 27, 224, 228

Antiochus Epiphanes, 154

Ascension of Jesus, 254–255

Barabbas, 232

Bartholomew. See *Nathanael.*

Bartimaeus, 178–179

Beatitudes, The, 64–65

Benedictus of Zachariah, 11–12

Bethany, 103, 143, 165, 166, 183, 184, 185, 186, 189, 206, 255

Bethlehem, 17–18, 19, 21, 22, 23

Bethphage, 184

Bethsaida (near Capernaum), 33, 77, 105, 140, 186

Bethsaida Julias, 116

Birth of Jesus, 17–19

Brothers of Jesus, 83, 97, 129

Burial of Jesus, 240

Caesar Augustus, 17, 19

Caesarea Philippi, 116, 117

Caiaphas (high priest), 27, 168, 206, 224, 225–226, 228, 229

Cana of Galilee, 34–35, 36, 47

Capernaum, 36, 47, 49, 51, 52, 53, 54, 56, 73, 77, 103, 105, 106, 107, 109, 122, 123, 124, 141

Chapel on the Mount of Beatitudes, 71

Chorazin, 77, 140

Church of the Annunciation, Nazareth, 25

Church of the Nativity, Bethlehem, 18

Circumcision of Jesus, 19

Cleansing of the temple, 36–37, 38, 185–186, 189

Corban, 111

Crucifixion of Jesus, 235–236

Dalmanutha, 114

Dead Sea, 27, 29, 100

Death of Jesus, 238

Decapolis, 53, 92, 113

Demon possession, 93

Divorce, 172–173

Egypt, 22–23, 24

Elijah (prophet), 27, 31, 49, 76, 101, 117, 119, 120, 121, 127, 238

Elizabeth, 7, 8, 10–11

Emmaus, 248–249

Ephraim, 168

Eschatological Discourse. See *Olivet Discourse.*

Feast of Unleavened Bread, 208

Festival of Dedication, 153, 154

Festival of Pentecost, 157

Festival of Tabernacles, 128, 129, 130, 157

Flogging of Jesus, 232

Gabriel (angel), 7, 8, 9, 10, 11

Galilee (province), 10, 17, 19, 23, 25, 29, 36, 45, 48, 51, 52, 53, 54, 62, 75, 80, 100, 101, 103, 123, 128, 129, 130, 131, 169, 172, 185, 186, 228, 230, 236, 244, 245, 247, 254

Galilee, Sea of; Lake Galilee, 23, 33, 36, 47, 50, 51, 62, 90–91, 103, 106, 113, 114, 116, 247, 251–252

Garden of Gethsemane, 63, 184, 189, 220–221, 223

Genealogies of Jesus, 12–14

Gennesaret, 106

Gentiles, 36, 98, 103, 104, 112, 113, 140, 150, 158, 169, 177, 178, 186, 192

Gerasene region, 91, 92

Gethsemane. See *Garden of Gethsemane.*

Golden Rule, 71

Golgotha, 235

Good Shepherd, 138–139

Great Commission, 254

Greeks, 186–188

Hanukkah, 154

Herod Agrippa I, 24

Herod Agrippa II, 24

Herod Antipas, 24, 41, 100, 101, 103, 112, 155–156, 189, 228, 231

Herod Archelaus, 23, 24

Herod Philip, 24, 41, 100, 117

Herod the Great, 7, 21, 22, 23, 24, 100

Herodians, 61, 193

Herodias, 41, 100

High Priestly Prayer, 219

Holy Spirit, 214, 216, 217

Hyperbole, 175

"I Am" statements of Jesus, 108, 111–112, 132–133, 138–139, 165–166, 213–215

Idumea, 62

Incarnation of Jesus, 6

Iturea, 27

Jairus, 93, 95

James, son of Alphaeus (apostle), 63–64, 127, 177–178

James, son of Zebedee (apostle), 50–51, 63–64, 77, 90, 94, 119, 124, 199, 221, 251

Jericho, 142, 178, 179

Jerusalem, 22, 24, 30, 31, 37, 40, 44, 53, 62, 80, 103, 110, 118, 123, 125, 128, 129, 130, 156, 176, 177, 183, 185, 247, 248, 255

Joanna, 80, 245

John (apostle), 50–51, 63–64, 77, 90, 94, 119, 124, 177–178, 221, 245–246, 251, 253

John the Baptizer, 6–8, 11–12, 27–30, 31–32, 33, 40, 57, 75–76, 100–101, 103, 112, 117, 121, 127, 154, 190, 199

Jordan River, 29, 30, 100, 113, 116, 154

Joseph (husband of Mary), 14, 15, 17, 18, 20, 22, 23, 24, 25, 96, 109, 129

Joseph of Arimathea, 39, 223, 240

Judas Iscariot (apostle), 63–64, 189, 207–208, 210–211, 223, 229

Judas, son of James (apostle), 63–64, 214

Judea (province), 10, 17, 21, 23, 40, 48, 51, 53, 54, 62, 75, 129, 155, 223, 228, 230

Judea, wilderness of, 6, 27

Kidron ravine, 223

Kingdom of God/Kingdom of heaven, 145

Lazarus, 40, 95, 103, 165–168, 169, 183, 206

Lebbaeus Thaddaeus. See *Judas, son of James.*

Levi. See *Matthew.*

Levites, 31, 142

Lord's Prayer. See *Model Prayer of Jesus.*

Lysanias, 27

Machaerus, 100

Magadan, 114

Magdala, 80, 114

Magnificat of Mary, 10

Malchus, 223

Martha, 40, 143, 165–168, 206

Mary (earthly mother of Jesus), 9–11, 12, 14, 15, 17, 18, 19, 20, 21, 23, 24, 25, 34–35, 83, 97, 129, 236

Mary Magdalene, 80, 236, 240, 243, 244, 246, 247, 250

Mary (mother of James), 243, 244, 245

Mary (mother of Joses), 240

Mary (sister of Martha and Lazarus), 40, 143, 165–168, 206–207

Mary (wife of Clopas), 236

Matthew (apostle), 13, 56, 63–64, 77

Memorial Supper, 189, 208, 212–213

Model Prayer of Jesus, 143

Mount Gerizim, 43

Mount of Olives, 131, 184, 185

Nain, 74, 95

Nathanael (apostle), 25, 33–34, 47, 63–64, 251

Nazareth, 9, 17, 18, 23, 24, 29, 34, 36, 48, 49, 83, 96–97, 130, 185

Nicodemus, 38–39, 131, 240

Olivet Discourse, 184, 198–202, 205

Passover Festival, 24, 36, 37, 104, 177, 179, 183, 189, 206, 208, 232, 234

Pentecost. See *Festival of Pentecost.*

Perea, 41, 100, 101, 103, 228

Peter. See *Simon Peter.*

Pharisees, 28, 32, 38, 39, 52, 55, 56, 57, 60, 61, 76, 78, 79, 80, 81, 82, 96, 103, 110, 111, 114, 115–116, 130, 131, 132, 133, 136, 137, 138, 146, 147, 148–149, 155, 156, 157, 159, 160, 163, 168, 170, 172, 175, 183, 185, 191, 192, 196–198, 241

Philip (apostle), 25, 33–34, 63–64, 104, 186, 213

Phylacteries, 196

Pilate, Pontius, 27, 152, 189, 223, 225, 228, 229–233, 235, 239, 241

Pool of Bethesda, 57

Pool of Siloam, 136

Post-resurrection appearances of Jesus, 247

Preparation Day, 241

Priests, 31, 130, 131, 142, 168, 183, 186, 189, 191, 206, 224

Prophetic Discourse. See *Olivet Discourse.*

Quirinius, 17

Resurrection of Jesus, 243

Ritual washings, 147

Rufus, 234

Sabbath controversies, 57–62, 135–136, 153, 156–157

Sadducees, 28, 114, 115–116, 193, 194

Salome (daughter of Herodias), 100

Salome (mother of James and John), 236, 243, 244

Samaria, 42, 51, 169

Samaritans, 42–44, 126, 135, 141

Sanhedrin, 39, 98, 155, 168–169, 183, 189–190, 223, 225, 227–228, 233, 240, 248

Scribes, 52, 55, 56, 80, 110, 111, 118, 121, 128, 132, 148, 159, 160, 186, 194, 195, 196–198, 206

Second coming, 150–151, 170, 171, 189, 201–202, 205

Sermon on the Mount, 64–73

Seven last words from the cross, 238

Seven signs of John's Gospel, 35

Sidon, 62, 112, 113, 141

Siloam. See *Pool of Siloam.*

Simeon, 20

Simon Peter (apostle), 33, 50, 52, 53, 63–64, 77, 90, 94, 106, 110, 117, 118, 119, 120, 123, 124, 126, 151, 175, 188, 199, 209, 210, 211, 221, 223, 226–227, 245–246, 247, 249, 251–253

Simon the Cyrenian, 234–235

Simon the leper, 206

Simon the Pharisee, 78–79

Simon the Zealot (apostle), 63–64

Skull, The, 235

Solomon's Colonnade, 153

Susanna, 80

Sychar, 42, 44

Tabernacles. See *Festival of Tabernacles.*

Tassels, 196

Teachers of the law, 54, 76, 141, 146, 147

Temptations of Jesus, 30–31

Theophilus, 5

Thomas (apostle), 63–64, 166, 213, 247, 250–251

Tiberias, 107

Tiberius Caesar, 27, 117

Trachonitis, 27

Traditions of the elders, 111

Transfiguration of Jesus, 119–120

Triumphal entry into Jerusalem, 184–185, 189

Tyre, 62, 112, 113, 141

Unforgivable sin, 81, 148

Valley of Hinnom, 125

Virgin birth of Jesus, 9, 129

Wise men visit Jesus, 21–22

Zacchaeus, 179–180

Zachariah, 7, 10, 11, 27

Zealots, 63

MIRACLES OF JESUS

1. Water into wine 34–35
2. A royal official's son healed 47–48
3. Miraculous catch of fish at Lake Galilee 51
4. A demon-possessed man healed at Capernaum 51–52
5. Peter's mother-in-law healed . . 52
6. A leper healed 54
7. A paralyzed man healed. . . 54–55
8. A lame man healed on the Sabbath. 57–58
9. A man's paralyzed hand healed on the Sabbath 61–62
10. A centurion's slave healed . . 73–74
11 A widow's son raised from the dead 74–75
12. A demon-possessed blind man healed 80
13. Stilling of the storm 90–91
14. A wild man among the tombs healed. 91–93
15. Jairus's daughter healed . . . 93–95
16. A woman with a hemorrhage healed 93–95
17. Two blind men healed. . . . 95–96
18. A demon-possessed deaf man healed 95–96
19. Feeding of the five thousand. 103–105
20. Walking on the water . . 105–107
21. The daughter of a Canaanite woman healed. 112
22. A deaf man healed. 113
23. Feeding of the four thousand 114
24. A blind man at Bethsaida healed 116–117
25. Transformation of Jesus before His disciples 119–120

26. A demon-possessed boy healed. 121–122
27. Production of a coin to pay the temple tax 123
28. A man blind from birth healed. 135–138
29. A woman with a crooked back healed 153
30. A man whose body was swollen with fluid healed . . 156–157
31. Lazarus raised from the dead 165–168
32. Ten lepers healed 169
33. Blind Bartimaeus healed. 178–179
34. Withering of a fig tree 185
35. Healing of the ear of Malchus 224
36. Resurrection of Jesus 243
37. Another miraculous catch of fish at Lake Galilee . . 251–252
38. Ascension of Jesus to the Father. 254–255

MAJOR PARABLES
OF JESUS

1. The two foundations (sand and rock) 73
2. The sower 84–85
3. The lamp on a lampstand 86
4. The wheat and the weeds. 87
5. The mustard seed 87–88
6. The yeast. 87–88
7. The hidden treasure. 89
8. The priceless pearl 89
9. The net 89
10. The landowner 90
11. The unforgiving slave . . 127–128
12. The good Samaritan . . . 141–142
13. The rich fool 149
14. The barren fig tree. 152
15. The large banquet 157–158
16. The lost sheep 159–160
17. The lost coin 160
18. The lost/prodigal son. . . 161–162
19. The dishonest manager. 162–163
20. The rich man and Lazarus 163–164
21. The persistent widow . . 171–172
22. The proud Pharisee 171–172
23. The vineyard workers . . 175–176
24. The minas 180–181
25. The two vineyard workers . . . 190
26. The vineyard owner. . . . 190–192
27. The wedding banquet 192
28. The ten virgins 202–203
29. The talents 203–204